Zeno Ackermann, Sabine Schülting
Precarious Figurations

Zeno Ackermann, Sabine Schülting

Precarious Figurations

Shylock on the German Stage, 1920-2010

DE GRUYTER

ISBN 978-3-11-073649-6
e-ISBN (PDF) 978-3-11-061792-4
e-ISBN (EPUB) 978-3-11-061559-3

Library of Congress Cataloging-in-Publication Data 2018965080

Bibliographic information published by the Deutsche Nationalbibliothek
The Deutsche Nationalbibliothek lists this publication in the Deutsche Nationalbibliografie;
detailed bibliographic data are available on the Internet at http://dnb.dnb.de.

© 2020 Walter de Gruyter GmbH, Berlin/Boston
This volume is text- and page-identical with the hardback published in 2019.
Printing and binding: CPI books GmbH, Leck
Cover image: iStock/Getty Images Plus/aerogondo

www.degruyter.com

Preface

It is a truth universally acknowledged that books are the products of intellectual cooperation. This is particularly true of this monograph, which is the outcome of several years of collaborative research, discussion, writing, and revision. It has originated from our research project entitled "Shylock und der (neue) deutsche Geist: Shakespeares *Der Kaufmann von Venedig* nach 1945" ("Shylock and the (new) German spirit: Shakespeare's *The Merchant of Venice* after 1945"), which was generously funded by the Deutsche Forschungsgemeinschaft (DFG) from 2008 to 2012. In the context of this project, many colleagues – in Germany and abroad – have given valuable suggestions, criticism, and advice. Some of them have offered us a forum in which we could present our ideas; others have accepted our invitation to come to Berlin and talk about their work. We cannot name everyone with whom we have discussed Shylock and *The Merchant of Venice* over the past decade, but our special thanks go to Shaul Bassi, Ingeborg Boltz, Elisabeth Bronfen, Tobias Döring, Anat Feinberg, Susanne Feldmann, Paul Franssen, Bernhard Greiner, Raphael Gross, Maik Hamburger, Tom Healy, Marion Hirte, Stefan Hofmann, Norbert Kentrup, Sarah Knor, Malte Kreutzfeldt, Lukas Lammers, Oliver Lubrich, Irmela von der Lühe, Julia Lupton, Irena R. Makaryk, Zoltán Márkus, Edna Nahshon, Avraham Oz, Jens Roselt, Hans Rübesame, David Schalkwyk, Guido Schenkel, Ludwig Schnauder, Michael Shapiro, Susanne Scholz, Stefanie Schüler-Springorum, Boika Sokolova, Wolfgang Türk, and Matthias Weiß. We would also like to thank our students with whom we have discussed Shakespeare's *The Merchant of Venice* in our seminars and lectures.

We are very grateful for the immense support we have been offered by archives and libraries, in particular the archives of the Akademie der Künste (Berlin), Deutsches Theater (Berlin), the theatre collection of the University of Cologne at Schloss Wahn, and the Shakespeare Research Library at the Ludwig-Maximilians University of Munich. A large number of theatres have sent us programmes, reviews, posters, as well as audio and video recordings of their *Merchant* productions. Our thanks go to Grenzlandtheater Aachen, ETA Hoffman Theater Bamberg, Badisches Staatstheater Karlsruhe, Theatersammlung des Stadtmuseums Berlin, Theater Biel Solothurn, Schauspielhaus Bochum, Theater Bonn, fringe ensemble (Bonn), bremer shakespeare company, Theater Bremen, Deutsches Rundfunkarchiv (Babelsberg), Staatstheater Cottbus, Staatsschauspiel Dresden, Theatermuseum Düsseldorf, Deutsches Theater in Göttingen, Städtisches Museum und Stadtarchiv Göttingen, Thalia Theater (Hamburg), Schauspiel Leipzig, Landestheater Linz, Theater an der Ruhr (Mülheim), Residenztheater München, Landesbühne Niedersachsen Nord, Theater Oberhausen, Staatstheater Stuttgart, Theater der Altstadt (Stuttgart), Landestheater Tübingen (LTT), Westdeutscher Rundfunk (Cologne), Stadttheater Wilhelmshaven, Schauspielhaus Zürich.

Last but definitely not least, there is a group of people who have worked in the background. They have supported us as research assistants, managed the budget, and helped us prepare the manuscript: Kathrin Bartha, Sophia Sam Davis, Steffen Donath, Aleksandra Ivanova, Manuela Kuhlen, Franziska Reinfeldt, and Wibke Joswig. Without their help we would not have been able to complete this book.

Zeno Ackermann and Sabine Schülting

Contents

List of Illustrations —— IX

Introduction —— 1

1 **Figuring Identity: Ruptures and Continuities from the Reinhardt Era to the Early Federal Republic (1905–1957)** —— 14
1.1 From the Reinhardt Era to the Rise of the Anti-Semitic Hegemony —— 19
1.2 The Theatrical Ratification of Genocide —— 43
1.3 Redemptive Figurations: The Post-War Period to the End of the 1950s —— 62

2 **Staging Remembrance: Refigurations on the West German Stage (1960–1990)** —— 83
2.1 The Transformation of Shylock into a Figure of Cultural Memory —— 88
2.2 Tactical Refigurations: Fritz Kortner, Peter Zadek, and George Tabori —— 98
2.3 The Diversification of the Shylock Figure: Holocaust Victims, Outsiders, and 'Rich Jews' —— 122

3 **Inheriting a Classic: Configurations of *Merchant* in the German Democratic Republic (1949–1990)** —— 137
3.1 Shakespeare and the 'Classical Heritage' —— 138
3.2 Absent Shylocks —— 145
3.3 Fritz Bennewitz's *Merchants* at Weimar (1976) and Leipzig (1988) —— 150
3.4 The Shylock Figure in the East-West Conflict —— 157

4 **After Remembrance? – Shylock in the Reunified Germany (1990–2010)** —— 162
4.1 Against Identification: Peter Zadek's 1988 Burgtheater Production —— 165
4.2 The "Shylock Syndrome": Dietrich Schwanitz's Close Reading of Anti-Semitism —— 171

4.3		The Theatre of Remembrance: Imperatives, Denials, and Transferences —— **175**
4.4		The Politics of Identity —— **190**
5		**"Forced Companionability": Conclusion —— 202**

Works Cited —— 207
1	Primary Texts and Critical Studies —— **207**
2	Reviews of Stage Productions of *The Merchant of Venice* —— **223**
3	Theatre Programmes and Theatre Websites —— **227**

Stage Productions of *The Merchant of Venice* in Germany and Austria (1933–2010) —— 228

Index —— 238

List of Illustrations

Figure 1: Stage plan for Max Reinhardt's 1913 production of *Merchant* at Deutsches Theater Berlin. Stage design: Ernst Stern; sketch by Rudolf Dworsky. *Shakespeare Jahrbuch* 50 (1914), 117. Courtesy of Deutsches Theater Berlin.
Figure 2: Fritz Kortner as Shylock in Max Reinhardt's 1924 production at Vienna's Theater in der Josefstadt. © Bruno Reiffenstein / Imagno / picturedesk.com.
Figure 3: Werner Krauß (Shylock) and Maria Holst (Portia) in the trial scene of Lothar Müthel's 1943 production at Vienna's Burgtheater. Courtesy of KHM-Museumsverband, Theatermuseum Wien.
Figure 4: Antonio (Heinrich Buchmann) and Bassanio (Andreas Wolf) asking Shylock (Wilhelm Meyer-Ottens) for credit in Gustav Rudolf Sellner's 1942 production at Stadttheater Göttingen. Courtesy of Deutsches Theater Göttingen.
Figure 5: Hilde Krahl (Portia), Ernst Deutsch (Shylock), and Wolfgang Spier (Antonio) in Erwin Piscator's 1963 production at Berlin's Freie Volksbühne. Photograph by Abraham Pisarek. Courtesy of Stiftung Stadtmuseum Berlin.
Figure 6: Fritz Kortner (Shylock) and director Otto Schenk during the shooting of the 1968 TV-adaptation. Courtesy of Österreichische Nationalbibliothek Wien (ÖNB Wien: CE 118/3).
Figure 7: Entrance of Bochum's Schauspielhaus with the poster advertising Peter Zadek's 1972 production. Film still from the WDR documentary *Hierzulande – heutzutage: Der Kaufmann von Venedig*, broadcast on 9 January 1973.
Figure 8: Photograph of the stage design of Fritz Bennewitz's 1976 production at Deutsches Nationaltheater Weimar. Photograph by Günter Dietel (Archiv der Akademie der Künste Berlin, Inszenierungsdokumentationen 173). Courtesy of Lore Dietel.
Figure 9: Gert Voss (Shylock) in Peter Zadek's 1988 production at Vienna's Burgtheater. © Gisela Scheidler, Archiv Burgtheater.
Figure 10: Renate Becker (Shylock) and Benno Ifland (Antonio) in Elmar Goerden's 2008 production at the Schauspielhaus Bochum. Photograph by Matthias Horn. Courtesy of Matthias Horn.
Figure 11: Caroline Ebner (Jessica) in Karin Beier's 1994 production at the Düsseldorfer Schauspielhaus. Photograph by Sonja Rothweiler. Courtesy of Sonja Rothweiler.

Introduction

"A borderline case": Erich Auerbach and Shylock

The German-Jewish intellectual Erich Auerbach (1892–1957) is not an obvious point of departure for a book on German responses to William Shakespeare's *The Merchant of Venice*. Although his seminal study *Mimesis: The Representation of Reality in Western Literature* (1946), written between 1942 and 1945 during the scholar's Istanbul exile, does contain a chapter on Shakespeare, Auerbach, who was a Romance philologist, did not write as a Shakespearean. The brief references to *Merchant* are scattered over a few pages in the Shakespeare chapter, which is primarily concerned with the playwright's mixed style.[1] And yet, Shylock is mentioned early on, in a passage on Shakespeare's "mixture of characters and the consequent mixture of tragic and comic elements." Despite Shakespeare's deviations from classical notions of genre and propriety, Auerbach observes, his tragic heroes are never low characters but are all "of high rank." Shylock, however, may be a "borderline case." While Auerbach acknowledges that Shakespeare's "pariah" is given powerful speeches "echo[ing] great humanitarian ideas,"[2] he has "no doubt [...] that the actors are wrong who have tried to make Shylock a tragic hero." With this rejection of a tragic Shylock, Auerbach challenges the understanding of the character that has prevailed since the late nineteenth century. In stark contrast to Hamlet, Lear, or Macbeth, Auerbach argues, Shakespeare conceptualized his Jewish moneylender as "a low figure, unworthy of tragic treatment, whose tragic involvement is conjured up for a moment, but is only an added spice in the triumph of a higher, nobler, freer, and also more aristocratic humanity."[3] He concludes: "Shylock is frankly a figure from farce. In the end, Shakespeare dismisses him, without greatness."[4]

For a reader at the beginning of the twenty-first century, it may seem irritating that Auerbach, a Jewish exile writing at the height of the Second World War, did not read Shylock as a representative of the victims of National Socialist persecution. Whereas Markus Moninger has posited that "Every single postwar

---

[1] We are quoting the fiftieth anniversary edition: Erich Auerbach, *Mimesis: The Representation of Reality in Western Culture*, trans. Willard R. Trask (Princeton: Princeton University Press, 2003), chapter 13: "The Weary Prince" (312–333).
[2] Auerbach, *Mimesis*, 313–314.
[3] Auerbach, *Mimesis*, 314.
[4] Auerbach, *Mimesis*, 314.

production of *The Merchant of Venice* remembers Auschwitz,"⁵ this inevitable association between *Merchant* and the Holocaust does not seem to apply to Auerbach's engagement with the play. His reservation has not gone unnoticed. In an article on "Auerbach in Exile," David Damrosch comments on Auerbach's distance to Shylock and the way in which the character's Jewishness is "recoded" through Auerbach's exclusive attention to his social status and personal features. Auerbach may not even have acknowledged Shylock as a Jew, Damrosch muses, or he may have wanted to preclude causal associations between the character's Jewishness and his flaws. One reason for this distance could have been Auerbach's attempt to ensure the impartiality of the researcher vis-à-vis the object of analysis.⁶ His "heedless Olympian serenity"⁷ regarding Shylock would then be one example of the ways in which Auerbach "both responded to his exile and refused to submit to it."⁸ In fact, it is exactly this detachment that Malachi Haim Hacohen finds so disconcerting:

> One wonders how Auerbach could maintain this interplay of proximity and distance facing the Holocaust. But the murder of the European Jews is not mentioned even once in *Mimesis* and appears not to figure in Auerbach's European crisis. Postbiblical Jews vanish from Auerbach's narrative of Western literature. He made a special effort to ignore them: In discussing Shylock as a (non-)tragic figure, he overlooked his Jewishness.⁹

However, Shylock is a name that resounds throughout Auerbach's Shakespeare chapter, second only to Hamlet, and more prominent than Lear, Macbeth, Prospero, and the chapter's eponymous "weary prince," Prince Hal from the two *Henry IV* plays. If Auerbach regards Shylock as a farcical and ultimately secondary character, why does he spend so many words on him?

The more closely one reads the chapter, the more obvious Auerbach's allusions to his own historical moment become. In relation to his speech in 4.1, in which Shylock justifies the righteousness of his bond through comparison

---

5 Markus Moninger, "Auschwitz erinnern: *Merchant*-Inszenierungen im Nachkriegsdeutschland," in *Das Theater der Anderen: Alterität und Theater zwischen Antike und Gegenwart*, ed. Christopher Balme (Tübingen: Francke, 2001), 229.
6 David Damrosch, "Auerbach in Exile," *Comparative Literature* 47.2 (1995): 103–104.
7 These are Auerbach's words for Shakespeare's treatment of Shylock (*Mimesis*, 314); they are quoted by Damrosch ("Auerbach in Exile," 104) as a fitting attribute of Auerbach's own discussion of the character.
8 Damrosch, "Auerbach in Exile," 115.
9 Malachi Haim Hacohen, "Typology and the Holocaust: Erich Auerbach and Judeo-Christian Europe," *Religions* 3 (2012): 617.

with the rights of a slaveholder (4.1.97–9),[10] Auerbach comments emphatically (a passage surprisingly ignored by Damrosch): "The pariah Shylock does not appeal to natural right but to customary wrong. What a dynamic immediacy there is in such bitter, tragic irony!"[11] The German original here reads "dynamische Aktualität"[12] ("Aktualität" means immediacy in the sense of topicality), thus establishing an implicit parallel to the war and the Holocaust. The next paragraph continues this topical reading. Looking for an example of the playwright's stylistic deviation from the classical model, Auerbach claims to "open a volume of Shakespeare at random." He then quotes the speech from *Macbeth* 3.6, in which Lennox refers to the murders committed by the protagonist, without actually naming him as the perpetrator. Instead, Lennox ironically comments on the official account of the events:

> [...] Only I say
> Things have been strangely borne. [...]
> [...] Did he [Macbeth] not straight
> In pious rage the two delinquents tear,
> That were the slaves of drink, and thralls of sleep?
> Was not that nobly done? Ay, and wisely too,
> For 'twould have angered any heart alive
> To hear the men deny't. [...] (3.6.2–16)

Auerbach writes that the inclusion of such lines "within the somberly tragic atmosphere" would have been "foreign to antiquity."[13] He reads them as a perfect example of the stylistic mix so characteristic of Shakespearean drama. But there is a subtext to the argument, which abruptly, and not altogether randomly, moves from Shylock to Lennox, from the Jewish character who believes in law and justice to the subject of a tyrannous regime who finds a language to talk about political murder. The connection between the two characters and the two plays is not merely in Shakespeare's "abundance of stylistic levels;" it is also Auerbach's concern with "moral phenomena"[14] that links Shylock's "tragic irony" with Lennox's bitter sarcasm. For Auerbach, it seems, both passages are comments on the (contemporary) individual faced with

---

10 William Shakespeare, *The Merchant of Venice*, in *The Norton Shakespeare*, ed. Stephen Greenblatt et al. (New York: W. W. Norton & Company, 1997). Unless specified otherwise, all quotes from Shakespeare follow this edition.
11 Auerbach, *Mimesis*, 323.
12 Auerbach, *Mimesis: Dargestellte Wirklichkeit in der abendländischen Literatur* (1946; Tübingen: A. Francke, 2001), 310.
13 Auerbach, *Mimesis*, 324.
14 Auerbach, *Mimesis*, 323.

inequality, tyranny, and murder. As Seth Lerer claims: "One reads these lines with an eye for the political, for the ways in which Auerbach inscribes that sense of isolation, hope, and moral judgment that runs throughout *Mimesis*."[15] Shakespeare thus seems to provide Auerbach with a means to address his own time.

In line with this reading, Damrosch suggests that many of the literary characters and personae discussed in *Mimesis* – including Rabelais's Alcofribas, Dante's Farinata, and Cervantes's Don Quixote – can be understood as alter egos of the scholar himself:

> Auerbach's descriptions of characters [...] often sound like self-portraits. [...] more particularly, these heroes reflect the *actual* experience of the critic who has assembled this gallery. In their multiplicity, Auerbach's heroes come to express elements both of his historical experience and of his response to it.[16]

Although Damrosch does not mention Shakespeare's Jewish character in this context, Auerbach's insistence on Shylock's farcical rather than tragic nature could also be interpreted as a bitterly ironic comment on his own situation as an outsider and exile in Istanbul as well as on his earlier misjudgement of his position as a Jewish professor at a German university. Indeed, for quite some time even after 1933, Auerbach seems to have continued trusting in the solidity of the German law, hoping that – as a decorated veteran of the First World War – he would be able to keep his post.

Nevertheless, there is no denying the fact that Auerbach fails to elaborate on Shylock's Jewishness. His only explicit reference is a brief comparison with Marlowe's "gruesome" Barabas, to whom Auerbach attributes more "greatness," even though "Shakespeare saw and stated the human problem of his Jew much more deeply."[17] Whereas some critics have regarded Auerbach's hesitancy towards Shylock as an indication of the assimilated Jewish intellectual's lack of identification with Judaism,[18] others have challenged this interpretation. Damrosch, for example, stresses that the famous introductory chapter of *Mimesis*, in which Auerbach contrasts Homer's *Odyssey* with the biblical story of Abraham's sacrifice of Isaac (Gen 22) and finds more depth in the latter, indeed estab-

---

15 Seth Lerer, "Auerbach's Shakespeare," *Philological Quarterly* 90.1 (2011): 37.
16 Damrosch, "Auerbach in Exile," 107.
17 Auerbach, *Mimesis*, 314.
18 See, e.g., Hacohen, "Typology and the Holocaust," 613–614 *et passim*. Hacohen sees Auerbach as a secular Jew who, in disacknowledging post-biblical Judaism, eventually subscribed to Christian supercessionism.

lishes the frame for a revision of Western literature from an unambiguously Jewish perspective. As he writes, paraphrasing Geoffrey Green:

> the apparently neutral juxtaposition of Genesis and the Odyssey serves as a powerful, and polemical, counter to anti-Semitic dismissals of Jewish culture, with Jewish psychological complexity and historical consciousness complementing – or even trumping – Winckelmannian Greek clarity and harmony.[19]

But if, in *Mimesis*, Auerbach sets out to rewrite the history of Western literature and re-appropriate it from the perspective of a Jewish philologist who had to flee from National Socialist Germany, he cannot *not* comment on one of the most important and contradictory Jewish characters that has emerged from this literary tradition. Rather than entirely deviating from Shylock's 'genealogy' and afterlife, Auerbach looks awry at his stage and literary history, confirming it and distancing himself from it at the same time. He seems to be aware of the danger inherent in a simplistic identification with Shylock, the stage Jew inherited from early modern English drama, who appears to confirm the anti-Semitic stereotypes that fuelled the murderous racism of Hitler's Germany.

Shylock in *Mimesis* does indeed appear as a complex figure, whose mere existence Auerbach sees as proof of Shakespeare's interest in "alien forms of life and culture":[20] "In Elizabethan tragedy and particularly in Shakespeare, perspective consciousness has become a matter of course."[21] Auerbach compares the dazzling multi-perspectivity of Shakespearean drama with the literature of Classical Antiquity and the Middle Ages, both of which he considers to be characterized by a "comparatively simple contrast of Greek or Roman versus barbarian or Christian versus heathen."[22] 'Shakespearean' secular culture, on the other hand, appears to complicate this kind of binary view.[23] In other words, the reference to Shylock helps Auerbach to propose Shakespearean drama as imagining (or prefiguring)

---

19 Damrosch, "Auerbach in Exile," 102. See also Avihu Zakai and David Weinstein, "Erich Auerbach and His 'Figura': An Apology for the Old Testament in an Age of Aryan Philology," *Religions* 3 (2012): 320–338.
20 Auerbach, *Mimesis*, 319.
21 Auerbach, *Mimesis*, 320. Auerbach developed the same idea in "The Idea of the National Spirit as the Source of the Modern Humanities," in *Time, History, and Literature: Selected Essays of Erich Auerbach*, ed. James I. Porter, trans. Jane O. Newman (Princeton: Princeton University Press, 2014), 61.
22 Auerbach, *Mimesis*, 320.
23 Cf. Damrosch, "Auerbach in Exile," 102.

"a tolerant secularism"[24] based on Jewish-Christian[25] traditions. This is what Edward Said celebrates in his introduction to the fiftieth anniversary English edition of *Mimesis*, where he describes Auerbach's deep belief in "the unity of human history, the possibility of understanding inimical and perhaps even hostile others despite the bellicosity of modern cultures and nationalisms."[26] For the postcolonial critic, this is one of the basic agendas of Auerbach's oeuvre, and it may also be one reason for the current renaissance of critical interest in Auerbach. In this light, *Mimesis* would suggest that *The Merchant of Venice* prefigured a Jewish-Christian cosmopolitanism – a cosmopolitanism that Auerbach actually may have been dreaming of in the 1940s.

Shylock is thus indeed "a borderline case" in Auerbach's account. He is and is not a Jew, both inviting and defying identification, a figure with tragic features who is not a tragic hero. Auerbach's Shylock is neither a 'round' character nor a realistic representation of a human being. Instead he is a figure – in the dual sense of a fictional character and a rhetorical device – that allows Auerbach to connect and contrast seemingly disparate topics and concerns: Christian and Jewish traditions in European literature or culture, classical and (early) modern literature, the acknowledgment of cultural differences in the European Renaissance and the hegemonic ideologies of National Socialism, the concern with moral questions in Shakespeare's plays and their topical resonance in the 1940s. Though he failed to acknowledge it explicitly, the ambivalently Jewish figure of Shylock was an important device in Auerbach's project of conducting traditional philology as a form of cultural critique.

---

24 Rey Chow, "'I Insist on the Christian Dimension': On Forgiveness ... and the Outside of the Human," *Differences: A Journal of Feminist Cultural Studies* 20.2/3 (2009): 241. For a very different interpretation of *Merchant*, see Susannah Heschel, "From Jesus to Shylock: Christian Supersessionism and 'The Merchant of Venice'," *Harvard Theological Review* 99.4 (2006): 424–425. In her reading, Shakespeare does not embrace Christian supersessionist theology but, quite to the contrary, "uses irony to call the categories of Christian theology into question" and to lay bare "the hypocrisy of Christian declamations through its literal and theologically figural transvestism."
25 In his "Introduction" to *Selected Essays of Erich Auerbach*, James I. Porter explains that he uses the term "Jewish-Christian" rather than "Judeo-Christian" as the one Auerbach preferred because "upon closer inspection [it] presents an unstable hyphenation of two religious traditions." (xlii–xliii).
26 Edward W. Said, "Introduction to the Fiftieth-Anniversary Edition," in Auerbach, *Mimesis*, xv.

Shylock Figurations

Erich Auerbach's resistance to conventional interpretations of Shylock is of crucial interest to our present study. This is not only due to the particular historical and individual situation in which this scholar was engaging with *The Merchant of Venice*. More fundamentally, our analysis of the play's diverging interpretations in Germany before, during, and after the Holocaust is decisively informed by Auerbach's take on Shylock as a complex construct rather than a psychologically coherent human being. Understood in this way, the figure of Shylock is key to research into the cultural history of *Merchant* on the twentieth-century German stage.

In *Blood Relations*, her seminal study on *Merchant*, Janet Adelman articulated her specific "perspective as a Jew" faced with Shakespeare's unsettling comedy and confessed to "the personal difficulty" experienced "in confronting this most painful of plays."[27] Adelman's monograph explores the ways in which *Merchant* is saturated with the theological discourses and ideological anxieties of early modern England. It is evident, however, that the particular pain felt by Adelman in encountering the text is due not only to its highly ambivalent stance towards medieval and early modern anti-Semitism, but also to its resonance with twentieth-century genocidal violence. In other words, even if *Merchant* is read historically, the Holocaust can still hardly be avoided. To modern readers and theatre audiences it seems proleptically inscribed into the very texture of the play, which evokes the murderous consequences of modern anti-Semitism as well as its historical pretexts. Dennis Kennedy has found a striking formulation for the phenomenon: "The external events of the Second World War have affected *Merchant* so thoroughly that it is fair to say that since 1945 we have been in possession of a new text of the play, one which bears relationships to the earlier text but is also significantly different from it."[28]

Focusing on the reception of *Merchant* in twentieth- and twenty-first-century Germany, our book will examine this "new text" – or rather, these multi-layered new *texts*. In doing so, however, we must also consider the ways in which "earlier text[s]" have lingered on, merging with new perspectives, complicating and sometimes subverting attempts at re-orientation. Looking at German theatrical practices and critical discourses from the Weimar Republic to the beginning of the new millennium, we attempt to show how and why the play – before the

---

27 Janet Adelman, *Blood Relations: Christian and Jew in* The Merchant of Venice (Chicago: University of Chicago Press, 2008), ix, vii.
28 Dennis Kennedy, *Looking at Shakespeare: A Visual History of Twentieth-Century Performance* (Cambridge: Cambridge University Press, 1994), 200.

Holocaust and after – has served both as a vehicle for the actualization of anti-Semitic tropes *and* as a staging ground for the critical exposure of the very logic of anti-Semitism, both as a metaphorical laboratory for negotiating the terms of Jewish integration *and* as a platform for affirmative postulations of a distinct Jewish identity, both as a reference point for attacks on liberal ideologies *and* as a staging ground for socialist visions of redemption.

Indeed, the most fundamental observation in relation to Shylock is that readers as well as scholars, directors, performers, and theatre-goers have been and remain puzzled over the significance and significations of 'Shakespeare's Jew.' A recent collection of essays, *Wrestling with Shylock*, edited by Michael Shapiro and Edna Nahshon, addresses the ways in which Jewish writers, critics, actors, and directors have responded to Shakespeare's *Merchant*, a play that has "engaged Jewish discourse for over 200 years" and "activates the sensitivities, fears, memories, and hopes encompassed in the Jewish experience as a minority group within a larger, primarily Christian society."[29] As an important contribution to this discourse, John Gross's massive study on Shylock represents both a formidable attempt to understand the character's impact and a self-conscious prolongation of his supposed mystery.[30] In a review of Gross's book, Robert Alter has wistfully demanded to know "Who is Shylock?," suggesting that it might be the very unanswerability of the question that proves so compelling. He posits that Shylock is made up of two very dissimilar character types, "in the representation of the suffering of a much-wronged outsider (the 'tragic' Shylock, as some critics would have it) and in the demonization of what in other comedies would be the figure of fun (the mythic Shylock)." Alter concludes: "perhaps the contradiction at the core of the character explains the power of this strange figure."[31] It is these contradictions, and the twentieth-century responses to them, that will be at the centre of our discussion. We will analyse Shylock as both a palimpsestic textual construct and the centre of an ideological arena where different discursive and performative strategies intersect and challenge each other.

In order to break free from the notion of 'character' and conceptualize the multi-layered cultural potentials and functions of Shylock, we rely on yet another text by Auerbach: his essay entitled "Figura," written in Istanbul in 1938. "Figura" traces the history of *figuratio* from classical rhetoric through the typological

---

29 Edna Nahshon, "Preface," in *Wrestling with Shylock: Jewish Responses to The Merchant of Venice*, ed. Edna Nahshon and Michael Shapiro (Cambridge: Cambridge University Press, 2017), xxii.
30 John Gross, *Shylock: A Legend and Its Legacy* (New York: Simon & Schuster, 1992), and *Shylock: Four Hundred Years in the Life of a Legend* (London: Chatto & Windus, 1992).
31 Robert Alter, "Who Is Shylock?" *Commentary* 96.1 (1993): 32.

(or figural) theology of the Church Fathers to its secularization in the works of Dante. For our purposes, the theological argument is less interesting than the aesthetic, epistemological, and ideological implications of figural interpretation, i.e. the understanding of persons and events from the Old Testament as anticipations of the New Testament (Adam, Moses, and Joshua would all be 'prefigurations' or 'types' of Christ). As Auerbach explains:

> Figural interpretation creates a connection between two events or persons in which one signifies not only itself but also the other – and that one is also encompassed and fulfilled by the other. The two poles of the figure are separate in time, but they both also lie within time as real events or figures.[32]

At the beginning of his essay, Auerbach stresses that *figura* "expresses something animated and lively, open-ended and playful."[33] He pays particular attention to the material and historical character of both poles, the figure and its fulfilment, and thus distinguishes figural prophecy from *allegoresis*.[34] The relationship between the two events or figures is neither causal nor allegorical. In the words of Hayden White, it is instead "a retrospective appropriation of an earlier event by the treatment of it as a figure of a later one."[35]

Understood in this way, *figuratio* can help us grasp the complicated significations and the precarious significance of the Shylock figure within German culture. We will thus pay attention to the juxtaposition of past, present, and future as well as to the ensuing tensions between outer form and meaning, symbol and material reality. Also, we will emphasize the processual nature or performativity of typological thinking as described by Auerbach. In doing so we are influenced by – and hope to add to – the career that the concept of 'figuration' has enjoyed in various disciplines since the late 1990s. Despite the prolix-

---

32 We are quoting from Jane O. Newman's excellent new translation of Auerbach's "Figura," in *Time, History and Literature: Selected Essays of Erich Auerbach*, 96. An earlier English translation by Ralph Mannheim was published in *Scenes from the Drama of European Literature: Six Essays* (New York: Meridian Books, 1959), 11–76. The original German version was published as "Figura," *Archivum Romanicum* 22 (1938): 436–489.
33 Auerbach, "Figura," 65.
34 Auerbach, "Figura," 83.
35 Hayden White, "Auerbach's Literary History: Figural Causation and Modernist Historicism," in *Figural Realism: Studies in the Mimesis Effect* (Baltimore: Johns Hopkins University Press, 1999), 90.

ity and proliferation of the term in musicology,[36] the fine arts, sociology,[37] and theatre and film studies,[38] there is certainly a common denominator to 'figuration.' In a very basic sense, it refers to processes of formation rather than to form, to the oscillating relationships between form and content, and to the performative aspects of a stage production rather than the assumed effects of this production.[39]

We want to suggest that 'figuration' can be productively adopted for making sense of the contradictory variety of ways in which Shakespeare's Shylock has been interpreted, realized, and discussed (not only) on the German stage:

1. First of all, the term figuration allows us to keep at bay the pressing but tortured discussion of "who Shylock is." It indicates that approaches to Shylock that try to understand him as a psychologically coherent *character* in the tradition of the nineteenth-century realist novel must fail to grasp his inherent contradictions. Instead, he can more productively be described as an over-determined dramatic figure in whose presentation on stage or screen various discursive implications come into play.[40] In this context, Auerbach's reference to the etymology of the term seems crucial: "*figura* comes from the same root as *fingere*."[41] Figures in this sense are always already a product of cultural discourses and artistic practices.

2. The concept of figuration facilitates a consideration of the heterogeneous yet connected temporal layers that are superimposed onto each other in productions of *Merchant:* the early modern period, the Enlightenment with its

---

[36] Alison Latham, "Figuration," in *The Oxford Companion to Music* (Oxford: Oxford University Press, 2011), http://www.oxfordreference.com/view/10.1093/acref/9780199579037.001.0001/acref-9780199579037-e-2510.
[37] See Norbert Elias, *What is Sociology?*, trans. Stephen Mennell and Grace Morrissey (London: Hutchinson / New York: Columbia Press, 1978), esp. 128–133.
[38] Marianne Shapiro, "Figuration," in *The Princeton Encyclopedia of Poetry and Poetics*, 4th ed., ed. Roland Greene et al. (Princeton: Princeton University Press, 2012), 486–487, https://www.degruyter.com/view/books/9781400841424/9781400841424.476/9781400841424.476.xml.
[39] See Gottfried Boehm, Gabriele Brandstetter, and Achatz von Müller, eds., *Figur und Figuration: Studien zu Wahrnehmung und Wissen* (Munich: Fink, 2007); Gabriele Brandstetter and Sibylle Peters, eds., *De figura: Rhetorik – Bewegung – Gestalt* (Munich: Fink, 2002); Bettina Brandl-Risi, Wolf-Dieter Ernst, and Meike Wagner, eds., *Figuration: Beiträge zum Wandel der Betrachtung ästhetischer Gefüge* (Munich: Epodium, 2000); Atsuko Onuki and Thomas Pekar, eds., *Figuration – Defiguration: Beiträge zur transkulturellen Forschung* (Munich: Iudicium, 2006). For an example for the new wave of interest in Auerbach, see Jonathan Holmes and Adrian Streete, eds., *Refiguring Mimesis: Representation in Early Modern Literature* (Hatfield: University of Hertfordshire Press, 2005).
[40] See also Heschel, "From Jesus to Shylock," 431.
[41] Auerbach, "Figura," 65.

contested emancipation (and assimilation) of Western Europe's Jewish populations, the Holocaust, the specific moment of each individual show, and also a recollection of earlier productions that "haunt"[42] the stage. Rather than assuming a simple merging of past and present, or a seamless actualization of the past, the concept of figuration addresses the equivocal and uneasy juxtaposition of these layers.

3. Figuration thus helps describe and problematize a complex and potentially daunting phenomenon that has shaped many post-war productions of *Merchant* in Germany and elsewhere: the tendency towards a secular – and not necessarily deliberate – typological approach that positions Shylock as an anticipation or prefiguration of the Jewish victims of the Holocaust. This approach may enter into strange and disconcerting constellations with attempts to 'understand' Shylock's apparent 'cruelty' in the vein of psychological realism.

4. The concept of figuration also allows an exploration of the tension between the role and its embodied representation on stage, by an actor whose corporeality, costume, language, gestures etc. 'configure' Shylock without the actor completely 'losing himself' (or sometimes herself) in the role. A study of the relationship between actor and role will reveal crucial insights into strategies of naturalization or de-naturalization, and the specific forms of reception that the respective configurations invite.

5. Following Norbert Elias, for whom 'figuration' is a way to study the "interdependence" and "constant flux in the grouping of players" in a given social scenario,[43] we understand Shylock as a relational figure whose meaning is only established in his interactions with other figures: with Antonio his antagonist; with Tubal his Jewish friend; with his daughter Jessica, who converts to Christianity; and with Portia, whose empowerment as a woman is closely linked to Shylock's disempowerment. Our comparison of individual performances over a longer period of time seeks to identify historical shifts in these constellations and account for the reasons why, at a particular historical moment, some relations are suddenly highlighted whereas others become less pronounced.

6. Finally, the concept of 'figuration' as propagated by Auerbach gestures to the entangled cultures of Christianity and Judaism. Like *Mimesis*, Auerbach's essay on "Figura" is a clear, albeit implicit, response to Christian self-iden-

---

[42] Marvin Carlson, *The Haunted Stage: The Theatre as Memory Machine* (2001; Ann Arbor: The University of Michigan Press, 2011).
[43] Elias, *What is Sociology*, 130–131.

tification against the Jewish tradition and marks a deliberate challenge to the separation between the Christian and Hebrew Bibles.[44] We do not claim to systematically continue this line of argument, but want to pay tribute to it. In addition, we will highlight interpretations that have used Shakespeare's *Merchant* in order to explore the entangled histories and cultural traditions of Jews, Christians, and, in recent years, also Muslims.

Calling such figurations 'precarious,' we wish to emphasize their instability, their dependence on context and circumstance, as well as the risky – and, in terms of potential effects, frequently counter-intuitive – ways in which they have been employed as interventions in cultural or political debates. In this way, our term 'precarious figurations' suggests research questions that go far beyond character analysis.

The Structure of the Book

Our study of the German reception of *The Merchant of Venice* is structured chronologically. Rather than narrating a linear and predominantly descriptive stage history, however, we seek to trace dominant traditions in the reception of the play since the early twentieth century and to identify those historical moments in which approaches to the play shifted. In particular, our analyses will focus on the ways in which the figure of Shylock has necessarily come to be both a device in, and a stumbling block for, attempts to bridge the fundamental "rupture in civilization"[45] brought about by the Holocaust. Testing the expectation that the year 1945 necessarily marks a decisive change in the German reception of *Merchant*, the investigation sets out from Max Reinhardt's spectacular productions of the play, revealing lines of continuity that run from the early twentieth century through Weimar and the National Socialist period, and well into post-war society and culture. Chapter 1 ("Figuring Identity: Ruptures and Continuities from the Reinhardt Era to the Early Federal Republic, 1905 – 1957") covers five decades of the play's twentieth-century reception history. It is followed by chapters on the period between the beginning of the 1960s and the end of the 1980s (Chapter 2: "Staging Remembrance: Refigurations on the West German Stage, 1960 – 1990"), and on recent developments since the early

---

44 Hacohen, "Typology and the Holocaust," 612–613.
45 The term was introduced by Dan Diner. See esp. Diner, ed., *Zivilisationsbruch: Denken nach Auschwitz* (Frankfurt/M.: Fischer, 1988).

1990s (Chapter 4: "After Remembrance? Shylock in Reunified Germany, 1990–2010"). A separate chapter (Chapter 3: "Inheriting a Classic: Configurations of *The Merchant of Venice* in the German Democratic Republic, 1949–1990") contrasts the ubiquity of *Merchant* on West German stages with the notable scarcity of productions in the German Democratic Republic, where the play was read in very different ideological frameworks.

Each of the main chapters centres on a number of major productions that can be taken to define a particular phase of reception. These include: Max Reinhardt's series of productions between 1905 and 1934, Lothar Müthel's infamous 1943 *Merchant* at Vienna, the allegedly 'philo-Semitic' renderings of Shylock since the late 1950s, the new departures taken by directors Peter Zadek and George Tabori between 1961 and 1988, Fritz Bennewitz's and Thomas Langhoff's *Merchants* in East Germany, and various productions by Hanan Snir, Karin Beier, Dieter Dorn, and Elmar Goerden between 1990 and the first decade of the new millennium. Our detailed discussions of these productions and their reception are based on diverse documents such as promptbooks and rehearsal notes, sketches and photographs, reviews, and (for more recent productions) video recordings as well as our own observations during performances. These sources constitute points of departure for wider explorations of discursive contexts in the theatre and beyond. Attention is also given to phenomena that have so far been neglected or overlooked, such as East German *Merchants* and the surprising wealth of productions in West Germany in the first half of the 1950s.

In these ways, *Precarious Figurations* interrogates several conventional frameworks of interpretation. Rather than automatically reading contradictory phenomena into a pre-established paradigm of Holocaust remembrance, our discussion seeks to do justice to the perplexing and contradictory range of approaches to the play. Even in productions that downplay or suppress the themes of anti-Semitism and the Holocaust, the traumatic memories connoted by the play necessarily remain present. As a result, topical productions of *Merchant* focussing on the alleged crises of contemporary Germany as a capitalist immigration society may seem to play the issue of Holocaust remembrance off against other issues, thus evoking and displacing the Holocaust at the same time. However, it can still be claimed that – even and especially in the present historical moment – the Shylock figure remains a potent obstacle against conscious or unconscious attempts to lay the ghosts of the past to rest, and to bridge the rupture in civilization. In fact, we will argue that both the precariousness and the potentials of German *Merchants* are due to Shylock's ultimate *dysfunctionality* as both a figure of identification and a figure of remembrance.

1 Figuring Identity: Ruptures and Continuities from the Reinhardt Era to the Early Federal Republic (1905–1957)

During the Second World War, Victor Gollancz strove to bring the extent of the genocide against Europe's Jews home to the British public.[1] Shortly after the war, when his estimations of the number of victims had proved horribly precise, the publisher brought out an important book by a German-Jewish emigrant who responded to anti-Semitism as a theatre enthusiast and literary scholar. In *Shylock: The History of a Character* (1947), Hermann Sinsheimer, who had been a prolific newspaper critic in Weimar Germany, examined Shakespeare's dramatic character in order to fathom "the European myth of the Jew." Interestingly, Sinsheimer attributed a dual function to Shylock as one of the myth's most significant devices. He treated Shakespeare's controversial character not only as a mainstay of anti-Semitic ideologies, but also as a staging ground for a resistant Jewish identity.

The position defined by Sinsheimer in the "Epilogue (Written in England)" that he appended to his study seems surprisingly optimistic as well as strangely ambivalent:

> In conclusion, I would say to my Jewish readers: let us acknowledge Shylock 'the Unwise' as the witness of our past enslavement as well as Nathan the Wise as a witness of our liberation. And let us praise Shakespeare as the genius who has given to the European myth of the Jew, as to many another myth and mystery of our earth, 'a local habitation and a name.'[2]

---

[1] Cf. Ruth Dudley Edwards, *Victor Gollancz: A Biography* (London: Gollancz, 1987), esp. 371–377. By the end of 1942, the devastating news of mass murder provoked Gollancz to write the highly influential pamphlet *Let My People Go: Some Practical Proposals for Dealing with Hitler's Massacre of the Jews and an Appeal to the British Public* (London: Gollancz, 1943).

[2] Hermann Sinsheimer, *Shylock: The History of a Character; or, The Myth of the Jew* (London: Gollancz, 1947); repr. as *Shylock: The History of a Character* (New York: Benjamin Blom, 1963), 144. Sinsheimer here quotes from *A Midsummer Night's Dream* 4.1.14–17. For a magisterial interpretation of Sinsheimer's book on Shylock, see Abigail Gillman, "Shylock in German-Jewish Historiography," in *Wrestling with Shylock: Jewish Responses to The Merchant of Venice*, ed. Edna Nahshon and Michael Shapiro (Cambridge: Cambridge University Press, 2017), 51–73. Gillman offers a comparison between Sinsheimer's book and Heinrich Graetz's 1880 essay "Shylock in der Sage, im Drama und in der Geschichte," strongly emphasizing how the former "embraces Shylock as an inspiring character on a par with the heroes of the Hebrew bible" (53).

It is likely that when he wrote these lines, Sinsheimer already knew that his brother Ludwig and his sister Eugenie had been killed in the Holocaust.[3] The bulk of his book on Shylock, however, had been penned earlier: in Germany, and in German, during the years 1936 and 1937. In a note dated "London, im Jahre 1946," which introduces the German edition (published in 1960 as *Shylock: Die Geschichte einer Figur*), Sinsheimer explained:

> At that time I was trying to get out of Germany – unsuccessfully. Being besieged from without and troubled from within, I resolved that if I could not get away from that polluted country, I would at least get away from those polluted times. On my 'flight' into the adventures of literature and history, I encountered, almost as a matter of course, Shylock: the mirror image of the European Jew as he has never existed, and the counterpoint of everything Jewish in its real form. I resolved to fathom his figure as thoroughly as I could. Thus, while all around the Nazis were staging their bloodthirsty and barbaric Shylockiads, I explored the realms of Shakespeare and of Jewish history.[4]

As the inverted commas indicate, the idea of fleeing anti-Semitic persecution by delving into scholarship on historical constructions of Jewishness may appear both understandable and strange. Still more startling are Sinsheimer's pervasive ambiguities. In the first of the two quotations above, the phrase "European myth of the Jew" stresses the constructedness of respective notions of Jewishness. However, there is also a second phrase, which lends weight to the construct as a "myth and mystery of our earth." Similarly, in the second passage, the solid "realms" of "Jewish history" blend with the more intangible "realms of Shakespeare." At work in both instances is a double move of foregrounding and simultaneously complicating well-rehearsed dichotomies such as 'history vs. myth,' 'fact vs. invention,' and 'reality vs. discourse.' Emphasizing the history-making power of fictions, Sinsheimer blurs the boundaries between two discrete dimen-

---

3 Cf. Hans-Helmut Görtz, *Hermann und Christobel Sinsheimer: Briefe aus England und der Pfalz*, ed. Gabriele Giersberg and Erik Giersberg (Neustadt/Weinstraße: Selbstverlag, 2012). See also Barbara Hartlage-Laufenberg, *Hermann Sinsheimer* (Berlin: Hentrich & Hentrich, 2012). Hermann Sinsheimer's brother Ludwig died in March 1942 in the camp of Gurs in Southern France. His sister Eugenie died at Theresienstadt in September 1942, and her husband Julius Reuter was apparently deported from there to Auschwitz. Karl, Hermann Sinsheimer's second brother, survived the war in a hideout in Germany. A third brother had already died before the First World War.
4 Hermann Sinsheimer, "Zur Vorgeschichte dieses Buches," in *Shylock: Die Geschichte einer Figur* (Munich: Ner-Tamid-Verlag, 1960), 8. This prefatory text was not included in the first (English) edition. The German original holds the tension between the two meanings of the German term 'Figur': as 'character,' in the general sense of a fictional personage, *and* as 'figure' in the specific sense of a representational or rhetorical device.

sions of "Jewish history": on the one hand, as a heritage handed down *by* Jews and, on the other, as a series of constructions *about* Jews. The twisted characterization of Shylock as "the mirror image of the European Jew as he had never existed" underlines this dual perspective.

Sinsheimer describes the process of how Shylock, a heterostereotypical figment of Jewishness, has fallen into history, thereby himself becoming a significant figuration of what it means to be Jewish in a world that defines itself in opposition to Jewishness:

> Shakespeare created the greatest Jewish character since the Bible. Necessarily, he has thus recorded Judaism – that is to say, he has made and written Jewish history. This book is intended as a tribute to him for this by interpreting Shylock from the Jewish point of view. In doing so, Shylock has to be treated, not only as a fictitious character, but also as a figure in Jewish history. His atmosphere is that of the sixteenth century, but, by virtue of Shakespeare's genius, he moves within the perennial destiny of the Jewish people from Biblical times down to the present day.[5]

The way that Sinsheimer slides between Shylock as "a fictitious character" and as "a figure in Jewish history" establishes Shylock as an important reference point for constructions of Jewishness from both the outside *and* the inside. Consequently, Shylock needs to be rejected and adopted at the same time. This take on the character also includes the possibility of turning him against the persecutors. Sinsheimer does so by addressing anti-Semitic discrimination and murder as a series of "bloodthirsty and barbaric Shylockiads."[6]

The precariousness of Sinsheimer's approach is underlined by the fact that he initially wanted to get his book printed in National Socialist Germany: "This book was to be published in Hitler's Germany. It had, not without trembling, been submitted to the Nazi Department authorised, or rather presuming, to censor Jewish manuscripts before publication by Jewish publishers for Jewish readers only, and, surprisingly enough, had passed."[7] Eventually, however, the further radicalization of persecution made it impossible to publish. In 1938, the year of the November Pogrom, Sinsheimer escaped to Palestine. From there he reached Britain, bringing his manuscript with him.

The complex perspective on Shakespeare's Jewish figure as fiction *and* fact, as myth *and* history, as a heterostereotypical figuration open to autostereotypical

---

[5] Sinsheimer, *Shylock: The History of a Character*, 17. This comes from one of two prefaces included in the English edition: "I. Preface written in Nazi Germany (Abridged)."
[6] Sinsheimer, *Shylock: The History of a Character*, 8; cf. 139.
[7] Sinsheimer, "Preface Written in England," in *Shylock: The History of a Character*, 18. This second preface of the English edition is dated "London. May 1943."

re-figurations is not unique to Sinsheimer. In his 1975 landmark study *Außenseiter* (*Outsiders*), the German-Jewish scholar Hans Mayer likewise chose Shylock as a seminal figuration of the socio-cultural positioning of Jews in Europe, specifically as "the phenotype for the Jewish emancipation that failed."[8] Similar to Sinsheimer, Mayer was both perplexed and fascinated by the ways in which the Shylock figure comprised completely different meanings and straddled mutually exclusive epistemologies.[9]

A related perspective is to be found in the meditations on Shakespeare's Jewish character that Heinrich Heine smuggled into his essays on *Shakespeare's Maidens and Women* (1839). Heine suggested that while the other Venetian characters invoked by Shakespeare were "long mouldered in the grave," Shylock must necessarily be "ever living."[10] And indeed, desperately seeking Shylock in contemporary Venice, Heine – or the speaker of his Shakespearean vignettes – eventually makes out his voice among the worshippers in a synagogue:

> I heard a voice in which tears flowed as they were never wept from eyes. There was a sobbing which might have moved a stone to pity – there were utterances of agony such as could only come from a breast which held shut within itself all the martyrdom which an utterly tormented race had endured for eighteen centuries.[11]

This imaginary encounter with an invisible yet audible Shylock transports Shakespeare's character into a twilight zone between fiction and reality, past and present, hetero- and autostereotype. Being appropriated as a Jewish figure of memory, this imaginary Shylock, although himself traumatically powerless, still functions as an agent of empowerment for the assimilated Jew Heine.

The writings of Heine, Sinsheimer, and Mayer demonstrate the special significance that German Jews attributed to the Shylock figure before, during, and after the period dealt with in the present chapter. This is the period from the early twentieth century to the end of the 1950s. The time under investigation thus includes the Second German Empire as well as that empire's demise in conse-

---

8 Hans Mayer, *Outsiders: A Study in Life and Letters*, trans. Denis M. Sweet (Cambridge, MA: MIT, 1982, pb. repr. 1984), 271.
9 On the one hand, Mayer insists that Shylock was "the character of a dramatist" (*Outsiders*, 271). On the other, he observes that "the wealth of individual and national traits in the rich Jew and usurer of Venice is surprising" (279). In relation to Jewish life in eighteenth-century England, it is stated that "reality ha[d] now caught up with Shakespeare's vision" (284).
10 Heinrich Heine, *Shakespeare's Mädchen und Frauen* (1838); English translation: *Shakespeare's Maidens and Women*, in *The Works of Heinrich Heine*, trans. Charles Godfrey Leland (London: Heinemann, 1906), 1: 398.
11 Heine, *Shakespeare's Maidens and Women*, 1: 401.

quence of the First World War; it comprises the attempt to forge a democratic Germany through the institution of the Weimar Republic as well as the destruction of that republic due to the machinations of the far right and due to the imperfect democratic allegiances of the elites; it reaches its nadir in the National Socialist dictatorship, which was backed by a majority of the German people and which culminated in the Second World War and the Holocaust; and finally, the chronological scope of this chapter will take us into the first one-and-a-half decades of the Federal Republic of Germany as one of two separate attempts to reconstruct a German nation that had been devastated not only by war but also by racist ideologies.

The shifting meanings attributed to Shylock within the half century covered by this chapter reflect the devastating developments and horrendous deeds that tore these decades apart. However, it is our proposition that there are also surprising lines of continuity in the cultural workings of the figure. In the following, we will investigate Shylock's ambivalent potential by focussing on two trajectories:

1. *Issues of power and powerlessness:* General cultural discourse and much of the scholarly criticism on *Merchant* have repeated, over and over again, the question whether the play should be read as 'comedy' or 'tragedy' and whether Shylock can be conceived of as a heroic character. Although these discussions are historically significant, the vague concepts of genre that underlie such debates hide another issue: Shylock's power or lack of power. Is he primarily a figuration of Jewish powerlessness and even a vehicle for disempowering Jews? Or can he be used as a reference point in order to construct resilient Jewish identities? It will be argued that these tricky questions dominated the history of the play's reception throughout the first half of the twentieth century.
2. *Figuration vs. identity:* As Heine's, Sinsheimer's, and Mayer's fascination with the relationships between history and myth indicates, the reception of *Merchant* was characterized by continual slippage between figurative and identitarian approaches. On the one hand, discourses and performances stressed both the play's and character's allegorical functions; from this perspective, *Merchant* appeared as a bold fiction, and Shylock as a completely imaginary figuration of Jewishness. On the other hand, and very often simultaneously, *Merchant* was seen and performed as a breathtaking drama of (Jewish) identity. In consequence, both play and character were inserted into history, and into the sociocultural realities of the day. Most often, the significance of particular contributions to the discourse lies within the specific way the two approaches (figurative or identitarian) were coordi-

nated, confused or played off against each other, rather than in a decision for one of the two.

During the chapter's investigation of Shylock's career for the first sixty years of the twentieth century, it will become evident that he functioned as a puzzle picture. Indeed, it is only in connection to specific contexts, configurations, and perspectives that Shylock took on his various meanings. These meanings have proven strangely flexible; they are likely to tilt as soon as the context changes. Of course, this is a general caveat. However, when we are dealing with a period characterized by affirmative conceptions of a 'German-Jewish symbiosis' as well as by the mass-murder of Jews at the hand and under the governing responsibility of Germans, it is particularly important to remind ourselves how loaded, complex, and contradictory the Shylock figure really is.

1.1 From the Reinhardt Era to the Rise of the Anti-Semitic Hegemony

"Drowned in a sea of music" – Max Reinhardt's Integrationist Design

The most influential production of *Merchant* in German history premiered in Berlin on 9 November 1905. Produced and directed by Max Reinhardt at his newly acquired Deutsches Theater, this *Merchant* addressed a late-Wilhelminian society that was torn between metropolitan attitudes of progressivism and the reactionary rhetoric of nationalism, between loud bursts of self-confidence and a pervasive undertone of insecurity. Shylock was played by the eminent Jewish actor Rudolph Schildkraut, whose son Joseph later claimed that this *Merchant* was "Max Reinhardt's greatest gamble, Rudolf Schildkraut's greatest victory, and Berlin's baptism as an artistic center of European liberalism."[12] This remark indicates the significance that could be attributed to the lavish production that Reinhardt put on right at the beginning of the twentieth century. Not only were elements of the 1905 *Merchant* emulated and resurrected by various other directors, but Reinhardt himself also repeatedly returned to his fabulous early success.[13]

---

[12] Joseph Schildkraut, *My Father and I* (1959), qtd. in Andrew G. Bonnell, *Shylock in Germany: Antisemitism and the German Theatre from the Enlightenment to the Nazis* (London: Tauris Academic Studies, 2008), 50–52.

[13] Cf. Jeanette R. Malkin, "Fritz Kortner and Other German-Jewish Shylocks before and after the Holocaust," in *Wrestling with Shylock*, ed. Nahshon and Shapiro, 198–223. In the context of her

After his first *Merchant* had been in the repertory for several years, the director presented a new version in 1913. This production, in which Albert Bassermann played Shylock, stayed on the programme right into the middle of the First World War. On 8 November 1918 – one day before Germany became a republic, and three days before the armistice was signed at Compiègne – a third major production of the play premiered at the Deutsches Theater. Shylock was played by yet another important member of Reinhardt's ensemble: Alexander Moissi. In 1921, the director also tried out the play at his grand new theatre for the masses, the Großes Schauspielhaus Berlin, with Werner Krauß as Shylock. Three years later, Reinhardt's last German-language production of *Merchant* took place in a more intimate environment, at Vienna's Theater in der Josefstadt, and it relied on a very different actor in the role of Shylock: Fritz Kortner. When these productions, spanning the period from 1905 to 1924, are considered together, we arrive at no less than 380 shows, some of which must have been watched by sizeable crowds.[14]

Reinhardt's productions of *Merchant* have been discussed in relation to the director's "project of a metropolitan, liberal theatre"[15] or as invocations of a "humanist world theatre."[16] From a different perspective, the Marxist critic Heinrich Braulich addressed the director's work up to the First World War as a prime example of "the romantic dream theatre of the bourgeois pre-war society." According to Braulich's admiring yet critical view, Reinhardt offered "the most complete expression of late bourgeois wishes, dreams and desires" and aimed at "entertaining the masses by means of total illusion."[17] Arthur Kahane, longtime assistant to Reinhardt, reported how the director himself saw this dimension of his work. Allegedly, Reinhardt declared:

---

essay on Kortner, Malkin also offers a brief general assessment of the significance of Reinhardt's productions of *Merchant* (see esp. 204–209).

14 For detailed data on Reinhardt's productions, see Heinrich Huesmann's compendium *Welttheater Reinhardt: Bauten, Spielstätten, Inszenierungen* (Munich: Prestel, 1983).

15 Peter W. Marx, "Die drei Gesichter Shylocks: Zu Max Reinhardts Projekt eines metropolitanen, liberalen Theaters vor dem Hintergrund seiner jüdischen Herkunft," in *Max Reinhardt und das Deutsche Theater*, ed. Roland Koberg, Bernd Stegemann, and Henrike Thomsen (Berlin: Deutsches Theater/Henschel, 2005), 51–59.

16 See Markus Moninger's important "Die Dramaturgie von *Merchant*-Inszenierungen in der Weimarer Republik," 2005, last modified 20 August 2018, in *Zukunft braucht Erinnerung*, accessed 8 September 2018, http://www.zukunft-braucht-erinnerung.de/die-dramaturgie-von-merchant-inszenierungen-in-der-weimarer-republik/, n. p.

17 Heinrich Braulich, "Das romantische Traumtheater der bürgerlichen Vorkriegsgesellschaft," in *Max Reinhardt* (Berlin: Henschelverlag, 1969), 63–157.

> What I have in mind is a theatre which will again give joy to people – which will elevate them above themselves, leading them out of the grey misery of their everyday lives into the bright and clear air of beauty. It is evident to me how much the audience is fed up with encountering, again and again, their own squalor even in the theatre. Instead, people yearn for brighter colours and a higher sense of being.[18]

Among the means for achieving such elevation were sheer technical perfection and lavish detail. Reinhardt's productions of *Merchant* offered not only a grand spectacle, but an overall sensory experience that included elaborate sound images as well as festive music that had been specially composed by Engelbert Humperdinck. A review of the 1905 production enthused:

> Setting: Venice. Time: the Renaissance. Dramatic poetry that avails itself of such a setting does not merely allow for but positively demands the full array of theatrical art, utmost sensual splendour and a thoroughly magical atmosphere. Indeed, productions of the play generally vie with each other in terms of colourful scenery and lavish decoration. Reinhardt, however, [...] has exceeded earlier productions in a way that leads to 'authenticity,' to a sense of being true to locality and history, to an illusion of reality that will be difficult to top in the future.[19]

The reviewer, Heinrich Hart, was particularly pleased with the last scene: "the park of Belmont with water in the background." As he confessed, he had "never seen anything more enchanting on the stage." Only "the glimmering of the stars" should perhaps have been done "in a more natural way": its golden splendour seemed a bit excessive to the critic. Hart also drew attention to a technical device that Reinhardt used to great effect: "Hail to the revolving stage!" the reviewer exclaimed emphatically. Through seamless transitions between scenes, Reinhardt had attempted to forge the divergent worlds and moods of the play into a consistent whole: "Thanks to the revolving stage we are at last able to see a *Merchant of Venice* as actually conceived by Shakespeare and not as botched together by adaptors." As Hart observed, previous productions had always created the impression that *Merchant* was "tragedy mixed with farce." In the version presented by the Deutsches Theater, however, "the entirety of the play is made to appear in its true form: as a free aesthetic play with serious-

---

18 Reinhardt according to Arthur Kahane, *Tagebuch des Dramaturgen* (1928), qtd. in Braulich, "Das romantische Traumtheater," 66.
19 Heinrich Hart, review of Reinhardt's 1905 production of *Merchant*, *Der Tag*, 11 November 1905, qtd. in Koberg et al., *Max Reinhardt*, 104.

ness and jest, using its theatrical gracefulness to enchant the audience and thus to win it over to a finer humanity."[20]

The German theatre scholar Markus Moninger observes that the revolving stage facilitated an almost filmic illusion of plasticity. He goes on to associate the stage setting with a specific ideational design: the Jewish quarter became part of a coherent representation of Venice as a maze of lanes, canals or bridges, while a tapestry of everyday noises that could be heard in all the city scenes corroborated this sense of interconnectedness.[21] The stage plan for the 1913 production (see figure 1) also suggests these programmatic leanings. Viewed from above, the revolving stage contains an urban landscape that is arranged around a canal spanned by bridges. Belmont (indicated as "Portia's room" on the plan) does not appear as a far-away realm, but as part of the city space. And "Shylock's house" can actually be seen to lean onto the outer wall of the large "court-room."

However, while Shylock and his Jewish world may have been integrated into the theatrical 'Venice,' they certainly were not centre stage. This impression is corroborated by the way in which Arthur Kahane presented the 1913 production to the German Shakespeare Society. In his talk, Reinhardt's assistant responded to the well-known tendency, initiated by Charles Macklin, Edmund Kean, and Henry Irving in eighteenth- and nineteenth-century England, of developing Shylock into a dominant virtuoso role, rendering him as a full-fledged tragic hero rather than a comedic character.[22] Kahane, however, clearly wanted to put Shakespeare's Jewish character back in his place: "The hero, the centre, the heart and the essence of this production is Venice. Not Shylock, but Venice. The eternally singing, eternally humming Venice. A city exulting with lust for life, indulgence, joy and exuberance."[23] The dramaturge went as far as ranking the Jewish character along with the side-roles of Morocco and Aragon: "Ultimately," Kahane argued, "Shylock also partakes in this pattern of the funny foreigner." In contrast to Portia's ridiculous suitors, however, there was allegedly something truly threatening about the revenge-thirsty moneylender. Characterizing Shylock as a version of the type of "the troublesome stranger" and as "an intrusive and uncanny guest," Kahane went on:

---

20 Hart, qtd. in Koberg et al., *Max Reinhardt*, 104.
21 Moninger, "Die Dramaturgie von *Merchant*-Inszenierungen," n. p.
22 For a stage history of Shylock, see John Gross, *Shylock: Four Hundred Years in the Life of a Legend* (London: Chatto & Windus, 1992); US edition: *Shylock: A Legend and Its Legacy* (New York: Simon & Schuster, 1992).
23 Arthur Kahane, "Max Reinhardt's Shakespeare-Zyklus im Deutschen Theater zu Berlin," *Shakespeare Jahrbuch* 50 (1914): 116.

1.1 From the Reinhardt Era to the Rise of the Anti-Semitic Hegemony — 23

We can be certain that he seemed quite as repelling and laughable and barbaric to Shakespeare as he does to the Venetians. For a moment, of course, the cheated Jew of the fairy tale bursts into the carefree bright sky of the Venetians like a dangerous thundercloud. As soon as Portia's word has dispelled the cloud and the danger, however, the full Venetian zest for life bursts forth in a shout of release. Joy makes itself heard twice as loud as before, and the memory of the uncanny and foreign is drowned in a sea of music.[24]

In Reinhardt's productions of *Merchant*, the "shout of release" mentioned by Kahane seems to have been staged in a pronounced manner. Apparently, it

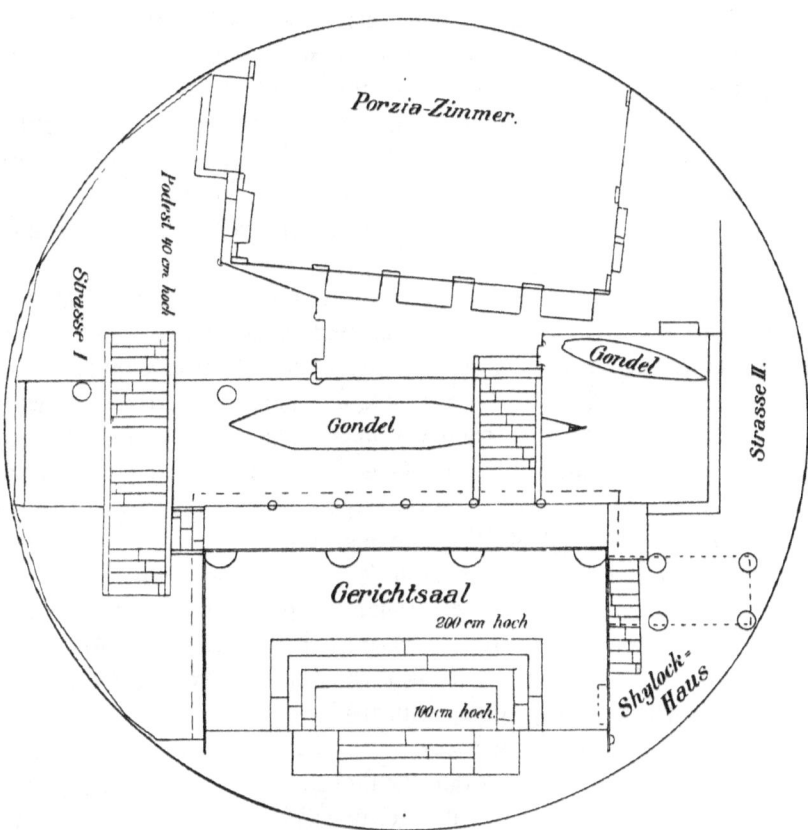

Figure 1: Stage plan for Max Reinhardt's 1913 production of *Merchant* at Deutsches Theater Berlin. Stage design: Ernst Stern; sketch by Rudolf Dworsky. *Shakespeare Jahrbuch* 50 (1914), 117. Courtesy of Deutsches Theater Berlin.

---

24 Kahane, "Max Reinhardt's Shakespeare-Zyklus," 117.

went forth after the critical moment in the trial scene when Portia intervenes with the words:

> Tarry a little. There is something else.
> [...] if thou dost shed
> One drop of Christian blood, thy lands and goods
> Are by the laws of Venice confiscate
> Unto the state of Venice. (4.1.300–307)

According to an account by Eduard von Winterstein, who played Bassanio in the 1905 production, there was then a long pause during which the action froze. Only after almost a minute of spell-bound silence came the massive cry of joy.[25] Interestingly, it is this theatrical device that Frederick Tollini sees as proof that Reinhardt's approach was not "simplistic," even though it was bent to indulge in the charms of Venice and to condone the faults of the Christians. According to this argument, the shout of the victorious majority was recognizable as an "excessive outburst," underlining the "hypocrisy of those who were most vociferous in their demand for justice," and perhaps even indicating their tendency towards dangerous "group hysteria."[26]

It is hard to decide whether such interpretations – interpretations that position Reinhardt's productions in accordance with late-twentieth-century attitudes – are accurate. The details of a historical stage event cannot be reconstructed from a few reviews and eyewitness accounts, and even if we were able to watch a show of the production, we would be led to recognize that theatrical performance resists the attribution of clear-cut significations. For the same reasons, Kahane's dismissive sketch of Shylock's role should not be read as a digest of fixed ideational content. It is more likely that it represents an apodictic formulation of ideas which were *at play* in Reinhardt's productions, vying with contrary ideas. Evidently, for all his painstaking planning of detail, the director conceived of the theatre as an open, discursive space in which various forces and dispositions were allowed to interact. As a consequence, Reinhardt's productions probably invited both sympathy with the supposed "zest for life" of the Venetians, *and* empathy with Shylock's situation as the outsider.

In this vein, Moninger suggests that the director rendered the trial scene as "a last minute rescue, by which the fun society was made to taste the potential consequences of their inhumanity." This interpretation resolves the contradic-

---

[25] Winterstein is referred in Frederick Tollini's analysis of the scene in *The Shakespeare Productions of Max Reinhardt* (Lewiston, NY: Edwin Mellen, 2004), 64–66.
[26] Tollini, *The Shakespeare Productions*, 64–65.

tions of Reinhardt's production by proposing a chiastic move: on the one hand, "in order to show Shylock in a positive light, it was necessary to also rehabilitate his judges;" while on the other hand, as Moninger observes with reference to Reinhardt's interpretation of Act 5 as a scene of reconciliation, "Shylock had to be sacrificed, as it were, in order to salvage the blocked-up humanity of the social community."[27]

The assessment of Reinhardt's productions depends on what exactly was "drowned in a sea of music" (Kahane). As we would like to suggest, characterizations of the director's work as "humanist world theatre" point to Reinhardt's attempt to reinstate the formulas of enlightened universalism. With respect to Jews, these formulas equated *emancipation* with *integration*, and they simultaneously made the promise of integration dependent on the minority's unqualified readiness to *assimilate*. In 1905, a real integration of Jews into German society and culture – one that would go along with a stable acknowledgement of the tremendous weight of Jewishness in that culture – may have appeared feasible, particularly in the context of Berlin's ongoing rise to becoming "an artistic centre of European liberalism" (Joseph Schildkraut).

Reinhardt's decision to give up his birth name, Goldmann, may be seen in the context of such demands (assimilation), promises (integration), and hopes (emancipation). However, the brutal destruction of these arrangements is documented by the way in which Reinhardt opened an autobiographical manuscript penned in 1943, a few months before his death: "Ich bin ein Jude." ("I am a Jew.")[28] Even before he was forced to flee Germany in 1937, the director certainly felt the strictures of assimilation and the frailty of the promise of integration. On the one hand, then, Reinhardt's productions were based on the wish to prolong an integrationist design, even if it rested on the prescription of assimilation. On the other hand, he also must have been motivated by an urge to question the very rules of the game. Viewed in this light, Reinhardt's take on *Merchant* was an attempt to engineer a balance between the discourse of identity and the discourse of assimilation, between the articulation and the submersion of Jewish difference. Such a precarious balance depended on a readiness to continuously displace Shylock into the realm of allegorical significance. This was Reinhardt's way of replicating Heine's approach: acknowledging Shylock's faltering voice while simultaneously pretending to be unable to see him.

---

27 Moninger, "Die Dramaturgie von *Merchant*-Inszenierungen," n. p.
28 Qtd. in Tollini, *The Shakespeare Productions*, 9.

Identifying Shylock – Rudolph Schildkraut and the Discourses of the Weimar Republic

There are many studio photos portraying Rudolph Schildkraut as Shylock in the context of Reinhardt's 1905 production. Even if we consider the difference between posing in the studio and performing on stage, the pictures betray a startling stylization of the figure. While the play's other characters (including Jessica) wore a historicist Renaissance costume, Shylock was clad in an outrageous fairy-tale garb that evoked contemporary concepts of the 'Orient.' In accordance with nineteenth-century practice, Schildkraut's make-up did not only boast conventional markers of Jewishness – a tousled beard, curled side locks, and an (indistinct) yellow badge – but it also played with the codified aesthetics of ugliness, particularly through an over-evident painted gap in the teeth. In addition, the photos show large gesticulating hands, on which the actor wore enormous rings with fake diamonds. As Peter W. Marx observes, this outward appearance already relegated Shylock to "comic marginality" in relation to the other characters on stage. Moreover, "such otherness also kept a potential Jewish audience – an audience for whom this image was even stranger than the appearance of Jewish migrants from Eastern Europe – from identifying with the figure." Instead of inviting identification, Marx argues, this Shylock was stylized to the point of turning into a "geometrical figure."[29]

Marx's use of the term "figure" is instructive. More precisely than the frequent remarks on the 'fairy-tale' qualities of Reinhardt's productions, the concepts of *figure* and *figuration* can help describe the director's tendency to bracket in Shylock's identity, deferring his literal significance as a Jew, and pushing him into the realm of the figurative: the realm of allegory or myth. The aim of this strategy was not simply escapist. Rather, Reinhardt's (neo-)romantic conception of theatre implied some kind of socio-cultural transformation. As we would like to claim, Shylock was the governing device by which the director regulated the movement between allegory and representation, between metaphorical and metonymical relations, between abstraction and identification.

This movement was mediated through a sliding between two dimensions of Shylock: on the one hand, as a figure in the sense of an artificial device and, on the other, as a figure in the sense of a character representing a specific social position or group. However, throughout the long period during which Reinhardt was engaged in producing *Merchant* – from his first production at Berlin's Deutsches Theater in 1905 to his very last production of the play, an outdoor per-

---

[29] Marx, "Die drei Gesichter Shylocks," 53.

formance at the Venice Biennale of 1934 – it became more and more difficult to maintain the precarious balance between figurative and identitarian approaches. As we shall see, the pervasive drive towards a drama of identity not only showed itself in the general cultural discourse on *Merchant* and in the work of other directors, but it also became manifest within the carefully calibrated design of Reinhardt's own productions.

Outside the theatre, the most consistent conceptualization of Shylock as a device of displacement and transformation was offered in an essay by Gustav Landauer. Landauer – Jew, socialist, anarchist, and Shakespeare scholar – was murdered when right-wing militia terminated the short-lived Bavarian Soviet Republic of 1919, in which he had served as commissioner for education and propaganda. His posthumously published Shakespearean essays were based on lectures given in Berlin during the First World War. The piece on *Merchant* ranks as one of the most influential – and one of the most interesting – German interpretations of the play. It clearly shows Landauer's esoteric anthropology, which made him read the twisted comedy as a fable of redemption. In this interpretation, Belmont figures as a blessed realm, presided over by Portia as the "highest and purest incarnation of light, colour, warmth and harmony."[30] As Landauer argued, even average and fallible human beings can hope to be eventually admitted into Portia's realm. This hope rests on a socialist theology that posits Shakespeare as a god-like inventor of the human:

> There is hardly another play by Shakespeare which moves us to such a degree of personal gratitude towards the poet, who, from his very heart, was lenient and kind towards all of us [...]. If he has admitted Bassanio, Antonio, Lorenzo, Jessica, Gratiano, and people of even lesser degree, then for us, too, the gate will not be locked.[31]

However, such universal redemption depends on the exclusion of one character: Shylock. He is interpreted as an allegory of humanity's conscious rejection of redemption. In this manner, Landauer defined a perspective from which it was possible to pity Shylock, and yet to ratify his destruction:

> It is us whom Shylock's furious and tortured cry follows. We are allowed and commanded to live, prosper and grow, even though the old man has been corrupted because of us, dying because of us like a wounded animal that has withdrawn into its hiding. [...] We – no matter whether we are men or women, Jews or Christians, but particularly the young folks – we may attend to our own affairs in work or play and hope for the kingdom to come, the king-

---

[30] Gustav Landauer, "Der Kaufmann von Venedig", in *Shakespeare: Dargestellt in Vorträgen* (Frankfurt/M.: Rütten und Loening, 1920), 1: 66.
[31] Landauer, "*Der Kaufmann von Venedig*," 90.

dom of souls bound and set free, of beauty and freedom, of mercy and harmony. Come, Jessica![32]

Landauer thus invited his readers to sympathize but not empathize with Shylock. More precisely, the persistent first person plural shows that Landauer wanted the audience to sympathize with Shylock and at the same time identify with the Venetian majority. This approach depended on reading both Shylock's Jewishness and the Venetians' Christianity (including their anti-Semitism) in an abstract way. Along these lines, Landauer envisaged a total reciprocal assimilation or a mutual dissolution of Jewishness and Christianity, which would prepare for the (socialist) "kingdom [...] of beauty and freedom, of mercy and harmony." Into this kingdom, Jessica was explicitly invited as a protagonist of sociocultural renewal. Shylock, however, had to be excluded, carrying the full burden of "our" common, historically determined guilt, shame, and hate. Shakespeare's Jewish character therefore came to be treated as a symbolic figuration of the burdens of unredeemed – pre-revolutionary – history. Thus, while Shylock represented "a dark, uncanny, hellish force," Landauer also pointed out that the pressure exerted by Shylock was in fact "reactive," so that "the fabled werewolf" had to be regarded as "the intellectually and spiritually significant representative of an abused and oppressed class."[33]

Given this stance, how did Landauer respond to Reinhardt's conception of *Merchant*? The socialist showed himself moved by Schildkraut's Shylock. However, he feared that the actor's approach to the role threatened to explode purely figurative readings by inviting not only sympathy for, but also identification with Shylock:

> The actor Schildkraut, whose Jewishness can be felt to tremble in its innermost humanity as he plays the role, consistently attempts to tone down harsh contrasts and to foreground sympathetic traits in Shylock. [...] There is in fact something to be said in support of such an approach. However, the more we force ourselves to hardness the closer we get to such Shakespearean figures.[34]

While Landauer's esoteric socialism overlapped with Reinhardt's romanticist leanings, the former's insistence on dogmatic "hardness" deviated from the polysemy of the latter's productions. In this context, Peter W. Marx's discussion of the 1905 production is again instructive. Marx acknowledges Reinhardt's tenden-

---

[32] Landauer, "Der Kaufmann von Venedig," 90.
[33] Landauer, "Der Kaufmann von Venedig," 60.
[34] Landauer, "Der Kaufmann von Venedig," 56–57.

cy to indulge in the pseudo-Renaissance rhetoric of splendour, music, and carelessness – a tendency that seems to underline Landauer's reading of the play: "The production presented lavish images that illustrated the zest for life and the vitality of a merry Renaissance city, which was made to appear yet more colourful and lively by the presence of the 'Other.'" However, Marx continues, Rudolf Schildkraut's representation of Shylock provided a counter-current to such surface tendencies and "opened up a space for reflection."[35] Indeed, the famous addition of a minutely choreographed and heart-breaking scene that showed Shylock returning to his empty house after Jessica's elopement is palpable proof of the director's and the actor's efforts to motivate the Jew's later behaviour.[36]

The difficulty of defining the thin line between figurative and identitarian approaches to Shylock comes to the fore in an essay on *Merchant* that the eminent philologist Friedrich Gundolf included in a 1928 study on Shakespeare. Gundolf was a member of the circle around Stefan George and had published a notable neo-Romantic study on "Shakespeare and the German Spirit" (*Shakespeare und der deutsche Geist*, 1911). He represents a tendency among assimilationist German-Jewish intellectuals to participate in a specific discourse on German cultural nationalism. On the one hand, he firmly refused to read Shylock as a representation of Jewishness: "Shylock's Jewishness, however impressive and authentic it may seem, is neither race nor rank but fairy-tale hue."[37] As Gundolf argued, "reading Brutus from the point of view of classical studies or Shylock from the point of view of race science is to confuse colour and essence: both are manifestations of eternal traits of humanity, rendered meaningful through historical substance."[38] On the other hand, Gundolf argued that Shylock could acquire universal significance exactly because he offered a strikingly authentic manifestation of Jewish specificity. In relation to Shylock's diction, Gundolf observed: "Biblical themes and a biblical tonality forge the heightened every-day speech of the Renaissance into a Jewish speech that is as real, as foreign, and as original as Caliban's mumbling. The point is not in imitating detail but in recreating the essence in a new medium."[39] It is possible to read

---

35 Marx, "Die drei Gesichter Shylocks," 53.
36 See Braulich, "Das romantische Traumtheater," 85–86, where Reinhardt's design for the realization of this scene in the 1934 production at Venice's Campo San Trovaso is quoted at length.
37 Friedrich Gundolf, "*Der Kaufmann von Venedig*," in *Shakespeare: Sein Wesen und sein Werk* (Berlin: Bondi, 1928), 1: 566.
38 Gundolf, "*Der Kaufmann von Venedig*," 574.
39 Gundolf, "*Der Kaufmann von Venedig*," 588.

Gundolf's essay as a forceful treatise against racialist delimitations of Jewishness. However, it is also striking how easily the text can be re-inserted into the very discourse of race that it aims to circumvent.

In the same year in which Gundolf's essay appeared in print, another important German-Jewish intellectual, Arnold Zweig, looked back on Schildkraut's Shylock in an unguardedly affirmative way. In his monograph *Juden auf der deutschen Bühne* ("Jews on the German Stage"), Zweig read Schildkraut's performance as a monument of the Jewish contribution to the German stage. He paid tribute to the kindness and benevolence initially shown by this Shylock. Zweig's main emphasis, however, was on the sheer power with which Schildkraut imbued the enraged Shylock:

> This Shylock is a real inhabitant of the Venetian Ghetto, a place where the forcefulness of a self-conserving Jewishness – a Jewishness defending itself in a most narrow space – is at home. You will not be allowed to spit into his beard with impunity. It is not a good idea to first mistreat and provoke him, and then to fall into his hands. [...] To pay back injuries point by point, this is what he is a man for. [...] Schildkraut's Shylock smells of onions and garlic – and this is a meal and a smell at least as good as slaughtered pigs and goat kids cooked in their mothers' milk. [...] The right of self-defence clearly is on his side, and he has a tremendous vital power that allows him to strike back even in situations when other types would have long since made an ideal of their serfdom. This is why Rudolf Schildkraut, fidgeting, plump, and producing guttural sounds, has been one of the most potent fascinations and shocks on the German stage.[40]

It is remarkable how much Zweig, writing more than twenty years after Schildkraut first played the role, diverged from earlier accounts. In 1905, a reviewer had observed about Schildkraut's Shylock:

> Without doubt, he wishes to assimilate himself without forsaking his religion. He wants to live in peace with these fine and powerful Christian merchants, and he wants to peacefully do business with them. Even in his speech and movements he attempts to flexibly adapt to the mores of the country.[41]

Furthermore, when Schildkraut's interpretation of Shylock was compared to that of his (non-Jewish) successor, Albert Bassermann, the forcefulness of the latter was usually contrasted to the frailty of the former: "With Bassermann in the role, the play appears tragic, grand, uneven, unjust, and unbearable. With Schildkraut it seems entertaining as well as a little bit sad, aesthetically satisfy-

---

[40] Arnold Zweig, *Juden auf der deutschen Bühne* (Berlin: Welt-Verlag, 1928), 178–179.
[41] Fritz Engel, *Berliner Tagblatt*, 13 November 1905; qtd. in Koberg et al., *Max Reinhardt*, 105.

ing and notably small."⁴² Zweig apparently saw a different Schildkraut from the one these critics had described.

At the same time, Zweig's insistence on the resilient power of Shylock cannot be read as a tribute to any kind of Jewish separatism. Quite to the contrary, *Juden auf der deutschen Bühne* was an attempt at upholding notions of a 'German-Jewish symbiosis' against the increasing anti-Semitism. In his preface, Zweig presented the German theatre as an example of propitious German-Jewish synergies. He explained how "the Jews, the Austrian Jews in particular," had "served the evolving German drama" and how they expected "to be eventually digested by the grand cultural organism of the German people."⁴³ Clearly, Zweig was not attempting to conjure up a Jewish counterforce to German culture, but rather to highlight Jews as an important presence within that culture. In terms of both his strength and his frailty, Schildkraut's Shylock seemed to be a case in point. Yet, Zweig was writing at a time when it was becoming more and more difficult to articulate Jewishness within an integrated German culture. The quoted passage is indeed an instance of "Jewishness defending itself in a most narrow space," and there was evidently a mounting awareness that it was not only a cultural position that needed to be defended, but the very lives of the Jews.

Inhabiting Shylock – Alexander Granach and Fritz Kortner

Zweig presented a double-sided picture of Schildkraut's Shylock: on the one hand, as a powerful character and, on the other, as a "fidgeting" and "plump" person with a "guttural" accent. At about the same point in time, the young actor Alexander Granach was yet more determined in drawing out Shylock's power, aiming to show him as an unqualified Jewish hero figure. Granach (1890–1945) was born in Galicia as the son of Jewish peasants. His passion for the theatre brought him to Berlin, where he originally worked as a baker. He first played Shylock in 1920, in a production at the Munich Schauspielhaus (director: Hermine Körner), and then again in 1924, at Berlin's Volksbühne (director: Fritz Holl). In terms of dramaturgical design, the second production in particular seems to have been close to Reinhardt's dramaturgical formula for the play. Granach had been a student at Reinhardt's acting academy, and he had sometimes stepped in as an understudy in Reinhardt's productions, for

---

42 Siegfried Jacobsohn, *Das Jahr der Bühne* 3 (1913/14); qtd. in Marx, "Die drei Gesichter Shylocks," 55.
43 Zweig, *Juden auf der deutschen Bühne*, 27–28.

example as Portia's servant Balthazar in a performance of *Merchant* on 26 May, 1914.⁴⁴ After the First World War – during which he had been drafted into the Austro-Hungarian Army – Granach returned to Germany and embarked on a splendid stage and screen career, performing in Murnau's *Nosferatu* (1922) among other films. His success continued after he had fled from Germany in 1933. As an emigrant, Granach lived in Poland, the Soviet Union, Switzerland, and the United States.⁴⁵

The theatre critic Hermann Sinsheimer, with whose study on Shylock we have opened this chapter, was among the actor's early supporters.⁴⁶ Granach evidently shared his mentor's fascination with Shylock. He devoted the entire concluding chapter of his memoirs – published in 1945, the year of his death – to Shakespeare's character, who emerges as both a canonical stage figure and an empowering Jewish role model. Granach talks about the injustice done to Shylock and recounts how, as a teenager, he resolved to devote his "entire life to slamming this injustice into the face of the world."⁴⁷ When he first played Shylock in Munich, the actor tacitly based his performance on a private fantasy concerning the character's fate after the verdict. Convinced that "never can a Shylock alter his faith,"⁴⁸ he conjured up an imaginary biography for Shylock after the trial. Escaping from Venice, Granach's Shylock eventually arrives in Galicia (Ukraine), where he remarries and becomes the progenitor of a large family. His children are described as "broad-shouldered, hard-working, and hungry for new experiences."⁴⁹ Granach imagined himself as a descendant of this Shylock. According to this fantasy, some of Shylock's offspring became actors, went West, and "discovered their forefather in the work of Shakespeare":

> From their parents and forebears they had learnt about Shylock's story of suffering. Now, on account of their kindred heart, they recognized him. And they played the character of their ancestor in a tragic and partisan manner, leaning on the genius of Shakespeare,

---

44 Huesmann, *Welttheater Reinhardt*, entry 715, n. p.
45 On Granach's life and work, see Irmela von der Lühe, "'Sogar das Sterben ist hier wunderschön: Grenzgänge des Schauspielers und Schriftstellers Alexander Granach," in *Anthropologien der Endlichkeit: Stationen einer literarischen Denkfigur seit der Aufklärung*, ed. Friederike Felicitas Günther and Torsten Hoffmann (Göttingen: Wallstein 2011), 208–218, and Zweig, *Juden auf der deutschen Bühne*, 149–156.
46 Zweig, *Juden auf der deutschen Bühne*, 152.
47 Alexander Granach, "Shylock," in *Da geht ein Mensch: Autobiographischer Roman* (Stockholm: Neuer Verlag, 1945), 421.
48 Granach, *Da geht ein Mensch*, 424.
49 Granach, *Da geht ein Mensch*, 427.

who has generously given so much power, so much life, so much sense of justice, and so much human dignity to a dark figure.⁵⁰

The German adverb we have translated as "in a partisan manner" is "parteiisch." It relates to the process of taking a position, either in the context of a lawsuit or in a political sense (such as acting in the interest of a specific political party). Granach's point is that in playing Shylock he allowed himself to be prejudiced in favour of a politically relevant Jewish position. This attitude is diametrically opposed to playing Shylock as an allegorical figure. As envisaged by Granach, Shylock emerges as a decidedly *Jewish* person of character. His power is not in wild outbursts, but in the quiet, although potentially desperate confidence of being in the right. Granach methodically blends his own biography with that invented for his Shylock, intending not merely to *play*, but rather to *inhabit* the character.

In the 1920s another young Jewish actor also offered resistance to the twin paradigm of assimilation and figurative displacement: Fritz Kortner (1892–1970).⁵¹ As an adolescent, Kortner had seen Schildkraut as Shylock in Vienna, where the Reinhardt ensemble had offered a guest performance of *Merchant*. In his autobiography, first published in 1959, Kortner remembered the tremendous impact of the experience:

> As represented by this Levantine arch-Jew, Shylock was utterly incapable of any evil intent. He softly endured the injustice he had to suffer, up to the point when it eventually became unbearable and when he burst forth in a frightening way. In his brute force and berserk wildness, something never before seen in Vienna, he continues to rank as a monument of the art of acting. In comparison to this performance contemporary takes on Shylock [...] almost appear to be drawing-room efforts.⁵²

---

50 Granach, *Da geht ein Mensch*, 427–428. On Granach's interpretation of Shylock in *Da geht ein Mensch*, see Nina Warnke and Jeffrey Shandler, "Yiddish Shylocks in Theater and Literature," in *Wrestling with Shylock*, ed. Nahshon and Shapiro, 74–75 and 96–98. Warnke and Shandler put the emphasis on how Granach, as a refugee from National Socialist Germany, portrayed Shylock in Warsaw in 1934.
51 A sensitive essay on Kortner's struggles with the role was offered by Ernst Theodor Sehrt, "Der Shylock Fritz Kortners," *Shakespeare Jahrbuch* (West) (1973): 78–96. See also Malkin's important essay "Fritz Kortner and Other German-Jewish Shylocks," esp. the section on "Kortner's Pre-War Shylocks" (209–216).
52 Fritz Kortner, *Aller Tage Abend* (1959; 4th ed., Munich: dtv, 1972), 56.

Insisting on the "brute force and berserk wildness"[53] that Schildkraut's Shylock displayed as a consequence of Jessica's elopement, Kortner – writing after the Holocaust and after his own exile and subsequent return to Germany – was yet more emphatic than Zweig about the power of the performance. However, Kortner also indicated that Schildkraut's forceful Shylock was contained by a dramaturgy that may have been politically naïve: "Looking back at it now, Reinhardt's entire production appears uncritical in its attitude towards society. Everybody was enchanting, happy, carefree, charming, melancholic – and Shylock was an isolated case, sad and pitiable but also heart-warming."[54]

Kortner first attempted to realize his own conception of Shylock in 1923, when he played the role at the Berlin Lustspielhaus for the avant-garde ensemble Die Truppe. Director Berthold Viertel originally aimed at an aesthetic of quasi-cubist abstraction, which would reduce the dramatic characters to the status of figurines. As an eyewitness recounted, in the first dress rehearsal, Kortner was put in "a black ton, which covered everything but his forearms." However, the actor was already well known and could take the liberty of making his point. As soon as he had spoken his first lines, he "tore this straitjacket to pieces and dressed in his own costume."[55] In the premiere he wore a yellow coat. As Moninger observes, it seems as if Kortner had "wrapped Shylock into the yellow badge as into a second skin, displaying the mark of enforced exclusion as a quasi-natural sign."[56] In this manner, Kortner countered Viertel's aesthetics of abstraction with a concrete symbolical gesture. His tearing of the original costume not only signalled resistance against the director's authority, but appears more widely significant as an act of rebellion against aestheticization and as a spectacular gesture of liberating Shylock from the strictures of depersonalization.

The title of a chapter in Richard D. Critchfield's biographical study of Kortner underlines this thrust in the actor's conception of the role: "Kortner as Shylock:

---

53 Kortner's expression is "Brachialgewalt und Wüstenwildheit." The second term, "Wüstenwildheit," can be read as a strange neologism that compounds 'Wüste' (desert) and 'Wildheit' (wildness) into the idea of a 'nomadic wildness' – an idea that may connect to the old figure of the Wandering Jew.
54 Kortner, *Aller Tage Abend*, 56.
55 Ernst Josef Aufricht, qtd. in Klaus Völker, "Berthold Viertels dramatische Opposition und sein Bemühen um ein Theater der Ensemblekunst im Berlin der Zwanziger Jahre," in *Der Traum von der Realität: Berthold Viertel*, ed. Siglinde Bolbecher, Konstantin Kaiser, and Peter Roessler (Vienna: Döcker, 1998), 115.
56 Moninger, "Die Dramaturgie von *Merchant*-Inszenierungen," n. p.

Reclaiming Jewish Identity."⁵⁷ "Identity" is also a key term in an essay by Critchfield that examines Kortner's autobiography as an exercise in "Self-Discovery as the Discovery of the Other." An alternative title offered for the essay reads "A Life and Career as Shylock." The story that Critchfield finds in Kortner's memoirs is the story "of a life, first spent fleeing but ultimately combating anti-Semitism; first rejecting, yet finally accepting Jewish identity" – and of doing so through repeated attempts of appropriating the Shylock figure.⁵⁸ The phrase "finally accepting Jewish identity" sounds deceptively simple. Kortner acted in a historical moment when a long tradition of anti-Semitism was finally striving for full political power. While in playing Shylock Granach evoked his personal background in the tight-knit Jewish communities of Galicia, Kortner could not build on a comparable alternative to the anti-Semitic societies of Germany and Austria. At the same time, he would not bow to the cliché of the 'good Jew' that European Christianity offered as the flip-side of its image of the 'evil Jew.' In consequence, Kortner's acceptance and performance of Jewish identity was not an uncomplicated process of coming into one's own. Rather, the actor boldly took possession of a bundle of explosive clichés and suffocating identity patterns, seeking to somehow control them and turn them around by the sheer force of his acting *and* his personality.

Contemporary accounts emphasize how radically Kortner insulated his 1923 Shylock against the image of Lessing's Nathan: "A Shylock devoid of humour, without the heart of the Jewish father, alien to the spirit of the wise Nathan. Only the blood-thirsty usurer, sewn into his prayer mantle as into a money sack."⁵⁹ Another review of the Viertel production also focused on Kortner's distinctive yellow mantle, and on the expressive pose with which he wore it: "There he stands, his body wrapped in the bulging yellow mantle, like the bogeyman, threatening, exactly according to the meaning of the Shakespearean fairy tale: 'the man that hath no music in himself' [...]." The text continues:

---

57 Richard D. Critchfield, "Kortner as Shylock: Reclaiming Jewish Identity," in *From Shakespeare to Frisch: The Provocative Fritz Kortner* (Heidelberg: Synchron, 2008), 47–50.
58 Richard D. Critchfield, "Fritz Kortner's *Aller Tage Abend*: Self-Discovery as the Discovery of the Other or a Life and Career as Shylock," in *When Lucifer Cometh: The Autobiographical Discourse of Writers and Intellectuals Exiled during the Third Reich* (New York: Peter Lang, 1994), 76.
59 Contemporary review, qtd. in Moninger, "Die Dramaturgie von *Merchant*-Inszenierungen in der Weimarer Republik," n. p. – Of course, the tallit is a shawl rather than a mantle. Indeed, photos of Kortner as Shylock in Reinhardt's 1924 Vienna production show him wearing an enormous mantle and a tallit *under* it.

> Thus, Kortner does not gloss over the beast even as he articulates Shylock's human pain and sobbing. [...] It is a strange experience when in front of the Duke a subdued roaring escapes from Shylock's throat, as from a tiger [...]; and when he finally creeps away, downwards, as into a thicket, Shylock almost resembles a wounded animal.[60]

Such descriptions of Kortner as Shylock betray the ubiquity of anti-Semitic formulae in Weimar culture. In this context, Kortner attempted to articulate several dimensions of the Shylock figure simultaneously. He approached the role from both the outside and the inside, as hetero stereotype and auto stereotype, as anti-Semitic figure and figuration of the actor's real Jewish identity. In doing so, he evidently tried to show what it meant to be Jewish in a rabidly anti-Semitic environment – but he also aimed at rebelling against and gesturing beyond the restrictions imposed by that environment.

In 1924, one year after playing Shylock under Viertel, Kortner joined the succession of actors who performed the role in Reinhardt's many *Merchant* productions. This was at Vienna's small Theater in der Josefstadt, where the director attempted to recover from the exacting experiments with a 'theatre for the masses' that he had been undertaking in Berlin since 1919. Not too much is known about the 1924 production (premiere: 26 May), which stayed on the programme for less than a month and reached only twelve performances.[61] However, a studio photograph of Kortner as Shylock, taken in that context, shows an enormous mantle that is reminiscent of the accounts of his previous performance with Viertel's troupe (see figure 2). The picture casts the actor in a striking pose, standing erect and sure-footed, with his arms folded and contracted eyebrows, as if proudly facing an adversary. The angle of the shot, looking up at Kortner's statue-like Shylock from below, contributes to the sense that this is a person of power and eminence.

In spite of the impressive look of his 1924 Shylock, Kortner later indicated a dissatisfaction with his early takes on the role: "I felt that my attempts had failed to represent the ethical vehemence of the character and of the play, the volcanic outburst, and the unarticulated mad cry that is born from the frustrated urge to make oneself understood."[62] The actor thought his conception of Shylock "came to fruition" only some years later, in a grand production of *Merchant* that Jürgen Fehling directed at Berlin's Staatstheater (premiere: 17 November 1927).[63] Inter-

---

[60] Qtd. in Moninger, "Die Dramaturgie von *Merchant*-Inszenierungen," n. p.
[61] Huesmann, *Welttheater Reinhardt*, entry 1487, n. p.
[62] Kortner, "Shylock," manuscript in the Kortner archive at Berlin's Akademie der Künste, qtd. in Critchfield, *From Shakespeare to Frisch*, 47n1.
[63] On Kortner's memories of the Fehling production, see Kortner, *Aller Tage Abend*, 241.

Figure 2: Fritz Kortner as Shylock in Max Reinhardt's 1924 production at Vienna's Theater in der Josefstadt. © Bruno Reiffenstein / Imagno / picturedesk.com.

estingly, the evolution of Kortner's performance in this production was furthered by tensions between the actor and the director. Kortner reports:

> The Shylock rehearsals in Berlin were pursued in a less polite way than in Vienna. Fehling indulged in frequent outbursts, and I also lashed out. I did not know what to do with his conception of Shylock, and he was embittered by mine. [...] The two of us [...] spurred each other on by the logic of opposition.[64]

That Kortner refers to the rehearsals as "Shylockproben" ("Shylock rehearsals") is revealing. Yet, although his own sense of importance may have played a role, Kortner appears to be right in explaining his fray with the director as disagreement about political strategies:

> It seems that Fehling was led by the laudable intention of avoiding to fuel the anti-Semitism that was already raging all around us. However, I was burning to be a Shylock who degenerates to inhumanity because of the inhuman treatment that he receives from his Christian environment.[65]

Rather than avoiding the rhetoric of an increasingly racist anti-Semitism, Kortner was bent on answering it in its own terms. The expressions "unmenschlich" and "Unmenschlichkeit" ("inhuman[e]" and "inhumanity") allow two opposed readings. On the one hand, they play into the racist idea that some human beings do not count as human beings. On the other hand, the terms articulate the very concept of humanity as a realm of irrevocable values and unalienable rights, which is anathema to reactionary ideologies. Kortner, who wrote about *being* rather than *acting* Shylock ("Ich aber brannte darauf ein Shylock *zu sein*"), did not simply refuse the logic of racism. Rather, he invited that logic onto the stage, there to do battle with it.

Kortner recounts that he and Fehling fought as much about the representation of the Christians as about the rendering of Shylock:

> Fehling shied back from showing Shylock's oppressors, none of whom is a true Christian, in quite such a revealing manner. He, the Aryan with a slight blotch in the generation of his grandparents, aimed at reconciliation; he wanted the tragedy of the single individual, while cutting out general implications that would take us beyond the specific case at hand. I, the blotch-less full Jew, wanted to settle the score, exposing the un-Christian hate (of the Christians) and the rotten morality behind the intoxicating colourfulness and carelessness.[66]

---

64 Kortner, *Aller Tage Abend*, 242.
65 Kortner, *Aller Tage Abend*, 242.
66 Kortner, *Aller Tage Abend*, 242.

By likening Fehling to Reinhardt,[67] Kortner conceives of his own approach to *Merchant* as a revolt against the tradition established by the great magician of the theatre. In the actor's view, the play should not be used for replicating the assimilationist paradigm but for exposing its falsity. Kortner wanted to "settle the score." In the face of an unconditional hate campaign against Jews, confrontation rather than reconciliation seemed the appropriate strategy. This is underlined by the martial rhetoric in which Kortner concludes his account of the 1927 production: "My Shylock, unsparing and making no concessions, achieved a grand victory." And referring to Julius Streicher's anti-Semitic weekly, Kortner remarks: "And the *Stormtrooper* spat venom."[68]

Degrading Shylock – Werner Krauß and the Rise of the Anti-Semitic Hegemony

Critchfield confirms that the National Socialists took Kortner's Shylock as an attack against themselves: "[T]he name Kortner and Shylock became inseparable in Nazi anti-Semitic propaganda. If Hitler was Germany and Germany was Hitler [...] then in the eyes of the Nazis Kortner was also Shylock and Shylock was Kortner."[69] However, at the beginning of the 1920s there was already another, very different Shylock at hand. For even before Kortner first performed the role in a major production, it had become part of the repertoire of Werner Krauß – the actor who later starred as Shylock in the infamous 1943 production at Vienna's Burgtheater. Playing the role at Berlin's Großes Schauspielhaus in 1921 (premiere: 12 March), Krauß had in fact been Kortner's immediate predecessor in Reinhardt's gallery of Shylocks. The *Shakespeare Jahrbuch*, the yearbook of the German Shakespeare Society, was remarkably unenthusiastic about that production as a whole. Krauß's Shylock, however, definitely left an impression on the reviewer: "With brusque and broad steps, sometimes nearly hopping, he paces the stage; shouting rather than speaking, wildly grotesque, almost

---

67 Cf. Kortner, *Aller Tage Abend*, 241.
68 Kortner, *Aller Tage Abend*, 242: "Mein Shylock, schonungslos und konzessionslos, errang einen Großsieg. Und der *Stürmer* spie Gift." The unusual compound "Großsieg" echoes the grandiloquent style of the pre-war period, as it was employed by the reactionary right in particular.
69 Critchfield, "The Nazis and Kortner: 'They hate you because of your aggressiveness'," *From Shakespeare to Frisch*, 51.

comical in the morbid suffering caused by his daughter's flight – this is how Werner Krauß draws Shylock."[70]

Peter W. Marx wonders why Reinhardt, who had cast Krauß as the clown Lancelot in his 1913 production, now let him play Lancelot's master as a kind of clown:

> From today's perspective, which is shaped by our knowledge about the Shoah, we cannot choose but read Krauß's representation of Shylock as a step on the way towards his stereotypical representation of five minor Jewish characters in Veit Harlan's film *Jud Süß* (1940) or in view of his clearly anti-Semitic interpretation of Shylock at Vienna's Burgtheater in 1943.[71]

As Marx suggests, the decision for Krauß is perhaps evidence of Reinhardt's political naivety.[72] At the same time, there may have been pragmatic reasons for casting Krauß. The Großes Schauspielhaus had originally been a market hall and later a circus. In 1919, the building was converted into a grand theatre, intended for Reinhardt's ambitious experiments with a theatre for the masses. The venue was enormous: it offered 3,200 seats and the stage was 55 metres wide.[73] In such a setting, Krauß's striding, hopping, and shouting may have been not only an idiosyncratic interpretation of the role, but also a sheer technical necessity. It is not unlikely that Reinhardt picked Krauß as Shylock because this actor knew how to make himself seen and heard even in such a large theatre.

Still, even Herbert Ihering – an important theatre critic of the Weimar Republic and staunch admirer of Krauß – pointed out that the representation of Shylock at the Großes Schauspielhaus was "evil." Ihering compared the Shylock of 1921 to Krauß's performance in contemporary films like *Freudlose Gasse* ("Joyless Street," 1925) or *Die Hose* ("The Trousers," 1927). He argued that the

---

[70] Walther Volbach, "Berliner Shakespeare-Vorstellungen: Spielzeit 1920/21," *Shakespeare Jahrbuch* 57 (1921): 146.
[71] Marx, "Die drei Gesichter Shylocks," 57.
[72] Marx, "Die drei Gesichter Shylocks," 57–58. Marx is aware that it is problematic to interpret Krauß's performance with hindsight. Indeed, in 1921 Krauß had not yet established himself as an anti-Semitic actor. When he was playing Shylock for Reinhardt, he was also starring in the lead role of *Nathan der Weise* (1922), a silent feature film by Manfred Noa. The characterization of the protagonist was ostentatiously 'philo-Semitic,' and the National Socialists tried to suppress the film. See Stefan Drössler, "Der Fall *Nathan der Weise*," booklet to the DVD of *Nathan der Weise* (Munich: Filmmuseum München, 2006).
[73] See Peter W. Marx, "Zirkus Reinhardt: Der Masse einen Ort und eine Gestalt geben," in *Max Reinhardt: Vom bürgerlichen Theater zur metropolitanen Kultur* (Tübingen: Francke, 2006), 83–117; see also Huesmann, *Welttheater Reinhardt*, 93, 135–137.

actor's take on Shakespeare's moneylender was based on the same merciless look on humanity – Ihering spoke of a kind of "evil eye" – that inspired his impersonation of petit bourgeois characters in the cinema. According to Ihering, the difference was that Krauß played Shylock not as a critique of contemporary society, but as a negative historical fantasy: "With heaving and tumbling steps Krauß shot into the arena, an evil, dangerous clown, a comical yet spooky Ahasver. [...] This reddish, ugly, joking devil, a distorted nightmarish imp had been spewed out by the hell of the Middle Ages."[74] Although he was writing from a different perspective, Hermann Sinsheimer's memories of the 1921 production show notable similarities to Ihering's account. Sinsheimer also referred to Krauß's strange manner of moving: "He seemed to tumble rather than walk." And like Ihering, Sinsheimer sensed a kind of medievalism in the performance: "Krauss ceased to be an actor playing the part of a Jew and took on the perplexing appearance of a medieval player in the part of a ghost."[75]

Performing Shylock in this "perplexing" way, Krauß was not necessarily pursuing direct ideological intentions. The actor's primary motivation may have been his unwavering desire to make the most of his histrionic strengths. Indeed, as will become clearer when we discuss the Vienna production of 1943, the ideological significance of Krauß's performance lay in his knack for *withholding* any personal investment in the role, and for doing so quite ostentatiously. This approach was bound to deflate the powerful performances of actors such as Kortner, who were constructing strong links between their own subject positions and the Shylock figure. If, according to Critchfield, "in the eyes of the Nazis Kortner was [...] Shylock and Shylock was Kortner," Krauß went out to steal the show, assuring his audience that Shylock was nothing but a nightmarish flicker emanating from the depths of history. Viewed from this perspective, it seems logical that, for all the noise the actor made in the role, "there was one passage that he surprisingly let drop." This was Shylock's famous monologue in Act 3 ("Hath not a Jew eyes?"). As the reviewer of *Shakespeare Jahrbuch* pointed out: "[T]his passage, which other actors render as an accusation directed at the whole of mankind, Krauß speaks almost in passing, in a conversational tone."[76]

Such a rendering of Shylock went against the established sensitivity to the tragic potentialities of the play. Indeed, the disintegration of the Weimar Republic and the rise of the anti-Semitic hegemony was accompanied by an increasing

---

[74] Herbert Ihering, *Werner Krauß: Ein Schauspieler und das neunzehnte Jahrhundert* (Berlin: Vorwerk 8, 1997), 59–60.
[75] Sinsheimer, *Shylock: The History of a Character*, 142.
[76] Volbach, "Berliner Shakespeare-Vorstellungen," 146.

insistence that *Merchant* ought to be performed as a comedy. Whereas Reinhardt's design rested on a balance between comedic and tragic, allegorical and identitarian approaches, the late 1920s witnessed a tendency to stick to the festive spirit of the magician's productions while at the same time stripping them of their finer meanings. An article in the magazine of Düsseldorf's municipal theatre, where a new production of *Merchant* premiered in September 1925, may serve as an example. It was noted that the director, Josef Münch, aimed at basing his production, "with an intensity that has seldom been achieved before," on "the principle of colour, gaudy and variegated colour, and on whirling movement." The text continues:

> Attempting to explain the director's conception one will not go wrong in assuming that he, too, shares the opinion (see our article on 'The Shylock Problem' in the last issue) that the poet originally intended his work to be nothing but an amusement for the crowd, a swirling comedy, which finds its most apt setting in a Venice illuminated by the southern glow and zest for life.[77]

In spite of the ostentatious good humour of the passage, it was certainly possible to combine the insistence on the play's "southern glow and zest for life" with an aggressive stance towards Shylock – a stance that consisted of downsizing and racializing the figure at the same time.

Such a perspective is evident from responses to a production that premiered at the Deutsches Theater am Rhein, a new branch of the Cologne public theatre, in September 1932 – on the eve of the National Socialists' accession to power. The director was Fritz Holl, in whose 1924 production Granach had starred as Shylock. As the reviewer of *Shakespeare Jahrbuch* pointed out, Holl now "reined in the Shylock tragedy": "It was in line with the director's conception of the play that Walther Richter completely refrained from investing Shylock with the demonic grandeur that some actors have displayed in the role, thereby destroying the play's character as a comedy."[78] At the same time, the text did not fail to quote a review of the same production in the *Kölnische Zeitung*. The passage demonstrates how a disempowered Shylock could be perceived from an anti-Semitic perspective:

> His appearance alone was repulsive and vermin-like rather than terrible. He had a gaunt, sickly pale and grubby face whose thin beard seemed to have been afflicted by an unappe-

---

[77] Städtische Theater Düsseldorf, "Zur Inszenierung des *Kaufmann von Venedig*," *Die Theaterwelt*, 16 September 1925, 27.
[78] Jürgen Weisker, "Theaterschau: Shakespeare auf der deutschen Bühne 1932/33," *Shakespeare Jahrbuch* 69 (1933): 210.

tizing lichen; below this a clumsy and fat body, which shuffled forward, waddling and staggering on its flat feet."[79]

According to this textual exercise in disgust, Richter's performance divested Shylock of all sympathetic traits. Consequently, the audience was absolved from nagging doubts concerning the legitimacy of his destruction – or so it seemed to the reviewer: "It goes without saying that the court verdict against such a Shylock failed to have the deep effect that a heroic rendering of the role inspires." Rather, as the text continues, "one was led to accept, without a split conscience, the sentence against Shylock as the well-deserved punishment for his mean intentions and character."[80] Interestingly, the very fierceness of the text betrays a need to manage insecurities concerning Shylock. In claiming that Richter's Shylock seemed "repulsive" ("widerlich") "rather than terrible" ("schrecklich") the critic was eager to assure his readers that Shakespeare's Jew lacked real power.

1.2 The Theatrical Ratification of Genocide

Evading Shylock? – National Socialist Insecurities

Four months after the premiere at Cologne Hitler was made chancellor. What happened to the Shylock figure in Germany under National Socialism? How was Shylock performed and interpreted at a time when Jews were increasingly threatened by persecution – a persecution that was to culminate in a systematic genocide pursued in many parts of Europe? On the whole, National Socialist cultural policy did not challenge the appropriation of Britain's national poet as a 'German classic.'[81] Simultaneously, the German Shakespeare Society was prepared, and in some ways eager, to bring its tradition of so-called 'Shakespeare-Pflege' – i.e. of 'cultivating' the bard's works in the German language

---

[79] Walter Schmits, *Kölnische Zeitung*, 13 September 1932, qtd. in Weisker, "Theaterschau: Shakespeare auf der deutschen Bühne 1932/33," 210. Cf. Bonnell, *Shylock in Germany*, 116.
[80] Schmits, qtd. in Weisker, "Theaterschau: Shakespeare auf der deutschen Bühne 1932/33," 210.
[81] See esp. Rodney Symington, *The Nazi Appropriation of Shakespeare: Cultural Politics in the Third Reich* (Lewiston, NY: Edwin Mellen, 2005). For an account of Shakespeare during the Nationalist Socialist Era, see also Andreas Höfele, *No Hamlets: German Shakespeare from Nietzsche to Schmidt* (Cambridge: Cambridge University Press, 2016), esp. chapter 6: "Third Reich Shakespeare," 192–226.

and on German soil – in line with the regime's major objectives.⁸² At the society's annual meeting in 1938, Rainer Schlösser, who held the position of a 'Reichsdramaturg' (Dramaturge of the Reich) in the Propaganda Ministry, spoke about "The German Shakespeare." He emphatically claimed Germany's right to the classic and pondered whether, in the course of time, Shakespeare's "motherland" might have forfeited such a claim.⁸³ A similar idea was expressed by the president of the society, Wolfgang Keller, in his opening speech at the society's meeting in 1940. Keller reminded his audience of the necessity of differentiating between Shakespeare and contemporary "British politicians and controlling stockholders that are fighting against the German Reich." Shakespeare lived in Elizabethan England, he explained, "which resembles today's Germany much more than the democratic or, rather, plutocratic, trading power, which now rules the British Empire."⁸⁴ Such pronouncements were part and parcel of a political readjustment of the Shakespeare Society, which also opened itself to racism and anti-Semitism. In 1936, Hans F. K. Günther was elected to the executive board. Günther, recently appointed as Professor for Race Science, Ethnic Biology, and Rural Sociology at Humboldt University Berlin, was an important protagonist in the attempt to turn National Socialist racism into a scholarly discipline. In 1937, the new board member opened the Shakespeare Society's annual meeting with a paper on a topic that had been famously discussed by the Jewish poet Heinrich Heine in 1839: "Shakespeare's Maidens and Women." Speaking a century after the publication of Heine's monograph, however, Günther argued from the perspective of eugenics.⁸⁵

Shylock was an important reference point for National Socialist propaganda. According to the protocols of his table talk, Hitler allegedly declared in 1942 that Shakespeare's character was a "timelessly valid characterization of the Jew."⁸⁶ This perspective was also stressed in contemporary criticism. An example is the introduction to a 1940 German edition of *Merchant* brought out by Velhagen & Klasing, a publishing house that had begun as publishers of religious litera-

---

82 See Ruth von Ledebur, *Der Mythos vom deutschen Shakespeare: Die Deutsche Shakespeare-Gesellschaft zwischen Politik und Wissenschaft 1918–1945* (Cologne: Böhlau, 2002).
83 Rainer Schlösser, "Der deutsche Shakespeare," *Shakespeare Jahrbuch* 74 (1938): 22.
84 Qtd. in Frank-Rutger Hausmann, *Die Geisteswissenschaften im 'Dritten Reich'* (Frankfurt/M.: Vittorio Klostermann, 2011), 593.
85 Hans F. K. Günther, "Shakespeares Mädchen und Frauen: Ein Vortrag vor der Deutschen Shakespeare-Gesellschaft," *Shakespeare Jahrbuch* 73 (1937): 85–108. Cf. Gerwin Strobl, "The Bard of Eugenics: Shakespeare and Racial Activism in the Third Reich," *Journal of Contemporary History* 34:3 (1999): 323–336.
86 Henry Picker, *Hitlers Tischgespräche im Führerhauptquartier* (Stuttgart: Seewald, 1983), 457 (entry for 24 July, 1942).

ture, but had come to endorse National Socialist ideology.[87] This edition of the play (reissued in 1943) was prepared by a schoolteacher, one Heinrich Lemcke, and was primarily aimed at German classrooms. Contrasting Shylock and Portia, Lemcke's introduction describes Shakespeare's Jewish character as a bloodthirsty moneylender, representative of a dark "realm of evil and cold hatred" and threatening the "sphere of the beautiful and the good" over which Portia reigns. Even if these lines show traces of Landauer's socialist reading of *Merchant*, Lemcke uses the praise of Portia as springboard for a National Socialist tirade on cultural politics. He starts out by quoting Alfred Rosenberg, a scholar and politician who was sometimes regarded as a mainstay of a National Socialist intelligentsia:

> In his book *Der Sumpf: Querschnitte durch das 'Geistes'-Leben der November-Demokratie* ("The Swamp: Cross-sections through the 'Intellectual' Life of the November Democracy") Alfred Rosenberg writes in the year 1930: "In Berlin, *The Merchant of Venice* is given, and – as always on this occasion – a swarm of Syrian Berliners sits down to defend Shylock and to let him appear as a noble martyr who is tortured by a crowd of brute non-Jews." In addition, Rosenberg reminds us of the moving remarks of a certain Shakespeare philology about the "raceless fairy-tale figure" Shylock and declares that in Shylock we are facing "the cruellest embodiment of the bloodiest system of exploitation realized in the person of the Jew."[88]

Lemcke thus reiterates Rosenberg's use of *Merchant* as a means of attacking the Revolution of 1918/19 and the Weimar Republic. The figurative interpretation of the play as a "fairy tale," which was associated with Max Reinhardt's productions, is taken as a symptom of everything found wrong with democratic governments and bourgeois culture. Lemcke suggests that the play would need to be won back as a perfect staging ground for National Socialist ideologies. At the same time, the editor picks up on the identitarian approach that Jewish actors such as Alexander Granach and Fritz Kortner had developed in reaction to Reinhardt's integrationist agenda. The schoolteacher and would-be propagandist attempts to turn the identitarian approach inside out: he proposes to see Shylock

---

[87] In the early 1940s, three new German editions of *Merchant* were published: the version edited by Lemcke; one edited in 1941 by Karl Schümmer for the Schöningh publishing house; and another one edited by Wolfgang Keller (Cologne: Schaffstein, 1940), then president of the German Shakespeare Society and editor of *Shakespeare Jahrbuch*.
[88] Heinrich Lemcke, "Zur Einführung," in William Shakespeare, *Der Kaufmann von Venedig*, trans. A. W. von Schlegel (Bielefeld: Velhagen und Klasing, 1940), iii. The date 1930 in the quote is not correct: Rosenberg's book was first published in 1927. By the term "Syrian race," Rosenberg referred to what he saw as the main enemies of the 'Nordic races,' including the Jews as well as the Roman Church, which supposedly had emerged from the 'oriental races.'

not as a complex figuration of Jewish predicaments in an increasingly anti-Semitic society, but as an exemplary embodiment of Jewish Otherness. Simultaneously, Lemcke suggests that a contemporary take on the play should stage National Socialist society as a "sphere of the beautiful and the good," i.e. as a realization of the redemptive utopia that the Jewish socialist Landauer – a victim of reactionary terror – had found in Shakespeare's comedy.

On the theatrical stage, however, there were evidently stumbling blocks that complicated the deployment of *Merchant* as a vehicle of National Socialist resentments. Despite the widespread assumption that the play "enjoyed special popularity from the outset" of the National Socialist ascendancy,[89] the number of productions at first decreased notably. According to the statistics of performance numbers published in *Shakespeare Jahrbuch*,[90] *Merchant* ranked first among Shakespearean plays in 1927. It held third place in 1928, 1929, and 1931, and fourth in 1932. During the theatrical season of 1933/34, the first season under Hitler's chancellorship, there were still nine new productions. However, numbers dropped to one or two for the following seasons. By 1941, performances had reached an all-time low of altogether three shows; *Merchant* held place twenty-one in the Shakespeare Society's listing for that year, ranking next-to-last, only ahead of *The Merry Wives of Windsor*.[91]

---

89 Gross, *Shylock*, 294. Cf. e. g. Gareth Armstrong, *A Case for Shylock: Around the World with Shakespeare's Jew* (London: Nick Hern, 2004), 46. Discussing anxieties that Shakespeare might have been "a Jew-hater," Armstrong explains: "The Nazis certainly thought he was. They encouraged productions of the play throughout the Reich during the thirties and the war years, and in Vienna, the Gauleiter commanded a performance on the grounds that 'every Jew active in Europe is a danger to European culture.'"

90 See the section "Theaterschau: Statistischer Überblick" in the annual issues of *Shakespeare Jahrbuch*. During the period under investigation these reports refer to the calendar year (not the theatre season) preceding their publication. For the time of the war, however, there are some irregularities. Thus, the stage statistics for the years 1941 and 1942 were listed only in the yearbook published in 1946, and there are no statistics for 1943 and 1944.

91 On the reception of *Merchant* in National Socialist Germany, see also Zeno Ackermann, "Shakespearean Negotiations in the Perpetrator Society: German Productions of *The Merchant of Venice* during the Second World War," in *Shakespeare and the Second World War: Memory, Culture, Identity*, ed. Irena R. Makaryk and Marissa McHugh (Toronto: University of Toronto Press, 2012), 35–62; and "'Ease and Deliciousness': *The Merchant of Venice* and the Performance of Ethical Continuity in National Socialist Germany," in *Renaissance Shakespeare / Shakespeare Renaissances: Proceedings of the Ninth World Shakespeare Congress*, ed. Martin Procházka, Michael Dobson, Andreas Höfele, and Hanna Scolnicov (Newark: University of Delaware Press, 2014), 238–248. See also Thomas Eicher, "Spielplanstrukturen 1929–1944," in *Theater im "Dritten Reich": Theaterpolitik, Spielplanstruktur, NS-Dramatik*, ed. Henning Rischbieter (Seelze-Velber: Kallmeyer, 2000), 302–308; Jörg Monschau, *Der Jude nach der Shoah: Zur Rezep-*

This hesitance to perform *Merchant* demands an explanation. Jessica's role in the plot was the most obvious reason. Put in racist terms, the comedy makes 'miscegenation' part of its happy ending. A potential solution was suggested by the author and translator Hermann Kroepelin in a 1936 letter to the Propaganda Ministry. Although he considered *Merchant* a play "that, on account of its other qualities, we would not like to do without," Kroepelin emphasized his aversion to showing the mixing of "Aryan blood with Jewish blood" on stage. His way out was to have Jessica, at the last moment, desist from marrying Lorenzo.[92] The head of the Propaganda Ministry's theatre department at the time was the same Rainer Schlösser who went on to speak about "The German Shakespeare" at the 1938 conference of the Shakespeare Society. Deviating from Kroepelin's suggestions, Schlösser preferred to turn Jessica into Shylock's non-Jewish foster-child. According to a list of suggested changes compiled by the Propaganda Ministry,[93] all passages referring to Jessica as a Jew or as the daughter of Shylock were to be dropped or rewritten.

These were not the only alterations mandated. The most drastic change in the Ministry's adaptation was to delete, entirely, Shylock's famous monologue in 3.1. It could be argued that Schlösser wished to evade the universalist humanism that can potentially be seen at work in this speech. We believe, however, that there were also different concerns – concerns relating less to the ideational potentials of the text than to the status and stature that the Shylock figure had acquired in the previous decades. We have already pointed out the remarkable insecurity towards Shylock betrayed by the racist 1932 review in the *Kölnische Zeitung*. Lemcke's attacks on established ways of playing or seeing Shylock, as well as Kroepelin's and Schlösser's extensive tampering with the text, show that this insecurity can be traced well into Hitler's Germany.

---

tion des Kaufmann von Venedig *auf dem Theater der Bundesrepublik Deutschland und der Deutschen Demokratischen Republik 1945–1989*, doctoral dissertation (Ruprecht-Karls-Universität Heidelberg, 2002), 19–25, and 68–87, published online at https://archiv.ub.uni-heidelberg.de/volltextserver/3530/; Symington, *The Nazi Appropriation of Shakespeare*, 244–251; Bonnell, *Shylock in Germany*, 119–169. – Most current studies take note of the decreasing performance numbers. However, focussing on the few productions that actually did take place, they still raise the impression that the play was a seminal tool of Nazi propaganda.

92 Hermann Kroepelin, preface to his adaption of *Merchant*; qtd. in Eicher, "Spielplanstrukturen 1929–1944," 304.
93 List qtd. in Eicher, "Spielplanstrukturen 1929–1944," 304–308.

The Return of a 'Classic' – Berlin 1942

When performance numbers for *Merchant* reached an all-time low in 1941, the stage had already been set for a return of the play. In the previous year, Schlösser had presented his suggestions for an adapted version to Goebbels. In an appended memorandum, the so-called Dramaturge of the Reich explained:

> In agreement with previous instructions, *The Merchant of Venice* has been kept from Berlin theatre programmes during the past years. In the meantime, however, a couple of stages in other places have tested out, with my permission, a slightly adapted version [...], which creates the impression that Jessica is not the Jew's daughter but merely his foster-child. [...] Accordingly, I do not see why we should continue to prevent performance of this classic in Berlin, in particular since skilful productions would actually be able to support our fight against the Jews.[94]

Within three days, Schlösser had the minister's approval. Berlin's private Rose-Theater, which had not been given the green light to put on *Merchant* in the 1937/38 season,[95] was now granted permission to do so, and the production eventually premiered in August 1942. Extant reviews refer to Jessica as Shylock's "adoptive daughter,"[96] which suggests that the production was indeed based on Schlösser's adaptation. The Rose-Theater followed the tradition of the Berlin 'Volkstheater' (popular theatre), which addressed a petit-bourgeois and working-class audience. It was in line with this tradition that the *Merchant* production sought a lively participation of the audience. The anecdote that Paul Rose placed extras in the auditorium who hissed and swore at Shylock during the fourth act, however, is hard to substantiate.[97] It may be a myth, based not only on a misreading of a review in the *Völkischer Beobachter*,[98] but also on a simplistic

---

94 Schlösser, memorandum to Goebbels, qtd. in Eicher, "Spielplanstrukturen 1929–1944," 308.
95 Cf. Ruth Freydank, "Die Klassiker als Herausforderung an eine Vorstadtbühne," in *Das Rose-Theater: Ein Volkstheater im Berliner Osten 1906–1944*, ed. Michael Baumgarten and Ruth Freydank (Berlin: Edition Hentrich, 1991), 154n24. According to this account, when Paul Rose submitted his list of plays for the 1937/38 season, the responsible supervisor in the Propaganda Ministry crossed out *Merchant* and inserted *Othello* in its place.
96 Wilhelm Grundschöttel, "Shylock im Fasching – Paul Rose inszeniert den Kaufmann von Venedig," *Völkischer Beobachter*, 2 September 1942, qtd. in Bonnell, *Shylock in Germany*, 157.
97 The anecdote is repeated by Joseph Wulf, *Theater und Film im Dritten Reich: Eine Dokumentation* (1964; Frankfurt/M.: Ullstein, 1989), 281; Bonnell, *Shylock in Germany*, 156; and Monschau, *Der Jude nach der Shoah*, 68.
98 Cf. Grundschöttel, qtd. in Bonnell, *Shylock in Germany*, 156: "And Paul Rose let the people's voice come down from the gallery, with cries of outrage and piercing whistles." The passage may refer to the Venetian populace placed on a gallery on stage rather than to the audience on the

conception of the workings of anti-Semitic propaganda during the National Socialist period.

In Berlin, Shylock was played by Georg August Koch, an active party member and professed anti-Semite.[99] The production, in which Shylock wore the traditional red beard of the stage Jew,[100] stressed the character's fundamental difference from the social majority. However, he was evidently meant to be a comical rather than a threatening Other. *Shakespeare Jahrbuch* commented: "In his *Merchant of Venice* at Berlin's Rose-Theater, Paul Rose openly displays his inclination towards comedy, or even towards commedia dell'arte. The play was rendered as a confrontation between clever people rather than as a struggle between law and mercy."[101] If Shylock was not portrayed as a demonic moneylender in the manner of *Jud Süß*, this does not mean that the Rose-Theatre did not offer an ideologically "skilful" production according to Schlösser's understanding. Indeed, if we consider Shylock's previous function as a staging ground for a resistant and powerful Jewish identity, the most important propagandistic task consisted in downsizing the figure into a laughingstock. It is telling that the *Völkischer Beobachter* – the party newspaper of the NSDAP – headed its review "Shylock during Carnival."[102]

When *Merchant* premiered in Berlin, the genocide that had begun simultaneously with the war had long since reached Germany. The yellow badge, which Jews in occupied Poland had to wear from the beginning of the war, was introduced in the 'Reich' in September 1941. Large-scale systematic deportations from Germany (and Austria) began in October 1941, and by the middle of 1942, the vast majority of the German Jews that had not previously emigrated had already been deported. Some of the victims had been murdered immediately after reaching their destinations outside the Reich.[103] It seems that the Rose production bowed to this terrible reality. Bonnell reads the design of Shylock's

---

balconies of the theatre. As to the stage setting of the production, see Beate-Ursula Endriss, *Shakespeare-Inszenierungen in Berlin 1933–1944*, doctoral dissertation (Freie Universität Berlin, 1994), 178.
99 Cf. Bonnell, *Shylock in Germany*, 158–161; Henning Rischbieter, "NS-Theaterpolitik," in *Theater im "Dritten Reich"*, ed. Rischbieter, 86.
100 Bonnell, *Shylock in Germany*, 157; cf. Endriss, *Shakespeare-Inszenierungen*, 178.
101 Werner Papsdorf, Ernst Leopold Stahl, and Carl Niessen, "Shakespeare auf der deutschen Bühne 1940/42," *Shakespeare Jahrbuch* 78/79 (1943): 133.
102 Grundschöttel, "Shylock im Fasching," qtd. in Bonnell, *Shylock in Germany*, 156–157, 218n205.
103 On deportations from Germany see Christopher Browning, *The Origins of the Final Solution: The Evolution of Nazi Jewish Policy, September 1939 – March 1942* (Jerusalem: Yad Vashem / Lincoln: University of Nebraska Press, 2004), esp. 375–398.

house, "a small booth-like structure with a pointed arched window and marked with a yellow star of David on top," as a deliberate allusion to the so-called 'Judenhäuser' ('Jewish houses').[104] Concentrating the victims in such houses was a preparation for deportation and murder. In consequence, the Rose production may be interpreted as linking Shakespeare's comedy – elusively but significantly – to the 'open secret' of the Holocaust.

"The hour of gladdening reward" – Göttingen 1942

The Rose production was the only attempt to stage *Merchant* in Berlin during the National Socialist period, but it proved remarkably successful.[105] In 1942 *Merchant* could also be seen at the municipal theatres of Görlitz and Göttingen. Indeed, while it would be wrong to claim that the implementation of the Holocaust in Germany was accompanied by an outright wave of *Merchant* productions, it is startling that the number of performances rose significantly. Whereas there were only three shows in 1941, the overall figure for 1942 amounted to seventy-two, which represented the highest number since 1933, and shot *Merchant* back up to fourth place in the Shakespeare Society's ranking.[106] This does not mean that Shakespeare's comedy turned into a theatrical mainstay of National Socialist propaganda. Rather, the shift in performance numbers is significant for suggesting that, in the context of the genocide, the play yet again seemed possible.

How was Shylock portrayed in this context? In his memoirs, the director Peter Zadek (whose own takes on Shakespeare's play will be discussed in the next chapter) stresses the force of a general European tradition in which Shylock was rendered according to ingrained fantasies of Jewish Otherness. Zadek recalls how his parents, Jewish refugees from Hitler's Germany, took him to see *Merchant* at London's Queen's Theatre in 1938. John Gielgud's Shylock in that

---

104 Bonnell, *Shylock in Germany*, 157. Bonnell refers to Wolfgang Znamenacek's set design for the production, which is held in the theatre archive of the University of Cologne at Schloss Wahn (graphic collection, no. 18151).
105 Cf. Egon Mühlbach's performance statistics for 1941 and 1942 as given in *Shakespeare Jahrbuch* 80/81 (1946): 113–121. By the end of 1942, the Rose production had reached no less than 50 performances, which is more than any other Shakespeare production that year.
106 The Rose production premiered on 31 August 1942. The premiere of the production at Göttingen's municipal theatre had been announced for 23 September, but the dating of contemporary reviews suggests that it took place a couple of days later. We have not been able to establish details about the production in Görlitz.

production came as a shock for the teenager: "Never before in my life had I seen a Jew as mean as the one played by Gielgud. I remember how my parents struggled to explain this Shylock to me."[107] As a contemporary review in the *New Statesman* observed, Gielgud combined "the squalor of a Transylvanian usurer" with "the ardour of an Old Testament prophet." This Shylock had "gummy, blinking eyes" that "suggested some nasty creature of the dark," and his "loquacious hands" communicated "as many inflections as his voice."[108]

It is often assumed that the Shylocks paraded on the stages of the so-called Third Reich must have been even more *outré* than the one played by Gielgud, and quite a few contemporary reviews confirm this assumption. Thus, in a much-quoted passage, Richard Biedrzynski wrote about the impact of Krauß's Shylock in the infamous 1943 production at Vienna's Burgtheater:

> And then, suddenly, as if it were an uncanny shadow, something revoltingly alien and astonishingly repellent drags itself across the stage: a marionette jingling its ducats, wearing a black gabardine and a garishly yellow synagogue shawl – the Shylock of Werner Krauß.[109]

The passage meets the general expectations concerning anti-Semitic propaganda. Intensifying trite clichés to the point of absurdity, it reveals both the simple-mindedness and the murderousness of National Socialist ideologies. If we look at photographs of the 1943 production, however, it is difficult to really see what Biedrzynski claims to have seen. A picture from the trial scene can serve as example (figure 3). Perhaps the pose of Krauß's Shylock – casually and provocatively leaning against a banister – catered to entrenched clichés of a presumed Jewish impertinence. Still, it is difficult to see the agile person in the picture as "revoltingly alien." And it is almost impossible to imagine this Shylock as "dragging" himself "across the stage."

The surviving photographs of Wilhelm Meyer-Ottens's Shylock in Gustav Rudolf Sellner's 1942 Göttingen production are even more difficult to pin down. One of the eight production photos held by Göttingen's municipal museum shows him pleading his case in the trial scene. Dressed in a black robe, standing erect with his eyes slightly raised, there is nothing in the outward appearance of this Shylock that could be described, in Biedrzynski's terms, as

---

107 Peter Zadek, *My Way: Eine Autobiographie 1926–1969* (Cologne: Kiepenheuer & Witsch, 1998), 106.
108 Anonymous review in the *New Statesman*, 1938; as quoted in Gross, *Shylock*, 179.
109 Richard Biedrzynski, *Schauspieler, Regisseure, Intendanten* (Heidelberg: Hüthig & Co., 1944), 35.

Figure 3: Werner Krauß (Shylock) and Maria Holst (Portia) in the trial scene of Lothar Müthel's 1943 production at Vienna's Burgtheater. Courtesy of KHM-Museumsverband, Theatermuseum Wien.

"repulsive" and "vermin-like." Evidently, this is not a "fat body" who may be caught in the act of clumsily "shuffling forward." Quite to the contrary, the person in the photo displays the posture of an authority figure. In a different context, this might be the representation of a venerated Jewish character – a Nathan, perhaps.

The discrepancy between visual and textual representations of Shylock reminds us of the complexity of anti-Semitic ideologies in general, and National Socialist propaganda in particular. The realization of a production's anti-Semitic potential depended on an interplay of performance and perception, of theatrical event and sociocultural context. In addition, it is important to consider the specific function of the theatre within the arsenal of National Socialist propaganda.[110] Whereas the mass media broadcast direct indoctrination, theatre lent itself

---

[110] For a critical assessment of the notion that the theatres represented islands of unadulterated art within National Socialist Germany, see Peter Mertz, *Das gerettete Theater: Die deutsche Bühne im Wiederaufbau* (Weinheim: Quadriga, 1990), esp. 41–53. See also Hans Daiber, *Schaufenster der Diktatur: Theater im Machtbereich Hitlers* (Stuttgart: Neske, 1995).

to more subtle techniques of affirmation. These were certainly more 'cultured,' but not necessarily less insidious than the propaganda tricks of papers such as *Der Stürmer* ("The Stormtrooper") or of films such as *Der ewige Jude* ("The Eternal Jew"). In this context, theatre reviews from the period should be regarded as acts of mediation; translating the complex language of the stage into the robust lingo of propaganda proper, they represent less a record of specific stage performances than a contemporary prescription for reading them.

It is thus difficult to say how palpably anti-Semitic the Göttingen production was. The passage on Sellner's *Merchant* in the respective stage report of *Shakespeare Jahrbuch* leaves room for speculation. According to the reviewers, the representation of Shylock was characterized by "a robust expressiveness," which included the traditional gesture of having the Jew whet the knife on the sole of his shoe during the trial scene. At the same time, the report contrasted the Göttingen production to that of the Rose-Theater, noting that the former "did not withhold the serious and tragic aspects of the play."[111] Reviews published in the *Göttinger Tageblatt* and the *Südhannoversche Zeitung* were more thoroughly committed to the well-rehearsed rhetoric of anti-Semitism. The latter made sure to spell out the topical character of *Merchant* within current contexts: "[T]he play demonstrates that anti-Semitism is not a recent National Socialist invention but that it has been alive for centuries among all Aryan peoples." The focus of the review, however, was not on Shylock, but on Portia. Once again, the clever heiress was praised for presiding over "the world of the beautiful, the bright and the good" – a world "which the Jew may only disturb but from which he remains excluded."[112] The *Göttinger Tageblatt* celebrated Portia along similar lines:

> It is not the Jew who is at the centre of the plot. It is not the 'God of Vengeance' who triumphs, but the God of Love 'from the sib of Dionysus and Venus.' The dark shadow that the spirit of the ghetto casts on the comedic cheerfulness of the play is warded off by the cunning of women who are in love and who are truly capable of loving – the sweetest fruit on the fairy tale tree of Shakespeare's poetry. This is where G. R. Sellner's beautiful production had its bearing. It was full of sunlight and cheerfulness, inspired by the music of Shakespeare's words.[113]

---

111 Papsdorf, Stahl, and Nießen, "Shakespeare auf der deutschen Bühne 1940/42," 133.
112 Anon., "Des Lebens ganze Fülle: Shakespeares *Kaufmann von Venedig* im Göttinger Stadttheater," *Südhannoversche Zeitung*, 28 September 1942. The name of the reviewer is illegible on the microfilm copy held in Göttingen's municipal archive.
113 Heinz Koch, "Das Spiel vom geprellten Juden: Shakespeares *Kaufmann von Venedig* im Stadttheater," *Göttinger Tageblatt*, 28 September 1942.

It is painful to see how this interpretation repeats formulae that Landauer had used in his utopian reading of *Merchant*. Accordingly, the main emphasis is not on the mobilization of anti-Semitic hate, but on the celebration of an assumed social regeneration: not on the abjectness of Shylock but on the goodness of those from whose society he is expelled.

This focus on the majority society and its supposed ethos had been prepared for by an article that the *Göttinger Tageblatt* published on the morning of the premiere. The author was the eminent scholar Herbert Schöffler, who had recently been appointed Professor of English Philology at the University of Göttingen. Historical accounts of English Studies in Germany have devoted particular attention to Schöffler – not because he was a clear-cut 'Nazi,' but exactly because his ideological positions seem vexingly contradictory.[114] Interestingly, Schöffler's article on *Merchant* shows hardly a trace of the conventional anti-Semitic indignation against Shylock. Rather than hate propaganda, it displays an ostentatiously neutral perspective, pondering with scholarly acumen how Shakespeare, who could not have known many Jews, was still able to draw a Jewish character so compellingly.

At the same time, Schöffler's article offered a veiled ratification of the expulsion and deportation of Jews from Germany. He dwelt on the fifth act of *Merchant* as an "hour of gladdening reward after all the tumult, when the Jew, the dark and demonic figure in the play, remains excluded not to be mentioned again," and then went on to argue that the comedy's resolution was "a doubly venerable monument of the intellectual and moral development of our cultural area."[115] Portia's outwitting of Shylock, and his consequent exclusion from the play could seem "doubly venerable" because an informed audience would be able to see the plot as a complex figuration of historical progress – a *figura* in the

---

[114] On Schöffler see Ludwig Pfeiffer, "Anglistik," in *Die Rolle der Geisteswissenschaften im Dritten Reich 1933–1945*, ed. Frank-Rutger Hausmann (Munich: Oldenbourg, 2002), 57–62. Frank-Rutger Hausmann views Schöffler more critically; see his *Anglistik und Amerikanistik im "Dritten Reich"* (Frankfurt/M.: Klostermann, 2003), 365–390. See also Zeno Ackermann, "Anglistik und Amerikanistik," in *Kulturwissenschaften und Nationalsozialismus*, ed. Jürgen Elvert and Jürgen Nielsen-Sikora (Stuttgart: Steiner, 2008), esp. 659–662. On a compromising post-war lecture in which Schöffler both exposed and condoned his sympathies for National Socialist policies, see Hermann Heimpel, "'Zur Lage': Eine Vorlesung des Professors für Englische Philologie, Herbert Schöffler, gehalten im Oktober 1945," in *Geschichtswissenschaft in Göttingen*, ed. Hartmut Boockmann and Hermann Wellenreuther (Göttingen: Vandenhoek & Ruprecht, 1987), 364–399.
[115] Herbert Schöffler, "*Der Kaufmann von Venedig*: Zu den kommenden Aufführungen in Göttingen – Von Professor Herbert Schöffler, Göttingen," *Göttinger Tageblatt*, 26/27 September 1942.

Figure 4: Antonio (Heinrich Buchmann) and Bassanio (Andreas Wolf) asking Shylock (Wilhelm Meyer-Ottens) for credit in Gustav Rudolf Sellner's 1942 production at Stadttheater Göttingen. Courtesy of Deutsches Theater Göttingen.

sense clarified by Auerbach, whose two poles are "separate in time," yet connected in terms of a redemptive historical logic.[116]

On the one hand, Schöffler suggested that the Shylock plot gestured towards the historical progression from ancient to more refined forms of justice: "Ancient laws, stemming from times when money was scarce, [...] allowed the creditor to mutilate a defaulting debtor. Our play represents the historical moment when outdated barbaric laws are mitigated and transformed."[117] On the other hand, Schöffler connected *Merchant* to the radical anti-Semitic politics pursued by the German government. This is brought home when he explains why the Shylock scenes, although they are not at the centre of the play, should be regarded as highly significant: "These scenes are particularly important since the art of acting the role is threatened to deteriorate quickly in Germany; for even today younger actors already need to be *told* by their elder colleagues how Jews are to be played."[118] Postulating that Jewish identity had already become a fading memory, Schöffler not only condoned the anti-Semitic politics of the regime, but also ratified their success. According to the article, Shylock was well on the way to becoming an empty signifier. In consequence, it seemed that *Merchant* could now be performed according to a new identitarian paradigm, using the play to stage the ethos of the German people as a 'Volksgemeinschaft' cleansed of Jewish influences. Perhaps a dyed-in-the-wool Nazi demagogue would have been unable to match the insidiousness of the anti-Semitic innuendos offered by the ideologically wavering conservative professor.

Extant stage photographs suggest that the Göttingen production really played along with the interpretative and ideological strategy suggested by Schöffler. According to the professor's approach, the representation of Portia and of the Venetians was at least as important as the representation of Shylock. Indeed, as a production photograph shows, Portia seems to have literally presided over the play, elevated on a dais, and seated on a sort of throne. Two surviving pictures demonstrate the positioning of the non-Jewish majority in relation to Shylock. In one of them, the grouping in the trial scene emphasizes Shylock's

---

116 Erich Auerbach, "Figura," in *Time, History and Literature: Selected Essays of Erich Auerbach*, ed. James I. Porter, trans. Jane O. Newman (Princeton: Princeton University Press, 2014), 96; see also our Introduction.
117 Schöffler, "*Der Kaufmann von Venedig.*" This may in fact be a valid perspective on the larger historical implications of the play; see Bernhard Greiner, "Is that the Law? Die Metaphorisierung des Rechts als Problem der Interpretation des *Kaufmann von Venedig*," in *Shylock nach dem Holocaust: Zur Geschichte einer deutschen Erinnerungsfigur*, ed. Zeno Ackermann and Sabine Schülting (Berlin: De Gruyter, 2011), 189–200.
118 Schöffler, "*Der Kaufmann von Venedig*," emphasis in the original.

difference and isolation. While his gaze is lost in the distance beyond the stage, all the other characters are looking towards him. They are united by a unanimous gesture of confronting the outsider.

Such a visual stylization of confrontation is even more clearly evident in another photograph, which shows Antonio and Bassanio asking Shylock for credit in scene 1.3 (figure 4). The way in which the Christian merchant faces the Jewish moneylender recalls the traditional iconography of the Archangel Michael, the vanquisher of Satan. In addition, Antonio's pose and mien are remarkably close to the codified image of the soldier-hero in fascist propaganda. Apparently, the other side of the romantic spirit and "comedic cheerfulness"[119] with which the production imbued the Venetian Christians was a merciless militancy. The pictures from scenes 4.1 and 1.3 show how this militancy surfaced at specific points in the performance. Indeed, the way in which the production absorbed the crimes against Jews into a utopian story of "ease and deliciousness"[120] – attempting to affirm the regime's anti-Semitic politics, and simultaneously to manage and mend their effects on the perpetrator society – smacks of the ethics of the SS. A pertinent analogy may be the secret speech to leading ranks of the SS delivered by Heinrich Himmler at Poznań in October 1943. Openly commenting on the difficulties of carrying out the genocide, Himmler declared: "To have endured this and at the same time to have remained – with exceptions due to human weakness – decent persons has made us tough."[121]

"Everything is bound to a middle" – Vienna 1943

Sellner had a great career in the theatre ahead of him, during which (as will be discussed later in this chapter) he returned again to *Merchant*. However, when he produced the play at Göttingen in 1942, he was relatively young and had not yet earned a grand reputation. In contrast, Lothar Müthel, the director of the 1943 Burgtheater production, was a theatre star. It had taken a fabulous salary to coax Müthel from Berlin to Vienna.[122] As managing director of the Burgtheater,

---

119 Koch, "Das Spiel vom geprellten Juden."
120 "Des Lebens ganze Fülle."
121 Heinrich Himmler, speech at Poznań, 4 October 1943, qtd. in International Military Tribunal, *Der Prozeß gegen die Hauptkriegsverbrecher vor dem Internationalen Militärgerichtshof: Amtlicher Wortlaut in deutscher Sprache* (Nuremberg: Internationaler Militärgerichtshof, 1947), 3: 559.
122 Müthel's original family name was Lütcke. On his role during the National Socialist period, see Daiber, *Schaufenster der Diktatur*, esp. 184. In January 1939, Müthel, who had previously

one of the leading German-language stages, he was expected to offer theatrical entertainment that would meet the standards of the Gauleiter Baldur von Schirach, whose father had managed the Deutsches Nationaltheater in Weimar and was now presiding over the Hessisches Staatstheater at Wiesbaden. While rumours that it was the Gauleiter's order to put on *Merchant* at Vienna's Burgtheater are hard to substantiate, the production that premiered on 15 May 1943 certainly represented the most important and most widely publicized staging of *Merchant* during the National Socialist period.[123] Inevitably, it seemed to represent something like an official pronouncement by the regime.

Müthel may have felt slightly uncomfortable in this exposed role. Apparently, he wanted to make sure that his efforts would be evaluated from the right perspective – not only by the National Socialists, but also by whoever would succeed them. This impression is raised by a long article that the director published in the *Neues Wiener Tagblatt* two days before the premiere. Müthel elaborated on his dramaturgical principles in staging Shakespeare's difficult comedy. Rather than emphasizing the meaning of the play within contemporary political contexts, he proceeded from an ostentatiously non-ideological standpoint, treating *Merchant* primarily as an aesthetic problem and quoting a series of sources. Müthel suggested that his main intention was to go behind recent distortions of the drama and to return to Shakespeare's original intentions. He explained that "under the influence of Jewry" a valuable tradition of performing the play as a "fairy-tale comedy" had been "interrupted." Shylock, who ought to be played as a "cheating fool and malicious idiot," had erroneously been transformed into the lead role.[124]

---

worked as a director at the Staatstheater Berlin, became managing director of the Burgtheater. According to Daiber, Müthel had been granted 60,000 Marks for his first year in Vienna, 70,000 for his second, and 80,000 for his third. Like Sellner, Müthel was able to splendidly continue his career after the war. In 1951, he became director of drama at the prestigious Schauspiel Frankfurt/Main.

123 On the Burgtheater production, see Ludwig Schnauder, "'The poor man is wronged!' Die Figur des Shylock in Inszenierungen am Burgtheater," in *Die Rezeption anglophoner Dramen auf Wiener Bühnen im 20. Jahrhundert*, vol. 2 of *Weltbühne Wien / World Stage Vienna*, ed. Ewald Mengel, Ludwig Schnauder, and Rudolf Weiss (Trier: WVT, 2010), 131–135; and Monschau, *Der Jude nach der Shoah*, 68–84. See also Charles Edelman's "Introduction" to *The Merchant of Venice*, Shakespeare in Production, ed. Charles Edelman (Cambridge: Cambridge University Press, 2002), 53–54, and Gad Kaynar-Kissinger, "*The Merchant of Venice* on the German Stage and the 1995 'Buchenwald' Production in Weimar," in *Wrestling with Shylock*, ed. Nahshon and Shapiro, 254–256.

124 Lothar Müthel, "Zur Dramaturgie des *Kaufmann von Venedig*," *Neues Wiener Tagblatt*, 13 May 1943.

In these disquisitions, the director may well have drawn on personal memory. For when he was still an actor, Müthel had been cast as Bassanio alongside Kortner's spectacular Shylock in Viertel's production of 1923. He must have been around at the rehearsal when Kortner tore his original costume to replace it with his yellow coat. Twenty years later, however, Müthel's *Wiener Tagblatt* article deflected from Kortner, instead connecting the transformation of the Shylock role to an obscure Italian actor who had toured Germany in the nineteenth century: if Shylock had "acquired a preponderance that completely destroyed the structure of the play," the director explained, this was due to "the epigones of the great Italian actor Novelli, who performed the scene of Shylock's return after Jessica's flight – a scene not even delineated in Shakespeare – as a grand tragic solo performance and made it into the virtual centre of the play."[125] It is indicative of Müthel's strategy of ostentatious abstraction that he played the game of resentment without even naming it.

A couple of days later, the newspaper in which Müthel had discussed his principles published an enthusiastic review of the premiere. The author was Siegfried Melchinger, who went on to become a highly influential theatre critic and scholar in post-war Germany.[126] Melchinger affirmed the dramaturgical principles previously expounded by Müthel and thought that they had in fact been realized by the Burgtheater production. In line with Müthel's argument, Melchinger downsized the weight of Shylock and put the emphasis on an assumed ethic and aesthetic totality of the play. According to the review, the director had achieved "less a new interpretation of Shylock than the restoration of the drama as a work of art." In particular, Melchinger stressed the production's truthfulness to Shakespeare's text. Allegedly, the director had "changed not a syllable and made hardly any cuts."[127]

At first sight, it may seem surprising that the surviving prompt-book for the Burgtheater production confirms this claim: apart from minor omissions that kept open the possibility that Jessica is not Shylock's daughter, only a few changes had been made in the text of the Schlegel translation. In contrast to the Propaganda Ministry's suggestions, Shylock's great monologue in 3.1 also

---

[125] Müthel, "Zur Dramaturgie des *Kaufmann von Venedig*."
[126] On Melchinger's career in National Socialist Germany, see Daiber, *Schaufenster der Diktatur*, 170–171. Daiber suggests that Melchinger was a competent theatre critic who initially made his way by systematically playing along with the rules of anti-Semitic rhetoric. For instance, he had claimed in relation to Kortner that the racial characteristics of Jewishness had been "hot-branded on his physiognomy."
[127] Siegfried Melchinger, "*Der Kaufmann von Venedig*: Müthels Neuinszenierung im Burgtheater," *Neues Wiener Tagblatt*, 17 May 1943.

seems to have been left untouched.[128] In fact, it is likely that the ideological value of *Merchant* as performed at the Burgtheater in 1943 did not really depend on the massive interventions into the play's substance that many commentators have taken for granted.[129] Rather, the ideological strategy with which Müthel complied consisted in affirming Shakespeare's role as a 'German classic,' appropriating his work even in the context of a Vienna whose Jewish inhabitants had only recently been expelled or deported. In such an environment, unobtrusive shifts in accentuation were sufficient to make an Elizabethan comedy sanction a totalitarian politics of exclusion and murder.

Apart from the production's truthfulness to the text of Shakespeare – or, to be more precise, to Schlegel's harmonizing translation – a second main point in Melchinger's review was Müthel's alleged achievement of offering a unified vision. According to Melchinger, the director had successfully pursued a strategy of "binding" the play together and of finding an ideal "middle" ("Bindung" and "Mitte" are the German keywords used by Melchinger). Strangely enough, achieving such a balance seems to have depended on an excessive "merriness":

> The laughter is carried from one sphere to the next. When Shylock appears, there is no longer the merest hint of seriousness. And even Shylock's merriness does not stick out in comparison to that of the other characters. Here, too, everything is bound to a middle.[130]

It is thus obvious that the "binding together" of the play was based on tying down Shylock. Jörg Monschau succinctly spells out the subtext of the quoted passage: "By 'Bindung' Melchinger really meant drowning out Shylock. This was realized by the seamless, inconspicuous and collective transition from general mirthfulness to the group derision of an involuntarily comical clown, who was still the enemy but had somehow lost the stature of a serious opponent." As Monschau observes, this indicates a shift from previous anti-Semitic propaganda: "What Melchinger describes as the gist of the performance already smacks of the arrogance of the victor."[131]

---

128 We are indebted to Ludwig Schnauder (University of Vienna) for providing us with a photocopy of the prompt-book for Müthel's production.
129 See, e.g., Oliver Rathkolb, *Führertreu und gottbegnadet: Künstlereliten im Dritten Reich* (Vienna: Österreichischer Bundesverlag, 1991), 162. Rathkolb argues that the Burgtheater production constituted a brutal "ideological (i.e. anti-Semitic) rape of the original text" (parenthesis in the original text).
130 Melchinger, "*Der Kaufmann von Venedig*." The last sentence of the quotation – which has no predicate and seems strategically vague – is difficult to render in English. In German it reads: "Auch hier also Bindung, Mitte."
131 Monschau, *Der Jude nach der Shoah*, 80.

As in Berlin and Göttingen the previous year, the main ideological significance of the Burgtheater production did not consist in fostering the cliché of the demonic Jew (though reviewers like Biedrzynski were certainly able to find it in Krauß's performance).[132] Rather, the production is remarkable for implicitly ratifying the deportation and murder of Austrian and German Jews. Not even the most indifferent member of the audience could have been unaware of the disappearance of Vienna's 200,000 Jewish inhabitants. Until the end of 1941, many had been able to emigrate, but almost all of the remaining 60,000 Jews had been deported between October 1941 and October 1942. It seems incredible that Melchinger should have spelt out the connotations that Shakespeare's assumed "fairy tale" had recently acquired, but it is difficult to read his following sentence in any other way: "Behind the Jew we can see the wicked man of the fairy tale, the unearthly man-eater, the bogey man, who, just like the witch, will finally have to be shoved into the oven."[133] Judging from Melchinger's review, expulsion, deportation, and genocide shimmered through the surface of the Burgtheater production with the irreversibility and intangibility of archetypes – archetypes waiting to be actualized by contemporary reviewers.

Müthel and many people in the audience must have sensed that the days of the 'Third Reich' were already counted when the Burgtheater production opened in May 1943. Fifteen months later, in August 1944, an order by Goebbels closed all German theatres.[134] However, only a couple of weeks after this had taken

---

132 Cf. Karl Lahm, "Shylock der Ostjude," *Deutsche Allgemeine Zeitung*, 19 May 1943. On the one hand, Lahm approved of Müthel's intention to render Shylock as a buffoon. Simultaneously, however, he pointed out that Krauß had delivered a Shylock who conformed to the "pathological image of the Eastern Jewish racial type."
133 Melchinger, *"Der Kaufmann von Venedig."*
134 Goebbels's order was not the end of the stage history of *Merchant* during the war. In the German-language front theatre of Minsk, a production of *Merchant* premiered in September 1943, exactly at the time when the so-called "German Ghetto" of the city was being liquidated. In her memoirs, *Das alltägliche Exil: Leben zwischen Hakenkreuz und Währungsreform* (Berlin: Dietz, 1982), actress Inge Stolten, who played Nerissa in this production, quotes from the anti-Semitic programme notes. She remembers that most of the stage hands and technicians were deported German Jews: "Today, I am sometimes led to believe that I was getting used to the Jews' fate. How else could it have been possible for me [...] to rehearse the role of Nerissa in *The Merchant of Venice* while the Jews were forced to stand by and listen to us?" (93). – Bonnell (*Shylock in Germany*, 165–166, 221n252) has information on a production of *Merchant* put on in September 1944 at Tatura Camp 3 in Victoria, Australia, by German prisoners of war. The programme notes contained racist quotations by Alfred Rosenberg and Hans F. K. Günther. For a discussion of a 1943 production by Polish officers in a POW camp at Murnau, Germany, see Krystyna Kujawińska-Courtney, "'In this Hour of History: Amidst these Tragic Events' –

effect, the famous director Veit Harlan contacted the Propaganda Minister to propose a film version of *Merchant*.[135] Again, the role of Shylock was to go to Werner Krauß, with whom Harlan had collaborated in the production of *Jud Süß*. Goebbels embraced the idea. Strangely enough, the regime was still considering lavish film productions even when defeat had become inevitable. It is yet more startling that *Merchant* should have been a candidate for such a terminal propaganda effort.

Kolberg, the film that Harlan was completing when he suggested the new project, told the story of a besieged town that held out against all odds at the time of the Napoleonic Wars. If such a story encouraged desperate acts of resistance, Shakespeare's troubling comedy was hardly suited to similar ends. Rather, it seems possible that *Merchant* may have been intended to represent a legacy that the faltering Nazi empire would leave behind. Indeed, the film project corroborates our argument that the place of *Merchant* within the ideological economy of National Socialist Germany was different from that of films such as *Jud Süß* or *Der ewige Jude*. In contrast to these films, National Socialist *Merchant* productions did not directly pave the way to murder. Rather, their function was in tacitly affirming as well as psychologically managing the Holocaust as an 'open secret' and *fait accompli*.

1.3 Redemptive Figurations: The Post-War Period to the End of the 1950s

The Problem of Continuity

In an important essay on West German productions of *Merchant*, Markus Moninger has stated: "Every single post-war production of *The Merchant of Venice* remembers Auschwitz. [...] In the period immediately after the war, there were reservations about performing the play. Ever since, however, it has been offering a stage for the drama of German post-war society's dealings

---

Polish Shakespeare during the Second World War," in *Shakespeare and the Second World War*, ed. Makaryk and McHugh, 122–142.

135 On the film project, see Bonnell, *Shylock in Germany*, 167–169; and Veit Harlan, *Im Schatten meiner Filme* (Gütersloh: Mohn, 1966), 199–205. See also Dorothea Hollstein, *Jud Süß und die Deutschen: Antisemitische Vorurteile im nationalsozialistischen Spielfilm* (Frankfurt/M.: Ullstein, 1983), 175–182. In contrast to Bonnell and Holstein, Harlan suggests that the idea for a film version had come from Goebbels.

with Auschwitz."[136] The last sentence draws attention to the momentous importance – the actual "drama" – of confronting the Holocaust. However, the terms "stage" and "drama" also indicate the theatricality – the performative quality and role-playing – that have frequently characterized such remembrance. At the same time, Moninger's words hint at the seminal role of the theatre as a medium for confronting the past.[137]

It is exactly because these notions are so pertinent that we set out, in the remainder of this chapter and in the following chapters, to complicate them. There are two main issues to be raised. Firstly, it is necessary to take a closer look at the supposed "reservations" against the play in the immediate postwar years. Secondly, we want to interrogate the assumption that the play's reception since 1945 and the concurrent refigurations of Shylock can be understood automatically and entirely in terms of Holocaust remembrance.

Extant analyses have suggested that *Merchant* was revived only at the end of the 1950s, when the outstanding Jewish actor Ernst Deutsch took on the role of Shylock. Moninger refers to Deutsch's earliest interpretation of the role in 1957 as "the first post-war portrayal of Shylock," and Hans-Peter Bayerdörfer commends the actor for creating "the first Shylock after the Shoah."[138] Along similar lines, Wilhelm Hortmann argues that after the war *Merchant* "was shunned as unapproachable for the time being on account of the crimes against the Jews. How to perform *Merchant* without seeming to add insult to injury was a question only solved by great Jewish actors of Shylock such as Ernst Deutsch and Fritz Kortner, and then only much later."[139] However, the focus on Deutsch and Kortner – and later on the renowned Jewish directors George Tabori and Peter Zadek,

---

136 Markus Moninger, "Auschwitz erinnern: *Merchant*-Inszenierungen im Nachkriegsdeutschland," in *Das Theater der Anderen: Alterität und Theater zwischen Antike und Gegenwart*, ed. Christopher Balme (Tübingen: Francke, 2001), 229–230. See also Zeno Ackermann, "Performing Oblivion / Enacting Remembrance: The Merchant of Venice in West Germany, 1945 to 1961," *Shakespeare Quarterly* 62.3 (2011): 364–395.
137 Cf. Peter Reichel, *Erfundene Erinnerung: Weltkrieg und Judenmord in Film und Theater* (Munich: Hanser, 2004).
138 Moninger, "Auschwitz erinnern," 231; Hans-Peter Bayerdörfer, "Shylock on the German Stage in the Post-Shoah Era," in *German Shakespeare Studies at the Turn of the Twenty-First Century*, ed. Christa Jansohn (Newark: University of Delaware Press, 2006), 207; cf. Bayerdörfer, "Shylock auf der deutschen Bühne nach der Shoah," in *Shylock? Zinsverbot und Geldverleih in jüdischer und christlicher Tradition*, ed. Johannes Heil and Bernd Wacker (Frankfurt/M.: Fink, 1997), 263–264.
139 Wilhelm Hortmann, *Shakespeare on the German Stage: The Twentieth Century* (Cambridge: Cambridge University Press, 1998), 182; cf. Hortmann, "Wo, bitte, geht's nach Belmont? Über ein Dilemma von Inszenierungen des *Kaufmann von Venedig* nach dem Holocaust," *Shakespeare Jahrbuch* 139 (2003): 218.

whose approaches to *Merchant* will be discussed in Chapter 2 – carries a danger of glossing over what was, in fact, a surprisingly lively, and at times surprisingly unrestrained, reception of *Merchant* in the theatrical mainstream of the 1950s.

The assumption that there were strict reservations concerning Shakespeare's comedy is correct only for the German Democratic Republic, where the play was first staged in 1976 and where it was only rarely performed afterwards (a phenomenon that will be discussed in Chapter 3). For West Germany the story is different. In Frankfurt (Main), an attempt to stage *Merchant* had been undertaken as early as December 1946. However, the plan was criticized by Holocaust survivors as well as by the general press. One journalist thought that the idea of putting on *Merchant* at this time bespoke "a lack of tact."[140] Eventually, Frankfurt's American military government stopped the production.[141]

In the following year, a member of an American UNESCO delegation intervened when he discovered that *Merchant* was given as assigned reading at a school in Wiesbaden (a city in the Southwest of Germany). The representative in question must have taken the occurrence very seriously, for he wrote directly to the American Secretary of War:

> It did seem to me that Germany in this day and age was an inappropriate place to teach *The Merchant of Venice*. [...] [The play] is so easily open to anti-Semitic reactions and interpretations, and the German teachers and German children have so long been conditioned to anti-Semitic reactions, that the book ought not to be used in German schools at this time under our auspices.[142]

As a result of this letter, the syllabus had to be changed and the reading of *Merchant* was discontinued.

The waning of occupational rule in West Germany, however, went along with a speedy return of Shakespeare's comedy. It could first be seen in 1948 at the Westdeutsches Landestheater (based in Siegburg, near Cologne), and a second post-war production was put on in Hamm (in the north-eastern part of the

---

140 Qtd. in Monschau, *Der Jude nach der Shoah*, 99.

141 For a detailed account of the aborted production at Frankfurt, see Monschau, *Der Jude nach der Shoah*, 97–105. Cf. Ernst Leopold Stahl, *Shakespeare und das deutsche Theater: Wanderung und Wandelung seines Werkes in dreiundeinhalb Jahrhunderten* (Stuttgart: Kohlhammer, 1947), 738–739.

142 Letter from James Marshall to Robert Patterson, 28 February 1947 (National Archives, Washington), qtd. in Wigand Lange, *Theater in Deutschland nach 1945: Zur Theaterpolitik der amerikanischen Besatzungsbehörden* (Frankfurt/M.: Lang, 1980), 323. See also Balz Engler, "The Noise That Banish'd Martius: *Coriolanus* in Post-War Germany," in *Renaissance Refractions: Essays in Honour of Alexander Shurbanov*, ed. Boika Sokolova and Evgenia Pancheva (Sofia: St Kliment Ohridski University Press, 2001), 179–186.

1.3 Redemptive Figurations: The Post-War Period to the End of the 1950s — 65

Ruhr area) in 1949. There were two productions in 1951, and two again in 1952, including a highly successful production at a major German stage: Bochum's Städtische Bühne. Another two premieres took place in 1953, and no less than five in 1954. Accordingly, *Shakespeare Jahrbuch* stated: "*Much Ado about Nothing, As You Like It, The Comedy of Errors*, and recently also *The Merchant of Venice*, while ranking clearly after the main plays in the Shakespeare repertoire, are an integral part of theatre programmes around the country."[143]

Our second caveat relates to the interpretation of the year 1945. Although the end of the war marked a dramatic rupture for Germans, the notion of a complete 'downfall' of the 'Third Reich,' resulting in a 'zero hour' ('Stunde Null') and a fresh start for German history obscures a complicated dialectic of continuity and change.[144] The post-war period in the narrow sense of the term – largely coterminous with Konrad Adenauer's chancellorship from 1949 to 1963 – was shaped by a generation who had already reached adulthood when National Socialism rose to power. As many former members of the NSDAP returned to positions in administration, politics, and culture, 'denazification' and 're-education' gave way to what Norbert Frei describes as an ambivalent strategy of managing the past ("Vergangenheitspolitik").[145] Amnesties for former National Socialists were combined with normative demarcations against National Socialism and with compensation for its victims. Suggestively, the totality of the measures undertaken in terms of compensation, reparation, and reconciliation were discussed as 'Wiedergutmachungspolitik,' i.e. as a 'politics of putting it right again.'

In this context, *Merchant*, with its emphasis on the relationships between Jews and the majority society, on debts and guilt, and on justice and mercy,

---

143 Wolfgang Stroedel, "Bühnenbericht 1954," *Shakespeare Jahrbuch* 91 (1955): 222. As the annual theatre reports in *Shakespeare Jahrbuch* show, the most popular Shakespeare plays were *Twelfth Night* and *Hamlet*. *A Midsummer Night's Dream* and *The Taming of the Shrew* were also performed frequently, while *Othello* and *Measure for Measure* enjoyed intermittent spells of popularity. If *Hamlet* (in some sense similar to Carl Zuckmayer's spectacularly successful *The Devil's General*, 1946, or Wolfgang Borchert's *The Man Outside*, 1946/47) was used to stage a highly theatrical sense of problematic selfhood, the ongoing predilection for *Twelfth Night* and *A Midsummer Night's Dream* betrays a need for stories of romance and reconciliation. The Belmont scenes in *Merchant* were usually rendered in a way that catered to these needs.
144 On the problematic relevance of the concept of a 'zero hour,' see Stephen Brockmann, *German Literary Culture at the Zero Hour* (Rochester: Camden House, 2009).
145 Norbert Frei, *Adenauer's Germany and the Nazi Past: The Politics of Amnesty and Integration*, trans. Joel Golb (New York: Columbia University Press, 2002). Golb's translation renders Frei's neologism "Vergangenheitspolitik" – perhaps not entirely convincingly – as "policy for the past."

became deeply significant. However, the reception of the play remained tied to a dominating concern for the identity of the German people – a people whose murderous ethnic homogenization was largely taken for granted. Consequently, the dominant motive behind post-war productions of *Merchant* was less the urge to remember the victims of Germany's crimes than the attempt to reconstruct a shattered nation through the restorative plot and cultural authority of Shakespearean comedy. Shakespeare in general and *Merchant* in particular became points of reference for constructing an imaginary continuity that seemed to reach back across the terrible rupture of the war and the Holocaust.

In reality, continuity was first of all an institutional and biographical fact.[146] The end of the war did not terminate the careers of many actors and directors who had been successful in Nazi Germany. Erich Ponto is a case in point. After Ernst Deutsch, Ponto was the most renowned Shylock of the 1950s. Like Deutsch, he also played Nathan in Lessing's drama and the heroine's father in the hugely successful stage adaptation of *The Diary of Anne Frank*. However, before he interpreted Shylock in accordance with the rhetoric of 'philo-Semitism,'[147] Ponto had offered a very different representation of Jewishness in the 1940 propaganda film *Die Rothschilds*.

Another example of artistic continuities can be seen in the splendid career of Gustav Rudolf Sellner, the director of the 1942 production at Göttingen, and a key protagonist of a renewed modernist aesthetic in the theatre of the Federal Republic. Sellner directed *Merchant* again in 1955 in Darmstadt. In a similar manner, Karl Pempelfort, who directed *Merchant* in Bonn in 1956, had also served as stage manager for a 1935 production in Königsberg (today's Kaliningrad). In his earlier function, Pempelfort had published a newspaper article that commented on Shylock and the Venetian Christians as representatives of different "worlds": "The true meaning of these two worlds can only be fathomed by us, who know that they are expressions of opposed racial characteristics."[148]

Still more significant than biographical continuities is the tenacity of anti-Semitic stereotypes in post-war reviews. Writing about a production of *Merchant*

---

146 On institutional, biographical, and aesthetic continuities between the theatre of the National Socialist period and that of post-war West Germany, see Mertz, *Das gerettete Theater*, esp. 39–101.

147 As the inverted commas indicate, 'philo-Semitism' has to be seen as a historical formation, an ambivalent posture that presupposes anti-Semitism and may imply anti-Semitic dispositions. Cf. Frank Stern, *Im Anfang war Auschwitz: Antisemitismus und Philosemitismus im deutschen Nachkrieg* (Gerlingen: Bleicher, 1991).

148 Karl Pempelfort, "Er besteht auf seinem Schein," *Königsberger Tageblatt*, 31 March 1935, qtd. in Wulf, *Theater und Film im Dritten Reich*, 281.

that premiered in Coburg in 1954, a critic described the representation of Shylock by actor and director Stefan Dahlen as follows: "His steady adherence to the Yiddish of Frankfurt's Jews, the frequent Hebrew invocations of God and the Devil, the gestures and facial expression of the typical Jew, all combined, resulted in a singularly impressive character study." At the same time, the review argued that Dahlen's tendency towards a "grave and heroic" Shylock "imperilled" not only "the play's character as a comedy," but also certain conventionalized patterns of ethnic identification: "This Shylock was German and heroic more than he was an incarnation of the mumbling and haggling little Jew who, afraid of his own courage, is finally cheated out of his reward."[149] Identifying heroism and cowardice as German and Jewish character traits respectively, the passage testifies to the tenacity of racist ideologies.

The review is indicative of what Norbert Frei describes as a "continued need" among Germans to prove their ongoing "solidarity" with the former National Socialist collective.[150] "National Socialism lives on, and even today we still do not know whether it is merely the ghost of what was so monstrous that it lingers on after its own death, or whether it has not yet died at all."[151] This was Theodor Adorno's assessment of contemporary Germany in his 1959 lecture on "The Meaning of Working Through the Past," which was broadcast on the radio in the following year. According to this analysis, the main problem was not manifest neo-fascism but the permanence of the sociocultural dispositions on which National Socialism had been based. Adorno demanded a real "working through" of the lingering past. This would be a critical and political process of transformation rather than the merely psychological exercise of "coming to terms" with history.

Adorno's demand also challenged those who attempted to use Shakespeare for resurrecting the cultural traditions of the past. Only two years after the war, Ernst Leopold Stahl published a comprehensive history of the Bard's reception in

---

149 ERES, "'Ich steh' hier auf meinen Schein!' Coburger Neuinszenierung des *Kaufmanns von Venedig*," *Neue Presse*, Coburg, 23 January 1954. As the reviewer notes, Dahlen had actually learnt Hebrew "in order to invest his Shylock with the right kind of jargon or with a correct dialect. Thus, Shylock can be heard to exclaim 'hochiéni elohai!' ('help me, oh my God')." Cf. Monschau, *Der Jude nach der Shoah*, 160.
150 Norbert Frei, *1945 und wir: Das Dritte Reich im Bewußtsein der Deutschen* (2005), extended ed. (Munich: Beck, 2009), 47. On the tenacity of the imaginative social integration effected by National Socialism, see also Theodor W. Adorno, "Was bedeutet: Aufarbeitung der Vergangenheit" (1959/60), trans. by Henry W. Pickford as "The Meaning of Working Through the Past," in *Critical Models: Interventions and Catchwords* (New York: Columbia University Press, 1998), esp. 95–96.
151 Adorno, "Was bedeutet: Aufarbeitung der Vergangenheit," 89–90.

Germany, in which he integrated the theatre of the National Socialist period into a teleological narrative. The chapter dealing with 1933 and the following years was titled "From Chaos to Order" – "chaos" characterizing both the turmoil created by the National Socialists in the lead-up to Hitler's chancellorship *and* the aesthetic experimentation of the Weimar period.[152] A similar attempt at simply continuing a long tradition was evident in *Shakespeare Jahrbuch*. As if it were a mere matter of course, the 1946 volume caught up on the incomplete theatre reports published during the last years of the war. In this context, an essay on the reception of Shakespeare during 1943 and 1944, again written by Stahl, first commented on the eminent stages of Berlin and Vienna, and then continued: "The most remarkable achievements on the stages of the Reich have already been dealt with in previous reports."[153]

If there was a general tendency to conceive of Shakespearean theatre as a tool for engineering continuity, director Heinz Hilpert was among the few who firmly excluded *Merchant* from such an agenda. When he was asked to direct the play he allegedly answered: "No, I will only put *The Merchant of Venice* on stage again when there are forty Jews in the stalls, ready to laugh about it."[154] However, this was not a majority opinion. On the contrary, it was frequently claimed that performing *Merchant* was a token of re-establishing a tradition that had been interrupted not only by the abuses of National Socialism but also by the interference of occupational administrations.

Especially after the Germany Treaty with the Western Allies and the Reparations Agreement with Israel had been signed in 1952, and after Adenauer had spoken of the "termination of the post-war era" ["Ende der Nachkriegszeit"] in 1953,[155] productions of *Merchant* were explicitly related to a general drive towards full sovereignty and total rehabilitation. Under the heading "Waiting

---

152 Stahl, *Shakespeare und das deutsche Theater*, 700–728. Stahl's heading ("Von der Unordnung zur Anordnung") contains wordplay: "Anordnung" means "order" in the sense of both "arrangement" and "command." However, Stahl was convinced that Weimar aesthetics had had to come to an end: "Efforts for the inauguration of a new artistic style [...] were conceivable only within the context of a changing form of government. The seizure of power by National Socialism in January 1933 created the outward conditions necessary for such efforts" (700). Stahl had been an important theatre critic during the National Socialist period.
153 Ernst Leopold Stahl, "Shakespeare im Aufführungsjahr 1943/44," *Shakespeare Jahrbuch* 80/81 (1946): 108.
154 Qtd. in Monschau, *Der Jude nach der Shoah*, 178. The original source of the anecdote is a 1956 theatre review in the *Süddeutsche Zeitung*.
155 Konrad Adenauer, second inaugural speech (1953), qtd. in Helmut Dubiel, *Niemand ist frei von der Geschichte: Die nationalsozialistische Herrschaft in den Debatten des Deutschen Bundestages* (Munich: Hanser, 1999), 45.

Period Over," a 1953 article in the daily *Rhein-Neckar-Zeitung* declared with reference to *Merchant:*

> Only if the Germans should be taken for an absolutely inferior species, a species with whom even the most subtle manifestations of art have negative consequences and result in barbaric reactions where others are emotionally moved and promoted in their humanity – only if the most steadfast adherents and admirers of Shakespeare should thus come to be viewed as utterly unpredictable and 'incorrigible,' it would be justified to withhold certain works of art from them.[156]

This goes further than hoping that the reception of Shakespeare might be instrumental in constructing continuity. The passage insists on the German *right* to stage a Shakespearean play, even one as problematic as the comedy about the condemnation and forced baptism of an unruly Jewish character. Moreover, the article from the *Rhein-Neckar-Zeitung* implies that Germans enjoy this right of staging the play *in compensation* for injuries that they have suffered as objects of denazification and re-education.

Self-Directed Compensation – Shylock and the National Regeneration of Germany

The first post-war production of *Merchant* on a really important German stage took place in 1952 at Bochum's Städtische Bühne. A local newspaper pointed out how director Hans Schalla had focused on the contrast between two worlds, a bright and a dark one. On the "bright side" ("Lichtseite") of the performance, Schalla is said to have displayed "the splendour and the glory, the wit and the amorous enchantment of the Venetian lovers, odd birds and cheerful fellows." From today's viewpoint at least, it seems remarkable how unquestioningly the critic, Leo Nyssen, described the Venetian Christians as paragons of virtue and the good life, commending actor Rainer Geldern for performing "a truly decent and virtuous Antonio." However, the review also applauded Schalla's production for placing one character firmly "outside the realm of mercy and grace": Shylock.[157] This illustrates that the interpretation of *Merchant* was still shaped by Gustav Landauer's seminal essay on the play.

---

[156] Emil Belzner, "Karenzzeit abgelaufen," *Rhein-Neckar-Zeitung*, 2 May 1953. Cf. Monschau, *Der Jude nach der Shoah*, 153.

[157] Leo Nyssen, "Lustspiel – dicht an der Tragödie," *Bochumer Anzeiger*, 24 September 1952.

Between 1952 and 1958, one in two programmes for productions of *Merchant* quoted Landauer, often extensively. There are two reasons for this. Firstly, as a Jewish and leftist victim of rightist political murder, Landauer – similar to Heine, who was quoted with even greater regularity – served as an alibi figure, disarming doubts about the appropriateness of showing a problematic Jewish character on the German stage. Secondly, Landauer's take on the play offered a vision of paradoxical redemption: a compensation for guilt that consisted in the (symbolic) exclusion of those against whom one had become guilty.

A dual perspective on Shylock's Jewishness is characteristic for the quoted review, as well as for many similar texts. On the one hand, Nyssen assures his readers that "there is no Jewish question in Shakespeare." Indeed, he frequently points to Shylock's status as a "figure," as if he wishes to foreground the character's dimension as an abstraction and a theatrical device: "One may say that the figure of the Jew in the play is the figure of the 'Other,' of the particular, the uncommon – similar to the figure of the moor in *Othello*, who was certainly not seen or designed by Shakespeare from the perspective of the 'racial.'"[158] On the other hand, the review explains that the playwright invested his "Venetian Hebrew" with "many character traits of his tribe." The ideological and social relevance of this perspective becomes apparent when Nyssen connects Shylock to an imagined powerful collective of Jews, writing that "whenever one of them is given an opportunity to strike back, he does not want to forego it and knows no forgiveness; he insists on his bond and on his hated enemy's pound of flesh." Thus, the Shylock figure serves as a container of various historical strata and discourses. It merges time-honoured mythical conceptions of Jewishness with the anti-Semitic propaganda of the National Socialists, and mixes both with the notion that Jews were unwilling to forgive the crimes of the Holocaust. Simultaneously, the image of the Jew as a dangerous Other and the image of the Jew as a powerless victim are blended with each other.

Nyssen's review betrays conflicting needs of confronting guilt and warding it off at the same time. This process and the resulting double bind for Shylock was made explicit in another review of the Bochum production. The text, by Albert Schulze Vellinghausen, was titled "Nach jenen Jahren – Hut ab vor Shylock!" ("After those years, hats off to Shylock!"). Besides the ominous phrase "those years," several other passages also hinted at the recent past. Thus, while the scenes dealing with Portia's suitors were playfully described as "a socially exclu-

---

[158] Nyssen, "Lustspiel – dicht an der Tragödie." Arguing that the figure/character Shylock is also a figure/figuration of the 'Other,' Nyssen's text slides between the two usages of the term in German.

1.3 Redemptive Figurations: The Post-War Period to the End of the 1950s — 71

sive entertainment of the highest order," Shylock's presence on stage came to be seen as deeply unsettling: "However, the Eternal Jew casts his uneerie, grandiose shadow into this aristocratic, if not to say snobbish, planetarium." This characterization was intended critically: what really seemed to cast its "shadow" over the performance was a murderous past in which stereotypes such as the "Eternal Jew" had played a central role. At the end of the review, the critic expressed his relief that the veiled confrontation with that past through the medium of Shakespeare's play had gone well: "Rightly, there was warm applause. Shylock was greeted with ovations. In part, these were in acknowledgement of his task to represent the shivers of history. Hats off!"[159] Strikingly, it is Shylock to whom the reviewer thus assigns the "task" of solving the knotty problems faced by German society. Shakespeare's Jewish character is expected to negotiate pervasive tensions between absence and presence, silence and confrontation, and also between a pre-occupation with the pains suffered by Germans and an acknowledgement of the crimes they had committed.[160] Shylock supposedly "represents" or even "stands in for" ("vertreten" is the German term) what is vaguely referred to as the "shivers of history." He is thus expected to open up the recent past to discursive treatment *without* making the events of that past explicit. Moreover, Shakespeare's fictional Jew has to serve as a figuration of the Jewish victims of the Holocaust *without* referring to any actual Jews with whom one would have to enter into a painful dialogue.

Wilhelm Hortmann has assumed that post-war productions of *Merchant* would necessarily have been informed by a desire to 'make amends' ('Wiedergutmachung') and to offer compensation: "During the 1950s and 1960s 'compensational' Shylocks dominated: they were brothers in spirit to Nathan the Wise, with Erich Ponto […] and Ernst Deutsch […] offering the most distinctive examples for this approach."[161] The responses to the Bochum production are among the numerous documents that complicate such an interpretation. In fact, compensation is itself a slippery concept. The notion of 'Wiedergutmachung' articulated an

---

159 A. S. V. [Albert Schulze Vellinghausen], "Nach jenen Jahren – Hut ab vor Shylock! Shakespeares *Kaufmann von Venedig* in Bochum," *Der Mittag*, 26 September 1952.
160 The preoccupation of post-war Germans with the pain that they themselves had suffered is the main thesis of Robert G. Moeller, *War Stories: The Search for a Usable Past in the Federal Republic of Germany* (Berkeley: University of California Press, 2001). See also Norbert Frei and Sybille Steinbacher, eds., *Beschweigen und Bekennen: Die deutsche Nachkriegsgesellschaft und der Holocaust* (Göttingen: Wallstein, 2001).
161 Hortmann, "Wo, bitte, geht's nach Belmont?," 218. Cf. Hortmann, *Shakespeare on the German Stage*, 255, where the term "expiation Shylocks" is used.

expectation that guilt could be converted into monetary debts.[162] An ethical imperative for compensation that, considering an 'industrialized' genocide, seemed impossible to fulfil was to be transformed into a manageable financial obligation. Moreover, the logic of 'Wiedergutmachungspolitik' included the promise that there would be a compensation for compensation: that there must be something to be gained in the process for Germany as a collective that had been shaken not only by guilt incurred but also by pain suffered during and after the war.

Viewed from the perspective of such a collective, *Merchant* had a lot to offer. After all, the play explores the topic of compensation in nearly all its potential ramifications: in the practical sense of compensation as a process of re-establishing equilibrium, in the financial and ethical sense of compensation as something offered to make up for debts or guilt, and also in the psychological sense of compensation as a process of displacing thwarted desires and aspirations. However, the passage in *Merchant* that seemed most pertinent to post-war German society was Portia's speech on "the quality of mercy" (much-quoted in German theatre programmes of the 1950s) and its assumption of a right to unqualified forgiveness:

> [...] Therefore, Jew,
> Though justice be thy plea, consider this:
> That in the course of justice none of us
> Should see salvation. We do pray for mercy,
> And that same prayer doth teach us all to render
> The deeds of mercy. [...] (4.1.192–97)

Nyssen, the first of the two critics of the Bochum production that we have quoted above, regarded "mercy" as the "leitmotif" of the play.[163] It is obvious that the appeal of *Merchant* in the early Federal Republic had much to do with this exchange of "mercy" and "salvation" for the demands of "justice." This was

---

162 On the ambivalence of the concept of 'Wiedergutmachung,' see Sigrid Weigel, "Shylocks Wiederkehr: Die Verwandlung von Schuld in Schulden oder: Zum symbolischen Tausch der Wiedergutmachung," *Zeitschrift für Deutsche Philologie* 114 (1995): 8–17. However, the notion of 'Wiedergutmachung' had originally been introduced in order to stress the *obligation* of 'making amends' for the crimes committed under National Socialism; cf. Hans Günther Hockerts, "Wiedergutmachung in Deutschland: Eine historische Bilanz 1945–2000," *Vierteljahrshefte für Zeitgeschichte* 49 (2001): 167–169. For a detailed account of compensational policy, see Constantin Goschler, *Schuld und Schulden: Die Politik der Wiedergutmachung für NS-Verfolgte seit 1945* (Göttingen: Wallstein, 2005).
163 Nyssen, "Lustspiel – dicht an der Tragödie."

already evident from the way in which Robert Michal, the moving force behind the aborted Frankfurt production of 1946, defended his project against its critics: "If this play should fail," Michal wrote, "then for us, too, there is no longer any hope for, nor any right to, mercy."[164]

The paradoxical idea of using Shakespeare's play to compensate oneself for the crimes one had committed also informed Gustav Rudolf Sellner's second production of *Merchant*, which premiered on 7 May 1955 at the renowned Landestheater Darmstadt (a city not far from Frankfurt). After the war, Sellner went through a period of philosophical reflection before he continued with his career. He later declared: "At that moment, it was of primary importance to resume the search for the essence of the human, the search for the lost image of man. I was looking for the magic spell, the formula."[165] The programme for Sellner's new *Merchant* suggests that the director hoped to rediscover "the lost image of man" not in the figure of Shylock but rather in contradistinction to it.

Sellner's "magic spell" was to be the ideal of forgiving mercy, and accordingly, the programme focussed on the theme of music and on the character of Portia. Besides the obligatory extract from Landauer's essay, there was also a piece on "Music in *The Merchant of Venice*." This contribution, specially written for publication in the programme, offered an interpretation not only of the play but also of Sellner's production. It raises the impression that the director translated Landauer's socialist mysticism into a conservative aestheticism. Suggesting that "music can balance out the scales of modernity," the author of the essay declared: "that it is the woman who cultivates music is also in line with Goethe's vision, for whom appealing to the mothers is more pertinent than trusting in the logism of the fathers."[166] In this interpretation, "the Jew Shylock" (as he was called in the programme) was cast to represent a "men's world" that seemed to have lost the right "balance between spirit and matter."[167]

In a later interview, published by *Shakespeare Jahrbuch* (West) in 1984, Sellner was asked what had motivated his production of *Merchant* so soon after the war. Even though the 1942 production was not mentioned in the interview, Sell-

---

164 Robert Michal, qtd. by Monschau, *Der Jude nach der Shoah*, 99.
165 Gustav Rudolf Sellner and Werner Wien, *Theatralische Landschaft* (Bremen: Carl Schünemann 1962), 27. As a contrast to Sellner's somewhat pompous story of introspection and redirection, see Mertz, *Das gerettete Theater*, 106: "These men – Gründgens and Sellner, Hilpert and Schäfer, Fehling and Müthel – were mired in the politics of the Third Reich to such an extent that within the new state they clung to their art world."
166 Landestheater Darmstadt, "Die Musik im *Kaufmann von Venedig*," *Das Neue Forum* 5 (1955/56): 2.
167 Landestheater Darmstadt, "Die Musik im *Kaufmann von Venedig*," 2.

ner's answer is instructive: "Our situation at the Darmstadt theatre. Apparently, we had already become a bit obsessed with a specific concept of philosophical theatre and with a theatre that could also be a kind of purgatory, so to speak – a purgatory also for the things from which we had only just emerged, from which we had escaped."[168] Sellner's responses are strategically vague. It is left open whether he interpreted *Merchant* as a play about guilt, about the ambivalence of the law, or about the puzzling "carelessness" of the Venetian "business world." Likewise, the fact that Shylock is a Jew is made to appear accidental and essential at the same time. However, Sellner's comments on Max Noack, who had played Shylock in the 1955 production, are fraught with significance: "Everybody who saw him as Shylock had to weep with him and for him. [...] I will never forget this suffering Shylock played by Noack, and I will always claim that it was right to attempt the play at that time."[169] The Shylock figure here serves as a fetish. It is used to contain the glaring contradictions of a specific conception of Germany's national regeneration in the double shadow of the Holocaust and of the National Socialist 'Community of the People' ('Volksgemeinschaft').

Personalizing Shylock

As we have seen, the Shylock figure served a double function in post-war West Germany. It was supposed to somehow address the quandaries of German guilt, while simultaneously articulating desires or demands for national regeneration, exculpation, and redemption. The problems created by such a multifarious approach come to the fore in Joachim Kaiser's *Kleines Theatertagebuch* ("Little Theatre Diary"), published in 1965. The book comprises an essay on *Merchant* in which the eminent critic displaced the problem of rehabilitating the perpetrator society into the problem of rehabilitating Shakespeare's fictional Jew. Kaiser asks: "Is it possible to save Shylock? Or do we have to let his soul go to hell, and Shakespeare's possibly most brilliant play with it?"[170] The heading of the respective chapter already answers the first of these questions: "Shylock Cannot Be Redeemed by Mortals."

---

[168] Sellner in Christian Jauslin, "Zu Gustav Rudolf Sellners Shakespeare-Inszenierungen: Gespräch mit dem Regisseur," *Shakespeare Jahrbuch* (West) (1984): 39.
[169] Sellner in Jauslin, "Zu Gustav Rudolf Sellners Shakespeare-Inszenierungen," 40.
[170] Joachim Kaiser, "Shylock ist auf Erden nicht zu helfen," *Kleines Theatertagebuch* (Reinbek: Rowohlt, 1965), 69.

Kaiser's position on whether German theatres should refrain from the play was equally clear: "I regard *The Merchant of Venice* as a test in democracy. For as long as theatres and TV stations skirt this play of Christian injustice and Jewish revengefulness [...], we will remain in a state of immaturity, not even being ready for a play that is more than 350 years old."[171] Kaiser was not convinced by the way in which renowned actor Erich Ponto had played Shylock in a famous production of the Wurttemberg Staatstheater in Stuttgart (premiere: 15 September 1956). As he wrote: "Shylock, who is craving revenge (and that for very good reasons), was rendered as a melancholy Nathan, a lenient Jew with eyes full of suffering, a victim praying for compassion, apparently grateful that he was suffered to breathe the air of Venice and to enter the Rialto."[172] Kaiser concluded: "Clearly, taming Shylock means betraying Shakespeare."[173] Indeed, actor Erich Ponto and director Werner Kraut had been at pains to achieve what Kaiser described as "saving" Shakespeare's play *without* letting Shylock "go to hell."

The programme for the Stuttgart production yet again started off with an extract from Landauer's essay on *Merchant*. This time, however, the passage chosen did not refer to Portia as a paragon of womanhood, nor did it dwell on the theme of mercy. Indeed, the new selection might almost be read as correcting the previous reception of Landauer's essay. One of the quotations was: "This work by the poet presents us simultaneously with the most boundless joy and deepest tragedy; the play does not only expose Shylock, it also exposes those on the other side, amongst whom we, as the audience, stand."[174] Moreover, the passages printed in the Stuttgart programme indicated the socialist direction of Landauer's allegory: "That pressure has such results holds true for all downtrodden people, not only for Jews but also for the mob that pours into the streets in times of riot and revolution, for the modern proletariat."[175]

At the same time, the Stuttgart production elevated Shylock far above the riotous "mob" of which Landauer had written. Under the heading "Shylock the Wise," the reviewer for the *Stuttgarter Nachrichten* described Ponto's performance as follows:

---

171 Kaiser, "Shylock ist auf Erden nicht zu helfen," 69.
172 Kaiser, "Shylock ist auf Erden nicht zu helfen," 69.
173 Kaiser, "Shylock ist auf Erden nicht zu helfen," 70.
174 Gustav Landauer, "Der Fall Shylock," in Württembergisches Staatstheater, *Der Kaufmann von Venedig*, theatre programme (Stuttgart, 1956/57), 3.
175 Landauer, "Der Fall Shylock," 4.

> There is sadness in his eyes and in his wonderful, sonorous voice. His mien is full of grief, even while he speaks of hate and revenge. It sounds much more truthful, and much more characteristic of this Jew's wisdom, when he declares that sufferance is the badge of all his tribe. [...] In spite of all the tragedy of his fate, this Venetian Nathan, set right by Ponto, is a man of honour through and through. [...] There is no question that the sympathy of the entire house is with him as he is threatened with enforced baptism, veils his head and exits as a broken man.[176]

In comparison to the material that we have presented so far, this passage indicates a completely different management of the protocols of identification. Deviating from the tradition of conceiving Shylock as an Other, Ponto's Shylock demanded thorough identification. His characterization as "a man of honour through and through" is striking. Whereas early post-war approaches had tended towards a paradigm of compensation through exclusion, conceiving Shylock as "a man of honour" meant performing a gesture of social inclusion, of restoring the injured dignity of the victims.

This approach also characterized a still more famous production of *Merchant* which premiered at Düsseldorf's Schauspielhaus on 9 July 1957. Directed by Karl Heinz Stroux and casting the eminent German-Jewish actor Ernst Deutsch in the role of Shylock, the Düsseldorf *Merchant* was tremendously successful. The production was invited to the 1957 Berlin theatre festival, where it incited a new debate on whether the play should be staged at all,[177] and it toured through Germany the following year. Indeed, the impact of Deutsch's Shylock on the German post-war image of the stage Jew can hardly be exaggerated.[178] The reviewer of *Der Mittag*, a West German daily, felt overpowered by the performance:

> It would hardly be possible to risk a Shylock these days if he were not played by a prominent Jewish actor. And, of course, this actor will be unable to forget the unbelievable trials that his people had to undergo. To Ernst Deutsch's impersonation of Shylock this fact lends a force and grandeur that is at times overpowering and breathtaking, an erratic loneliness belonging to a pained soul.[179]

---

176 Hermann Missenharter, "Shylock der Weise," *Stuttgarter Nachrichten*, 17 September 1956. The light irony of the description emphasizes the difference of Ponto's Shylock from the established take on the role.
177 Cf. Monschau, *Der Jude nach der Shoah*, 195–200.
178 Cf. Evelyn Deutsch-Schreiner, "Die Opfer schützen die Täter," in *Theatralia Judaica II: Nach der Shoah. Israelisch-deutsche Theaterbeziehungen seit 1949*, ed. Hans-Peter Bayerdörfer (Tübingen: Niemeyer, 1996), 111–113.
179 Erwin Laaths, "Der elisabethanische Shylock – ehedem und heute," *Der Mittag*, 9 September 1957.

The critic was obviously unaware that Deutsch was in fact the *first* Jewish actor to play Shylock in Germany since the end of the Weimar Republic, and that many non-Jewish actors had done so since 1945. Moreover, the text betrays the difficulties of coming to terms with such a Shylock, and with the past he was taken to embody. However, in the case of Deutsch's Shylock, exclusion was not an option. With his breathtaking "force and grandeur," he constituted a presence that – although it may have been imbued with "erratic loneliness" – was not to be erased in the fifth act. In fact, to make sure that Shylock was both understandable and unavoidable, Stroux had not shied away from considerable intrusions into the established text of *Merchant*. Thus, Shylock's monologue from the third act ("Hath not a Jew eyes?") was moved into the latter half of the trial scene.[180]

Deutsch had been one of the most successful actors of the Weimar Republic, both on stage and on screen. He had left Germany in 1933, working in Prague, Vienna, and London, before he emigrated to the United States in 1938. As early as 1947, the actor had returned to Vienna, and from 1951 he was again to be seen on the stages of Berlin. An international audience would have known Deutsch mainly as Baron Kurtz in Carol Reed's film *The Third Man* (1949). In Germany, Austria, and Switzerland, however, his signature roles were Nathan (in no less than eleven productions between 1954 and 1968), Otto Frank in the stage version of *The Diary of Anne Frank* at Düsseldorf's Schauspielhaus (1956), and Shylock (in altogether four major productions premiering between 1957 and 1967).[181] Beginning with the role of Nathan and then continuing with Shylock, Deutsch broke with the traditions of representing Jews, avoiding the customary fake Yiddish accent, the sloped body, the wild gestures, and shuffling gait. Instead, he played a 'noble Jew,' self-assured, religious, and with a fine humour: a man whose suffering was dignified, silent, and internal.[182]

Jörg Monschau has characterized the 1957 Düsseldorf production as "seemingly joining all the efforts to rehabilitate Shylock which had been undertaken in Germany since 1945 into one major project that would finally conclude the 'Nathanization' ('Nathanisierung') of this Shakespearean character."[183] We have suggested a different interpretation of the post-war German reception: not as an effort to 'rehabilitate Shylock,' but as an attempt at rehabilitating the German national collective at Shylock's cost. Accordingly, we would like to suggest a different understanding of Deutsch's – and also of Ponto's – perfor-

---

[180] Theaterarchiv der Stadt Düsseldorf: sound recording of the premiere of the 1957 production.
[181] See Chapter 2 for a discussion of Deutsch's performance in Erwin Piscator's 1963 production of *Merchant* at Berlin's Freie Volksbühne.
[182] Cf. Deutsch-Schreiner, "Die Opfer schützen die Täter," 111–112.
[183] Monschau, *Der Jude nach der Shoah*, 174.

mance, arguing that their grand and sympathetic rendering of the role actually constituted a new departure. Now the idea was to offer compensation *for* the murderous persecution of Jews, not merely compensation *to* a shattered German majority society.

The triptych of male Jewish father figures created by Deutsch between 1954 and 1968 is fascinating: its facets combined the role of the enlightened Jewish philosopher and the assimilated Jewish bourgeois with that of the cruel Jewish usurer. As the play with which Berlin's Deutsches Theater had opened its first post-war season on 7 September 1945, Lessing's *Nathan the Wise* had gained immense popularity in Germany and Austria. More than a hundred productions were put up in the first decade after the war. To a certain extent, productions of *Nathan* were intended as symbolic ruptures with the past, offering allusions to anti-Semitism, persecution, and the genocide.[184] With Frances Goodrich and Albert Hackett's dramatization of *The Diary of Anne Frank* (1955), which took the German-speaking stages by storm in the season 1956/57, references to the genocide became more explicit.[185] Like Nathan in Lessing's play, however, the Jewish characters in *The Diary of Anne Frank* refrained from openly accusing the Germans.[186]

It seems amazing that Shylock, a figure driven by the logic of justice and revenge, should have joined these 'noble' Jews in the late 1950s. Looking back at the 1957 Düsseldorf production, theatre critic Johannes Jacobi recalled in 1960 how Deutsch had played Shylock as an Old Testament figure: "Mad, entirely uncomprehendingly, Deutsch's eyes stared into the void, when the Venetian Duke appealed to the Jew's mercy. Mercy is unknown in the Old Testament, and Deutsch played Old Testament. [...] It is unforgettable how these eyes expressed the suffering and the knowledge of millennia."[187] It seems yet more significant that Jacobi underlined the differences between the three Jewish figures impersonated by Deutsch:

---

[184] Cf. Hans-Peter Bayerdörfer, "'Ewiger Jude' und 'Israeli': Stationen der 'Nathan'-Rezeption in der Bundesrepublik," in *Theatralia Judaica II*, ed. Bayerdörfer, 77–79.
[185] *The Diary of Anne Frank* (1956) was played throughout Germany and Austria; cf. Deutsch-Schreiner, "Die Opfer schützen die Täter," 102.
[186] Cf. Deutsch-Schreiner, "Die Opfer schützen die Täter," 112; see also Anat Feinberg, "Vom bösen Nathan und edlen Shylock: Überlegungen zur Konstruktion jüdischer Bühnenfiguren in Deutschland nach 1945," in *Shylock nach dem Holocaust*, ed. Ackermann and Schülting, 45–46; and Feinberg, *Wiedergutmachung im Programm: Jüdisches Schicksal im deutschen Nachkriegsdrama* (Cologne: Prometh, 1988), 5–32.
[187] Johannes Jacobi, "Der aktuelle Shakespeare," *Die ZEIT*, 5 February 1960.

1.3 Redemptive Figurations: The Post-War Period to the End of the 1950s — 79

> It was Deutsch's third Jewish role in Düsseldorf, after Lessing's *Nathan* and Father Frank in *The Diary of Anne Frank*. To those who had seen his wise Nathan (also on TV), it would have seemed as if in the narrative of the fate of his people the whole suffering of Jewry had taken form in the personal experience of the actor. And then this entrancing but dangerous Shylock![188]

As Jacobi's observations indicate, Nathan and Shylock could be interpreted as figurations of potential Jewish stances towards post-war Germany, pitting forgiveness and revengefulness against each other. Judging from most contemporary comments, however, the larger part of the audience ignored such tensions. Indeed, Deutsch wore nearly the same costume in both roles: a simple but elegant long velvet caftan, a heavy 'golden' chain round his neck, and a kippa. In addition, both stage figures had a well-groomed beard and short payot (see figure 5). These outer similarities supported the tendency to confound Deutsch's Shylock and Deutsch's Nathan. Following Marvin Carlson, this process can be described as a "ghosting," in which "the body of an actor, already a complex bearer of semiotic messages, will almost inevitably in a new role evoke the ghost or ghosts of previous roles if they have made an impression on the audience."[189] Deutsch's Nathan and Otto Frank 'ghosted' his Shylock, thereby 'ennobling' Shakespeare's cruel Jew, or in fact conflating the three characters into one single figure: the post-war German 'noble' stage Jew.[190] As his biographer Georg Zivier claims, Deutsch deleted previous 'images' of Shylock so that "in the future, everyone who is not hopelessly prejudiced will reject negative or caricatured interpretations" of the role.[191]

A second form of ghosting contributed to this ennobling of the Shylock figure. For the German audience, the personal experiences of Deutsch, who had himself suffered anti-Semitic persecution and had lost family members in the Holocaust, legitimated and authenticated his performance as an actor.[192]

---

[188] Jacobi, "Der aktuelle Shakespeare."
[189] Marvin Carlson, *The Haunted Stage: The Theatre as Memory Machine* (2001; Ann Arbor: The University of Michigan Press, 2011), 8.
[190] One reviewer of the 1957 Düsseldorf *Merchant* wrote: "Shylock does not have to be excused by Nathan. In Ernst Deutsch they both live on in their uniqueness. Shylock can adopt the lustre of his benevolent clansbrother with good conscience." Paul Hübner, "Herrliches Weltheater um ein Pfund Fleisch," *Rheinische Post*, 9 September 1957; qtd. in Monschau, *Der Jude nach der Shoah*, 185.
[191] Georg Zivier, *Ernst Deutsch und das deutsche Theater: Fünf Jahrzehnte deutscher Theatergeschichte. Der Lebensweg eines großen Schauspielers* (Berlin: Haude & Spenersche Verlagsbuchhandlung, 1964), 107.
[192] Cf. Bayerdörfer, "Ewiger Jude und Israeli," 80.

Figure 5: Hilde Krahl (Portia), Ernst Deutsch (Shylock), and Wolfgang Spier (Antonio) in Erwin Piscator's 1963 production at Berlin's Freie Volksbühne. Photograph by Abraham Pisarek. Courtesy of Stiftung Stadtmuseum Berlin.

However, this identification of Deutsch with Shylock (and vice versa) was frequently connected to a racist or racialist logic. The critic of the *Frankfurter Nachtausgabe*, for example, referred to the assumed facts of "race, tribe (*Volk*), and blood" in order to explain Deutsch's impressive rendering of the role.[193] Deutsch's body was thus taken to physically connect Shakespeare's fictional early-modern Jew to the victims of the Holocaust. This confusing identification offered the naïve promise that attending a show could function as some kind of 'compensation.' A critic reviewing a guest performance of the Düsseldorf production at Wilhelmshaven wrote that it seemed as if the audience, with their overwhelming applause for Deutsch, "wanted to compensate him for what he had suffered from the Venetians."[194]

---

[193] Gerhard Schön, "Deutschs Shylock: Ein Mono-Drama," *Frankfurter Nachtausgabe*, 15 September 1957; cf. Monschau, *Der Jude nach der Shoah*, 187.
[194] "'Der Kaufmann von Venedig' im Stadttheater," *Nordwestdeutsche Rundschau*, 17 February 1958, qtd. in Monschau, *Der Jude nach der Shoah*, 192.

1.3 Redemptive Figurations: The Post-War Period to the End of the 1950s — 81

With a view to these processes of displacement, Markus Moninger discusses Deutsch's interpretation under the heading "Losing His Own Voice" ("Verlust der Eigenrede"). He points out how the actor's stylization of Shylock catered to the needs of the German majority society.[195] Such a critique of 'philo-Semitic' clichés is pertinent. However, an important facet of Deutsch's (and Ponto's) rendering of the role should not be overlooked: the deviation from an earlier phase of post-war reception that had continued the tropes of National Socialist anti-Semitism and resulted in an exclusion of Shylock as a Jew who provoked shameful memories.

It may come as a surprise that director Peter Zadek, who was known for exposing 'philo-Semitic' arrangements and whose re-interpretations of *Merchant* Moninger acknowledges as important departures, attributed a decisive role to Deutsch's interpretation. In the first volume of his memoirs, Zadek stated in 1998:

> And Ernst Deutsch played Shylock as the noble Jew. At the time, I thought this was a mistake. Today, I think that Deutsch's interpretation was necessary and entirely justified. It could not have been done any other way. You had to find a means of transition, a passable way. The fact that the play was put on so early after 1945 was more important than the fact that Shylock was too much of the noble Jew.[196]

The notion of "a means of transition, a passable way" takes into account the dialectic at work in the post-war reception of *Merchant* – a dialectic of confrontation and evasion, of compensating a shattered German nation and compensating its victims. Historian Nicolas Berg has observed about post-war German discourses:

> The half-hearted concessions, desperate rescue operations for tradition, construed suppositions and shallow excuses [which characterized debates after the war] should not be seen as the opposite of thinking about National Socialism and its legacies. Rather, these phenomena constituted the medium in which such thinking about the past could take place.[197]

Zadek's (re-)evaluation of Deutsch's interpretation proceeds from an awareness that the notion of the 'noble Jew' was not an automatic given, even after the Holocaust. Moreover, as we have argued, the 'nobility' projected by Deutsch included an unavoidable demand for inclusion and citizenship. Although he seemed to play along with the psychological needs of the German majority soci-

---

[195] Moninger, "Auschwitz erinnern," 230–234.
[196] Zadek, *My Way*, 315.
[197] Nicolas Berg, "Lesarten des Judenmords," in *Wandlungsprozesse in Westdeutschland: Belastung, Integration, Liberalisierung 1945–1980*, ed. Ulrich Herbert (Göttingen: Wallstein, 2002), 138.

ety, Deutsch actually returned to Alexander Granach's precept of performing Shylock in a "partisan manner," insisting not only on the tragic "power," but also on the "human dignity" and the "life" of the character.[198] In these ways, Deutsch had begun to break open the cage of figuration – not only by returning Shylock to the realm of personal significance but also by indicating the Holocaust as a literal fact.

---

198 Granach, *Da geht ein Mensch*, 427.

2 Staging Remembrance: Refigurations on the West German Stage (1960–1990)

We finished the last chapter with the suggestion that Ernst Deutsch's Shylock interpretations – in 1957 at the Schauspielhaus Düsseldorf, 1963 at the Freie Volksbühne Berlin, and 1967 at Vienna's Burgtheater – initiated a new approach to the play: the connection of *The Merchant of Venice* and Holocaust remembrance, which was to become the dominant form of reception in the following two decades. Two major cultural debates contributed to this revision. They included, firstly, the key events confronting German society with the National Socialist past and the Holocaust, in particular the Eichmann trial at Jerusalem (1961) and the Frankfurt Auschwitz trials (1963–1965), whose extensive media coverage caused an unprecedented public discussion about the genocide. Secondly, the refigurations of *Merchant* were also the result of a wide-reaching politicization of German theatres during the 1960s and 1970s.

These two ruptures in the post-war consensus were closely related. To a considerable extent, the challenges to theatre conventions in West Germany were voiced and represented by actors and directors of the Weimar avant-garde, some of them Jewish, who had been forced to emigrate after 1933 and remigrated to Germany after the war: among them were Fritz Kortner, Ernst Deutsch, Therese Giehse, Wolfgang Heinz, Wolfgang Langhoff, Berthold Viertel, Bertolt Brecht, and Erwin Piscator. They were joined by a younger generation of Jewish remigrants, such as Peter Zadek and George Tabori, who brought with them the experience of British and American theatre and film. These remigrants were key players in the process of modernizing the German theatre, often referred to as the transition to a *Regietheater* ('directors' theatre').[1] Yet these changes were difficult and slow, as Klaus Wannemacher has pointed out. This was firstly due to the fact, already discussed in the last chapter, that many theatre directors and managers had kept their posts at the end of the war. Secondly, modernization was hindered by the resilience of authoritarian and anti-democratic convictions, which blended with the new anti-communism of the Cold War.[2] Many West Germans longed for an end of the Allied denazification policy,

---

[1] For a discussion of the connection between the avant-garde theatre of the early twentieth century and the experiments undertaken in the second half of the century, see Marvin Carlson, *Theatre Is More Beautiful than War: German Stage Directing in the Late Twentieth Century* (Iowa City: University of Iowa Press, 2009), x.
[2] Klaus Wannemacher, "Der Amnesie des Publikums begegnen: Nachkriegstheater als Inkubator des 'Aufarbeitungs'-Diskurses," in *Erfolgsgeschichte Bundesrepublik? Die Nachkriegsgesell-*

a return to 'normality,' and material comfort. The theatre, as well as other art forms, catered to this mentality by offering light entertainment, by celebrating a transhistorical humanism, and by painstakingly holding on to "what was considered the essence of German high culture."[3]

The core ideas of this kind of apolitical theatre were summarized in the so-called "Düsseldorfer Manifest," a manifesto published in October 1952. It had been initiated by actor and director Gustav Gründgens, who had pursued a very successful theatre career throughout the National Socialist period. Signed by a considerable number of German theatre managers, directors, dramaturges, and publishers, the manifesto defended "the unadulterated reproduction of poetry" as the sole guarantor of "a healthy and true tradition," against "non-objective influences on the composition of repertoires and against an arbitrary interpretation of poetry through unjustified experiments, which thrust themselves between the work and the audience."[4] This position was confirmed during the Darmstädter Theatergespräche in 1955, a meeting on cultural politics and the role of the theatre, chaired by Rudolf Sellner, the director of the 1942 *Merchant* at Göttingen (see Chapter 1). Bertolt Brecht was not among the participants, but in a letter to the meeting he broached the issue of theatre's engagement with the modern world.[5] His (Marxist) conclusion, that theatre had to represent the world as changeable, caused a heated debate in which actor and director Will Quadflieg demanded the "anatomical" separation between humanism and politics. Otherwise, he claimed, theatre would sacrifice the ideal of aesthetic "purity" and run the risk of participating in "sedition and massification" ("Verhetzungen und Vermassungen").[6] On the surface, this claim for theatre's abstinence from politics appears well-intentioned, given the appropriation of the arts for National

---

schaft im langen Schatten des Nationalsozialismus, ed. Stephan A. Glienke, Volker Paulmann, and Joachim Perels (Göttingen: Wallstein, 2008), 263–291, esp. 265–274. The persistency of anti-democratic structures at German theatres also affected the remigrants. For more than a decade, Piscator, the eminent director of the Weimar Republic, had to work as a guest director at various city theatres until he was eventually assigned director of the Volksbühne in Berlin in 1962. Fritz Kortner was even less successful and remained a guest director until his death in 1970; cf. Wannemacher, "Amnesie," 266, 272.

3 Carlson, *Theatre*, xi.
4 "Düsseldorfer Manifest," qtd. in Johannes Jacobi, "Wohin steuert das Theater?," *Die ZEIT*, 16 October 1952.
5 Brecht's letter was read out by his dramaturge Hans-Joachim Bunge; cf. *Darmstädter Gespräch: Theater*, ed. Egon Vietta (Darmstadt: Neue Darmstädter Verlags-Anstalt, 1955), 276–277.
6 Will Quadflieg, in Vietta, *Darmstädter Gespräch*, 284. See also Peter Reichel, *Erfundene Erinnerung: Weltkrieg und Judenmord in Film und Theater* (Munich: Carl Hanser Verlag, 2004), 216.

Socialist propaganda between 1933 and 1945. However, in its implied rejection of artists from the political left and the GDR, most prominently Brecht, the plea was also a symptom of the Cold War. As the last chapter has shown, the celebration of a universal humanism – allegedly preserved by the classical authors – actually prevented the real 'working through' of the past. Throughout the 1950s, the contributions of German theatres to National Socialist power and propaganda remained largely unacknowledged, and there was no attempt to explicitly address the issue of guilt and remembrance. It is crucial to bear in mind that none of the directors and actors who returned from enforced exile supported this notion of a non-ideological theatre.[7]

It was only in the 1960s that considerable changes took place in German theatres. They were triggered not least by the public debates about the Holocaust, to which the theatres both responded and contributed. Klaus Wannemacher even refers to the post-war stage as an "incubator" of cultural remembrance.[8] The first major theatre events to deal explicitly with the Holocaust were Rolf Hochhuth's historical play *Der Stellvertreter* (1963, "The Deputy"), which addressed the inactivity of Pope Pius XII in the face of the Holocaust,[9] and Peter Weiss's *Die Ermittlung* (1965, "The Investigation"), a documentary drama on the first Frankfurt Auschwitz trial. These thematic shifts coincided with the retirement of a considerable number of German directors and their replacement by a younger generation.[10] Erwin Piscator, who had been appointed managing director at the Freie Volksbühne Berlin in 1962, was a crucial figure. In 1963, he directed *Der Stellvertreter*, which met with a huge media response. Two years later, in October 1965, Piscator initiated the multiple-stage debut of Weiss's *The Investigation* at fourteen theatres in East and West Germany. His German collaborators were the Suhrkamp publishing house and Peter Palitzsch.[11] They were joined by the Royal Shakespeare Company's Aldwych Theatre in London, where the production was directed by Peter Brook.[12] *The Investigation* was

---

[7] Markus Moninger, *Shakespeare inszeniert: Das westdeutsche Regietheater und die Theatertradition des 'dritten deutschen Klassikers'* (Tübingen: Max Niemeyer Verlag, 1996), 73.
[8] This is indicated in the title of Wannemacher's article: "Nachkriegstheater als Inkubator des 'Aufarbeitungs'-Diskurses".
[9] For Reichel (*Erfundene Erinnerung*, 226), Hochhuth's play initiated the debate on Auschwitz on the German stage.
[10] The major change took place in 1972 when Gustav Rudolf Sellner, Hans Schalla, and Karl Heinz Stroux all retired.
[11] In 1966 Palitzsch became director of the Schauspiel Stuttgart.
[12] On *The Investigation* in the context of Holocaust remembrance see Robert Cohen, "The Political Aesthetics of Holocaust Literature: Peter Weiss's *The Investigation* and Its Critics," *History and Memory* 10.2 (1998): 43–67.

based on documents from the Auschwitz trial by witnesses, perpetrators, and judges, which were put together in a "blend of Brechtian and surrealist aesthetics."[13] Inspired by Dante's *Divina Comedia*, the play is structured into 'Cantos,' which mark the victims' passage through the topography of the camps, from their arrival at the ramps to the furnaces. The play was a key event that contributed to making the Holocaust tangible for public debate in Germany and on the German stage.[14] It also initiated the revival of documentary theatre in Germany in the 1960s, not least through the influence of Piscator, who had been one of the main representatives of political and documentary theatre in the Weimar Republic.

In addition to documentary drama, it was the classics through which theatre conventions were challenged. For the traditionalists, the classical authors were seen as the best means to fulfil what was considered the primary function of the theatre, namely to preserve cultural traditions and to be "uplifting and spiritual"[15] by communicating universal truths. Even when, in the course of the 1960s, the debates on the role of the stage in post-war Germany were losing their sharpness, not least through a new concern with modernization, the ideal of universalist humanism was still reiterated. In an article in the *Shakespeare Jahrbuch* (West) of 1965, Siegfried Melchinger[16] explored these questions under the title "Shakespeare heute" ("Shakespeare today"), thus quoting the title of the German translation of Jan Kott's *Shakespeare Our Contemporary*, which had been published a year previously. Melchinger contends that Shakespeare has to be modernized, but for him modernization included the preservation of the plays' transhistorical meaning.[17] It was exactly this approach to the classics that directors like Peter Zadek attacked, and for him it was *through* the classics that this attack had to be launched. In an interview, reprinted in the programme to his production of *Merchant* at Schauspielhaus Bochum in 1972/73, Zadek stressed: "We have to assume that the audience knows the play. And the rules

---

13 Cohen, "The Political Aesthetics," 50.
14 Cf. Reichel, *Erfundene Erinnerung*, 240. Reichel maintains that *The Investigation* contributed to "modelling" the Auschwitz Trials into a "political myth."
15 Carlson, *Theatre*, xi.
16 On Melchinger's role during the National Socialist period, see Chapter 1. After the war, he became one of the most important West German theatre critics and, in 1963, professor at the University of Music and Performing Arts at Stuttgart.
17 Siegfried Melchinger, "Shakespeare heute," *Shakespeare Jahrbuch* (West) (1965): 75–76.

of well-known plays are like traffic-lights. A convention."[18] He set out to change them.

As we will argue in this chapter, *The Merchant of Venice* became an important site of this struggle over the classics and their contribution to the cultural remembrance of the Holocaust. This implied major shifts in the refiguration of both Shylock and the play:

1. *The transformation of Shylock into a figure of cultural memory:* The 1960s witnessed a number of productions by major directors, and with important actors in the role of Shylock. It was particularly in the media coverage of these productions that the transformation of Shylock into a memory figure took place. Critics repeatedly asked *whether* the drama should still be performed and, if the answer was positive, *how* it could be played "after Auschwitz."[19]
2. *Tactical refigurations: The Merchant of Venice* turned out to be a key play for a number of remigrants who became eminent players in German theatre from the 1960s onwards: Fritz Kortner, George Tabori, and Peter Zadek. They combined new forms of Holocaust remembrance with theatrical innovation: the one becoming the precondition of the other. Stressing the necessity of putting *Merchant* on stage, and repeatedly returning to it throughout their career, they offered radical transformations of the play that revolved around the figure of Shylock. These refigurations were 'tactical' in that they responded to a particular historical moment and/or cultural location.
3. *The diversification of the Shylock figure: Holocaust victims, outsiders, and 'rich Jews':* The late 1970s and the 1980s marked a new phase of *Merchant* reception, which was characterized by the individualization and psychologization of the Shylock figure as well as by a new interest in economic questions. In the 1980s, the contentious figure of the 'rich Jew' surfaced in several public debates in which the relevance of the past for post-war Germany was as much at stake as the position and the role of Jewish communities in Germany.

---

18 Peter Zadek in an interview with Hartmut Gehrke and Karsten Schälike, in Schauspielhaus Bochum, *Der Kaufmann von Venedig*, theatre programme (Bochum, 1972/73), 28.
19 For a discussion of Shylock as a memory figure, see Sabine Schülting, "Shylock als Erinnerungsfigur," in *Shylock nach dem Holocaust: Zur Geschichte einer deutschen Erinnerungsfigur*, ed. Zeno Ackermann and Sabine Schülting (Berlin: De Gruyter, 2011), 103–116; and Schülting, "'Remember Me': Shylock on the Postwar German Stage," *Shakespeare Survey* 63 (2010): 290–300.

2.1 The Transformation of Shylock into a Figure of Cultural Memory

"Mannheim was right to stop the production of *The Merchant of Venice*,"[20] the German weekly *Die ZEIT* commented on 5 February 1960. The Nationaltheater Mannheim had engaged director and theatre manager Hans Schalla (Bochum) for a production of *Merchant*, with Hanns-Ernst Jäger as Shylock, who had already played the role in Schalla's Bochum production in 1952. However, the Mannheim *Merchant* never made it to the premiere. The rehearsal period was overshadowed by a sudden wave of anti-Semitic daubing on synagogues and in Jewish cemeteries, which had started in Cologne in the night of 25 December 1959 and had soon spread throughout Germany and other European countries.[21] In this situation, the Mannheim theatre manager, Hans Schüler, was apprehensive about the potential effects of *Merchant*, and decided to stop the production. He replaced it with Erwin Sylvanus's *Korczak und die Kinder* ("Korczak and the Children," 1957), a play about the Polish-Jewish pedagogue Janusz Korczak, who had been murdered in the concentration camp of Treblinka. The programme contained a detailed statement on the political role of theatres, which ended with the following explanation by the dramaturgue Heinz Knorr:

> The Nationaltheater is dedicated to art. It keeps away from party politics and the politics of the day. But it also raises its voice in the battle against inhumanity and indifference, for justice and freedom, even if sometimes this may be uncomfortable for parts of the audience. This includes not only the staging of plays that touch on these issues, but – as an exception – also their non-staging, as for example in the case of *The Merchant of Venice*. This play was misused by various directors and theatre managers of the Hitler era for anti-Jewish propaganda and could, for this reason, despite the full appreciation of the ingenuity of its author, shock Jewish members of the audience, as has already happened elsewhere.[22]

Media reactions were hostile. In a radio review broadcast on WDR (West German Broadcasting, the public broadcasting station in North Rhine-Westphalia), Knorr's decision was severely criticized as "giving way to anti-Semitism."[23] A critic writing for the Bavarian local newspaper *Neue Presse Coburg* dismissed Schü-

---

[20] Johannes Jacobi, "Der aktuelle Shakespeare," *Die ZEIT*, 5 February 1960.
[21] See Jörg Monschau, *Der Jude nach der Shoah: Zur Rezeption des Kaufmann von Venedig auf dem Theater der Bundesrepublik Deutschland und der Deutschen Demokratischen Republik 1945– 1989*, doctoral dissertation, Ruprecht-Karls-Universität Heidelberg, 2002, 204–211, accessed 8 September 2018, https://archiv.ub.uni-heidelberg.de/volltextserver/3530/.
[22] Qtd. in Monschau, *Der Jude nach der Shoah*, 211; cf. also 209–213.
[23] Qtd. in Jacobi, "Der aktuelle Shakespeare." Cf. also Monschau, *Der Jude nach der Shoah*, 206.

ler's concerns as absurd, falling "from one extreme into another," and exemplifying what the critic diagnosed as an exaggerated and hypocritical post-war sensitivity. Claiming to oppose insincere political correctness (while deliberately alluding to the strong undercurrent of anti-Semitism in 1950s Germany), he wrote: "As soon as Jewish people appear on stage, the Germans get nervous. When today someone sets out to produce Shakespeare's *Merchant of Venice*, a dozen democratically re-educated former supporters of the great and small German Reich cry out that this could hurt their Jewish fellow-citizens."[24] He added how well Ernst Deutsch had approached the role of Shylock only a few years previously. Deutsch reminded him of Heine's famous account of a performance in London, according to which a woman in the audience cried out during the fourth act: "The poor man is wronged!"

The reference to Ernst Deutsch comes as no surprise. Indeed, at the time, hardly any comment on German *Merchants* failed to mention his interpretation of the role. Deutsch brought about a double shift in the understanding of the Shylock figure, which would prove dominant in the following decades: firstly, the promotion of the Shylock figure to the protagonist of the play; and secondly, his transformation into a figuration of Jewish Holocaust victims. Deutsch's noble Shylock, victimized by Venetian society, became the blueprint for interpretations of the role in the 1960s and 1970s. He constituted the recognizable figure through which cultural remembrance of the Holocaust was performatively re-enacted.

This shift of focus on Shylock was apparent in two major productions in 1963, one directed by Peter Palitzsch and the other by Erwin Piscator. On 20 June 1963, Palitzsch's *Merchant* premiered at Ballhof Hannover. The programme highlighted the role of Shylock through an excerpt from Hermann Sinsheimer's monograph:

> Shylock – his name and nature, his claims and arguments, his faith and fortune – is 'liquidated' and disposed of. [...] The romanticism of life, which he had dared to disturb, is re-established. Venice and Belmont, the spirit of the sixteenth century and of youth, music, and poetry, love and light-heartedness are the surviving victors. The times are no longer out of joint. They have deprived the Jew of his name and being.[25]

The production highlighted Shylock's disenfranchisement and destruction. According to the reviews, Kurt Ehrhardt played an impressive Shylock: less a

---

24 H. G. Sellenthin, "Die Angst vor Shylock," *Neue Presse Coburg*, 14 April 1960.
25 Hermann Sinsheimer, "Shylock," in Landestheater Ballhof, Hannover, *Der Kaufmann von Venedig*, theatre programme (Hannover, 1963), n. p. We are quoting from the English translation of Sinsheimer's monograph, *Shylock: The History of a Character* (London: Gollancz, 1947), 113.

noble philosopher than the "epitome of the persecuted,"[26] whose hatred was the result of his endless suffering in the hypocritical Venetian society in which he was an outsider. One reviewer stressed that it might be possible to see the performance in the company of a Jewish friend, but impossible not "to feel ashamed because there are so many Venetians in the world."[27]

Erwin Piscator's production of *Merchant* at Freie Volksbühne Berlin, which premiered a few months later (1 December 1963), was more explicitly political. Piscator understood the role of the post-war German stage as that of a "moral institution" and wanted the theatre to address post-war amnesia, thus contributing to the acknowledgement of Germany's "overwhelming guilt."[28] As he explicated in his foreword to *The Deputy*, he saw his new post as an opportunity: "When in spring 1962 I was chosen as art director of Freie Volksbühne in Berlin, I was resolved to use precisely the instrument of the popular stage [*Volksbühne* means 'popular stage' in German], a popular stage repertoire, to stop the general forgetfulness, the general wish to forget the things of our recent history."[29]

Piscator's concern with the German past can be traced back to the early 1950s, when he returned to Germany from his exile in the United States. As early as 1952, his *Nathan the Wise* at the Schauspielhaus Marburg sought to address racism and anti-Semitism, as well as the German refusal to confront the genocide.[30] About a decade later, in 1963, the year that had started with the premiere of *The Deputy* at Freie Volksbühne, Piscator turned to *Nathan's* shadow play, *The Merchant of Venice*, to also revise it from a post-Holocaust perspective. Somewhat surprisingly, perhaps, he followed Stroux in casting Ernst Deutsch as Shylock. Wannemacher suggests that Piscator's main motive behind this decision may have been the attempt to hold the prominent actor

---

26 Gerd Schulte, "Shakespeares Shylock und die Taugenichtse," *Hannoversche Allgemeine Zeitung*, 22 June 1963.
27 Wolfgang Tschechne, "So viele Venezianer: Zu Shakespeares 'Kaufmann von Venedig' in Hannover," *Hannoversche Rundschau*, 22 June 1963.
28 Erwin Piscator, "Die Bühne als moralische Anstalt in der Prägung dieses Jahrhunderts," in *Theater der Auseinandersetzung: Ausgewählte Schriften und Reden* (Frankfurt/M.: Suhrkamp, 1977), 138.
29 Erwin Piscator, "Vorwort zum 'Stellvertreter'," in *Aufsätze – Reden – Gespräche*, vol. 2 of *Schriften*, ed. Ludwig Hoffmann (Berlin: Henschelverlag, 1968), 302.
30 Cf. Hans-Peter Bayerdörfer, "'Ewiger Jude' und 'Israeli': Stationen der 'Nathan'-Rezeption in der Bundesrepublik," in *Theatralia Judaica II: Nach der Shoah. Israelisch-deutsche Theaterbeziehungen seit 1949*, ed. Bayerdörfer (Tübingen: Niemeyer, 1996), 78; Klaus Wannemacher, *Erwin Piscators Theater gegen das Schweigen: Politisches Theater zwischen den Fronten des Kalten Kriegs (1951–1966)* (Tübingen: Niemeyer, 2004), 30–35.

at Volksbühne.³¹ As Piscator explains in the programme to *Merchant*, he had initially intended to cast Deutsch in the title role of *Don Carlos* but had been forced to change his plans because the Berlin Schiller Theater was already working on that play.³² The pragmatism of this explanation is strangely at odds with the general tone of the programme, in which a detailed article on "The Problem of the Performance" focuses on the question of whether and how *Merchant* can be played in post-war Germany. Deutsch's interpretation of Shylock is presented as the only possible solution to the problem: "In our opinion, this [...] more or less philo-Semitic understanding of Shakespeare's play is the *correct* one, it is correct in the view of the historical events. In this context the question is not important whether such an understanding is in line with Shakespeare's intention." In the German debate on post-war *Merchants*, this is one of the first explicit acknowledgements that the play's meaning may depend more on the historical context of the production than on a hypothetical authorial intention. The text contends that the "sad events of the most recent past" require the focus on the "tragedy of Shylock, his disenfranchisement and destruction, which he suffers as a representative of his people." Antonio and Gratiano are neither "Hitler nor Eichmann," the text concludes – consciously or unconsciously echoing Hannah Arendt's observations on the Eichmann trial in Jerusalem, which were published in *The New Yorker* in early 1963.³³ The Venetians rather represent the "'little' anti-Semites [...] whose anti-Semitism [...] is difficult to grasp in everyday reality."³⁴ It was this everyday anti-Semitism that the production sought to highlight, and this was supported in the programme through quotes from a large number of critical studies on *Merchant* dealing with Shylock and the tradition of anti-Semitism.

Stage design and costumes stressed the confrontation between Shylock and the Venetians. Hans Ulrich Schmückle's stage was inspired, as he writes, by Vittore Carpaccio's late fifteenth-century painting *Miracle of the Cross at the*

---

31 Cf. Wannemacher, *Piscators Theater*, 191.
32 Cf. Freie Volksbühne Berlin, *Der Kaufmann von Venedig*, theatre programme (Berlin, 1963/64), 2. This rather banal explanation of why he chose to produce this contentious play was widely criticized. See e.g. Friedrich Luft's review "Wie man Shakespeare schändet," *Die Welt*, 3 December 1963; Wolfgang Werth, "Shylock gegen Shakespeare," *Deutsche Zeitung*, 9 December 1963; Irma Reblitz, "Piscators 'Kaufmann von Venedig'," *Rhein-Neckar Zeitung*, 13 December 1963.
33 Freie Volksbühne Berlin, "Zum Problem der Aufführung," in *Der Kaufmann von Venedig*, theatre programme (Berlin, 1963/64), 3; emphasis in the German original. Arendt would turn these articles into a book, published later in the same year: *Eichmann in Jerusalem: A Report on the Banality of Evil* (New York: Viking Press, 1963).
34 Freie Volksbühne Berlin, "Zum Problem der Aufführung," 3.

Ponte di Rialto, whose spatial design it recreated.³⁵ During the scenes set in Venice, the stage was framed by large buildings on the left (the Venetian palazzos) and the right (the ghetto), which were meant to highlight the differences between "the luxurious extravagance and playboy-like quality of the Venetian-Christian establishment, on the one hand, and the darkness and barrenness of the Jewish ghetto on the other."³⁶ A fragile-looking 'Rialto' bridge was the only connection between the two opposite spaces. The Venetians, dressed in identical costumes and wearing blond wigs, appeared as a "compact bloc confronting the Jew," as costume designer Sylta Busse suggested. "In *Merchant* this clique (with their shared world view and shared interests) embody the brutality, cruelty and arrogance of the 'Aryan race' that centuries later felt justified to send Jews (preferably in their entirety) to the gas ovens."³⁷

Piscator's unpublished prompt-book indicates that the director had initially planned to add a long new scene after 2.7, showing Shylock in the very moment when he realizes that Jessica has eloped. The scene was intended to have him run through his house and call for Jessica and his ducats with increasing despair. His cries would have been imitated sneeringly, first by Salerio and Solanio, and then by a large carnival parade. The scene would have ended with the sounds of the carnival slowly disappearing, Shylock shouting "Jessica" for the last time, and then remaining alone on the dark stage, with the curtain falling for the interval.³⁸ However, this additional scene, which had been intended to underline Shylock's exclusion from an anti-Semitic society, was omitted due to technical reasons, as a brief note in the final version of the prompt-book reads.³⁹

Apart from projections on the curtain, which commented for example on the naval power of Venice and the exclusion of Jews from the Venetian trade,⁴⁰ the version that was eventually played did not contain additional material. It relied on a slightly modernized version of August Wilhelm Schlegel's translation, but

---

35 The suggestion may have come from the programme to Zadek's Ulm production of *Merchant* in 1961, which showed a small reproduction of the painting.
36 Hans-Ulrich Schmückle and Hermann Kleinselbeck, "Notizen für die Szene zu 'Der Kaufmann von Venedig' von William Shakespeare," in Hans-Ulrich Schmückle and Sylta Busse, *Theaterarbeit: Eine Dokumentation*, ed. Eckehart Nölle (Munich: Theatermuseum, c. 1975), 75.
37 Sylta Busse, "Vorschläge für Erwin Piscator zur Kostümgestaltung der 'Clique' ... im *Kaufmann von Venedig*," in Schmückle and Busse, *Theaterarbeit*, 90.
38 Erwin Piscator, "Regiebuch" (*Der Kaufmann von Venedig*, Freie Volksbühne Berlin, premiere: 1 December 1963), Archiv der Akademie der Künste Berlin, Piscator 555, n. p.
39 Piscator, "Regiebuch," Archiv der Akademie der Künste Berlin, Piscator 557, n. p. We could not find any reference to the nature of these "technical reasons."
40 Cf. Piscator, "Regiebuch," Archiv der Akademie der Künste Berlin, Piscator 556–560. Cf. also Wannemacher, *Piscators Theater*, 193.

the text had been carefully revised in order to shift audience sympathy from the Venetians to Shylock, and support the interpretation of the play as Shylock's tragedy. This included considerable cuts to Portia's speech on the quality of mercy (in 4.1) and the banter between Lorenzo and Jessica (at the beginning of 5.1). Those lines by Shylock that would have rendered him a heartless character were also left out – most importantly, his curse "I would my daughter were dead at my foot and the jewels in her ear! Would she were hearsed at my foot and the ducats in her coffin!" (3.1.74–76).

Piscator's notes contain close descriptions of how individual scenes were to be played. The end of the trial scene is of particular interest: when the Duke pronounces his "pardon" (4.1.364), Shylock falls down on his face and has difficulty getting up again when Portia asks him whether he was "contented" (4.1.388). With a voice that is only barely audible, he answers in the affirmative, enshrouds his face with his mantle and leaves the stage slowly, with staggering steps, silently watched by everyone until Gratiano yells after him: "In christ'ning shalt thou have two godfathers" (4.1.394). The last lines of the play were slightly rearranged so that Portia, informing Lorenzo about Shylock's "special deed of gift" (5.1.291), would have the last word. Everyone leaves the stage except for Jessica, who – clad in a grey gown – slowly moves downstage, with a startled expression on her face, and her hands in front of her mouth while a large image of Shylock's face is projected onto the back wall.[41]

The production showed the contradictions inherent in Piscator's balancing act between Deutsch's consensual 'philo-Semitic' interpretation of the Shylock figure and Piscator's own political agenda for West German theatres. With sixty-one shows, the production was very successful with the audience, and Deutsch guaranteed reviews that were at least partially positive, as he played again the 'noble' Shylock that was unanimously praised. Critics were less merciful when it came to the political connotations of the production. Writing for *Frankfurter Rundschau*, Ethel Schwirten criticized Erwin Piscator as a "political teacher" whose use of Shakespeare's comedy for the "contemporary reflection on the unresolved past" was "too forced" and did not do justice to a play that offered "enough examples of beautiful humanity as well as examples of exaggerated resentment to appeal to the conscience also in our times."[42] The reviewer for the Berlin evening newspaper *Der Abend* concluded: "From a political perspective, Piscator is certainly right. But from a Shakespearean, he is wrong."[43] It was

---

41 Piscator, "Regiebuch," Piscator 556, n. p.
42 Ethel Schwirten, "Piscators politischer Shylock," *Frankfurter Rundschau*, 5 December 1963.
43 Heinz Ritter, "Nur Ernst Deutsch," *Der Abend*, 2 December 1963.

this conflation of 'the classics' with politics that reviewers criticized, and they were particularly unhappy about what they considered the destruction of the 'poetry' of the play.⁴⁴

One reason for the critical reviews may have been the East-West conflict, and the West German rejection of political theatre, associated with Brecht and the GDR stage. It is telling that among the few voices to praise the production was a review in the GDR theatre journal *Theater der Zeit*.⁴⁵ The influential West German critic Friedrich Luft, however, writing for *Die Welt*, summarized the production as an instruction on "How to Violate Shakespeare."⁴⁶ Like all the other critics, he excluded Deutsch's Shylock from these slating remarks. Arguably, it was Deutsch who allowed Piscator to make a political statement on the Holocaust without completely alienating his audience. His Berlin *Merchant* was one in a series of plays directed by Piscator which all addressed the Holocaust: most notably, *Nathan the Wise*, *The Deputy* and, two years after *Merchant*, *The Investigation*. They complemented, and indirectly commented on, each other and thus contributed to Piscator's idea of a political theatre actively supporting a culture of remembrance. Wannemacher stresses the importance of his productions for the eventual change taking place on West German stages:

> Without the cautious efforts of Piscator, who in his late work became again a pioneer of the theatre, including authentic primary texts, well-balanced concepts of directing and an unpretentious staging, a contribution of the theatre to bringing about insights that had been long due would have been difficult to convey against the backdrop of the Cold War.⁴⁷

The beginning of the Auschwitz Trial, with its intensive media coverage, only three weeks after the premiere of Piscator's *Merchant* reinforced the topicality of the production. It is possible that this event added a layer of meaning to the production, which critics at the beginning had been unwilling or unable to see, and contributed to its eventual success. Such a view would be supported by the profound transformation of critical responses to *Merchant* productions in the following years. From the end of 1963 onwards, reviewers increasingly noted that the Holocaust had changed the play and its traditional reception. Only half a year after Piscator had been attacked for his inattention to the 'poetry' of *Merchant*, one reviewer of a *Merchant* production remarked: "an attitude

---

44 Cf. Walther Kersch, "Shakespeare ohne jede Poesie," *Der Tagesspiegel*, 2 December 1983.
45 Cf. Wannemacher, *Piscators Theater*, 194. On *Merchant* in the context of the Cold War, see Chapter 3.
46 This was the title of his review: "Wie man Shakespeare schändet."
47 Wannemacher, "Amnesie," 287.

that is primarily determined by the aesthetic is no longer possible today." His words implicitly suggested that the Holocaust had added a further layer of meaning to the play, which was automatically actualized in performance: "to all the injustice that Shylock has to suffer – not without his own fault – the spectators add what has happened since. Their main sympathy is now directed at the Shylock figure; everything that is said by Shylock is received with more attentive ears than ever before."[48] Several other productions, many of them in the provinces, triggered similar reviews. It is probably not too far-fetched to assume that these reactions were informed less by the specificity of the individual performance than by the media coverage on the Eichmann and the Auschwitz Trials. One reviewer explicitly commented on these repercussions. He recorded that German TV stations were concerned about the plan to broadcast the 1964 production at Deutsches Theater Munich, in which Ernst Deutsch was again cast as Shylock, "because of the topic." "It is also likely," he mused, "that the Auschwitz Trial has played a role."[49]

Despite the increasing willingness of directors and critics to relate *Merchant* to the Holocaust, the awkwardness of the vocabulary for the genocide is striking. Programmes and reviews were characterized by evasive references to "this vexed story," "the events of the recent past," "all the horror," "the brown years," and "the hundreds of thousands of Shylock tragedies of our times."[50] It was only in the course of the 1960s, and through the Auschwitz Trials, that Adorno's phrase "after Auschwitz" eventually became accepted, functioning as a "chiffre," the name of a place "that replaces the nameless victims and marks not merely the destruction of persons but also the erasure of their names, i.e. the erasure of the name per se."[51]

It is also at this time and in these reviews that the myth of *Merchant*'s absence from the immediate post-war stages was born: the review of the 1962 *Merchant* at Heidelberg was even headed with the statement "Seventeen years

---

48 Hanns Braun, "Der Kaufmann von Venedig," *Süddeutsche Zeitung*, 25 July 1964.
49 kth, "Buckwitz kommt doppelt," *Abendzeitung*, 8 April 1964.
50 Quotes are from R. K., "Oldenburgisches Staatstheater: 'Der Kaufmann von Venedig' von Shakespeare," *Münsterländische Tageszeitung*, 16 January 1963; U. R., "Shylock heute," *Stuttgarter Zeitung*, 16 January 1964; Jan Herchenröder, "Shakespeares 'Kaufmann von Venedig'," *Lübecker Nachrichten*, 1 September 1964; k. u., "Das Problem läßt sich nicht überspielen," *Die Rheinpfalz*, 22 October 1962.
51 Mirjam Wenzel, *Gericht und Gedächtnis: Der deutschsprachige Holocaust-Diskurs der sechziger Jahre* (Göttingen: Wallstein, 2009), 240–241. For a discussion of the name 'Auschwitz' in Adorno's philosophy, see also Detlev Claussen, "Nach Auschwitz: Ein Essay über die Aktualität Adornos," in *Zivilisationsbruch: Denken nach Auschwitz*, ed. Dan Diner (Frankfurt/M.: Fischer, 1988), 54–68.

later Shylock is given back to us,"⁵² as if *The Merchant of Venice* had been a precious item among the spoils of the war, which, seventeen years after the end of the war, was eventually returned by the allied powers. Apparently, it was no longer conceivable that productions of *Merchant* could have taken place *before* Ernst Deutsch shaped the post-war Shylock figure. The implications of this myth, namely that the "ban on the play ha[d] been broken" and that *Merchant* was again "playable" on German stages, was interpreted by some as an indicator of a redeemed nation: "the full recovery of the general state of mind" of the nation.⁵³ It is crucial to comprehend the implications of this stance, and thus the ambiguity of the new connection between *Merchant* and cultural remembrance: a theatre's decision to mount *Merchant* would not necessarily have indicated the wish to address the Holocaust, but could just as well have been motivated by the attempt to celebrate the end of the post-war era and to openly display 'normality' in West Germany – not least in clear opposition to the other German state, where the play was still conspicuously absent from the stage (see Chapter 3). This is corroborated by the fact that – in contrast to the political frameworks established by the reviewers – most productions do *not* seem to have referenced the Holocaust explicitly.⁵⁴

In the 'Shakespeare year' of 1964, in which the quatercentenary of Shakespeare's birthday was celebrated, and which was also 'Year One' after the separation of the German Shakespeare Society into an eastern and a western branch (see also Chapter 3), such a return to 'normality' was crucial. The Shakespeare Society West registered more than 200 Shakespeare productions with almost 4,000 shows in the year 1964, in addition to opera, musical or TV adaptations, which was more than twice the number of previous years. Compared to the numbers for the tragedies (eight *Hamlet* productions with 378 shows, ten *King Lears*, and nine *Macbeths*) and the popular comedies (e.g. fifteen productions of *A Midsummer Night's Dream* with more than 200 shows), the numbers for *Merchant* were not impressive. In addition to the remounting of a previous production at Hannover, there were five new productions of *Merchant* in West

---

52 Heinz Luckow, "Siebzehn Jahre danach wird uns der Shylock wiedergegeben," *Heidelberger Tageblatt*, 18 October 1962.
53 Paul Hübner, "Porzias Heiratslotterie," *Rheinische Post*, 28 September 1964.
54 This also seems to have been the case with the *Merchant* at Deutsches Theater Munich, in which Ernst Deutsch had again been cast for the role of Shylock. The production was criticized by many as naïve and undecided, as one of the "misdirected attempts in the Federal Republic to cope with the 'unresolved past,' without either understanding its origin or soberly facing the truth." Wilhelm Unger, "Die Tragödie des venezianischen Juden ist keine Tändelei," *Kölner Stadt-Anzeiger*, 30 July 1964.

Germany: at Württembergische Landesbühne Esslingen (11 January 1964), Deutsches Theater Munich (23 July 1964), Bühnen der Hansestadt Lübeck (9 September 1964), Städtische Bühnen Krefeld-Mönchengladbach (22 September 1964), and Stadttheater Cuxhaven (29 November 1964). But despite these low numbers, half a page of the stage report in *Shakespeare Jahrbuch* was dedicated to *Merchant*, emphasizing that the "play that has been shunned for years reached more than 100 shows." The author concedes that "the inhibition against the scrupulous matter cannot be discarded, despite assertions to the contrary."[55] Nevertheless, the report implies that the productions of *Merchant* contributed to a successful celebration of the quatercentenary. This ambiguity was typical: on the one hand, the intricate links between the Shylock figure and the long tradition of anti-Semitic ideology turned any production into a precarious project, while on the other, the desire to stage the play was all too obvious. Shylock, as a figure of cultural memory, was thus often also interpreted as a figure that encouraged (or sanctioned) forgetting.

More often than not, therefore, moral or political reservations were quickly dismissed. One of the most problematic absolutions was offered in the programme for the production at Stadttheater Gießen (3 November 1968), in a short article written by German author Bernt von Heiseler. In 1933, von Heiseler had become a member of the NSDAP, and even though he later distanced himself from the Nazis, his political stance was that of a Christian nationalist who was still defending "some of the original social and national demands" of National Socialism in 1951.[56] The decision to use someone like von Heiseler as an authority on *Merchant* must seem inappropriate today, but in the late 1960s, von Heiseler was a renowned author, a member of the German Academy of Arts and the German Academy for Language and Literature, and a recipient of the Konrad Adenauer Prize (in 1967). In his article for the Gießen production, von Heiseler contended that it was only the "hypersensitivity towards all things concerning Jews" that prevented German audiences from realizing that Shakespeare's Shylock was not really related to the "Jewish question" at all. Shylock was intended neither to represent "*the* Jew," he claimed, nor to be played as a tragic character.[57] Other comments were less ideological, but frequently, it was suggest-

---

55 Karl Brinkmann, "Bühnenbericht 1964," *Shakespeare Jahrbuch* (West) (1964): 344.
56 Bernt von Heiseler, "Unser Dienst am Frieden: Ansprache auf der Herbsttagung 1951 der 'Deutschen Akademie für Sprache und Dichtung'," in *Zwischen Kritik und Zuversicht: 50 Jahre Deutsche Akademie für Sprache und Dichtung*, ed. Michael Hackmann and Herbert Heckmann (Göttingen: Wallstein, 1999), 293.
57 Bernt von Heiseler, "Zu Shakespeares Komödie 'Der Kaufmann von Venedig'," in Stadttheater Gießen, *Der Kaufmann von Venedig*, theatre programme (Gießen, 1968), 71.

ed that the play would only be safe from anti-Semitic "misunderstandings" if it was acknowledged firstly, that Shakespeare's original was neither "political nor tendentious," and secondly, that there had not been any Jews in Shakespeare's England.[58] It was this second argument, a clear rejection of the interpretation of Shakespeare's play as a figuration of the Holocaust, that was reiterated like a mantra in comments on the play until the late 1980s. It seemed to absolve Shakespeare from all accusations of anti-Semitism and productions of *Merchant* from reproducing Nazi ideology. "To sum up," one critic wrote on the production at Koblenz in January 1967, "by no means does *The Merchant of Venice* have to be set on the list of casualties of the unresolved German past, as some one hundred and ten-percent democrats had demanded after the war. Thank God!"[59]

2.2 Tactical Refigurations: Fritz Kortner, Peter Zadek, and George Tabori

The widespread consensus on post-war *Merchants*, strangely oscillating between Holocaust remembrance and forgetting, was disrupted by the work of Fritz Kortner, Peter Zadek, and George Tabori – all of them Jews who had been in exile. It has frequently been noted that their takes on Shakespeare's play were iconoclastic, breaking with the conciliatory *Merchants* of post-war Germany, and offering radical alternatives to the noble Shylocks in the tradition of Ernst Deutsch.[60] All of them returned to *Merchant* more than once during their careers, developing various figurations of Shylock. Kortner, who had played Shylock in four productions before the war (see Chapter 1), returned to the role at the age of seventy-six, in Otto Schenk's 1968 TV adaptation (broadcast in Germany on 2 March 1969). Peter Zadek directed the play four times: first in the English Midlands at the end of the 1940s with Jack Boyd-Brent as Shylock; soon after his return to Germany in Ulm in 1961, in Bochum in 1972, and eventually in 1988 at the Vienna Burgtheater. George Tabori offered three different *Merchants*, or rather, adaptations and spin-offs of the Shakespearean play: *The Merchant of Venice (As Performed in Theresienstadt)* was shown at the Berkshire Theater Festival in Stockbridge, Massachusetts, in 1966. The title of his Munich adaptation of 1978 quoted

---

[58] G., "'Der Kaufmann von Venedig': Richard Flatters Neuübersetzung im Großen Haus des Badischen Staatstheaters," *Badische Neueste Nachrichten*, 8 March 1966.
[59] Wolfgang Eschmann, "Sieg der Liebe und der Gnade: Der Jude Shylock als tragische Figur," *Rhein-Zeitung*, 17 January 1967.
[60] See Anat Feinberg, "Against 'False Piety': George Tabori and *The Merchant of Venice*," *Shakespeare Jahrbuch* 149 (2013): 104.

Shylock's lines in 3.1: *Ich wollte, meine Tochter läge tot zu meinen Füßen und hätte die Juwelen in den Ohren: Improvisationen über Shakespeares Shylock* ("I would my daughter were dead at my foot and the jewels in her ear: Improvisations on Shakespeare's Shylock"). In 1989, Tabori returned to the play for the last time, when he included a scene based on *The Merchant* in his *Verliebte und Verrückte* ("Lovers and Lunatics") in Vienna.

In an interview on the occasion of his production of *Merchant* at Vienna in 1988, Peter Zadek was asked why he had so often directed this play. He answered that it was a play about a Jew in a non-Jewish society and thus resonated with his own experience more closely than any other play.[61] But biographical explanations cannot fully explain this continuous interest in *Merchant*, which for Anat Feinberg was an explicit decision for Shylock (and against Nathan) as a figure if not of identification, then of respect.[62] The productions were designed not as timeless realizations of a canonical play, but as tactical comments or interventions, made for a particular stage and its respective audience. Kortner's, Zadek's, and Tabori's interpretations were divergent contributions to the same project, namely the deliberate appropriation of the Shylock figure for an analysis of German anti-Semitism and the Holocaust, combined with a more general attack against the conventions of the West German stage.

Our understanding of tactics follows Michel de Certeau's differentiation between strategy and tactics in *The Practices of Everyday Life*. In contrast to a political or military strategy, developed by "a subject of will and power," a tactic is the momentary appropriation of a place by an individual who tests boundaries and bends dominant rules. It is "a calculus which cannot count on a 'proper' (a spatial or institutional localization)," but comes from the margins and "insinuates itself into the other's place."[63] The refigurations of Shylock by Kortner, Zadek, and Tabori were indeed tactical interventions which positioned themselves in the force field of cultural politics. The rules they were faced with were the dominant discourses on the Second World War and the Holocaust, but also the conventions of the theatre, including the interpretation of the classics. De Certeau suggests the practice of reading to be one of the most basic

---

[61] Peter Zadek, "Ein Interview für das *profil* mit Sigrid Löffler anläßlich der Inszenierung von *Der Kaufmann von Venedig* in Wien (1988)," repr. in *Das wilde Ufer: Ein Theaterbuch*, ed. Laszlo Kornitzer (1990, Cologne: Kiepenheuer & Witsch, 1994), 253.
[62] Cf. Anat Feinberg, "Vom bösen Nathan und edlen Shylock: Überlegungen zur Konstruktion jüdischer Bühnenfiguren in Deutschland nach 1945," in *Shylock nach dem Holocaust*, ed. Ackermann and Schülting, 50.
[63] Michel de Certeau, *The Practice of Everyday Life*, trans. Steven Rendall (Berkeley: The University of California Press, 1984), xix.

forms of tactic: the reader "insinuates into another person's text the ruses of pleasure and appropriation," as de Certeau writes; he thus becomes a 'poacher,' or a temporary lodger, who "transforms another person's property into a space borrowed for a moment by a transient."⁶⁴ Kortner, Zadek, and Tabori were readers in this sense, inhabiting, appropriating, and transforming Shakespeare's text and the Shylock figure. Their borrowings were tactical and transient interventions explicitly located in time and space.

"From another age" – Fritz Kortner's Shylock

Fritz Kortner was "the only man in the German theatre who, although he was away from Germany for so long, has managed to link the pre-Hitler era with the theatre today,"⁶⁵ Peter Zadek wrote in a 1959 article for the journal of the Association of Jewish Refugees in Great Britain. This link became evident in Kortner's return to the role of Shylock for a film version in 1968, a co-production of the Austrian TV and the German WDR. Directed by Otto Schenk, an influential Austrian director of opera and drama, actor, and theatre manager, the film was designed around Kortner, who turned it into a reminiscence of his 1927 interpretation of the figure, when he had last played Shylock in Fehling's Berlin production as the "breakthrough of a century-old outcry," as he described it in 1966.⁶⁶ Schenk's screen adaptation had been initiated by a documentary film in 1966, directed by Hans Jürgen Syberberg, which shows Fritz Kortner at Kammerspiele Munich in December 1965, during a disk recording. Kortner speaks Shylock's lines in 1.3 and his famous monologue in 3.1, and comments on his understanding of the role.⁶⁷ In the course of the shooting, Kortner then agreed to play the role once more – even though he had already ended his career as an actor.

This screen version shows Shylock as a revenant of Kortner's pre-war Shylock: an old Jew with tallit and kippa, a thin white beard and tangled hair,

---

64 De Certeau, *Practice of Everyday Life*, xxi.
65 Peter Zadek, "Fritz Kortner: The Last of the Lions," *AJR Information* 14.9 (1959): 9.
66 This is Kortner's phrase ("Durchbruch eines jahrhundertealten Schreis") from Jürgen Syberberg's 1966 film on Fritz Kortner, *Fritz Kortner spricht Monologe für eine Schallplatte* (Syberberg Filmproduktion / Preiserrecords, 1966). For Kortner's Weimar Shylocks, see also Chapter 1.
67 This is the second of Syberberg's Kortner films, and like his first (filmed in 1965), it is a low-budget film in black and white. The setting is a table, in front of the stage of the Kammerspiele. Kortner's interlocutor is director August Everding. The scenes are accessible on YouTube at <https://www.youtube.com/watch?v=9GB6Jaas3oO> (in German), accessed 8 September 2018.

Figure 6: Fritz Kortner (Shylock) and director Otto Schenk during the shooting of the 1968 TV-adaptation. Courtesy of Österreichische Nationalbibliothek Wien (ÖNB Wien: CE 118/3).

already visually an outsider in the society around him (see figure 6). His thirst for revenge is unquenchable, and the mutual hatred driving the plot around his bond is strangely at odds with the love plot, which is played as a shallow romantic comedy. The Belmont scenes seem stage-like and the acting artificial; the costumes have a folkloristic touch. One of Kortner's biographers, Peter Schütze, sees this as a serious flaw of the film. For him, the Christians are too "harmless," "pale," and "modern," and compared to them Kortner's Shylock is a "man from another, a remote age," who through the "intensity" of his acting appears "age-old, opera- or aria-like."[68] Yet what Schütze sees as a shortcoming can also be understood as a deliberate comment on post-war Germany.

Kortner's Shylock does indeed interrupt an atmosphere that much resembles that of a *Heimatfilm* ('homeland film'), a film genre that was eminently popular

---

68 Peter Schütze, *Fritz Kortner* (Reinbek bei Hamburg: Rowohlt, 1994), 70.

in Germany and Austria in the 1950s.[69] The early *Heimatfilm* showed idyllic rural landscapes and dealt – often in a melodramatic plot – with love, friendship, and family life in a small village. This timeless world offered audiences respite from both the National Socialist past and the bleak present in post-war Germany, where towns and cities were lying in ruins. As Alexandra Ludewig has argued: "The unblemished ideal of the Alpine sublime and of iconic rural landscapes provided a positive representation of German life which seemingly pre-dated National Socialism and was thus a pseudo-carefree and, above all, natural alternative."[70] The slogan of the German film industry – "Mach Dir ein paar schöne Stunden – geh ins Kino" ("Spend a few pleasant hours – go to the movies!")[71] – advertised German cinema as a medium of entertainment and distraction. Some examples of the *Heimatfilm* genre were remakes of the motion pictures produced by Goebbels's UFA studio. New productions cautiously alluded to the problems of the post-war society, such as homelessness and displacement, but they did so primarily by addressing "the plight of the common man,"[72] to which they offered simple solutions. The happy ending, usually a marriage between the protagonists, combined an ideal of personal happiness with the renewal of the community (and the exclusion of outsiders). The films thus catered to the emotional disposition of the German audience,[73] particularly their desire to forget the war and National Socialism, by offering the fantasy of a pre-industrial society, and of static and homogeneous communities.

The Belmont scenes in Schenk's *Merchant* are marked by the same artificial settings that are so typical of the *Heimatfilm*, in which "the screen became a looking glass into the future via the past, presenting images of well-kept, civilized, cultured, refined, and clean people and environments."[74] Shylock resembles the outsiders in the *Heimatfilm*, who remain marginalized if they do not submit to the norms of the majority society.[75] Kortner's Shylock is indeed a misfit, an old Jew, unkempt, shabby, and unrefined, driven by his growing hatred: a killjoy from a different age, disturbing the sentimental atmosphere

---

[69] Between 1949 and 1964, 24% of all film productions in West Germany were *Heimatfilme*; cf. Irmgard Wilharm, "Filmwirtschaft, Filmpolitik und der 'Publikumsgeschmack' im Westdeutschland der Nachkriegszeit," *Geschichte und Gesellschaft* 28.2 (2002): 282.
[70] Alexandra Ludewig, *Screening Nostalgia: 100 Years of German Heimat Film* (Bielefeld: transcript, 2011), 178. The genre became more critical in the late 1960s and 1970s.
[71] Qtd. in Gerhard Bliersbach, *So grün war die Heide: Der deutsche Nachkriegsfilm in neuer Sicht* (Weinheim: Beltz, 1985), 28.
[72] Ludewig, *Screening Nostalgia*, 182.
[73] Ludewig, *Screening Nostalgia*, 185.
[74] Ludewig, *Screening Nostalgia*, 183.
[75] Ludewig, *Screening Nostalgia*, 201.

and threatening the happiness of the young lovers. The ending of Schenk's film seems to reproduce the conventional endings of the *Heimatfilm*, which confirm the exclusion of the outsider, relegating him to the margins of the plot. But Kortner's Shylock seeks to take revenge on the society for this exclusion. As such, he represents the 'dark shadows' that the *Heimatfilm* was meant to dispel, and confronts the audience with their unacknowledged past.

Kortner's Shylock is a deeply religious man whose original benevolence eventually gives way to hatred because he suffers a constant series of anti-Semitic defamations and attacks. In Syberberg's documentary film of 1966, Kortner explains that he has always understood Shylock as a man who silently communes with his god. He developed the same idea in Schenk's film: Kortner's Shylock interprets Antonio's losses as divine signs confirming the rightfulness of his bond. But from the moment in which he enters the courtroom, he meets with the aggression of the 'Venetians.' He is rudely shoved forward by one of the guards to the bar behind which the Duke is sitting, as if he, Shylock, were the defendant rather than the claimant. The judge's ideological bias against the Jew is suggested by a crucifix on the wall next to the Duke, and during the trial Shylock is shouted and spat at by Bassanio, Gratiano, and the others. When Nerissa arrives as Bellario's messenger, Shylock is surrounded by a menacing group of men. One of them clandestinely takes his knife, but when he is about to stab Shylock, he is held back by Gratiano, who whispers into his ear. Like the others around him, he starts to grin, suggesting that everyone except for Shylock has become aware of the trick that will be played on him. The trial is clearly just a farce. After Portia's "Tarry a little" (4.1.300), it takes a few seconds of incredulous silence before the whole audience understands the trick and breaks out in laughing cheers. Portia's language, aggressively emphasizing the word *Jude* ('Jew'), brands Shylock as an outsider who cannot expect mercy. This is met by the audience's sneering shouts, until the scene eventually turns into a pogrom of sorts, with the Venetians dancing and laughing while the guards are manhandling Shylock. When they take away the money bags that Bassanio has given him, a few handfuls of coins fall to the ground and immediately the general attention shifts from Shylock to the money – a scene not only identifying the Venetians as the real moneygrubbers but also recalling the looting of Jewish property during the November pogroms of 1938. When eventually Shylock understands that he is being forced to consent to his own conversion, he raises his eyes in mute despair, then draws his tallit over his face, and asks permission to leave. This is the gesture of prayer, and in Syberberg's film Kortner actually suggests that his Shylock would chant a subdued prayer. When the camera follows his exit through the door into a vacant hallway, its bareness disconcertingly symbolizes the 'disappearance' of the Jews in the genocide.

This interpretation is supported by the last scene, on the surface following the Shakespearean original. However, the film does not end with a celebration of the young lovers, as a traditional *Heimatfilm* would, but with the dialogue between Lorenzo, played by Klaus Höring as a womanizer, and Gertraud Jesserer's Jessica. The last take shows a close-up of her face against the dark sky, with tears running down her cheeks. Quite obviously, she is not merely lamenting her lost love but also mourning her father's fate. As the last picture of a film that in the trial scene suggests parallels between Shakespeare's Venice and National Socialist Germany, Jessica's tears gain a more general significance. She transforms into the figure of the survivor who testifies to the genocide and mourns the dead. A similar solution was chosen in the nearly contemporaneous National Theatre production of 1970, directed by Jonathan Miller, and starring Laurence Olivier as Shylock. At the end, Jessica (played by Louise Purnell) remained alone, utterly distressed by the news about her father's legacy. In the film version of 1973, adapted and directed by John Sichel, the off-screen intoning of the Kaddish, part of Jewish mourning rituals, underscored her symbolic reconversion to Judaism.

Schenk's film was an act of cultural memory, not merely recalling and reiterating Kortner's pre-war interpretation of the role, which had already commented on the anti-Semitism of the National Socialists (see Chapter 1). More importantly, Kortner's figuration of Shylock in the late 1960s established a multi-layered temporal palimpsest that invited a figural interpretation: the close connection between the increasing anti-Semitism of the 1920s, the emigration of the Jews in the 1930s, the Holocaust, and the problematic relationship between Germany and its small Jewish population after the war. The link between the various layers of meaning of the Shylock figure was established (and authenticated) through the actor's body, and more specifically, through the body of a Jewish actor who had been constructed by the National Socialists as the "Demonstrationsjude" ("the stereotypical Jew") in their invective against the theatre.[76] In Kortner's performance, Shylock could be seen simultaneously as a Jewish forefather from the Old Testament (as many critics noted), an anti-Semitic construct (which would still have been remembered by the post-war

---

[76] Cf. Günther Rühle, "Rückkehr in ein verwüstetes Land," *Theater heute* 45.12 (2004): 28–29. See also Michael Bachmann, "Fritz Kortner on the Post-War Stage: The Jewish Actor as a Site of Memory," in *Jews and Theater in an Intercultural Context*, ed. Edna Nahshon (Leiden: Brill, 2012), 197–217.

audience), a ghostly representative of the Jewish victims of the Holocaust, and the 'real' body of the Jewish actor.

More than representing a mere homage to an ageing actor and director, which it certainly also was, the TV-production introduced a new phase of reception. Its deviation from both the figure of a noble Shylock and sentimental German cinema was eminently political, and it was received as such when it was first broadcast on German TV, on 2 March 1969.[77] The film was accompanied, on that same Sunday night, by a round-table discussion on WDR, which brought together representatives of German cultural life: the authors Günter Grass and Paul Schallück, director Peter Stein, author and critic Rudolf Krämer-Badoni, Professor of Pedagogy Hartwig von Hentig, and rabbi Emanuel Schereschewsky. Strangely enough, the panelists did *not* read the film as an instance of cultural remembrance, but rather as a problematic production that could present an obstacle for the implementation of democracy in West Germany. Chaired by Claus Helmut Drese, then general director of the theatre at Cologne, the panel was entitled "Darf der Jude wieder böse sein?" ("May the Jew be evil again?").[78] It addressed the question of whether the film encourages anti-Semitism and, as Drese put it, whether Germany in 1969 was "mature enough" to "suffer" such an interpretation. The debate revolved around Kortner's figuration of the "evil Jew," as many saw him. Peter Stein was an exception. He praised Kortner's analytical approach to the figure, which for him showed how Shylock consciously resorts to the stereotype as a reaction against the Venetians' anti-Semitism. Stein described Kortner's/Shylock's resistance to integration, and his insistence on his cultural difference and the discreteness of his history, as the only way to impact on the public debate.

Other participants in the discussion were less convinced. They feared that Schenk's film might not only confirm the anti-Semitic prejudices of the older generation, but would also encourage the emerging anti-Zionism of leftist groups, which had been reinforced by the Six-Day War of 1967. As Krämer-Badoni observed, Kortner's interpretation of the role also ran the risk of confirming anti-Semitic prejudices because the figure was *embodied* (rather than *played*) by a

---

[77] The film had been shown on Austrian TV (ORF) on 26 October of the preceding year.
[78] This question has a further layer of meaning if read against the scandal around Kortner's *Don Carlos* at the Schiller Theater in Berlin in 1950. During the last act, "actors dressed as soldiers in black fired in the direction of the audience" (Bachmann, "Fritz Kortner," 198), thus leading to tumultuous scenes among spectators, to anti-Semitic audience responses, and scathing reviews which ignored the obvious reference to the Holocaust. Bachmann quotes contemporary reviews that stress the parallels between Kortner's King Philipp in *Don Carlos* and his pre-war Shylock (cf. 203).

Jew. The position held by Günter Grass, who would win the Noble Prize in Literature in 1999, was different. He saw the film as a laudable step on the way back to normality, going beyond the distortions of philo-Semitic idealization, and offering a "whole picture" of "the Jews" including the "dark sides."[79] Interestingly, it was rabbi Schereschewsky who reminded his interlocutors of the long history of Jewish actors and directors in Germany. He quoted Ernst Simon's plea, made in 1929, to acknowledge Shylock rather than the pale Nathan as a "tragic brother."[80]

"Embarrassments" – Peter Zadek's *Merchants*

Peter Zadek was strongly impressed by Kortner's work. He saw him as "the last of the lions," a representative of 'old school' directors, his work "big and full, but without pomposity, without pretentiousness." Zadek first met Kortner after his return to Germany (in 1958), when preparing a feature about the actor-director for British TV (which was broadcast on 7 June 1959). In the September issue of *AJR Information*, Zadek describes his impression of Kortner:

> What he hates more than anything in the world is the empty phrase, the pretentious gesture, the carbon copy, the cliché. He humanises even the great heroic tragedies and, even more, the great heroic characters. I suppose the mistrust of heroes is a very Jewish trait [...]. [W]hen Kortner spoke of the corruption of the German language under the Nazis, the way it had become pompous and hollow, full of sound and fury and empty of meaning, I could see what he had against heroes. [...]. His own function as far as the German language was concerned, Kortner described as 'ein Zersetzungsprozess' – a necessary and deliberate process of decomposition, undoing what nearly twenty years of false values had stultified.[81]

Kortner and Zadek shared this aversion to heroism and (tragic) heroes. And like Kortner, Zadek regarded *The Merchant of Venice* as a play that was crucial for this project.

Zadek's first German *Merchant* at Städtische Bühne Ulm concentrated on the figure of Shylock and its stage history. The programme compiled excerpts from

---

[79] In hindsight, his words resonate uncannily with later debates on his biography and his position towards Israel. His 2012 poem "Was gesagt werden muss" ("What must be said"), an explicit attack on Israel's nuclear programme, generated a massive controversy, not least because only six years previously Grass had admitted that as a young man he had been a member of the SS.
[80] Ernst Simon, "Lessing und die jüdische Geschichte," *Jüdische Rundschau*, 22 January 1929, repr. in Simon, *Brücken: Gesammelte Aufsätze* (Heidelberg: Verlag Lambert Schneider, 1965), 218.
[81] Zadek, "Fritz Kortner," 8.

2.2 Tactical Refigurations: Fritz Kortner, Peter Zadek, and George Tabori

texts by Hermann Sinsheimer, Alfred Polgar (on Shylock's plea), and Cecil Roth (on Jewish life in the ghetto), but it also included the passage from Kortner's autobiography *Aller Tage Abend* (1959) on his Shylock for Fehling's Berlin *Merchant* in 1927 (see Chapter 1). To this was added a series of portraits of famous nineteenth- and early twentieth-century actors in the role of Shylock, including August Wilhelm Iffland, Friedrich Mitterwurzer, Albert Bassermann, Ludwig Devrient, Rudolf Schildkraut, and Fritz Kortner. This line-up suggested a continuity between pre-war *Merchants* and Zadek's own production, excluding the three decades between 1930 and 1960 and, significantly, also Deutsch's Shylock, which we discussed in the previous chapter. It is somewhat surprising that Zadek's 1961 *Merchant* – seven years before Schenk's film and two years before Piscator's Berlin *Merchant* – was celebrated by critics and audiences alike, despite the fact that it showed Norbert Kappen as a bloodthirsty Shylock, a Jewish figure form the ghetto, devoid of any "false romanticizations," as critic Hellmuth Karasek judged.[82] One explanation for this success could be that Zadek, in contrast to other directors, decided to emphasize rather than downplay the comedic character of the play, and to complement the focus on Kappen's evil Shylock with an extremely witty Portia (played by Elisabeth Orth).

This same combination between popular comedy and critical deconstruction also characterized Zadek's Bochum production of 1972, in which farce and slapstick were even intensified, often at the expense of the spoken word.[83] For Zadek, entertainment was a prominent part of the dramatic experience.[84] This applied particularly to productions of the classics, which he wanted to open up to a more general audience beyond the educated middle classes.[85] Like the Ulm *Merchant*, the Bochum production revolved again around Portia and Shylock, but they were now conceptualized in a more radical way to 'decompose' the traditional romantic comedy that had dominated the post-war reception of the play. In Zadek's version, which disassembled the play into its various plots and scenes, there was neither poetry nor nobility. This was supported by drama-

---

82 Hellmuth Karasek, "Shylock im Ghetto," *Stuttgarter Zeitung*, 13 February 1961.
83 Parallel actions were shown on stage, distracting the attention of the audience. In addition, almost every reviewer noted that the characters' lines were difficult to understand. The actors shouted, spoke very fast, or mumbled, and Ulrich Wildgruber's clown Lancelot Gobbo spoke in a Swabian dialect.
84 Wilhelm Hortmann speaks of Zadek's concern with offering "a full, i.e. sensual and visceral theatre event," in *Shakespeare on the German Stage: The Twentieth Century* (Cambridge: Cambridge University Press, 1998), 258.
85 Astrid Herbold, "*Der Kaufmann von Venedig* (1972)," *Vom Elefanten zum Intendanten: Peter Zadeks Shakespeare-Inszenierungen am Schauspielhaus Bochum* (Herne: Verlag für Wissenschaft und Kunst, 1997), 23.

turge Karsten Schälike's translation, which modernized the traditional Schlegel version and dispensed with blank verse. Whereas Rosel Zech's Portia was foolish and undignified, focusing in the trial scene exclusively on her performance of masculinity and thus leading to complete verbal and physical confusion, Hans Mahnke played Shylock as an embodiment of anti-Semitic clichés. He wore a dirty baggy cloak and a *kippa*, large rings glittered on his fingers, and he had the mannerist gestures and the lisping voice of the traditional stage Jew.[86] Again, like in Ulm, the programme contextualized the figure both in its critical and stage history as well as in the context of Holocaust remembrance.[87] In an interview on the production, which was also printed in the programme, Zadek stressed that he wanted to show a *Merchant* that was "embarrassing" for the audience: "unpleasant, disgusting, abominable, gross, unnuanced, undifferentiated, etc."[88]

Clearly, the most provocative of these "embarrassments" was the figure of Shylock – and this was not confined to the show alone but began already at the entrance of the theatre. A huge poster showed the visual stereotype of the bloodthirsty Jew with a long crooked nose, tousled hair and beard, an oversized skull cap, and a caftan-like garment. This figure approaches his victim with a raised dagger and open mouth as if to devour him (see figure 7). The male victim, on the left, passively submits to the violence, thus assuming the posture of the Christian martyr St. Sebastian – an association that was suggested by the reproduction of Andrea Martegna's painting of *Saint Sebastian* (1456–1459) in the programme. A rope invited spectators to 'give life' to the stereotype and raise the figure's arm that held the dagger. "It was a shocking do-it-your-self Shylock," Georg Hensel judged in a review.[89] Among the heated responses that the poster evoked, there was also a long article published in a Jewish weekly, where it was described as an anti-Semitic attack "right into the heart of reconciliation," as the title of the review read.[90] Even more embarrassing was Hans Mahnke's Shylock:

---

[86] See Volker Canaris, *Peter Zadek: Der Theatermann und Filmemacher* (Munich: Hanser, 1979), 175; Herbold, "*Der Kaufmann von Venedig*," 37.
[87] It contained, among other texts, a quote from Hannah Arendt's *Vita Activa* (1960); a juxtaposition of two photographs, one showing the Warsaw Ghetto, the other a picturesque Italian estate; the passage from Kortner's comment on his 1927 Shylock; and Polgar's plea for Shylock.
[88] Peter Zadek and Karsten Schälike in an interview with Hartmut Gehrke during the rehearsals: "Gespräch mit Peter Zadek und Karsten Schälike," in Schauspielhaus Bochum, *Der Kaufmann von Venedig*, theatre programme (Bochum, 1972/73), 28.
[89] Georg Hensel, "Laudatio auf Peter Zadek," in Peter Zadek, *My Way: Eine Autobiographie 1926–1969* (Cologne: Kiepenheuer & Witsch, 1998), 549.
[90] Anon., "Der Versöhnung mitten ins Herz," *Allgemeine Wochenzeitung der Juden in Deutschland*, 26 January 1973.

evil, repulsive, and tasteless, as most papers noted. "A Shylock from Hitler's times"⁹¹ was how he appeared to the reviewer for the German weekly *Der Spiegel*.

Figure 7: Entrance of Bochum's Schauspielhaus with the poster advertising Peter Zadek's 1972 production. Film still from the WDR documentary *Hierzulande – heutzutage: Der Kaufmann von Venedig*, broadcast on 9 January 1973.

The stage had been constructed by René Allio, the French stage designer and later film director; it was an asymmetric maze of long wooden runways on which black slates had been glued. Suggesting the bridges of Venice, they extended several metres into the auditorium, thus allowing Shylock to come very close to the spectators. The reviewer for *Süddeutsche Zeitung* asserted that, compared to the society of farcical popinjays on high platform shoes, the Shylock figure was thoroughly explored and precisely drawn, "the only human being," "irritating, virtually archaic, slow-witted, not up to date." But Mahnke's Shylock did not invite audience identification, and it iconoclastically attacked the figure of the 'noble' Jew, as the reviewer emphasized: "This was aimed at the heart of

---

91 Anon., "Ein Shylock wie aus Hitlers Zeiten," *Der Spiegel* (8 January 1973): 96–97.

philo-Semitic prudery, this was 'embarrassing.'"[92] The last act did not offer any reconciliation, when at the end of the show Shylock remained alone on an empty stage.

Zadek's fourth production of *Merchant* at the Vienna Burgtheater in 1988, which will be discussed in more detail in Chapter 4, moved the setting to the international world of modern businessmen, where Portia's question "Which is the merchant here, and which the Jew?" (4.1.169) caused some confusion. Once more, Zadek had redesigned the figure: For the first time on a German-speaking stage, Shylock was *not* visibly marked as a Jew. Gert Voss as Shylock was a broker like the others: an assimilated Jew in a society where (verbal) stereotyping was an obvious strategy to defeat economic competitors. In the late 1980s, this was a pertinent answer to the political situation in Austria. The election of President Kurt Waldheim in 1986, who as an intelligence officer in the German Wehrmacht seems to have been implicated in war crimes, had caused massive international protests, and led to the US-government declaring him a persona non grata. Parallel to this debate, a new political party had emerged, which would play a crucial role in the following decades: the Austrian Freedom Party (FPÖ), a right-wing populist party under its leader Jörg Haider, who brought nationalism and anti-immigration politics onto the agenda. Against this emergence of a 'New Right,' Zadek's production insisted that Shylock belonged to and would remain in Venice. Christian society could not ward off those whom they had constructed as 'others' or 'foreigners,' since the boundary between the self and its others had become blurred.

"Improvisations" – George Tabori's Adaptations

George Tabori's adaptations of *The Merchant of Venice*[93] were the most experimental among all post-war approaches to the play. They were designed, firstly, as explorations of the question of figuration: namely, how to play Shylock after the Holocaust, and how to do so with non-Jewish actors and for a predominantly non-Jewish audience. Secondly, this was accompanied by an investiga-

---

92 Reinhard Baumgart, "Shakespeares krauser Reichtum," *Süddeutsche Zeitung*, 3 January 1973.
93 For a more detailed discussion of Tabori's productions, see also Sabine Schülting, "Evoking the Holocaust in George Tabori's Productions of *The Merchant of Venice*," in *Wrestling with Shylock: Jewish Responses to* The Merchant of Venice, ed. Michael Shapiro and Edna Nahshon (Cambridge: Cambridge University Press, 2017), 224–242.

tion of "Shylockism,"[94] as Feinberg has claimed, referring to the study of the various interpretations of Shylock through time. Tabori's adaptations probed into the figure of the Jewish moneylender and positioned it between anti-Semitic stereotyping on the one hand, and a figure open to resistant readings on the other. This included, thirdly, the juxtaposition of various temporal and spatial layers: of early-modern England, Germany during the National Socialist regime, and the respective moment and place of performances in post-war America, Germany, and Austria. These layers were interconnected through repetition, allusion, and transformation, suggesting a figural interpretation in which the past anticipated the present, and the present reiterated the past, and in which one setting was a "retrospective appropriation" and interpretation of another one.[95] *Merchant* thus complemented Tabori's so-called "Holocaust Plays,"[96] opening up a way of addressing the past – not least through the precarious trope of Shylock's pound of flesh: "Historians speak of six million murders – a statement that is meaningless like rubbish. However, if one considers that it was six million times one murder, one returns to Shylock's pound of flesh."[97] Six years after Zadek's take on the play, the notion of an "embarrassing" Shylock, who confronts the audience with their own prejudices and disrupts their passive complacency, would also be the dominant idea for Tabori's Munich adaptation of *Merchant*.

In Tabori's first production, at the Berkshire Theater Festival in 1966, *The Merchant of Venice* was a play within the play, which Jewish prisoners of a concentration camp had to perform for an SS audience. In his unpublished production notes, Tabori relates the idea for his first *Merchant* to the (unconfirmed) legend that the play had been put on stage in a concentration camp, probably Theresienstadt.[98] Tabori was interested in imagining whether such a

---

[94] Anat Feinberg, *Embodied Memory: The Theatre of George Tabori* (Iowa City: The University of Iowa Press, 1999), 218.
[95] Hayden White, "Auerbach's Literary History: Figural Causation and Modernist Historicism," in *Figural Realism: Studies in the Mimesis Effect* (Baltimore: Johns Hopkins University Press, 1999), 90.
[96] The term refers to Tabori's *The Cannibals* (1968), *Mutters Courage* (1979; "My Mother's Courage"), *Jubiläum* (1983, "Jubilee"), and *Mein Kampf* (1987, "My Struggle"); see Feinberg, *Embodied Memory*, 195–262.
[97] George Tabori, "Es geht schon wieder los," in *Unterammergau oder Die guten Deutschen* (Frankfurt/M.: Suhrkamp, 1981), 203–204.
[98] Tabori even considered the (unlikely) possibility that such a performance may have happened at Auschwitz. George Tabori, "For B. H." (typescript), in "Regiearbeiten: *The Merchant of Venice* (As performed in Theresienstadt)" (Stockbridge, Berkshire Theatre Festival, premiere: 19 July 1966), Archiv der Akademie der Künste Berlin, Tabori 3079, n. p. French-Canadian direc-

production, even if it had been mandated by SS officers, would have allowed some kind of "defiance,"[99] and this became the main idea behind the production. The inherent contradictions of the play – as a product of anti-Semitism that simultaneously lends itself to appropriation against the anti-Semites – was at the centre of the Berkshire production. The resulting ambivalence towards the Shylock figure, encompassing rejection and acceptance at the same time, was played out on the stage. According to the reviews, Alan Epstein in the role of the prisoner-actor who had been forced to play Shylock with a long false nose and a pathetic wig made of red yarn was extremely funny, showing the moneylender as a "deliberately gross, slimy, and caricatured role." However, the audience's laughter was not innocent and reminded them of their complicity in perpetuating the anti-Semitic cliché: "You see, he seemed to say, we Jews really are funny. But don't forget, you made us this way, we're doing it for you, so don't think you're superior to Antonio."[100]

In the trial scene, the prisoner was no longer willing to embody this anti-Semitic figure. He took off his wig and nose, and ceased to speak in the "horrendous Yiddish accent" of the previous scenes. In his normal voice, he asked "What judgment shall I dread, doing no wrong?"[101] – thus appropriating Shylock's very words against the Nazi terror, even though he knew that his resistance would lead to his certain death. While the other prisoners tried to silence him and convince him to play along, he suddenly attacked the Nazi guard with the moneylender's knife. But before he could act out his revenge, he was shot. The play closed with the other prisoners silently carrying his corpse away. That frame and the play within the play became intricately interrelated, thus blurring the dividing line between actor(s) and role(s): Epstein, the Jewish prisoner, and Shylock. Shylock was an anti-Semitic stereotype, but at the same time he figured the Jewish victims of the genocide as well as a phantasmagoria (or ideal) of the Jewish avenger.

---

tor Tibor Egervari, born into a Hungarian Jewish family before the Second World War, did base an adaptation of *Merchant* on the fiction of a performance of the play at Auschwitz; see Tibor Egervari, "Shakespeare's *Merchant of Venice* in Auschwitz," in *Shakespeare and the Second World War: Memory, Culture, Identity*, ed. Irena R. Makaryk and Marissa McHugh (Toronto: University of Toronto Press, 2012), 274–285.

99 George Tabori. "Programm notes" (typescript), in "Regiearbeiten: *The Merchant of Venice* (As performed in Theresienstadt)" (Stockbridge, Berkshire Theatre Festival, premiere: 19 July 1966), Archiv der Akademie der Künste Berlin, Tabori 3065, 1.

100 Anon., typescript of an untitled article on Tabori's Berkshire *Merchant*, in "Regiearbeiten: *The Merchant of Venice* (As performed in Theresienstadt)," Archiv der Akademie der Künste Berlin, Tabori 3079, 14.

101 Anon., typescript of an untitled article on Tabori's Berkshire *Merchant*, 13, 22.

For his Munich production Tabori had initially intended to reproduce the idea of *Merchant* as a play within a play, performed at a concentration camp. In 1978, the merging between performance and reality would have gone even further than in the previous production. Tabori had sought to gain permission to use the site of the former concentration camp at Dachau, near Munich, as an improvised stage. The performance would have started with spectators being brought to the camp in buses, suggesting the imprisonment and deportation of the Jews. Tabori later changed his plans and decided to have the first three acts played in the theatre and only 4.1, the trial scene, in Dachau. However, permission for this was denied by the municipal authorities so that the production had to be relocated to the improvised stage of a small rehearsal room of Kammerspiele, which seated only one hundred spectators, thus offering a very intimate atmosphere.[102]

The ensuing redesign led to an even more pronounced focus on the question of how to play Shylock. The adaptation took the form of a collage, combining passages from Shakespeare's play, anti-Semitic songs and jokes, and new material such as a "concentration camp narrative" and a scene, entitled "Kristallnacht" ("The Night of Broken Glass"), about the pogroms in Germany and Austria in November 1938. The love plot around Portia and Bassanio had been cut entirely. Some scenes, such as "Antonio ist traurig" ("Antonio is sad"), "Bassanio braucht Geld" ("Bassanio needs money"), and "Shylock macht ein Angebot" ("Shylock makes an offer"), were closely linked to the Shakespearean original, which was played in the classical Schlegel translation. But others were adapted and played in various improvisations like in jazz music. In an interview published in the daily *Süddeutsche Zeitung* on 17 November 1978, two days before the premiere, Tabori explained that they did not want to offer "an interpretation in the sense of Kortner or Olivier," but rather reflect on the difficulties of staging the play in post-war Germany:

> Almost all our actors are young, and there is no Jew among them. So it was crucial how one can play a Jew; how one can play a Jewish girl ([...] because in this production, just as in Shakespeare's times, there are only male actors, also because men and women were separated in Dachau); and how one can play the experience of the concentration camp.[103]

As in the Berkshire production, Tabori's systematic meta-dramatic design focused on the actor and the tension – rather than identification – between

---

102 For a detailed account of Tabori's productions, see Feinberg, *Embodied Memory*, 209–224.
103 George Tabori, "Das Einmalige wiederholen: Gespräch mit George Tabori über sein Münchner Shylock-Projekt," *Süddeutsche Zeitung*, 17 November 1978.

actor and role. In Munich, this was enhanced by the multiplication of the figure, which was played by all of the actors. In 2.5, for example, when Shylock takes his leave from Jessica, exhorting her to lock the doors and keep an eye on the house, Shylock appeared in four variations, all products of Jessica's fantasy: "a Jewish patriarch, a benevolent, a mythical and a poetical [father]."[104] Another scene, only reported in 2.8 of Shakespeare's play, showed Shylock's outrage at Jessica's elopement. It was played thirteen times, by all thirteen actors in their individual interpretations, transforming the scene alternately into slapstick, burlesque, tragedy, and so on. One actor expressed his grief in a low and subdued voice; another ran over the stage screaming and howling; a third was convinced that Shylock had spoken in dialect; a fourth imitated Fritz Kortner playing Shylock; and a fifth transformed the scene into a musical.[105] By thus staging a variety of possible figurations rather than giving a single interpretation of scene and role, Tabori underscored the bewildering array of interpretations that Shakespeare's Shylock invites and challenged the idea that any single version could be the correct one. The production drew attention to the contradictory facets the figure had acquired over time, facets that – like in a cubist painting – could not be reassembled to form a coherent whole.

Perhaps taking up Zadek's suggestion, Tabori has also called this multi-faceted Shylock a "*Peinlichkeit*,"[106] an embarrassment, which confronts spectators with events they would rather forget.[107] Compared to Zadek's understanding of the term, 'embarrassment' gained a further, corporeal dimension in Tabori's production. The German word *peinlich*, which etymologically comes from *Pein* (pain), can mean 'embarrassing' and 'uncomfortable,' 'overly exact' and 'precise,' or, in an archaic sense, 'related to the body' and 'by means of physical torture.' It was this third aspect that Tabori also explored. To call Shylock a *Peinlichkeit* would thus suggest a link between the embarrassment the figure has caused on the stage, Shylock's pedantic insistence on the letters of the law, and the physical violence of anti-Semitism. In addition, the figure as conceptual-

---

104 George Tabori, *Ich wollte meine Tochter läge tot zu meinen Füßen und hätte die Juwelen in den Ohren: Improvisationen über Shakespeares Shylock. Dokumentation einer Theaterarbeit*, ed. Andrea Welker and Tina Berger (Munich: Hanser, 1979), 49.
105 Georg Hensel, "Shakespeare, Jazz und Judenhaß: George Taboris Shylock-Improvisationen," *Frankfurter Allgemeine Zeitung*, 23 November 1978.
106 Tabori, *Improvisationen über Shakespeares Shylock*, 11.
107 See also Iwona Ubermann's study of Tabori's "Holocaust plays": *Auschwitz im Theater der "Peinlichkeit": George Taboris Holocaust-Stücke im Rahmen der Theatergeschichte seit dem Ende der 60er Jahre* (Munich: Dissertationsverlag NG Kopierladen, 1995). "Theater der Peinlichkeit" can be translated as 'theatre of embarrassment.'

ized by Tabori affected the audience and was painful for them as well – even in a literal sense. Tabori had always sought to include the audience in the performance and disrupt their passivity towards the events on stage. In the Berkshire *Merchant*, for example, they saw themselves transformed – through the arrangement of the stage – into the SS audience in the concentration camp for whom the Jewish prisoners had to perform the play. Any reaction to the events on stage was thus always already compromised and became meaningful in the frame story.

In Munich, the involvement went a lot further.[108] There was no spatial separation between audience and stage. The show started with a "Ballad of Shylock," based on a text by Samuel Pepys from the seventeenth century, during which all thirteen actors, with false noses looking like the anti-Semitic stereotype from *Der Stürmer*, prowled through the audience and whispered anti-Semitic jokes into spectators' ears. This was followed by a dumb show, in which puppets, wearing shabby clothes, each displaying a yellow star, and carrying suitcases, were violently 'tortured' and then destroyed with knives, electric drills, or acid. The broken parts – puppet arms, heads, and feet – were distributed as 'gifts' among the audience. The remaining pieces, together with the puppets' clothes, were put in plastic bags and thrown on a pile under the piano at the centre of the room, where a pool of theatre blood was slowly spreading across the floor. One of the actors entered, calling "Jessica," and started to cry when he found a bloody ring in one of the bags. The audience thus became part of the show, not merely psychologically but also physically participating in the disturbing events from which they could not distance themselves.

Radically deviating from the tradition of German Shylocks represented by Ernst Deutsch, Tabori's Shylocks did not trigger emotions like pity or sympathy. Spectators who had expected to see a sentimentalized *Merchant* rejected the production as "tasteless." The critic writing for the conservative newspaper *Die Welt* saw nothing but a cultivation of naïve anti-Semitism and added that only the fact that Tabori was a Jew himself and had "lost" [sic!] family members through the Nazis could protect him from accusations of anti-Semitic propaganda.[109] But the majority of the reviews were enthusiastic. Lucidly commenting on the forcefulness of the event, one theatre critic saw the broken puppets as metaphorical representations of the historical rupture caused by the Holocaust, i.e.

---

108 The extensive documentation of the production, edited by Andrea Welker and Tina Berger, provides ample insight into the rehearsal period; cf. Tabori, *Improvisationen über Shakespeares Shylock*.
109 A. W. "Shylock im Souterrain," *Die Welt*, 23 November 1978.

the literal cracks that in Tabori's *Improvisations* were no longer "papered over" but staged as a "Menetekel" (i.e. a writing on the wall).[110]

Lovers and Lunatics (1989),[111] a six-hour collage about Shakespearean lovers, reduced *The Merchant of Venice* to the Trial Scene and the confrontation between Shylock and Portia. This encounter was the penultimate scene of the show, sandwiched between *Antony and Cleopatra* and *Romeo and Juliet*. It reimagined the configuration between the two characters, played by Tabori (who was already 75 years old) and Hildegard Schmahl, as one oscillating between affection, or even love, and antagonism. Feinberg comments:

> Portia and Shylock are two aging partners, worn out by endless disputes and unable to resolve the differences between them. While she still hopes he will for once reveal his feelings and display a touch of human warmth, he maintains a cool aloofness and, no less embittered than she is, feels that 'she does not really listen to me.'[112]

This adaptation did not merely suggest that Shylock and Portia are the real protagonists of the 'comedy,' but also implied that they are in effect dependent on each other. Shylock was already marked as an outsider and a victim of physical abuse when he first entered the stage after the *Antony and Cleopatra* scene, with a bloody dressing covering his left eye. Immediately, the other actors/characters on stage expressed their physical disgust, coughing and making gestures as if to disperse a bad smell. It seemed all too clear why Shylock demanded his bond. But he was a pathetic avenger. When in his monologue he reached the line "And if you wrong us, shall we not revenge?" (3.1.52), he drew out a clasp knife but did not manage to open it and had to ask Portia for assistance. With clear sympathy for him, she appealed to his mercy, his reason and his affection or love, but became more and more impatient when he remained obstinate.

In a newspaper article, it was reported that during a rehearsal of the scene, Tabori as Shylock suddenly exclaimed in response to Schmahl's/Portia's lines: "For the umpteenth time, Hildegard, how often do I have to tell you that I insist on my bond." It remains unclear whether this was a joke or an unplanned outburst, in which Shylock suddenly came to figure Tabori himself, whose father had been killed at Auschwitz. Against the background of Holocaust remem-

---

110 Michael Krüger, "Menschen-Spiele: Anmerkungen zum Münchner Shylock," *Theater heute* 20.2 (1979): 4.
111 The production premiered on 14 March 1989. Our comments are based on the video recording of the performance of 20 May 1989, held by the Tabori Archive at Akademie der Künste Berlin.
112 Feinberg, *Embodied Memory*, 170. (Feinberg quotes Tabori here.)

brance, the encounter between Shylock and Portia on stage was simultaneously that between Tabori and Schmahl, and that between a survivor of the Holocaust and a representative of the majority society asking for, or even demanding, his mercy. This particular moment was singled out for comment by the critic for *Der Standard:*

> Nobody who has survived Auschwitz can be tolerant; no, he won't listen to her questions, he won't react – and this is the worst one can do to someone. Hildegard Schmahl has problems understanding why as Portia she suddenly approaches him so scathingly, so aggressively. The scene is breathtaking in its truthfulness.[113]

Feinberg reads this figural interrelation along similar lines, as an allegory, actualized in a post-Holocaust situation, of "the history of friction and distrust between Jews and Christians, a rupture which left them both scarred."[114] As in Tabori's previous adaptations, various temporal layers merged, and the relation between perpetrators, bystanders, and survivors of the Holocaust surfaced. After Portia had pronounced her verdict, Shylock took off his hat and crumpled it in his hands, while suddenly experiencing a fit of coughing. He choked and collapsed on the stairs at the back of the stage – a drastic proof that he was, indeed, not well. When he sat up again, he had transformed into Romeo, who then spoke – first in English, then in German – the lines from 2.2 ("But soft, what light through yonder window breaks" etc.). But there was no romantic beauty in this *Romeo and Juliet*, which did not show Romeo and Juliet as young lovers but rather as aging actors who, in Feinberg's words, "senescent and disillusioned, [were] only play-acting the juvenile lovers, rehearsing the passionate heroes they [could] never really *be*."[115] Their love scene was informed by the same lack of communication as the preceding episode from *The Merchant of Venice*, and Romeo's handkerchief with which he dried his tears was the one that Shylock had just used to polish his knife. Shylock appeared as a figuration of Romeo, thus haunting the greatest love story of all time.

---

113 Anon., "Utopisches Illyrien und Pandämonium der Liebe: George Tabori über seine Entdeckungsreise durch Shakespeares Leidenschaften, Kulturpolitik und experimentelles Theater," *Der Standard*, 13 March 1989.
114 Feinberg, *Embodied Memory*, 170.
115 Feinberg, *Embodied Memory*, 171.

"Circumstantial dramaturgy"

In a similar way to how Tabori's Munich adaptation of *Merchant* referred to the site of the former concentration camp at Dachau, Hanan Snir gestured towards Buchenwald, the concentration camp near Weimar, in the Weimar *Merchant* of 1995 (discussed in more detail in Chapter 4). In both Tabori's Munich and Snir's Weimar productions, the spatial location of the performance added a layer of meaning to the play and suggested links between the events on stage and the actual history at the former concentration camps. Snir's dramaturge, Gad Kaynar, has used the term "circumstantial" to describe a kind of dramaturgy which pays particular attention to the context of the performance.[116] For Zadek in Bochum, such a "circumstantial" dramaturgy was also characteristic. It included, in addition to the debates on Holocaust remembrance, a consideration of the tradition and economic situation of the theatre, the social and cultural specificity of the city of Bochum, and the demographic composition of the audience.

Merchant was Zadek's second production as artistic director at the Bochum Schauspielhaus, following its long-time director Hans Schalla. On taking office, Zadek was faced with the task of attracting new audiences to a theatre that, in the preceding years, had witnessed a slow but steady decline in the number of spectators.[117] Although in the 1970s, Bochum was already slowly turning into the cultural centre of the Ruhr area that the city is today, it was still strongly influenced by its tradition as a mining town with a large working class. At the same time, the Bochum Schauspielhaus, a subsidized municipal theatre, was looking back at a long history closely connected to the political self-representation of Bochum, which can be traced back to the 'Shakespeare weeks' introduced in 1927 by theatre director Saladin Schmitt. Zadek sought to break with this tradition of Shakespeare worship, while simultaneously opening the theatre to a broader section of the Bochum population, including the youth. He started with a revue based on Hans Fallada's novel of 1932, *Kleiner Mann, was nun?* ("Little Man, What Now?"), which he and Tankred Dorst had adapted for the stage. The play critically reflected on the tensions in Weimar Germany immedi-

---

[116] Gad Kaynar, "Pragmatic Dramaturgy: Text as Context as Text," *Theatre Research International* 31.3 (2006): 247. See also Kaynar's discussion of the Weimar production in Gad Kaynar-Kissinger, "*The Merchant of Venice* on the German Stage and the 1995 'Buchenwald' Production in Weimar," in *Wrestling with Shylock*, ed. Nahshon and Shapiro, esp. 260–272.

[117] On Zadek's time in Bochum see Klaus Völker, *Peter Zadek: Mit dem "Fertigen" gab er sich nicht zufrieden* (Berlin: Hentrich & Hentrich, 2011), 46–51; and Herbold, "*Der Kaufmann von Venedig*."

ately before Hitler's rise to power: the carelessness of the world of art in the face of increasing social conflicts, and a new sentimentalism and individualism despite an increasing coercion to uniformity.[118] *Merchant* followed only three months later, approaching the German past from a different perspective, thus complementing the previous production and juxtaposing the adaptation of a popular novel with a Shakespearean classic. Like the previous production, however, it was characterized by the same combination of entertainment and cultural analysis. With thirty-one shows between December 1972 and June 1973,[119] and more than 23,000 tickets sold, *Merchant* was the second most important production of the season, surpassed only by *Kleiner Mann*. The productions were accompanied by substantial programmes in A4-format – magazines rather than leaflets, which brought together background information, relevant critical articles on the plays, interviews, and high-quality production photographs.

What worked very well for Bochum, however, did less so in Berlin. In May 1973, at the Theatertreffen, the important theatre festival in (West-)Berlin, Zadek's *Merchant* met with hostile reactions.[120] The festival audience was different from the one at Bochum: more sophisticated, familiar with Shakespeare, and expecting to see what the festival promised, namely the ten most remarkable stage productions of the year. Apparently, they were annoyed by what they may have regarded as an excess of theatricality, farce, and slapstick, inadequate for both the context and the serious topic.

Zadek's *Merchant* thus serves as a good example for how circumstances influence the recognition and success or failure of a production. The same would be true for Arie Zinger's Cologne *Merchant* of 1979. Born in Israel, Zinger moved to Germany in 1976 since when he has worked as a director at various major German theatres. Capitalizing on the debates around German *Merchants* since the early 1960s, the Cologne Schauspielhaus marketed its own production with the headline "Israeli stages the 'Jew's play'" ("Israeli inszeniert 'Judenstück'"). This appeared on posters placarded throughout the city, thus highlighting what they wanted to be perceived as an extraordinary event: that a young

---

118 Hellmuth Karasek, "Revue der Arbeitslosen," *Die ZEIT*, 29 September 1972.
119 Cf. Herbold, "*Der Kaufmann von Venedig*," 32; Christian Jauslin even speaks of fifty shows altogether; see "Bühnenbericht 1973 und Verzeichnis der Shakespeare-Aufführungen 1973," *Shakespeare Jahrbuch* (West) (1974): 231.
120 See, e. g., Heinz Ritter, "Ein Märchen-Unhold," *Der Abend*, 19 May 1973; Hagmuth W. Brockmann, "Wahrheit zwischen vielen Gags," *Spandauer Volksblatt*, 20 May 1973; Horst Winderboth, "Shakespeare – heiß umstritten," *Berliner Morgenpost*, 20 May 1973; Georg Lentz, "Der Clown von Venedig," *B.Z.*, 21 May 1973; Günter Grack, "Spektakel um Shylock," *Tagesspiegel*, 20 May 1973. See also Monschau, *Der Jude nach der Shoah*, 301.

Jewish director, born in Israel, put on an allegedly anti-Semitic play. However, although it caused an extensive media echo that included a TV panel discussion, the production was not a success: it was slated by most critics and booed by the opening night's audience.[121]

As Zadek's former assistant in Bochum, Zinger was strongly influenced by his approach to directing, and this included his take on *Merchant*. Like Zadek before him, Zinger imagined Shylock as a product of the world in which he lived, whose anti-Semitism had left its marks on his body. Dressed in a long black coat, which established a stark contrast to Antonio's white suit, Hermann Lause played an unsympathetic Shylock whose cultural difference was stressed. Dramaturge Volker Canaris wrote in his production notes:

> And the different culture, history, religion: the kippa, the shirt with the ritual fringes, the sidelocks. In particular the reference to what during the rehearsals was summarized under the keyword 'Old Testament.' Sentences that make Shylock great, foreign, which isolate him because they come from another conceptual world.[122]

Shylock's difference was easily transformed by the other characters into the anti-Semitic stereotype: Antonio wrote the word '*Jude*' ('Jew') into the Star of David that Shylock had drawn on a table, thus transforming the symbol of Judaism into the Jew's badge which was compulsory for Jews during National Socialism. Zinger explained in an interview aired on Deutschlandfunk on 25 October 1979, a day after the premiere, that he wanted to confront the audience with the repressed past. This contextualisation of the play in a discourse of cultural remembrance was more explicit than in Zadek's *Merchant*, and it was performed on stage through acts of physical violence against Shylock, anti-Semitic jokes told by Lancelot, and by visual icons like the Jew's badge. At the end of the violent encounter with Salerio and Solanio, Zinger reproduced the iconic photograph of the Warsaw Ghetto, which shows a group of women and children, SS men in the background with guns, and a little boy at the centre raising his hands in the gesture of helpless surrender.[123]

The audience was evidently displeased by what many described as an excruciatingly long and boring show. There were only a few supportive voices, which

---

121 Cf. Gerhard Stadelmaier, "Shylock hat keine Chance," *Stuttgarter Zeitung*, 27 October 1979.
122 Volker Canaris, "Beobachtungen, Überlegungen, Fragen bei den Proben," qtd. in Günther Rühle, "Wie zeigt man auf Wunden: Arie Zinger inszeniert in Köln Shakespeare's 'Kaufmann von Venedig'," *Theater heute* 20.12 (1979): 9.
123 This visual parallel was highlighted by dramaturge Volker Canaris in the programme, qtd. in Rühle, "Wie zeigt man auf Wunden," 9. See also Monschau, *Der Jude nach der Shoah*, 361.

suggests that the problem may not have lain exclusively with an inexperienced young director but also with the audience, who may have been expecting a more conciliatory show. Gerhard Stadelmaier, one of the most influential West German theatre critics writing for *Frankfurter Allgemeine Zeitung*, was fascinated by the production and praised Zinger as a "merciless director," whose greatness showed in the cynical dissection of "the banality of evil" (Arendt) and the presentation of a powerless Jewish character. But the Cologne audience was apparently yearning for a sentimental resolution, for the Christian ideology of grace (that Portia had arrogantly demanded from Shylock),[124] so that they "drowned one of the most haunting recent productions in a storm of boos. They didn't know better. No wonder!"[125] Stadelmeier's review was entitled "Shylock has no chance" – thus connecting his fate in the fictional world with his defeat in the theatre and associating, by implication, the Cologne audience with the Venetians.

* * *

In 1981 the Old Vic toured Europe with *The Merchant of Venice*. The Arts Council of Great Britain had withdrawn funding so that 1981 was the company's last season before the theatre was sold in the following year. In May 1981, the production could be seen in the south-west of Germany and in Switzerland: in Ludwigshafen, Stuttgart, Wiesbaden, and Zurich. Most reviewers praised the troupe's professionalism and acting skills, and they liked director Timothy West as Shylock. However, they were surprised by what many considered an astonishingly conservative and unsophisticated production, stubbornly faithful to Shakespeare's lines, and failing to activate any political subtext. The reviewer for *Bergsträßer Anzeiger*, a provincial newspaper, judged: "For our taste something is missing."[126] "The English are more unencumbered because excesses against the Jews did not happen there,"[127] was the explanation, in the clumsy phrasing that is so characteristic for *Merchant* reviews in post-war Germany. The reactions to the tour exemplify that within less than two decades, *Merchant* productions had changed so thoroughly under the influence of the German 'director's theatre' and the debates on the Holocaust that an apolitical approach to the play was deemed inappropriate. Disregarding whether their interpretations would please everyone, Jewish actors and directors had set standards against which new productions were frequently judged. Throughout the late 1970s and the 1980s,

---

124 This is Canaris' description of the trial scene, qtd. in Rühle, "Wie zeigt man auf Wunden," 9.
125 Stadelmeier, "Shylock hat keine Chance."
126 Wilhelm Ringelband, "Abschied vom Old Vic," *Bergsträßer Anzeiger*, 19 May 1981.
127 Doris M. Trauth, "Das Spiel von Liebe und Haß," *Die Rheinpfalz*, 15 May 1981.

Kortner's and Zadek's names kept reappearing in reviews and theatre programmes as the yardsticks of critics or points of directorial self-identification. In particular, they had convinced directors, critics, and probably also theatregoers that the play was eminently political in post-war Germany.

2.3 The Diversification of the Shylock Figure: Holocaust Victims, Outsiders, and 'Rich Jews'

German theatres' interest in *Merchant* resurfaced at precisely those moments when public debates were revolving around cultural remembrance. This was not the case in the mid-1970s, when production numbers decreased significantly, with only one production in 1973, two in 1974, and no West German productions between 1975 and 1977.[128] This changed again in the last years of the decade, with two productions in 1978 (Tabori's Munich adaptation and a *Merchant* in Lübeck) and four in 1979 (Cologne, Würzburg, Bielefeld, and Baden-Baden). These later productions roughly coincided with the broadcasting of the NBC series *Holocaust* on the third programmes of West German TV between 22 and 27 January 1979. *Holocaust* has been described by historians as "a caesura in media history and the history of remembrance." Watched by millions of German spectators, it dominated the general public debate for several weeks and had an immediate political and legal impact when the Bundestag, the West German parliament, revoked the limitation period for murder – thus making possible the future prosecution of crimes committed during 1933 and 1945.[129]

In his historical overview of post-war films about the era of Nationalist Socialism, Frank Bösch describes the success of *Holocaust* as the "expression of a long-term change in the public culture of remembrance," which had already manifested itself, in the previous year, in the commemoration of the November pogroms and the heated debates around the case of Hans Filbinger,[130] and which

---

128 Monschau (*Der Jude nach der Shoah*, 334–336) explains this as an effect of the shift of public interest to the terrorism of the so-called 'Baader-Meinhof Gang' (the Red Army Faction, RAF), which had started in the early 1970s and peaked in the "German Autumn" of 1977.

129 Frank Bösch, "Film, NS-Vergangenheit und Geschichtswissenschaft," *Vierteljahrshefte für Zeitgeschichte* 54 (2007): 2. See also Matthias Weiß, "Sinnliche Erinnerung: Die Filme *Holocaust* und *Schindlers Liste* in der bundesdeutschen Vergegenwärtigung der NS-Zeit," in *Beschweigen und Bekennen: Die deutsche Nachkriegsgesellschaft und der Holocaust*, ed. Norbert Frei and Sybille Steinbacher (Göttingen: Wallstein, 2001), 71–102.

130 Anon., "Affäre Filbinger: Was Rechtens war...," *Der Spiegel* 20 (15 May 1978): 23–27. In August 1978, Filbinger, a member of the conservative Christian Democratic Union, had to resign from his post as Minister President of Baden-Württemberg after a public debate about his role as

was also evident from the great public interest in the Düsseldorf Majdanek Trial (1975–1981).[131] At the same time, Bösch argues, *Holocaust* paved the way for medial representations of the genocide that paid attention to everyday life, told stories of individual Jewish victims, and reflected on the role of the German population. Both the affective impact brought about by the personalization of the victims and the interlacing of micro- and macro-history contributed to the success of *Holocaust*.[132] There were, however, also critical voices: Elie Wiesel, Holocaust survivor and recipient of the Nobel Peace Prize in 1986, called the series a "trivialization of the Holocaust."[133] In a similar vein, Peter Zadek characterized the series and its echo as hypocritical feel-good TV: "Personally, after all the prattling of the press [...] I can no longer hear or see the word 'Jew.' And it's not that it disgusts me, but it sucks."[134]

Merchant productions of the late 1970s and early 1980s formed part of the intensive public debate that had been furthered by *Holocaust*, and they adopted some of the series' representational strategies. Whereas Tabori and Zadek had explored, and iconoclastically deconstructed, the different facets of the Shylock figure, directors now sought to construct Shylock as a 'realistic' individual. This was the case in Peter Palitzsch's Düsseldorf production of 1981, which found a striking image for the isolation of Shylock. After Stefan Wigger's Shylock had spoken the line "What judgement shall I dread, doing no wrong?" (4.1.88), he froze at the apron of the stage, and remained there during the entire interval, staring into the auditorium. For the critic of *Westdeutsche Zeitung*, this was the climax of the show: "Again the Jew is isolated, left alone – a performance cannot describe Shylock's situation more succinctly." He recounts the reaction of a ten-year-old boy who seemed to have understood Shylock's affliction and, during the interval, repeatedly went to the stage, looking up at Wigger/Shylock as if to comfort him.[135] A similar solution was found for the last act. Shylock remained on stage, leaning against a wall, isolated from the rest of the charac-

---

a navy judge during the war. The catalyst was a remark by Rolf Hochhuth, who had called Filbinger "Hitler's navy judge," who even after the end of the war had judged German soldiers according to Nazi laws.

131 In this trial at Düsseldorf, which lasted until 1981, sixteen former SS-members, camp officials, and guards were accused of war crimes in the extermination camp of Majdanek, near the city of Lublin in occupied Poland.
132 Cf. Reichel, *Erfundene Erinnerung*, 249–263, esp. 259–262.
133 Elie Wiesel, "Trivializing the Holocaust: Semi-Fact and Semi-Fiction," *New York Times*, 16 April 1978.
134 Peter Zadek, "Holocaust (1979)," repr. in Zadek, *Das wilde Ufer*, 244.
135 Dieter Westecker, "Die Pause ist der einsame Höhepunkt," *Westdeutsche Zeitung*, 28 September 1981.

ters. With the comic scenes considerably cut, *Merchant* was played as the tragedy of Shylock, although in some reviews Antonio was identified not merely as Shylock's economic antagonist, but also as a complementary figure, a second outsider, a closeted homosexual.[136]

Except for Shylock's kippa and a Star of David scrawled onto a wall by one of the Venetians, ethnic or religious differences between the Jew and the mainstream of Venetian society were not visually highlighted. Some critics regarded this as the opening up of the play for other cultural conflicts, as for example the controversial debate about the situation of the so-called 'Gastarbeiter' (literally 'guest workers'), the migrant workers who had come to Germany since the middle of the 1950s.[137] They saw their impression confirmed by a passage from Heinrich Heine's *Shakespeare's Maidens and Women*, which was quoted in the theatre programme for the production, and in which the author contends that

> The genius of Shakespeare rises still higher over the petty strife of two religious sects, and his drama shows us neither Jews nor Christians, but oppressors and oppressed, and the madly agonised cries of exultation of the latter when they can repay their arrears of injuries with interest. There is not in this play the least trace of difference in religion [...].[138]

Although a corresponding tendency towards allegory would indeed be observable in some productions from the 1980s onwards, it does not really seem to have dominated Palitzsch's *Merchant*, which did in fact reference Judaism. The visual cues were complemented by an article in the programme, entitled "The Rich Jews in Germany," which suggested a link between Shylock and (affluent) Jews in post-war Germany. Despite those references, what the production did not show was the conventional stage Jew marked by his caftan, long beard, and payot. Some reviewers took this as an indication of Palitzsch's de-politicization or even 'belittlement' of the play.[139] The reactions show that the iconicity of the stage Jew was considered inseparable from the Shylock figure. Any changes to the convention were resented – from Zadek's inflation of the stereotype into caricature in the early 1970s to Palitzsch's almost complete abandonment of

---

136 See e.g. Reinhard Kill, "Ein Macht-Spiel?," *Rheinische Post*, 28 September 1981.
137 Rainer Hartmann, "Der Schmerz des Außenseiters," *Frankfurter Neue Presse*, 29 September 1981.
138 Heinrich Heine, *Shakespeare's Maidens and Women*, vol. 1 of *The Works of Heinrich Heine*, trans. Charles Godrey Leland (London: William Heinemann, 1906), 378. The programme quotes from the German original.
139 Cf. e.g. Kill, "Ein Macht-Spiel?," and Eo Plunien, "Außenseiter gegen Playboys," *Die Welt*, 28 September 1981.

the visual stereotype. One reviewer of the Düsseldorf *Merchant* spoke of an "elimination of everything Jewish and thus of everything that is racially problematic,"[140] his unhappy phrasing inadvertently connecting Palitzsch's production and the genocide. Monschau similarly concludes that in Palitzsch's version the "enormity disappeared which had been ascribed to the conflict after 1945, and thus also Auschwitz, which until then had almost always been associated when Shylock's fate was shown."[141] Paradoxically, therefore, the assumption was that the reference to Auschwitz required the reiteration of the iconic figure that had emerged from the history of anti-Semitism. The longevity of stage conventions is one explanation for this surprising response to Palitzsch's *Merchant*. In addition, in his traditional costume, Shylock remained a recognizable figure of the stage, a bogeyman (or victim) from ancient times, and thus located at a safe distance from the here and now of the performance and the actual relations towards the Jewish population in Germany.

It was indeed Shylock's topicality that was evoked by the article on rich Jews in the programme to Palitzsch's production. Authored by the German-American author Irene Dische, it focused on Jewish speculators in Frankfurt – the brothers Rosen, Simon Perel, Josef Orgler, Josef Buchmann, and Ignatz Bubis, who were described as a fairly homogenous group of Holocaust survivors with a Polish background. After the war, they had soon become rich. Dische gives a detailed account of the display of wealth at a Bar-Mitzwa celebration in West-Berlin, a level of prosperity that was allegedly based on the Jews' clever profiteering: aggressive real estate speculation. It was their childhood experiences in the camps, Dische suggests, that had prepared them for the harsh business world and made them immune to criticism. "In reality," Dische writes, "the newly rich Jews of Frankfurt were again the classical middlemen: they did the dirty work for the city and the banks, who profited from their willingness to take on bad publicity and financial risks. [...] After a while, the word 'speculator' had become synonymous with 'Jew' [...]." Clearly, Dische's article is characterized by the same ambivalence towards the rich Jews that she diagnoses for the West German society of the 1970s and early 1980s: "It was thought that the Jews were embarrassing and fascinating."[142]

---

140 Hans-Jörg Loskill, "Nur Wigger überzeugt als Shylock," *Westdeutsche Allgemeine Zeitung* (Essen), 14 October 1981.
141 Monschau, *Der Jude nach der Shoah*, 373.
142 Irene Dische, "Die reichen Juden in Deutschland," repr. in Schauspielhaus Düsseldorf, *Der Kaufmann von Venedig*, theatre programme (Düsseldorf, 1981), n. p. The text had originally been published in Hans Magnus Enzensberger's journal *TransAtlantik* 6 (1981): 14–25.

The Jewish community protested against this article in an open letter of 9 October 1981, signed by Werner Nachmann, then chairman of the Central Council of Jews in Germany, and addressed to Günther Beelitz, the artistic manager of the theatre. Nachmann criticized the implied comparison between Shylock and contemporary German Jews, which in his reading supported anti-Semitic stereotypes. "Did you want to inform your audience that one of the greatest playwrights in occidental history not merely captured the type of the Jew around 1600, but – with extensive prophetic anticipation and in a universally valid way – also the German Jew in the last third of the 20th century?"[143] Quite distinct from the position held by rabbi Emanuel Schereschewsky in the debate on Schenk's TV *Merchant* discussed above, the Jewish community refused to identify with Shylock and the notion of Jewish usury and economic unscrupulousness that he represented in Dische's reading. This was a different figure than the one Kortner and Schereschewsky had in mind: the disenfranchised outsider, the target of racist stereotyping, and a revenant of the victims of the Holocaust.

The conflict was ended when the contentious article was deleted from the programme and a brief explanatory statement added that the article's "general tenor could have led to unintentional anti-Semitic misunderstandings."[144] The affair does not merely reveal the inevitably political nature of every production, but it is also indicative of a new figuration of Shylock and the shift of emphasis to economic conflicts – an interpretation that had always been prevalent in East German responses to the play (see Chapter 3). This was supported by the new translation offered by Shakespeare scholar Klaus Reichert, which employed contemporary economic vocabulary. The translator's introduction to the play in the programme informed the spectator that the production intended to offer a new perspective that deviated from conventional approaches to Shylock:

> In 1905 Albert Bassermann in Max Reinhardt's production played Shylock as a villain; in 1943 Werner Krauss played him as a comical figure, evoking disgust; and after the war Ernst Deutsch and Fritz Kortner showed the oppressed creature. Today's interpretation will be based on the complete play and thematize the opposition Shylock/Antonio as a sign of a socio-economic contradiction.[145]

Palitzsch's production is an interesting example of the conflation of different discourses that are characteristic of *Merchant* in the 1980s. Without offering an

---

143 Werner Nachmann, "Warum? Offener Brief an den Intendanten des Düsseldorfer Schauspielhauses, Günther Beelitz," *Berliner Allgemeine jüdische Wochenzeitung*, 9 October 1981.
144 Qtd. in Monschau, *Der Jude nach der Shoah*, 375.
145 Klaus Reichert, "William Shakespeare: Der Kaufmann von Venedig," in Schauspielhaus Düsseldorf, *Der Kaufmann von Venedig*, theatre programme (Düsseldorf, 1981), n. p.

integration of these perspectives, it juxtaposed Holocaust remembrance, the psychological investigation of outsiders, and a new interest in what Reichert called the "socio-economic contradiction" at the core of the play. The production thus resonated with two influential and contradictory studies of *Merchant* and the Shylock figure which had been published in the second half of the 1970s: Hans Mayer's long chapter on Shylock in *Außenseiter* (1975; Engl. trans. *Outsiders*, 1982) and Christian Enzensberger's reading of *Merchant* in his monograph *Literatur und Interesse* (1977, "Literature and Interest"). Mayer was a Jewish remigrant, whose parents had been murdered in Auschwitz. Returning to Germany in 1945, he worked as a journalist before he was appointed Professor of Literary Studies at the University of Leipzig. In 1963, he left the GDR and became professor at Technical University Hannover two years later. Mayer's influential study took its point of departure from the alleged failure of the bourgeois Enlightenment. Focusing on three groups of 'existential' outsiders – women, homosexuals, and Jews – Mayer discusses processes of in- and exclusion, and their literary repercussions, since the Renaissance. Shylock is analysed as a figuration of the Jewish outsider in a secularised Europe, which – against its own claim – does not accept Jewish difference but uses it to justify the exclusion of Jews from full citizenship.[146] The focus on Shakespeare's *Merchant* also allows Mayer to explore the antagonism of the two outsiders of early modern Europe – Shylock the Jew and Antonio the homosexual,[147] who do not unite in "a community of outsiders."[148] Deviating from the Marxist emphasis on economy, Mayer agrees with Adorno that the "justifiable, often repeated, often merely formally made denunciation of social reification and self-alienation remains itself an expression of reification as long as the concrete suffering of the individual human being is set aside with an allusion to a whole humanity that must be saved."[149]

It seems as if Christian Enzensberger represented the kind of reasoning against which Mayer was writing. Christian Enzensberger, the brother of philosopher Hans Magnus Enzensberger, was Professor of English Literature at Ludwig Maximilians-Universität Munich. Informed by materialist interpretations of the play, not least by Marx's "On the Jewish Question" and his scattered references to Shylock in *Capital*, Enzensberger read *Merchant* as revolving around the economic changes occurring at the end of the feudalist period, most particularly

---

146 Hans Mayer, *Outsiders: A Study in Life and Letters*, trans. Denis M. Sweet (Cambridge, Mass.: MIT, 1982, pb. repr. 1984), 285. Mayer's more complex argument is developed in his long chapter on Shylock (267–395).
147 Cf. Mayer, *Outsiders*, 279–280.
148 Mayer, *Outsiders*, 401.
149 Mayer, *Outsiders*, 401.

the conflict between maritime trade and usury. For him, Shylock sought to resist the capitalist utopia of free exchange – not only of money and goods, but also of people – represented by the merchant Antonio. Adopting Marx's suggestion, Enzensberger regarded "the question of the racism of the play as solved," and described Shylock as an "embodiment of usury," since "Shylock's world is never extended into what is actually religious, nor into the Judaism of the Talmud."[150]

Both Mayer's and Enzensberger's readings of the play were frequently quoted in programmes to productions from the mid-1970s onward, even though Holocaust remembrance remained an important point of reference for directors, dramaturges, and critics alike. However, despite this continuity, there were some voices that pronounced a new era for German *Merchants*, in which the play could eventually be liberated from the legacy of the past.[151] One critic even suggested – in a more than unhappy phrasing – an end of the "forty-year close season" for post-war Shylocks, in which, allegedly, only Jewish actors like Deutsch and Kortner had been able to play a revengeful Jew.[152] Perhaps as a result of these shifts, the Shylocks of the late 1970s and 1980s lost the mythical grandeur of Kortner's and Deutsch's interpretations and became more human, psychologically 'round' characters.[153] This resulted in remarkable contradictions: between individualization and generalization, between Shylock's diverging roles as the target of racist discrimination and his economic agency, and between his figuration of Holocaust victims and his reference to Jews in contemporary post-war Germany.

Individual productions often highlighted one of these aspects without necessarily ignoring the others, but also without consciously addressing the tensions and contradictions. The Heilbronn *Merchant* (premiere: 9 January 1982) was a guest production by Jaroslav Gillar, a Czech who lived in Zurich. Gillar stressed the economic complications of the play in a show that paid deference to the

---

150 Christian Enzensberger, "Das Schöne im Warentausch: William Shakespeares *Kaufmann von Venedig*," in *Literatur und Interesse*, vol. 2 (Munich: Hanser, 1977), 29, 30.
151 They thus anticipated to some extent the arguments in the so-called 'Historians' Quarrel' of the late 1980s.
152 Wolfgang Butzlaff, "Kiel: Ein nachdenklicher 'Kaufmann von Venedig'," *Lübecker Nachrichten*, 17 April 1985.
153 The programme for the production at Badische Landesbühne (premiere: 6 October 1981) contained hypotheses on the psychological motivation of the characters, which were based on current debates in developmental psychology. Cf. Badische Landesbühne Bruchsal, "Einige Vorüberlegungen zur Inszenierung: Vor Probenbeginn," in *lb Texte: William Shakespeare: Der Kaufmann von Venedig. Eine Komödie*, theatre programme (Bruchsal, 1981/82), 19–22.

tradition of commedia dell'arte.¹⁵⁴ At Staatstheater Darmstadt (premiere: 13 June 1986) a voluminous programme contextualized the play through reference to the early modern debates on money economy, usury, maritime trade, and the Merchant Adventurers.¹⁵⁵ For director Jens Pesel these issues were closely connected with the topic of xenophobia – not least through Shylock's reference to slavery (in 4.1.89–97), which Pesel read as a comment on the early modern slave trade.¹⁵⁶ Economic conflicts were also underscored in the productions at Bremen (premiere: 20 January 1989, dir. Kurt Hübner) and Dortmund (premiere: 11 February 1989, dir. Annegret Ritzel). In contrast, Alfred Kirchner's *Merchant* at Residenztheater Munich (premiere: 13 January 1984) highlighted the outsider topic. Shylock and Antonio wore almost identical timeless costumes so that "Shylock's stigma was barely visible,"¹⁵⁷ as one critic wrote. The production revolved around the hatred between the two men, both outsiders and thus parallel figures – the Jew Shylock (Walter Schmidinger) and the homosexual Antonio (Martin Benrath). A *Merchant* in the spa-town of Baden-Baden in 1979 (premiere: 16 February 1979), a few years previously, had shown a gay Antonio, thereby leading to homophobic reactions. Referencing the TV-series *Holocaust* (and not the historical event!) in its title ("How about Shylock after 'Holocaust'?"), a reviewer criticized this production with reference to Stroux's 1957 *Merchant* in Düsseldorf. He stressed that in the 1950s, Deutsch's Shylock had convinced him that the play could indeed be played "after Auschwitz." Yet in the Baden-Baden production, he did not find anything of the "colourful and splendid world theatre" that had impressed him earlier. The production was described as "bad" and "inexcusable," and he bemoaned in particular the homoerotic subtext of the show:

> In the society around the beautiful Portia [...] the perfumed-effeminate affectation of the men is particularly revolting; camouflaged behind faddish fashions, partly fancy-dress ball, partly homoerotic display, it creates a bracing climate which has to be contradicted and denounced [...] in order to prevent the installation of certain forms of behaviour on the stage of the spa town.¹⁵⁸

---

154 Peter Sachse, "'Der Kaufmann von Venedig' als bunte Commedia dell'arte," *Heilbronner Stimme*, 11 January 1982.
155 Staatstheater Darmstadt, *Der Kaufmann von Venedig*, theatre programme (Darmstadt, 1986).
156 Interview with Jens Pesel, "Shylock ist in erster Linie Kaufmann," *Darmstädter Echo*, 28 May 1986.
157 Hans Krieger, "Melancholisches Märchen," *Nürnberger Nachrichten*, 16 January 1984.
158 Paul Hübner, "Wie steht es mit Shylock nach 'Holocaust'?," *Badisches Tagblatt* (Baden-Baden), 19 February 1979.

Holocaust remembrance was instrumentalized for conservative sexual politics or, more explicitly, the denunciation of male homosexuality. Until 1994, male homosexuality was a criminal act in the Federal Republic, according to Section 175 of the German Criminal Code. During the Nazi era, c. 10,000 homosexual men had been sent to concentration camps. After the war, paragraph 175, together with its Nazi amendments, was confirmed in West Germany and formed the basis for the persecution and conviction of tens of thousands of homosexual men. The paragraph was repealed in 1994, but it took German Parliament more than two further decades, until June 2017, to rehabilitate and compensate the victims of this law.[159]

In the mid-1980s, during the so-called 'AIDS crisis,' male homosexuality was a topic frequently addressed by the media, but we are not aware that this also impacted *Merchant* productions. Instead, two other controversies seem to have been more relevant, one of them being the so-called Bitburg incident. In May 1985, on the occasion of the fortieth anniversary of Germany's capitulation, Chancellor Helmut Kohl and the American President Ronald Reagan had planned to visit the military cemetery of Bitburg as a gesture of reconciliation, imitating the handshake of Kohl and the French President François Mitterand at Verdun in 1984. What at first appeared as a facile comparison of the First and the Second World Wars caused a massive national and international outcry, particularly in the US and among Holocaust survivors, when it became public that the cemetery also contained graves of men who had served in Hitler's Waffen-SS. Kohl insisted on the event, thus aggressively continuing his politics of 'normalization.' During a visit to the Knesset in January 1984, Kohl had offended his hosts when he claimed for himself the "blessing of late birth" ("Gnade der späten Geburt") with regard to the Holocaust, denying any personal guilt and proclaiming an unproblematic relationship between post-war Germany and Israel. This was in clear opposition to the gesture of former Chancellor Willy Brandt, who in 1970 had knelt before the memorial of the Warsaw Ghetto. The Bitburg controversy ended with what was less a compromise than a problematic equation of German soldiers and the victims of the Holocaust, when a visit to the former concentration camp of Bergen-Belsen was added to the schedule of Reagan's state visit. The event was discussed in the German media, with intellectuals like Jürgen Habermas and Günter Grass criticizing the visit, and conservative journals such as the *Frankfurter Allgemeine Zeitung* defending it. Surprising-

---

159 See e.g. Burkhard Jellonnek: *Homosexuelle unter dem Hakenkreuz: Die Verfolgung von Homosexuellen im Dritten Reich* (Paderborn: Schöningh, 1990); Clayton J. Whisnant, *Male Homosexuality in West Germany: Between Persecution and Freedom, 1945–69* (Basingstoke: Palgrave Macmillan, 2012).

ly, the Jewish community in Germany largely abstained from the debate. This would change considerably in another controversy.

1985 also saw the announcement of the premiere of *Der Müll, die Stadt und der Tod* ("Garbage, the City, and Death"), which had been planned for October at the theatre of Frankfurt (Main). It was a new play by film director Rainer Werner Fassbinder, loosely based on Gerhard Zwerenz's novel *Die Erde ist unbewohnbar wie der Mond* (1973; "The Earth is as Uninhabitable as the Moon"). The plot connected the topic of real estate speculation and modernization in the Frankfurt Westend with the situation of underprivileged social groups and left-wing protest in the aftermath of the students' revolts of the 1960s. The eleven scenes of Fassbinder's play revolve around the miseries of life in modern Western societies – a life associated with capitalist speculation, corrupt municipal authorities, and social outcasts like prostitutes, pimps, transvestites, and homosexuals. At the centre of the play is "The Rich Jew," a real estate investor, who is driven by his will to "revenge himself on the common people."[160] He thus embodies the ruthlessness and cynicism of the city, whose authorities protect him because he is a Jew, as he says. He becomes the client of Roma B., a prostitute, who suffers from consumption and is ill-treated by Franz B., her homosexual husband and pimp. "The Rich Jew" uses Roma in order to approach her father, Herr Müller, a singer in a transvestite bar, whom he suspects to be responsible for the death of his parents during the Holocaust. Müller is a self-declared "technocrat,"[161] who does not repent his crimes and anticipates the victory of fascism. The most explicit anti-Semitic ideas are voiced by Hans von Gluck, another businessman and a rival of "the Rich Jew." In a long monologue, he fantasizes about the death of "The Rich Jew" in the gas. At the end of the play, "The Rich Jew" gives in to Roma's demands, who is weary of life. He kills her but is protected by the corrupt police, who accuse Franz of the murder.

Written in 1975, *Der Müll, die Stadt und der Tod* was initially planned for performance at the avant-garde theatre TAT (Theater am Turm).[162] This never worked out, however, and Fassbinder left the theatre in July of the same year.[163] When

---

160 Rainer Werner Fassbinder, *Der Müll, die Stadt und der Tod. Nur eine Scheibe Brot* (Frankfurt/M.: Verlag der Autoren, 1998), 56.
161 Fassbinder, *Der Müll, die Stadt und der Tod*, 83.
162 For a detailed timeline of the controversy, see the appendix in Fassbinder, *Der Müll, die Stadt und der Tod*, 101–118.
163 In May 1976, *Schatten der Engel* (*Shadow of Angels*), the film adaptation of Fassbinder's play, directed by Daniel Schmid, was Germany's official contribution at the Cannes film festival. When the festival management refused to comply with the demand of the Israeli delegation to withdraw the film retroactively, the Israelis left under protest.

the text was brought out by the renowned Suhrkamp publishing house in 1976, it was immediately denounced as anti-Semitic – most prominently by critic Joachim Fest writing for the conservative newspaper *Frankfurter Allgemeine Zeitung*, who accused Fassbinder of "left-wing fascism."[164] Suhrkamp rejected the accusation but withdrew the book all the same. The play was republished in 1978, together with material on the controversy. Fassbinder had decided that the play should not be performed during his lifetime so that it was only in 1984, two years after his death, that the Schauspielhaus in Frankfurt considered a production directed by Palitzsch. Again, the idea was abandoned after a meeting with the Jewish community of Frankfurt. In 1985, after a few other failed initiatives to stage the play, the Schauspielhaus undertook a new attempt under its new director Günther Rühle. Surprisingly, this was the same Rühle who only one year previously, then as feuilleton editor for *Frankfurter Allgemeine Zeitung*, had written a scathing article against a planned performance at the newly renovated Alte Oper, the former opera house. Rühle had left the newspaper at the beginning of 1985.[165] His announcement to the press, in September 1985, that *Der Müll, die Stadt und der Tod* was considered for production, immediately sparked a heated debate. "The Rich Jew" was understood by many as a reference to Ignatz Bubis, a real estate investor in Frankfurt and a liberal politician, who would later become chairman of the Central Council of Jews in Germany. The play was interpreted as a critique of the same group of rich Jews in post-war Germany that Irene Dische had portrayed in her article for Palitzsch's production discussed above. As in Düsseldorf, the bone of contention was the stereotype of the 'rich Jew.' Seyla Benhabib has suggested that in addition, the Jewish community, yearning for middle-class normality in post-war Germany, resented the association with the play's social outcasts, with sexual deviancy and social destitution: "In the aftermath of the Holocaust, there is no glory in the kind of otherness that Fassbinder attributes to the Jews. There is no redemption through his ruthless critique of the normality into which they have fallen and within which they live in post-war Germany."[166]

Whereas the Jewish community as well as other organisations (including the Christian churches and the more conservative political parties) protested against the production, it was defended by leftist intellectuals and artists, who insisted upon the freedom of art. At the opening night, on 31 October 1985, the stage was

---

[164] Joachim Fest, "Reicher Jude von links," *Frankfurter Allgemeine Zeitung*, 19 March 1976.
[165] Cf. Andrei S. Markovits, Seyla Benhabib, and Moishe Postone, "Rainer Werner Fassbinder's *Garbage, the City and Death*: Renewed Antagonisms in the Complex Relationship between Jews and Germans in the Federal Republic of Germany," *New German Critique* 38 (1986): 9.
[166] Markovits, Benhabib, and Postone, "Rainer Werner Fassbinder's *Garbage*," 19.

occupied by the opponents of the production. A fervent discussion followed until the audience was eventually sent home. On 4 November a 'rehearsal' was shown to a select audience of media representatives, most of whom defended the production in their subsequent reviews. After an official letter of protest from the Knesset to the German government, a number of (unsuccessful) lawsuits against the theatre, and a petition of renowned theatre directors from all over Germany in support of the production, the theatre eventually announced to withdraw it for the time being. By the end of the 1980s, the debate had slowly died down.[167]

During the controversy, "The Rich Jew" was frequently compared to Shakespeare's Shylock. In an article for *Theater heute*, Peter von Becker suggested that Fassbinder, who had worked with Zadek in the latter's first season at the theatre of Bochum,[168] had designed "The Rich Jew" on the model of Zadek's/Mahnke's Shylock: "an agglomeration of man and monster," a "cliché." Although Fassbinder does not bear comparison with Shakespeare, von Becker argues, he employs the same strategy – namely the inclusion of the stereotype of the 'rich Jew' – to achieve the aesthetic and affective impact of his play.[169] The parallels between the two plays and the two Jewish figures were so apparent that critics of contemporaneous *Merchant* productions frequently referred to the Fassbinder controversy, while theatres initially sought to discourage comparison.

At the Landesbühne Hannover, where *The Merchant of Venice* (directed by Reinhold Rüdiger) premiered on 8 January 1986, the development of the controversy in parallel with the rehearsal period had apparently been followed with some anxiety. Since it was too late to postpone or cancel the production, it was decided to introduce the show with a prologue, spoken by the actor playing Shylock (Gerd Peiser).[170] "Esteemed audience," he began, "please don't take offence if we show Shylock as Shakespeare wrote him," and then stressed that

---

167 In the following years, some German theatres organized scenic readings and public discussions of *Der Müll, die Stadt und der Tod*. The play was eventually performed – for the first time on a German stage – in 2009 at the theatre of Mühlheim an der Ruhr.
168 In his autobiography, Zadek notes that the discussions on *Merchant* for the Bochum production in 1972 were the most interesting – due to the topical debates (including propaganda against Israel) and the people he had brought together at the theatre, "as for example Fassbinder and a few other anti-Semites" (*My Way*, 319).
169 Peter von Becker, "Fast verspielt: Das Theater als unmoralische Anstalt? Beobachtungen und Fragen zum Frankfurter Fassbinder-Streit," *Theater heute* 26.12 (1985): 6, 7.
170 See Landesbühne Hannover, *Der Kaufmann von Venedig*, theatre programme (Hannover, 1985/86), n. p.

the plot was prone to misunderstandings, due to the German past.[171] He asked the spectators to enjoy the play without prejudice because it was the aim of the comedy "to show human improvidence, hatred, and love."[172] Some reviews criticized the prologue as a wishy-washy statement in an overall complaisant production, which lacked the courage to thoroughly address a contentious topic. One critic assumed that through the prologue's reference to the Shakespearean 'original,' director Rüdiger had sought to re-invoke a prelapsarian state of innocence, which had irrevocably been lost – "after Auschwitz, after Frankfurt, [...] in January 1986."[173] The same triangulation of Auschwitz, the Frankfurt Fassbinder controversy, and *The Merchant of Venice* was repeated in many reviews on productions in the following year (in Darmstadt, Tübingen, and Moers).

The production at Landestheater Tübingen, which premiered a year after the Fassbinder controversy (12 September 1986, dir. Johannes Klaus), made the reference explicit, not merely in the programme, which focused on anti-Semitism, but also on stage, where Lancelot Gobbo quoted the Fassbinder controversy verbatim. Michael Wittenborn's Shylock seems to have been developed on the model of Kortner's.[174] But the references to the Holocaust were more pronounced than in the 1968 film: at the end of the trial scene, Shylock – speaking his "Nay, take my life and all" (4.1.369) – tore open his jacket, disclosing a Jew's badge and the striped shirt worn by concentration camp prisoners. The production was accompanied, on 6 October, by a panel discussion with the Jewish journalist Henryk M. Broder, who had been a major player in the Fassbinder controversy.[175] In a book-length study of the enduring force of anti-Semitism, entitled *Der ewige Antisemit* ("The Eternal Anti-Semite," 1986), Broder had launched an attack against what he saw as a new anti-Semitism of the left, disguised as anti-Zionism.[176]

---

[171] Qtd. in anon., "Tragische Elemente bestimmten Sinn der Komödie Shakespeares 'Kaufmann von Venedig in der Aula'," *Neustädter Zeitung*, 22 January 1986.
[172] Qtd. in anon., "Rüdigers Shylock kann nicht mehr mißbraucht werden," *Hannoversche Allgemeine Zeitung*, 22 January 1986; and anon., "'Der Kaufmann von Venedig' – ein Schauspiel in Vers und Prosa," *Helmstedter Blitz*, 12 February 1986.
[173] Hans-Christian Winters, "Frühshakespearesche Unschuld gibt es nicht mehr," *Göttinger Tageblatt*, 14 January 1986.
[174] Christoph Müller, "Tübingen: Vom Rialto direkt nach Auschwitz," *Theater heute* 27.11 (1986): 53–54.
[175] Cf. anon., "Shylock," *Schwäbisches Tagblatt Tübingen*, 3 October 1986.
[176] Due to Broder's personal accusations against his person, Rühle, the Frankfurt theatre manager, obtained an interim injunction against Broder's book.

More than a mere reference to the Frankfurt controversy, the Tübingen *Merchant* was framed and played as a counter-argument to Fassbinder's play. The same was true for the production in Moers, directed by Holk Freytag, where the premiere (on 21 November 1986) was preceded by a scenic reading of Jochen von Lang's documentation of the Jerusalem Eichmann trial, *Das Eichmann-Protokoll* (1983). Eichmann's proposition during the trial was spoken by the same actor that would also play Shylock, Hans-Christian Seeger. Following Zadek's take on the play, the Moers Shylock was also played as a "monster," speaking artificial Yiddish, and using the gestures that were common to the stage Jew.[177] Against the backdrop of the emerging Historians' Quarrel, the debate on the historical 'status' of the era of National Socialism and the Holocaust, and the latent anti-Semitism that had been diagnosed in the Fassbinder controversy, the production at Tübingen and Moers deliberately took sides and rejected any relativization of the Holocaust.

In conclusion, we would like to return to Peter von Becker's article on the Fassbinder controversy in *Theater heute*, which explores in detail the positions of the various actors in the controversy: the political superficiality and carelessness of the play's defenders; the Holocaust survivors' apodictic claim of being entitled to define anti-Semitism; the increasing self-confidence of the Jewish community in Frankfurt, which for the first time after the war successfully positioned itself in a political debate; the artists who insisted on the freedom of art and of expression; the personal feud between Rühle and Fest, former colleagues at *Frankfurter Allgemeine Zeitung*; and the hypocrisy of bourgeois critics of the play, who were eager to use the accusation of anti-Semitism for an attack on what they considered to be crude expressionism or even 'degenerate' modern art. The debate was therefore far more than a disagreement on the question of whether a second-rate play was anti-Semitic. Seyla Benhabib is thus right in arguing that *Der Müll, die Stadt und der Tod* was "not a social realistic play about the housing battles in Frankfurt. Rather, the play has become a metaphor for how, 40 years after the end of the Second World War, Germans and Jews understand the meaning of their past, how they remember it, and the images of self and other they're willing to live with."[178]

Although no post-war production of Shakespeare's *Merchant* had triggered such a vehement debate, the arguments pro and contra Fassbinder's play resonated with some of the discussions sketched in this chapter: the debate on art

---

177 Cf. Karen Giese, "Shylock als Projektion," *Rheinische Post*, 11 November 1986; Wolfgang Platzeck, "Blick durchs Teleobjektiv," *Westdeutsche Allgemeine Zeitung*, 25 November 1986.
178 Markovits, Benhabib, and Postone, "Rainer Werner Fassbinder's *Garbage*," 12.

and aesthetic conventions; the tension between freedom of expression and ethical obligations; the tendency to pit anti-Semitism, economic exploitation, and homophobia against each other; and the situation of German Jews in the majority society. In the 1980s, these frictions increasingly revolved around the figure of the 'rich Jew,' both Fassbinder's and Shakespeare's, and the question of how a Jewish figure can or should be played on the post-war German stage. In the debates on Shakespeare's Shylock from the 1960s to the 1980s, there was a tendency to accept, albeit willy-nilly, offensive Jewish characters if they were played by Jewish actors or if the production was directed by a Jew. This is perhaps one reason why von Becker concludes his article on the Fassbinder controversy with the suggestion that a more experienced director, with some standing, should produce the contentious play, and the names he mentions are Peter Zadek and George Tabori.[179] Neither of the two took on the challenge.

---

[179] Cf. von Becker "Fast verspielt," 9.

3 Inheriting a Classic: Configurations of *Merchant* in the German Democratic Republic (1949–1990)

On 17 March 1985, *The Merchant of Venice*, directed by Thomas Langhoff, premiered at Deutsches Theater in East Berlin. After *Merchants* in Weimar (1976), Greifswald (1978), Meiningen (1982), and Dresden (January 1985), this was only the fifth production of the play to be staged in the German Democratic Republic. Before German reunification in 1990, two further productions on GDR stages would follow: one in Nordhausen (1986), and one Leipzig (1988). Compared to the play's rich stage history in the Federal Republic, with around ninety productions before reunification, this reticence is remarkable. Director Fritz Bennewitz had first brought *Merchant* to East German stages with his Weimar production in 1976, and he returned to the play in September 1988. But it was Langhoff's 1985 Berlin *Merchant* that received the widest and most controversial media response, in both East and West Germany. Whereas West German reviews criticized what they saw as an unconvincing interpretation of the Shylock figure,[1] East German critics – despite some praise for the humanism and realism of the production[2] – detected anti-Semitic stereotypes and posed the old question of whether the play should be staged at all in (East) Germany.[3] This chapter will trace the developments that led to the confrontation between East and West over Shakespeare's play and the figure of Shylock at the centre of this controversy. This will include, firstly, a discussion of the possible reasons

---

[1] Michael Stone, "Nicht zu rechtfertigen. Premiere in Ost-Berlin: 'Der Kaufmann von Venedig'," *Der Tagesspiegel*, 24 March 1985; Gerhard Stadelmaier, "Kein Visum für Shylock: Thomas Langhoff inszeniert Shakespeare in Ost-Berlin," *Stuttgarter Zeitung*, 23 March 1985; Ernst Schumacher, "Gewagt, doch nicht gewonnen: Shakespeares 'Kaufmann von Venedig' im DT," *Berliner Zeitung*, 22 March 1985; Hartmut Krug, "Konflikte im Weichzeichner: Shakespeares 'Kaufmann von Venedig' in Ost-Berlin," *Zitty*, 7 June 1985.

[2] Gerhard Ebert, "Die humanistische Aussage eines klassischen Werkes neu entdeckt," *Neues Deutschland*, 23/24 March 1985; Jochen Gleiß, "Masken des Realen: Thomas Langhoff inszenierte Shakespeares 'Der Kaufmann von Venedig'," *Theater der Zeit* 6 (1985): 14–15. The weekly *Die Weltbühne* even featured a debate on *Merchant*, which was continued over three issues: Günther Cwojdrak, "Shakespeares Kaufmann, Barlachs Boll," *Weltbühne* 14 (2 April 1985): 426–428; Henryk Keisch, "Nochmals zum 'Kaufmann von Venedig'," *Weltbühne* 23 (4 June 1985): 716–718; Henryk Keisch, "Nochmals zum 'Kaufmann von Venedig' (II)," *Weltbühne* 24 (11 June 1985): 745–747.

[3] See e.g. Helmut Ullrich, "Da ist ein Mensch in seinem Widerspruch: Zu Shakespeares 'Kaufmann von Venedig'," *Neue Zeit*, 20 March 1985.

for the long absence of *The Merchant of Venice* from GDR stages. Secondly, we will discuss the three productions realized by Bennewitz and Langhoff, as well as the debates surrounding them, showing that throughout the four decades of the GDR's existence, *Merchant* was indeed considered a 'precarious' play.

Especially until the 1980s, East German responses differed considerably from those in the West. The discursive contexts in which *Merchant* was read comprised Marxist-Leninist interpretations of Shakespeare, the socialist approach to the 'classical heritage,' and the undeclared ban on *Merchant* in the Eastern bloc. This was complemented by the impact of the Cold War on the cultural sphere, by the political distance to the state of Israel, and the particular forms of remembering the Second World War in a self-declared anti-fascist state. As a consequence, East German scholarship on *Merchant* showed a tendency, widely unacknowledged, to disregard, or at least downplay, the figure of Shylock and its implications. Instead, it focused on the play's specific economic and political configurations – most notably on the early modern juxtaposition of feudalism and early capitalism, represented in the confrontation between Antonio and Shylock.

Before the 1980s, Holocaust remembrance was not only avoided, but was even declared a lamentable misreading of the play. When from the late 1970s the play appeared on the stage, the tensions between official ideology and theatre practice became apparent. Robert Weimann has suggested that "East German post-war theatre and criticism constituted a public site on which cultural communications inhabited an ambivalent space between political control and unorthodoxy, between ideological dogma and a search for a forceful, irrepressible performative."[4] As a result, in East German *Merchants* of the 1980s, the Shylock figure sometimes disrupted the economic configuration that was supposed to be at the centre of the respective production.

3.1 Shakespeare and the 'Classical Heritage'

After the war, theatres in the Eastern and Western zones of Germany almost invariably reopened with classical plays. As already mentioned in Chapter 1, this practice was initiated by Deutsches Theater Berlin under the management of Gustav von Wangenheim, a former Reinhardt actor and a Communist, who

---

[4] Robert Weimann, "Ideology and Performance in East German Versions of Shakespeare," in *Shakespeare in the Worlds of Communism and Socialism*, ed. Irena R. Makaryk and Joseph G. Price (Toronto: University of Toronto Press, 2006), 346.

had left Germany in 1933 and gone into exile in the Soviet Union. *Nathan the Wise*, directed by Fritz Wisten,[5] premiered on 7 September 1945; it was followed, on 11 December, by *Hamlet*, directed by von Wangenheim himself. This *Hamlet* developed the conventional conception of the Danish Prince as an allegory of Germany facing a time 'out of joint.' But what on the surface looked like a continuation of pre-war traditions was in fact a contradictory response to the historical moment, featuring a mixed cast of actors and actresses, from former stars of the National Socialist stage to opponents and exiles. Maik Hamburger underscores the incongruous nature of the production, which picked up "the threads of liberal discourse of the 1920s, as though nothing had occurred in between," but on the other hand was also motivated by an evident "desire for a radically new start with a socialist perspective."[6] Indeed, von Wangenheim's *Hamlet* anticipated aspects that would become characteristic of Shakespeare productions in the German Democratic Republic. Seeking to awaken "new hopes for the future," thus "spurring people to activity," von Wangenheim stressed both Hamlet's "will to change historical circumstances by action" and Fortinbras's continuation of "Hamlet's historical mission."[7]

Almost two decades later, von Wangenheim's dramaturge, Armin-Gerd Kuckhoff, compiled a voluminous monograph on Shakespeare's plays: *Das Drama William Shakespeares* (1964). At that time, Kuckhoff was director of the Theatre College Leipzig and a member of the executive committees of the Federation of Theatre Professionals of the GDR (Verband der Theaterschaffenden der DDR) and of the German Shakespeare Society. Published in the year of the quatercentenary of Shakespeare's birth, and immediately after the separation of the German Shakespeare Society into an Eastern and a Western branch, it was the first comprehensive Marxist-Leninist analysis of Shakespeare's dramatic

---

5 Wisten, an Austrian Jew, had worked as an actor and director in Stuttgart until he was banned from the stage in March 1933. He joined the newly established Jüdischer Kulturbund (Cultural Federation of Jews) and worked as a director at its Berlin theatre. During the November pogroms of 1938, he was arrested but released after three days with the order to continue his work at the theatre. In 1941, the Jüdischer Kulturbund was dissolved and most of its members were deported. Because of his non-Jewish wife, Wisten escaped deportation and survived. See *Fritz Wisten: Drei Leben für das Theater: Stuttgart 1919–1933. Jüdischer Kulturbund 1933–1941. Berlin 1945–1962*, ed. Akademie der Künste Berlin (Berlin: Hentrich, 1990).
6 Maik Hamburger, "Shakespeare on the Stages of the German Democratic Republic," in Wilhelm Hortmann, *Shakespeare on the German Stage: The Twentieth Century* (Cambridge: Cambridge University Press, 1998), 372.
7 Hamburger, "Shakespeare on the Stages," 370–371. See also Lawrence Guntner, "In Search of a Socialist Shakespeare: *Hamlet* on East German Stages," in *Shakespeare in the Worlds of Communism and Socialism*, ed. Makaryk and Price, esp. 179–180.

oeuvre for a German readership. Kuckhoff reads Hamlet as a man at the turn of two epochs, who "[i]n the name of his humanist ideas [...] has to oppose the old disappearing order, which dissolves in cynicism, egotism, immorality, a chaotic struggle of all against all, in rebellions and intrigues."[8] This was also Shakespeare's own perspective, Kuckhoff argues. Even though Shakespeare was not a revolutionary and never addressed the class struggle explicitly, his plays were both progressive and popular, in the sense of being connected to the people – hence the eminent role Kuckhoff ascribes to Shakespeare as a precursor of socialist art. In particular, Kuckhoff praises Shakespeare's embracement of dramatic realism: "not a static image of an unchanging state of things but the artist's struggle with the problems of a continually changing reality."[9] He finds this realism summarized in Hamlet's admonition to the players that the purpose of acting "is to hold as 'twere a mirror up to nature [...] and the very nature of the time his form and pressure" (3.2.20 – 22).[10] Kuckhoff concludes his *Hamlet* chapter with a brief comment on von Wangenheim's 1945 production, which, he contends, showed

> what strong and positive impulses [...] can emanate from a correct production of *Hamlet*, in line with Shakespeare's intentions [...]. The democratic regeneration [*Erneuerung*] could only be realized through the collective social practice of everyone and the social awareness of all those truly interested in the reorganization.[11]

Shakespeare appears as a founding father of the GDR, "risen from ruins / And facing the future," as the first lines of the national anthem of the GDR read.

The East German approach to Shakespeare – as well as to other 'classics' such as Goethe, Schiller, Lessing or Herder – was based on the concept of 'heritage' (*Erbe*), which had developed in Marxist thought since the 1930s. A theoretical basis for this was provided by Marx's introduction to his *Eighteenth Brumaire of Louis Bonaparte* (1852), especially the insistence on the historicity of human practice and the laws of historical development. The assumption was that all great artists, disregarding their respective class backgrounds, captured the

---

[8] Armin-Gerd Kuckhoff, *Das Drama William Shakespeares* (Berlin: Henschel, 1964), 257.
[9] Kuckhoff, *Drama*, 23.
[10] Similar ideas were voiced by Shakespeareans in the Soviet Union; see e.g. Alexander Anikst, "Shakespeare – A Writer of the People" (1959), in *Shakespeare in the Soviet Union: A Collection of Articles*, ed. Roman Samarin and Alexander Nikolyukin, trans. Avril Pyman (Moscow: Progress Publishers, 1966), 113 – 139. See also Robert Weimann, "A Divided Heritage: Conflicting Appropriations of Shakespeare in (East) Germany," in *Shakespeare and National Culture*, ed. John J. Joughin (Manchester: Manchester University Press, 1997), 181 – 182.
[11] Kuckhoff, *Drama*, 277.

conflicts of their times as well as the progressive forces generating social change.¹² A teleological narrative established a connection between the dissolution of feudal bonds in the sixteenth century and the emergence of capitalism, the Enlightenment, the bourgeois revolutions, and, eventually, socialism. The concept of 'heritage,' in stark contrast to that of 'tradition' in the West, proposed not merely a conscious recognition of works of art that supported this continuity between past, present, and future. 'Heritage' also implied a historical subject, preserving it and profiting from it. Karl Robert Mandelkow has described the term as a "Kampfbegriff" ("discursive weapon") against bourgeois art, a weapon

> which includes a specific subject of inheritance, the working class, and thus, on the basis of an almost strictly juridical use of the legal term, refers to the exclusive claim of this heir to the heritage. 'Heritage,' in this sense, signifies ownership, and it is the prerogative of that class to whom the historical perspective of the future belongs to claim ownership.¹³

In his article on 'heritage' in the 1970 issue of *Shakespeare Jahrbuch*,¹⁴ Kuckhoff underscores the innovative quality of such an approach. By treating Shakespearean drama as heritage, he claims, GDR theatres have opened up new layers of meaning without succumbing to the dangers of "pseudo-actualization" and the "depersonalization of the human being" into a passive object of history, which allegedly characterized theatre productions in the FRG.¹⁵ The phrasing draws attention to the divergent concepts of dramatic character in East and West Germany. Whereas in the West, from the late 1960s onwards, directors like Tabori, Zadek, and others sought to deconstruct the Shylock figure, and explore its potentials and limits, East German productions were supposed to

---

12 Anselm Schlösser concludes his *Shakespeare: Analysen und Interpretationen* (Berlin: Aufbau-Verlag, 1977) with a chapter on Shakespeare as an anticipatory thinker (459–494).
13 Karl Robert Mandelkow, "Die literarische und kulturpolitische Bedeutung des Erbes," in *Die Literatur der DDR*, ed. Hans-Jürgen Schmitt (München: dtv, 1983), 78. Kuckhoff describes the "attitude to heritage [...] as a means in the struggles of the present" ("Erbe – Gegenwart – Prognose," *Shakespeare Jahrbuch* 106 [1970]: 34). See also Michael D. Richardson, *Revolutionary Theater and the Classical Heritage: Inheritance and Appropriation from Weimar to the GDR* (Bern: Peter Lang, 2007).
14 We do not adopt the title *Shakespeare Jahrbuch Ost* ("East") for the yearbook published by the society based in Weimar. Indeed, their claim to the title of Deutsche Shakespeare-Gesellschaft with the *Shakespeare Jahrbuch* as their yearbook was legally correct. The society's counterpart in West Germany (Deutsche Shakespeare-Gesellschaft West) was founded only after the separation, hence the title of their yearbook: *Shakespeare Jahrbuch* (West). For a historical account of the separation, see Ruth von Ledebur, *Deutsche Shakespeare-Rezeption seit 1945* (Frankfurt/M.: Akademische Verlagsgesellschaft, 1974), 129–142.
15 Kuckhoff, "Erbe," 40, 45–46.

follow the anti-experimental principles of Socialist Realism and render psychologically credible characters, representing their respective class. Shylock, however, certainly did not lend himself to being the hero of socialist art, "depict[ing] reality in its revolutionary development."[16]

Kuckhoff's statement also demonstrates that, in the context of the Cold War, the contemporary stage and the idea of dramatic character were construed as forming an ideological battlefield, on which the inheritance battle was fought. There is a certain irony to the fact that the German Democratic Republic should have appropriated one of the most important writers of the Western canon for the cultural policy of a socialist state. Paradoxically, the political invocation of Shakespeare as the champion of a socialist future was embedded in a conservative cult of the classics. This cult was explicitly opposed to the proletarian and avant-garde art of the Weimar Republic, denounced as 'formalism,' as well as to the artistic experiments of Western postmodernity. Consequently, from the late 1960s onwards, the East German museumization of the classics was criticized by left-wing Western artists and intellectuals as an indicator of the thoroughly bourgeois nature of GDR 'socialism.'[17] And yet, as Robert Weimann has convincingly argued, the East German insistence on the cultural and political functions of the Shakespearean stage, as well as the attempt to gauge the relevance of early modern drama for the present anticipated (and later shared) some concerns with New Historicism and Cultural Materialism. To a certain extent, therefore, and despite its otherwise conservative tendencies, GDR Shakespeare Studies was closer to the new paradigms in the international Shakespeare scholarship of the 1980s than the philological focus on Shakespeare's works that dominated West German publications of the period.[18]

The quatercentenary in 1964 was turned into a major national celebration of Shakespearean heritage. Already in 1963, a committee in charge of the preparation of the festivities had been established, with more than fifty members stemming from politics, the theatre, and academia. The programme included an eight-day academic conference at Weimar (19 to 27 April), with a festive ceremony and a concert, around eighty stage productions throughout the GDR, exhibi-

---

16 Maxim Gorky, qtd. in Brandon Taylor, "Socialist Realism: 'To depict reality in its revolutionary development'," in *Adventures in Realism*, ed. Matthew Beaumont (Hoboken: Wiley, 2008), 142–157.
17 Cf. Mandelkow, "Die literarische und kulturpolitische Bedeutung," 79–80.
18 Weimann, "A Divided Heritage," 193.

tions, and a *festschrift* edited by the Shakespeare scholar Anselm Schlösser.[19] The opening lecture at the Weimar conference, which was broadcast on radio and TV, was held by Alexander Abusch, the Minister of Culture. Summarizing the official approach to Shakespeare, Abusch celebrated Shakespeare as a realist and humanist, and criticized productions in the Federal Republic – most notably a *King Lear* at Bochum, in the tradition of the Theatre of the Absurd – as driven by "irrealism," "anti-humanism," "nihilism," and "late-bourgeois decadence."[20] Shakespeare was called upon as a brother in arms in the Cold War.

It must be pointed out, however, that the approach to Shakespeare in the German Democratic Republic was never monolithic. Indeed, Socialist Realism as it had developed in the Soviet Union on the model of the nineteenth-century novel was constantly clashing with the tradition of the Weimar avant-garde and the principles of Brechtian theatre, which proved to be surprisingly persistent even though they were not officially supported.[21] Furthermore, there was a tension between performance and ideology, which has been explored by Robert Weimann in his seminal study *Shakespeare and the Popular Tradition in the Theatre* (1976; German original 1967). Referring to the early modern theatre, but with obvious implications for East German Shakespeare productions, Weimann explores the way in which performance could challenge "the authority of any attempt to validate a particular signification in a given historical situation."[22] In addition, the German Democratic Republic was never isolated from debates in the West, nor did cultural politics remain constant throughout the four decades of its existence. The late 1960s and early 1970s marked a period of cultural and political change also in East Germany.[23] When, in 1971, Erich Honecker won the power struggle with Walter Ulbricht and became General Secretary of the Central Committee of the SED (Socialist Unity Party), he

---

19 Anselm Schlösser (ed.), *Shakespeare-Jubiläum: Festschrift zu Ehren des 400. Geburtstages William Shakespeares und des 100jährigen Bestehens der Deutschen Shakespeare-Gesellschaft* (Weimar: Hermann Böhlaus Nachfolger, 1964).
20 Alexander Abusch, *Shakespeare: Realist und Humanist, Genius der Weltliteratur* (Berlin: Aufbauverlag, 1964), 35, 36.
21 Weimann, "A Divided Heritage," 189.
22 Lawrence Guntner, "Introduction. Shakespeare in East Germany: Between Appropriation and Deconstruction," in *Redefining Shakespeare: Literary Theory and Theater Practice in the German Democratic Republic*, ed. Lawrence Guntner and Andrew M. McLean (Newark: University of Delaware Press / London: Associated University Presses, 1998), 41. See also Weimann, "Ideology and Performance," 341.
23 Mandelkow, "Die literarische und kulturpolitische Bedeutung," 105.

proclaimed a new openness in the fields of literature and art.[24] After a decade in which the so-called 'Bitterfelder Weg' ('The Bitterfeld Way')[25] had obliged writers to address the needs of the working class – not least by working in factories themselves and by supporting workers in their artistic production, the aesthetic dimension of art (in addition to its ideological function) was acknowledged for the first time, and artists were encouraged to explore the conflicts and contradictions of reality.[26] However, the forced expatriation of poet and singer-songwriter Wolf Biermann, who, in 1976, after a tour in the Federal Republic, was not re-admitted into the GDR and was deprived of his citizenship, revealed the difference between political theory and practice. The measure initiated a new phase of reprisals against critical artists and eventually prompted a veritable wave of emigration. It was only in the 1980s that a new openness to and eager reception of theoretical debates in the West became really palpable. This was also the time when the German Shakespeare Society based at Weimar started to invite British and American Shakespeareans (among them Susan Bassnett, Walter Cohen, John Drakakis, Stephen Greenblatt, Graham Holderness, Murray Krieger, and Kiernan Ryan) to their annual meetings, which attracted large numbers of scholars, students, teachers, and other Shakespeare aficionados.[27] Weimann asserts that this interest in international (i. e. Western) Shakespeare Studies was at least partly due to their relevance for "indigenous needs and problems,"[28] including the precarious relationship between art and political power.

The theatre did indeed play an important political function in the German Democratic Republic – a function that was not merely, and perhaps not even primarily, confined to reproducing the dominant ideology. More importantly, the theatre has been described as one of the few social arenas that functioned as a "public sphere," which otherwise did not exist in the GDR.[29] The ephemeral

---

[24] Erich Honecker, "Für das Wohl des arbeitenden Menschen all unsere Kraft: Bericht des Zentralkomitees an den VIII. Parteitag der Sozialistischen Einheitspartei Deutschlands, 15. bis 19. Juni 1971," in *Reden und Aufsätze*, vol. 1 (Berlin: Dietz Verlag, 1975), 198.
[25] Bitterfeld is an industrial town in the federal state of Saxony-Anhalt. The term 'Bitterfelder Weg' goes back to a conference of writers, at the Electrochemical State Combine Bitterfeld, on 24 April 1959.
[26] Otto F. Riewoldt, "Theaterarbeit: Über den Wirkungszusammenhang von Bühne, Dramatik, Kulturpolitik und Publikum," in *Die Literatur der DDR*, ed. Hans-Jürgen Schmitt (Munich: dtv, 1983), 171.
[27] The reports on the Weimar conferences in *Shakespeare Jahrbuch* speak of 1,200 to 1,500 participants annually.
[28] Weimann, "A Divided Heritage," 194.
[29] Lawrence Guntner, "Preface," in *Redefining Shakespeare*, ed. Guntner and McLean, 13; and Guntner, "In Search of a Socialist Shakespeare," 177. Guntner's argument is echoed by Weimann

nature of a stage production was more difficult to control than radio, TV, or the print media. Direct censorship was rare, but theatres had to have their annual repertoires approved of by the Ministry for Culture so that in many cases potentially contentious productions would have been avoided as a form of self-censorship.[30] Dramaturges, supporting directors in realizing their (ideologically correct) productions, were also in charge of putting together and documenting the concept of the respective production, which would be submitted to the Ministry with the request for approval.[31] Yet, although as academics dramaturges were very close "to the institutionalized apparatus of doctrinaire ideology," their approach had to be negotiated in their interaction with theatre people, who, "thanks to the symbolically encoded order of their work, enjoyed a much greater margin of experimentation and unorthodoxy."[32]

Once it had been given green light, a play would make its way to the stage. Sometimes a production was indeed stopped after a few shows,[33] but these were rare cases. Indeed, from the 1950s to reunification, Shakespeare was repeatedly staged not only to reiterate, but also to challenge the hegemonic approach to the classics and GDR cultural politics. Examples range from Heinar Kipphardt's satire on cultural bureaucracy, *Shakespeare dringend gesucht* ("Desperately Seeking Shakespeare"), which premiered at Deutsches Theater Berlin on 28 June 1953, to a number of "subversive Shakespeare"[34] productions in the 1960s and 1970s, and Heiner Müller's seminal *Hamletmaschine* (1979) and *Hamlet/Maschine* (1990), the latter of which responded to the end of the GDR.

3.2 Absent Shylocks

Whereas *Hamlet* was a crucial play for the negotiation of the German reception of Shakespeare, the classical heritage, and the role of the theatre in a socialist state, *Merchant* is just as interesting for the extent to which it was ignored or,

---

in "Ideology and Performance," 332. A similar argument is also made by Riewoldt, "Theaterarbeit," 135.
30 In 1973, a subdivision, the Direktion für Bühnenrepertoire was introduced as the authority in charge of theatre repertoires. Cf. Guntner, "In Search of a Socialist Shakespeare," 177.
31 Cf. Eva Walch, "Dramaturgische Blicke auf zwei Inszenierungen von Thomas Langhoff am Deutschen Theater," *Shakespeare Jahrbuch* 140 (2004): 154–155.
32 Weimann, "Ideology and Performance," 331.
33 Alfred Dresen's *Hamlet* at Greifswald in 1964 was taken off the programme after twelve performances and was criticized as an instance of "left-wing radicalism" (Guntner, "In Search of a Socialist Shakespeare," 186).
34 Gunter, "Introduction," 43.

rather, consciously avoided. This is true not only for the German Democratic Republic, but also for the whole Eastern Bloc between 1945 and c. 1990.³⁵ With respect to the Soviet Union, Mark Sokolyansky even calls *Merchant* a "half-forbidden play." He explains:

> If earlier *The Merchant of Venice* was not recommended for production as an "anti-Semitic play," since the late 1940s, when anti-Semitism became an essential component of the state politics, the play began to be even more persistently alienated because the words "Jew" and "Hebrew" are used in its text too often and not always with a negative connotation. Soviet ideologists feared that free interpretations of the play could be comprehended as a *sui generis* apology of ethnical Jews.³⁶

It can be assumed that this rejection of the play in Soviet cultural politics was one of the main reasons for its subsequent neglect in the German Democratic Republic (as well as in other countries in Eastern Europe), although we are not aware of any historical documents that explicitly acknowledge the impact of Stalinist anti-Semitism on the reception of *Merchant* in East Germany. On the contrary, most scholars reiterated the argument that productions of the play might rekindle latent anti-Semitism. In his 1964 monograph, Kuckhoff claims that a play about a money-lending Jew, in a world where anti-Semitism is still existent, would be challenging for any theatre:

> The theatre has to ask itself whether it can trust its audience, whether it can guarantee that a production does not awake the remnants of anti-Jewish resentments, the very resentment that has been bred for several centuries. Only those are entitled to this glorious play by Shakespeare, the great humanist, who have 'clean hands' that are not stained by the blood, the thousandfold murder, of defenceless Jews; only those who have not gambled away the grace to claim this play their own.³⁷

Apparently, the caveat was read by most theatre practitioners as it was intended: that the play was taboo because the Shylock figure was too precarious. In his

---

35 Boika Sokolova, in an unpublished paper ("'Mingled Yarn': Perspectives on *The Merchant of Venice* in East European Contexts") given at the World Shakespeare Conference 2016 at Stratford-upon-Avon, counted merely seven productions of the play between 1945 and 1989, in addition to the seven productions in the GDR: three in Hungary, two in Poland, one in Bulgaria, and one in Serbia. After the Revolution of 1917, the play disappeared from Russian stages; Mark Sokolyansky lists one production in Estonia in 1958 and one in Georgia in 1984; cf. his "The Half-Forbidden Play in Soviet Shakespeare Criticism of the 1920s–50s," *Multicultural Shakespeare: Translation, Appropriation and Performance* 6/7 (2010): 77, accessed 8 September 2018, http://dspace.uni.lodz.pl:8080/xmlui/handle/11089/1508
36 Sokolyansky, "The Half-Forbidden Play," 75.
37 Kuckhoff, *Drama*, 528.

historiographical account of "Shakespeare on the Stages of the German Democratic Republic," Maik Hamburger also speaks of the "odium of anti-Semitism" with which *Merchant* was "burdened" in East Germany.[38] It seems that some did not understand the undeclared ban, or refused to accept it. According to Hamburger, there were a few initiatives to stage the play in the 1960s – among others by Wolfgang Langhoff at Deutsches Theater in 1962. But most directors and theatre managers, Hamburger assumes, would not even have tried to put the play on. The actual reasons for this self-censorship are difficult to gauge, and Hamburger bases his own account on oral information given to him in conversations and interviews.[39] In our archival research we have come across the unpublished correspondence between the translator Rudolf Schaller and the Akademie der Künste der DDR (Academy of the Arts of the GDR), who were paying him a monthly allowance for his translation of Shakespeare plays into German. He was requested to submit quarterly reports on the progress of his work. In three of his letters to the Academy – of 12 March, 17 July and 7 December 1959 – Schaller informed his patrons that he was working on a translation of *Merchant*, which would be staged by the Theatre of Zwickau in a production directed by Gerhard Erfurt and scheduled for 3 March 1960.[40] The December letter was the last time Schaller mentioned this production.

In the following year, however, it was not *Merchant* that premiered in Zwickau but a popular Chinese play entitled *Hirse für die Achte* ("Millet for the Eighth [People's Army]"), on 21 April, directed by the same director that Schaller had mentioned in his letter. The German translation of *Hirse für die Achte* had premiered in 1954 at the Berliner Ensemble and was broadcast in the same year on East German television. It is not clear what happened to the Zwickau *Merchant*. A simple explanation would be that Schaller, who was apparently suffering from health problems, was just taking too long to complete his translation. However, given the reservation to *Merchant* in the German Democratic Republic at least until the mid-1970s, it is just as possible (and even more probable) that the Theatre of Zwickau's annual repertoire for 1960 was rejected by the authorities, leaving them eager to look for a replacement for the conten-

---

38 Hamburger, "Shakespeare on the Stages," 421.
39 Maik Hamburger, "Unser Shakespeare – Ein Judenfeind? *Der Kaufmann von Venedig* auf den Bühnen der DDR," in *Shylock nach dem Holocaust: Zur Geschichte einer deutschen Erinnerungsfigur*, ed. Zeno Ackermann and Sabine Schülting (Berlin: De Gruyter, 2011), 85–86.
40 Letter by Rudolf Schaller to Gert Hillesheim, Deutsche Akademie der Künste, Sektion Dichtkunst und Sprachpflege (Academy of Arts, Section Literature and Language), 7 December 1959, unpublished typescript, in "Vorgänge um Shakespeare-Übersetzung von Rudolf Schaller," Archiv der Akademie der Künste Berlin, AdK-O 0858.

tious Shakespeare comedy, for a play that would be both ideologically safe and popular with the audience.

Adel Karasholi's response to Bennewitz's Weimar production of 1976 suggests another reason for the scarcity of *Merchants* on East German stages.⁴¹ In an article entitled "Die Figur des Shylock in heutiger Sicht" ("The Figure/Character of Shylock from a Contemporary Perspective"), Karasholi reiterates the dominant approach to Shylock in the Eastern Bloc, proposing that with this figure, Shakespeare did not intend to represent "a member of a suppressed minority but rather the *type* of a usurer."⁴² Like others before him, Karasholi supports this claim with the standard argument that there were no Jews in Shakespearean England. He is well aware that the two approaches to Shylock are mutually exclusive. In order for the figure to typify the cruelty of early modern capitalism, Shylock's representation as a victim of Venetian anti-Semitism in the trial scene must be excluded: "Sympathy with his plight [...] must not deceive us about the basic character of the figure as a usurer, as a capitalist, whose action is dominated by his pursuit of money."⁴³

Karasholi quotes Kuckhoff's admonition to theatres, but then stresses that it is "difficult to imagine that in the GDR of today, there are any remnants of anti-Semitic race-baiting which could be evoked in a production of the play."⁴⁴ For Karasholi, a new problem was much more urgent, represented in particular by the older generation. It is not their latent anti-Semitism, he writes, but, on the contrary, their philo-Semitism that is problematic against the backdrop of the contemporary conflict between Israel and Palestinians:

> particularly with people belonging to the middle or older generations, one still encounters great difficulties in making them comprehend the question of Palestine from a class perspective. It is not infrequently that a necessary, a class-specific view remains inaccessible to them, and this is because of their universal, unhistorical, and purely emotional attitude towards this problem. Whenever they cannot find any counter-arguments, they ask: Why don't the Arabs let the Jews, who have suffered so much, live in peace!⁴⁵

---

41 Poet, essayist, and translator Adel Karasholi was born in Dasmaskus in 1936. He went into exile when the Union of Arabic Writers was banned in 1959, and eventually settled in Leipzig. From 1969 to 1993, he taught at the University of Leipzig.
42 Adel Karasholi, "Die Figur des Shylock in heutiger Sicht," *Shakespeare Jahrbuch* 113 (1977): 64; emphasis added.
43 Karasholi, "Die Figur des Shylock," 67.
44 Karasholi, "Die Figur des Shylock," 64.
45 Karasholi, "Die Figur des Shylock," 64–65.

Karasholi continues with a brief excursus to Fritz Kortner's TV-version of Shylock, which we have discussed in the previous chapter. This Shylock had corroborated the famous verdict invoked by Heinrich Heine: "The poor man is wronged." It is perfectly possible, Karasholi admits, that such a view of the character may express a sincere humanism. Nevertheless, he adds that more often than not in the Federal Republic, it has been manipulated for the purposes of imperialist propaganda: "They mystify anti-Semitism and thus try to eventually distract from the deep causes of the emergence of fascism as a specific form of imperialism, which is the very precondition of such race-baiting."[46]

Karasholi's article corroborates Sokolyansky's assumption that, besides the explicit anti-Israeli stance of the 1960s and 1970s, it was also Soviet and East German anti-Semitism that was at the base of the ban on *Merchant* in the Eastern Bloc. Impacted by the anti-Semitic purges in the Stalinist USSR, the early GDR had also witnessed the marginalization of Jewish victims of National Socialism, who soon after the war were relegated to a rank lower than that of the communist "*fighters* against fascism." In addition, up to the mid-1950s, prominent members of Jewish communities and those speaking up in favour of Jewish survivors faced accusations of being imperialist or Zionist agents. They were excluded from the socialist party, and were threatened with persecution and imprisonment so that many fled to West Germany.[47] For Jeffrey Herf,

> [t]he marginalization and forgetting of the Jewish catastrophe in postwar East Germany was due to a combination of long-dominant traditions of Marxist-Leninism, the interaction of German nationalism and German communism, and Stalin's and East German Stalinists' use of the Jewish question to tar opponents with the brush of disloyalty in the early years of the Cold War.

The Holocaust was not forgotten, but it was relegated to the "margins of East Germany's official anti-fascist political culture."[48] On the international arena, the GDR rejected US and Israeli demands for financial 'compensation' of Jewish survivors with the argument that the anti-fascist state of the GDR was not the legal successor of Nationalist Socialist Germany. This policy would not change

---

46 Karasholi, "Die Figur des Shylock," 65.
47 See Annette Leo, "Als antifaschistischer Staat nicht betroffen? Die DDR und der Holocaust," in *Deutschland, Israel und der Holocaust: Zur Gegenwartsbedeutung der Vergangenheit*, ed. Bernd Faulenbach and Helmuth Schütte (Essen: Klartext, 1998), 95. According to Leo, 500 Jewish citizens left the GDR in the years 1952–1953. See also Jeffrey Herf, *Divided Memory: The Nazi Past in the Two Germanys* (Cambridge, MA: Harvard University Press, 1997), 69–161. According to Herf, only 4,500 Jewish survivors were staying in the Soviet zone of occupation in 1945 (70).
48 Herf, *Divided Memory*, 157–158, 161.

fundamentally until the 1980s, even though the Eichmann trial in Jerusalem (1961) brought the Holocaust back into public debate.⁴⁹

The considerable ideological shift between the 1960s and the 1970s becomes apparent when Kuckhoff's and Karasholi's discussions of *Merchant* are compared. In 1964, Kuckhoff argued that the play, whose primary conflict he identified as being the economic opposition between Antonio and Shylock, had been misread because Shakespeare had designed one of the antagonists as a Jew. Kuckhoff continued:

> The confusion of interpretation is understandable because of the particular political and human accentuation that the Jewish problem has received in the history of Europe. When we think of Shylock, the thousandfold, millionfold disaster that race-baiting and Christian fanaticism has inflicted on Jews, again and again (to the ultimate horror, augmented to a barely comprehensible excess by the fascist 'final solution of the Jewish question,' the most cruelly organised pogrom that world history has witnessed) cannot be banned from the mind and the heart.⁵⁰

A mere decade later, Karasholi relativized the impact of the Holocaust on any reading and future production of *Merchant*. In the 1970s, Holocaust remembrance through the figure of Shylock was potentially suspect of imperialist and Zionist ideology.

3.3 Fritz Bennewitz's *Merchants* at Weimar (1976) and Leipzig (1988)

When, in the mid-1970s, the eminent East German Shakespearean Anselm Schlösser published his essay on "Dialectic in *The Merchant of Venice*,"⁵¹ he omitted all references to twentieth-century politics. Schlösser focused on the dialectical structure of the play – the relations between Venice and Belmont, Shylock and Antonio, usury and humanity, and comedy and tragedy. Deviating from the two traditions represented by Kuckhoff and Karasholi respectively, Schlösser marginalizes Shylock's Jewishness, and the Shylock figure in general, by describing him as a mere type that shows Calvinist traits: he is a miser, and

---

49 Cf. Leo, "Als antifaschistischer Staat nicht betroffen?," 98–99.
50 Kuckhoff, *Drama*, 527.
51 The article was first published in the East German journal *Zeitschrift für Anglistik und Amerikanistik* 23.1 (1975): 5–11. A revised German version was then reprinted in *Shakespeare Jahrbuch* 113 (1977): 135–144, and, in the same year, in Schlösser's collection of essays *Shakespeare: Analysen und Interpretationen*, 290–303.

hostile to art.⁵² Schlösser republished his article on *Merchant* in a collection of Shakespearean essays in 1977, writing in the introduction that they were "intended to provide [...] contributions or suggestions for conceptions of stage productions."⁵³ Indeed, the manuscript of the German version of Schlösser's article is frequently quoted in the comprehensive documentation of Bennewitz's Weimar production of *Merchant* (premiere: 11 April 1976), where it is identified as a major inspiration.⁵⁴ It seems that Bennewitz's embracement of this interpretation – the avoidance of both Holocaust remembrance and topical allusions to Israel, and, by implication, the marginalization of the Shylock figure – was the precondition for the first GDR production of *Merchant* to be realized in Weimar in April 1976, only one year after the publication of Schlösser's article.

"The stage history of this play is full of contradictions, which originally – particularly with regard to the role of Shylock – were closely related to the social and ideological position of the respective reader."⁵⁵ This sentence introduces the "Conceptual Considerations" in the documentation of Bennewitz's production at Deutsches Nationaltheater Weimar. In contrast to what such a statement would have implied in West Germany in the mid-1970s, the author – presumably dramaturge Dieter Görne – stresses that "the fascist attempts to falsify *The Merchant of Venice* into an anti-Semitic propaganda piece are explicitly excluded as *distortions*". The claim is that the interpretation at the basis of the Weimar production is closer to Shakespeare's presumed original play than "later insinuations"⁵⁶ – by implication, West German productions. The Weimar *Merchant*, at least according to its documentation, sought to shift attention away from Shylock and proposed Antonio as the character around whom the various strands of the plot revolved. Although the documentation briefly mentions that Shakespeare's Shylock is a Jew and thus a member "of a minority that had been persecuted for centuries and whose personal and professional freedom was reduced to a mini-

---

52 Schlösser, *Shakespeare*, 293.
53 Schlösser, *Shakespeare*, 5. Kuckhoff similarly presented his 1964 monograph on Shakespeare as a book providing "scholarly help to theatre specialists, actors, directors, dramaturges." (Kuckhoff, *Drama*, 15)
54 Since 1967, each stage production had to be documented for the Verband der Theaterschaffenden der DDR (Organization of Theatre Practitioners in the GDR). All material on a production was collected, including the programme, posters, a detailed dramaturgical concept, the promptbook, rehearsal notes, as well as reviews. Cf. Annemarie Matzke, *Arbeit am Theater: Eine Diskursgeschichte der Probe* (Bielefeld: transcript, 2012), 107–108.
55 "Konzeptionelle Überlegungen," in the theatre documentation for Fritz Bennewitz's production of *Merchant* at Deutsches Nationaltheater Weimar (premiere: 11 April 1976), unpublished typescript, Archiv der Akademie der Künste Berlin (Inszenierungsdokumentationen 173), 1.
56 "Konzeptionelle Überlegungen," 1–2 (emphasis in the original).

mum,"⁵⁷ there is no explicit attempt at establishing a link between Shylock and the Jewish victims of the Holocaust. On the contrary, in an interview for the weekly *Wochenpost*, director Fritz Bennewitz stressed that the question of whether the play is pro- or anti-Semitic fails to recognize its dialectical structure and its main concern with class conflicts.⁵⁸

The stage design supported Schlösser's reading; it offered a spatial configuration of what he had described as the dialectical relation between the two settings of the play: Venice and Belmont. A circular upper stage, covered with a white cloth, was erected on a fragile pillar on the left, with the 'Venetian' buildings of the lower stage on the right (see figure 8). A white curtain at the centre of the upper stage showed the silhouette of a Renaissance palace: Belmont. Venice on the lower stage appeared disordered, with casks and crates half covered by fishermen's nets on the left, and a staircase leading up to a building with doors and a window, in front of a painted scenery showing Venice. During the Belmont scenes, this lower part of the stage remained dark. The two settings appeared as opposites, dark versus light, the harsh reality of Venice versus the idyll of Belmont. And yet they were interconnected, with the superstructure of Belmont resting on the economic basis of Venice. In an article on their production, Bennewitz and Görne explained that in their reading Belmont was only a utopian space on the surface, but in fact depended on Venice, without which it would not have been able to survive.⁵⁹ In presenting the basic conflict of the play as one between commercial and financial capitalism, represented by Antonio and Shylock respectively,⁶⁰ the production adopted the conventional reading of *Merchant* as a play on the economic and social changes during the Renaissance. The conflicts at the core of the play are not solved in the last act, Schlösser admits, but at the same time, they are not impossible to solve, as "recent bourgeois criticism" seems to take for granted:

> Even though the play does not offer ready-made answers, it does not conclude in a dead end. It is exactly because the problems are shown in their whole complexity that they so

---

57 "Konzeptionelle Überlegungen," 10.
58 Cf. Interview with Fritz Bennewitz, "Ein Theater stellt sich den Forderungen unserer Zeit," *Wochenpost* 41 (1976).
59 Fritz Bennewitz and Dieter Görne, "Shakespeares *Kaufmann von Venedig* im Deutschen Nationaltheater Weimar," *Shakespeare Jahrbuch* 113 (1977): 58. See also Schlösser, *Shakespeare*, 290–291.
60 Bennewitz and Görne, "Shakespeares *Kaufmann von Venedig*," 60; cf. Schlösser, *Shakespeare*, 294–295.

urgently demand an answer which the spectators are called on to find. Further reflection in the direction suggested by the play means progress.[61]

Quoting this sentence, the documentation describes a production that would have invited the audience to shift attention from the fate of the individual figure to a potential (socialist) resolution of the economic conflicts. In his review for *Theater der Zeit*, Jochen Gleiß reiterated this interpretation, suggesting that the play was not about the question of "my nose versus your nose, but naked economic interests."[62]

Figure 8: Photograph of the stage design of Fritz Bennewitz's 1976 production at Deutsches Nationaltheater Weimar. Photograph by Günter Dietel (Archiv der Akademie der Künste Berlin, Inszenierungsdokumentationen 173). Courtesy of Lore Dietel.

---

61 Schlösser, *Shakespeare*, 303; quoted also in Bennewitz and Görne, "Shakespeares *Kaufmann von Venedig*," 62–63.
62 Jochen Gleiß, "Ein Kaufmann für Belmont," *Theater der Zeit* 7 (1976): 10.

Despite this flippant attempt at discarding the issue of anti-Semitism and downplaying the relevance of the Shylock figure, it turned out to be difficult to avoid. In an interview, Bennewitz acknowledged the symbolic nature of Weimar and the particular responsibility of its theatre, which emerged from the proximity and antagonism of "Frauenplan and Buchenwald,"[63] the centre of Weimar Classicism and the site of the former concentration camp. In other words, the Shylock figure resurfaced in various ways, and its Jewishness was acknowledged, despite Bennewitz and Görne's conceptual attempts to relegate Shylock to the margin. Shylock was played by Victor Dräger as a Jew, in his traditional stage costume, with a long dark coat and a kippah. He turned out to be the gravitational centre of the production, at least for most of the critics, who applauded Dräger's interpretation of the role. All of the reviews praised Bennewitz for bringing the play to an East German stage, but they also all addressed the precarious nature of the Shylock figure. In the words of one reviewer, Georg Menchén: "Shylock. One can turn it this way or the other, argue for or against the 'comedy,' but in the end the play depends on how this Jew is deciphered."[64] Menchén adds a brief overview of twentieth-century interpretations of the role, from Albert Bassermann in Reinhardt's 1913 *Merchant* to Ernst Deutsch in Piscator's 1963 production, and Hans Mahnke in Zadek's *Merchant* of 1972 (see Chapter 2). Although Menchén characterizes the latter production as an instance of "a completely uninhibited pop version of a theatre of alienation" and a proof of Zadek's ideological insecurity, he acknowledges it as an important take on the play. It showed Mahnke's Shylock, "the monstrous equivalent of a werewolf-like world, which – addressing the concrete context of the Federal Republic – could indeed lead to strong effects."[65] The Weimar *Merchant* is positively contrasted with its counterparts in the Federal Republic, but by force of comparison, it is included into a general *German* stage history of the play, before and after the war.

Although intended as a comment on the emergence of capitalism in early modern England, the critics thus read the production in the context of more recent political conflicts: the cultural competition with the Federal Republic, but also, and even more importantly, the legacy of National Socialism. Several reviews reiterated Kuckhoff's stance and explained the long absence of *Merchant* from the stages of East Germany through reference to the Holocaust and the persistence of anti-Semitic stereotypes. Georg Antosch, writing for *Neue Zeit*,

---

[63] Bennewitz, "Ein Theater stellt sich," 15.
[64] Georg Menchén, "Von der Notwendigkeit menschlicher Bewährung," *Thüringische Landeszeitung*, 17 April 1976.
[65] Menchén, "Von der Notwendigkeit."

the official newspaper of the Christian Democratic Union in the GDR, claimed that the impact of the play on three different generations was at stake:

> those that still remember Max Reinhardt's affectionate banter with a serious subject, those for whom Werner Krauß had to convey the 'pathological image of the racial type of the eastern Jew,' and the young generation who – unburdened by prior knowledge – understand and use the theatre for the here and now.[66]

It had been necessary, Gleiß adds, to first "remove unseemly prejudice and redeem the anti-Semitic mortgage," thus suggesting that in 1976 the "social conditions [were] eventually ripe" to approach the play again.[67] Bennewitz's production appears to give proof of a new state of grace for the GDR, whose hands are not (or no longer) stained.

However, the fact that Bennewitz's production did *not* open during the Weimar Shakespeare conference but more than a week before its beginning, and that it was accompanied by a discussion on Shakespeare's play in a conference seminar,[68] indicates the precarious quality of this *Merchant*, which seemed to stubbornly resist the dominant ideology – despite the massive apologetic textual production surrounding it. Almost imploringly, Kuckhoff wrote in the 1977 issue of *Shakespeare Jahrbuch:* "It is a fact that is as important as it is gratifying that in the vivid discussions on the concept and the details of the Weimar production, the problem of the 'Jew' Shylock was not an issue. It shows that in our Republic the subjugation of anti-Semitism is absolutely secure."[69]

Twelve years later, in Leipzig in 1988, Bennewitz staged a *Merchant* (premiere: 2 September) with Shylock at the centre of the play. The programme focuses almost exclusively on him, quoting extensively from Gustav Landauer's 1920 essay on *Merchant*,[70] and reiterating his acknowledgment of Shylock's Jewishness: "Shylock is a human being, Shylock is a Jew!"[71] This production actually resembled West German productions in figuring Shylock as a victim

---

66 Georg Antosch, "Anregung zu erneuter Erprobung: Gedanken zu Shakespeares 'Kaufmann von Venedig'," *Neue Zeit*, 26 May 1976.
67 Gleiß, "Ein Kaufmann für Belmont," 10. See also Rainer Kerndl, "Shakespeares 'Kaufmann' wieder auf der Bühne," *Neues Deutschland*, 4 May 1976.
68 The contributions were documented in the *Shakespeare Jahrbuch* of the following year (vol. 113, 1977). The volume contains four articles on *Merchant*, by Anselm Schlösser, Thomas Sorge, Dieter Görne and Fritz Bennewitz, and Adel Karasholi.
69 Armin-Gerd Kuckhoff, "Shakespeare auf den Bühnen der DDR im Jahre 1975," *Shakespeare Jahrbuch* 133 (1977): 193.
70 See Chapter 1.
71 Schauspielhaus Leipzig, *Der Kaufmann von Venedig*, theatre programme (Leipzig, 1988), n. p.

of anti-Semitism. At the beginning of the play, one Venetian wrote with chalk the racist word "Judensau" ("Jewish sow") onto the door of Shylock's house. In the year of the fiftieth anniversary of the "The Night of Broken Glass" (the 1938 November pogrom), this was an explicit reference to the National Socialist period, which remained visible throughout the production. The play did not end in Belmont, but rather had a last scene that showed Shylock as an old and broken man, trying to wipe away the graffiti. Similar to the spatial layout of the stage in Weimar, the Belmont scenes in Leipzig were also played on a circular upper stage, covered with a purple ceiling. But with its sloping plane, this Belmont did not offer stable ground. In addition, it was built on top of a city with a Jewish cemetery. The reviewer for *Theater der Zeit* wrote: "The conflict pertains entirely to Shylock."[72]

The Leipzig stage gave ample testimony to the changes within East German memory culture during the 1980s. Although the precedence of Communist fighters against Nazism was not officially challenged, the Holocaust was duly acknowledged, for the first time, in the commemoration of the November pogroms. The dilapidated graveyard on the Leipzig stage represented the Jewish cemeteries in Berlin and other cities that were put in order in 1988, and it also referred to the large Jewish cemetery of Berlin Weißensee, which had been endangered by a road-building scheme. In the same year, Erich Honecker personally laid the foundation stone for the rebuilding of the New Synagogue in Berlin's Oranienburger Straße. According to Annette Leo, this late acknowledgement of the Holocaust in the last years of the German Democratic Republic was brought about by the state's attempt to normalize its relationship to the churches, and the slow resumption of diplomatic relations with Israel in order to benefit from better trade conditions with the United States. Leo adds that the general attitude towards the Jewish victims of National Socialism may also have changed because a considerable part of the GDR population would have followed the broadcasting of *Holocaust* on West German TV.[73]

The comparison of the Weimar and the Leipzig productions shows an increasing divergence between scholarship and theatre practice in the German Democratic Republic. Whereas Bennewitz's Weimar production – at least according to its official documentation – reiterated the hegemonic approach to the Shylock figure in East German scholarship, his Leipzig production openly acknowledged the changing cultural climate of the 1980s. Reviewers, however,

---

[72] Bernhard Scheller, "Düstere Komödie – Römerdrama – Trauerspiel: Welttheater? Shakespeare-Inszenierungen in Erfurt, Leipzig und Weimar," *Theater der Zeit* 12 (1988): 19.
[73] Cf. Leo, "Als antifaschistischer Staat nicht betroffen?," 101.

noted these changes with some dismay. The critic for *Theater der Zeit* bemoaned the pessimism at the end of the Leipzig *Merchant* and recalled Bennewitz's more hopeful Weimar production. Rainer Kurt Langner, reviewing the Leipzig production for the radio, concluded that "this production does not want to, and cannot, forget Auschwitz" – only to add that he was not completely convinced by this interpretation.[74]

3.4 The Shylock Figure in the East-West Conflict

Thomas Langhoff's production at Deutsches Theater Berlin (premiere: 17 March 1985) showed a similar interest in the Shylock figure although the official concept of the production – as submitted to the Cultural Ministry – at least to some extent reproduced the hegemonic economic reading of the play, stressing that Shylock's Jewishness was merely "functional."[75] And yet the various documents compiled in the theatre documentation draw a more ambiguous picture. There are extensive quotes from critical studies on the play and on Shylock, from Nicholas Rowe to John Russell Brown, the majority of which were written by Anglo-American Shakespeare scholars. In addition, the documentation includes an overview of various international productions, including John Barton's *Merchant* in Stratford-upon-Avon in 1978 (with Patrick Stewart in the role of Shylock) and the 1980 BBC adaptation, but also the Berlin *Merchants* of the 1920s with Fritz Kortner, and Zadek's Bochum (1972) and Palitzsch's Düsseldorf (1981) productions. There is an obvious interest in relating Langhoff's production to the play's (Western) stage history and the recent figurations of Shylock in the FRG, against which earlier GDR studies recede to the background. The East German reticence towards *Merchant* is implicitly criticized by comparing the brief stage history of the play on GDR stages to the large number of productions in the FRG, and adding that "after the Second World War no produc-

---

[74] Rainer Kurt Langner, radio review of *The Merchant of Venice* at the Schauspielhaus Leipzig (dir. Fritz Bennewitz, premiere: 2 September 1988), *Stimme der DDR*, 11 September 1988, Deutsches Rundfunkarchiv.

[75] Thomas Langhoff and Eva Walch (?), "Überlegungen zur Neuinszenierung von 'Der Kaufmann von Venedig' (1984/85)," in theatre documentation for Thomas Langhoff's production of *Merchant* at Deutsches Theater Berlin (premiere: 17 March 1985), unpublished typescript, 2 vols., Archiv der Akademie der Künste Berlin (Inszenierungsdokumentationen 584), vol. 1, 1.

tion can circumvent the problems raised by the figure of Shylock, as long as one does not avoid them and the play altogether."[76]

The theatre documentation does not focus exclusively on Shylock, but there is a pronounced interest in this figure, its various interpretations in criticism and on the stage, as well as related plays with Jewish protagonists, such a Christopher Marlowe's *The Jew of Malta* (c. 1590), Gotthold Ephraim Lessing's *Die Juden* ("The Jews," 1749), Rainer Werner Fassbinder's *Der Müll, die Stadt und der Tod* ("Garbage, the City, and Death," 1981), and Arnold Wesker's *The Merchant* (1976). In the 1985 theatre documentation, therefore, not much is left of the earlier dismissal of the precarious nature of the play or the simple confirmation of GDR anti-fascism.

The stage at Deutsches Theater Berlin had been designed by Pieter Hein. With boxes in red velvet, which surrounded the central stage on three sides, it reduplicated the auditorium of the theatre so that the spectators became witnesses of the trial scene, sitting opposite, and thus mirroring, the actors playing the Venetians. Shylock was played by Fred Düren, one of the most important and successful actors of the GDR, who had been engaged at Deutsches Theater since 1958. But it was not merely Düren's experience and fame that made this casting so interesting, but a conscious merging between actor and figure, which we have already discussed with regard to Kortner's Shylock (see Chapters 1 and 2). Langhoff had chosen him because he knew that at this time, Düren was already preparing for his conversion to Judaism. Shylock would be his last role at Deutsches Theater. In 1986, he left the stage and emigrated from the German Democratic Republic to Israel two years later. He settled with his family in Jerusalem, where he lived until his death in 2015. He studied Hebrew and the Torah and, in the 1990s, received the *smicha* to become a rabbi.[77]

In Langhoff's production, there were clear parallels between Shylock and Antonio, which were stressed through their costumes, dark elegant suits that created a stark contrast to the extravagant clothes and masks of the Venetians. In retrospect, dramaturge Eva Walch commented: "Two equal competitors were facing each other, both in their way loners and outsiders in the light-hearted,

---

[76] Langhoff and Walch, "Überlegungen zur Neuinszenierung von 'Der Kaufmann von Venedig' (1984/85)," 1.
[77] Karl-Heinz Müller, "Stationen des Schauspielers Fred Düren," in Fred Düren, *Ich muß ja den Weg gehen, den ich gehen kann: Schauspieler in Berlin – Jahre in Jerusalem*, ed. Karl-Heinz Müller (Berlin: Das Neue Berlin, 2007), 16–19; see also sle, "Der Schauspieler Fred Düren ist tot: Eine deutsche Theaterlegende," *nachtkritik.de*, 8 March 2015, accessed 8 September 2018, https://www.nachtkritik.de/index.php?option=com_content&view=article&id=10655:2015-03-08-15-51-34&catid=126:meldungen-k&Itemid=100089.

aggressive pleasure society of Venice during carnival."⁷⁸ Indeed, Langhoff's *Merchant* seems to have been the first East German production that openly acknowledged Antonio's homosexuality. Thus concentrating on the two outsider figures and the relation between them, the production 'forgot' about its alleged focus on the economic conflict. A similar decision on the configuration between the two antagonists would be made by Dieter Dorn in his Munich production in 2001 (see Chapter 4); but already in 1970, Laurence Olivier in Jonathan Miller's production for the National Theatre London had played Shylock as a businessman, whose costume did not differ from that of his Christian counterpart. Peter Zadek would resort to this decision in the same year as Langhoff, in his production at the Vienna Burgtheater (see Chapter 4).

Although Langhoff's and Düren's figuration of Shylock thus showed considerable parallels to those in West Germany, Gerhard Stadelmaier, the influential West German theatre critic, described Düren's Shylock as a "pale [...] caricature of a Jew,"⁷⁹ recognizable only through his kippah. For him, the Berlin Shylock was not Jewish enough, but resembled all the other capitalists. In a way, then, this reviewer again conjured up the figure of the late nineteenth-century 'stage Jew' with a caftan, long beard, and kippah, which was becoming increasingly rare also on West German stages. Stadelmaier took the absence of the iconic figure as clear evidence of the shortcomings of Langhoff's production, which – allegedly – only half-heartedly addressed Holocaust remembrance. As Stadelmaier put it, with his usual taste for polemics:

> The GDR, according to the GDR, has overcome fascism, which for example, as it was said back then, had 'settled the Jewish question.' In that way the GDR, together with fascism, has also overcome the Jewish question. Since the GDR, rejoices the GDR, has also overcome capitalism, a capitalist Jew [...] is somehow doubly foreign to it. And doubly unreal. Thus Thomas Langhoff protects the GDR [...] not only against the reality of Venice. Also this Jew, Shylock, [...] this hell of a monstrous Jew, the most human invention of the theatre because he is its most vicious one, only appears in East Berlin as a Fata Morgana. He has no visa for the GDR.⁸⁰

Many other Western critics echoed these polemics, despite the fact that the production did not differ considerably from contemporaneous West German productions.⁸¹

---

78 Walch, "Dramaturgische Blicke," 157.
79 Stadelmaier, "Kein Visum für Shylock."
80 Stadelmaier, "Kein Visum für Shylock."
81 Our comments are based on the theatre's video recording of the production.

In its deviation from the teleological socialist narrative, the fragility of its ending (Antonio and Jessica remained alone on the stage, not participating in the general celebration), and its emphasis on the decadence and artificiality of the Venetian and Belmont societies, Langhoff's *Merchant* to some extent anticipated Bennewitz's Leipzig refiguration. One scene that was mentioned in all West German reviews (and by hardly any East German critic) is scene 2.2, in which Lancelot ponders whether he should leave his master, Shylock. This was turned into an allusive scene, suggesting a potential flight from East to West Germany. With three bricks, Ulrich Mühe's Lancelot built a 'wall,' while speaking the lines in which the servant disputes with the 'fiend.' Whereas Lancelot's 'good' self spoke Saxonian (i.e. an East German) dialect, the 'fiend' responded in High German (associated with the West). The latter won over, and Lancelot eventually jumped over the wall.

It is not clear whether this scene was simply too dangerous to be discussed in the East German media, but the theatre was also confronted with other problems. Eva Walch mentions that they received several negative letters responding to the production, one of which was written by a woman who saw it characterized by a "most bitter anti-Semitism" and demanded it to be taken from the repertoire.[82] Some reviews in the East German press had a similar tendency, among them Ernst Schumacher's article in *Berliner Zeitung*:

> Despite its aesthetic qualities, this performance of *The Merchant of Venice* at Deutsches Theater [...] could not convince me that it is adequate to put this Shakespeare play on the stages of this country. [...] No, all historical references that Shakespeare meant less the Jews than the usurers are in vain: the shadows of the recent German history are cast too powerfully over this play for to see it played here and now without discomfort.[83]

After East German scholars had argued for twenty years that *Merchant* had to be read economically and that anti-Semitic effects were no longer possible in the GDR, the new awareness of the Holocaust posed fresh problems for GDR critics when they were literally faced with the Shylock figure. Wolfgang Gersch, writing for *Die Tribüne*, the weekly of the FDGB (the association of East German trade unions), remarked: "History is still bleeding and the doom of misunderstanding is nigh."[84] Whereas West German critics attacked the production for its evasive stance towards Shylock's Jewishness, East German reviewers seemed to consider the production as latently anti-Semitic. Reminding us of the impossibility to

---

82 Quoted in Walch, "Dramaturgische Blicke," 158.
83 Schumacher, "Gewagt, doch nicht gewonnen."
84 Wolfgang Gersch, "Die Welt des Geldes und die Welt des Schönen: Der Kaufmann von Venedig am Deutschen Theater Berlin," *Tribüne* 58 (22 March 1985): 4.

reconstruct a performance on the basis of reviews, the debate on Langhoff's *Merchant* also exemplifies the extent to which the figure of Shylock was used as a pawn in the cultural antagonism between the two German states throughout the four decades between the end of the war and German re-unification.

4 After Remembrance? – Shylock in the Reunified Germany (1990 – 2010)

Focussing on the last decade of the twentieth century and the first of the new millennium, this chapter takes our investigation to the threshold of the present moment. We are thus entering a terrain that we cannot yet pretend to grasp securely or to historicize. Indeed, the period under investigation seems particularly dynamic and contradictory. It begins with the breakdown of the GDR and the reunification of Germany – a process that was as sudden as it was momentous.[1] On both sides of the erstwhile border between the two Germanies, the speedy integration of the states of the former GDR into the political and economic structures of the FRG created tremendous pressures and vast possibilities. This was taking place within a wider framework of international processes, among them the closer integration of the European Union and the increasing 'globalization' of economic and cultural exchange. In these contexts, the liberal-conservative government of Chancellor Helmut Kohl pursued a rigorous policy of economic liberalization, which was continued by the coalition of the Social Democrats with the Green Party that came to power in 1998. Chancellor Gerhard Schröder's Agenda 2010, a rigorous reform programme begun in 2003, drastically cut welfare services.

In this heterogeneous socioeconomic climate – a climate defined by stock market wonders as well as by financial crisis and social insecurity – the economic implications running through *The Merchant of Venice* seemed newly relevant. Whereas in the 1980s the play was often seen as a significant document of the early history of capitalism, since the 1990s it has frequently been approached from a presentist angle. The terms 'global' and 'globalization' have become standard ingredients in theatre programmes and reviews, where they are used as shorthand descriptions of current economic conditions and structures of feeling. Thus, in 2008, the Landestheater Tübingen (LTT) updated Shakespeare's text by introducing Antonio not only as a "modern capitalist," but also as a "global player" dealing in "international future bonds."[2] And in 2009, the preview for a production at Berlin's Gorki Theatre described *Merchant* as "a classic of global-

---

[1] For a concise account of 'reunification,' see Karl-Rudolf Korte, "Die deutsche Wiedervereinigung," in *Die Bundesrepublik Deutschland: Eine Bilanz nach 60 Jahren*, ed. Hans-Peter Schwarz (Cologne: Böhlau, 2008), 181– 203.
[2] Landestheater Tübingen, "Der Kaufmann von Venedig," accessed 8 September 2018, http://alt2.landestheater-tuebingen.de/spielplan/der-kaufmann-von-venedig-1953. (The date for the premiere on this website is not correct.)

ization drama."³ In the following, we will discuss how this urge for adapting Shakespeare's play to current concerns has affected the mnemonic implications of *Merchant*.

It is yet more significant for our project that the breakdown of the GDR and the transition to an expanded new Germany went along with the renewed articulation of the notion of the people as a 'Volk.' It was through the ubiquitous slogan 'Wir sind das Volk!' ('We are the people!') – and by placing the emphasis on the initial pronoun – that demonstrators in the GDR expressed their dissent with the governmentality of 'actually existing socialism.' Shortly after, only the definite article '*das*' had to be exchanged for the numeral '*ein*' to shift the meaning of the slogan, from reclaiming political agency to demanding national unity: 'Wir sind *ein* Volk!' ('We are *one* people!'). It would be utterly mistaken to reduce the claims of the East German 'Monday demonstrations' in 1989/90 to mere instances of the newly emerging xenophobic nationalism that Germany, like many other European countries, is witnessing right now. However, the persistent appeal to a German nationhood – and the ways in which West German opinion makers echoed the appeal – certainly meant a breach of the political decorum that had been established in post-war Germany. Now, the rhetoric of nationhood and nationalism was no longer taboo, and it would soon resonate in the collective consciousness.

The frustration of the high hopes that many Germans, particularly in the East, had placed on reunification gave a particular edge to such lingering nationalism. This became evident in connection to another major topic that started to dominate political debates: immigration.⁴ It came as a shock that a series of xenophobic attacks – in both East and West Germany – should follow on the heels of reunification. Partly driven by the events and partly driving them, the government restricted the right of asylum that the constitution of 1949 had granted in response to the experience of National Socialism and the Holocaust. The so-called 'Asylum Compromise' was passed by parliament in 1993, making it more difficult for refugees to claim asylum. At the same time, the period under investigation has brought a growing recognition of Germany's character as a country shaped by immigration. The two momentous political acts in this field were the reform of the citizenship law in 1999/2000 and the so-called Immigration Law of 2004. The full name of the latter was Act for Controlling and Limiting Immigration and for Regulating the Residence and Integration of EU

---

3 Anon., "Mitten ins System: *Gomorra* und *Der Kaufmann von Venedig*," *Berliner Zeitung*, 25 September 2009.
4 See Ulrich Herbert, *Geschichte der Ausländerpolitik in Deutschland: Saisonarbeiter, Zwangsarbeiter, Gastarbeiter, Flüchtlinge* (Munich: Beck, 2001).

Citizens and Foreigners, thus interconnecting an older discourse of ethnic homogeneity with the emergent concept of a multicultural immigration society.

To a certain extent at least, German reunification marked a departure from the 'lessons learnt from the past.' At the same time, apprehensions that the unified Germany would break free from the imperative of remembering have proven unjustified.[5] Quite to the contrary, the public representation and official commemoration of 'the German past' have intensified. On the sixtieth anniversary of the breakdown of the National Socialist regime, the Memorial to the Murdered Jews of Europe was inaugurated. Transforming a large area in the centre of the German capital into a permanent site of Holocaust memory, the memorial manifests the continuance of what historian Reinhart Kosselleck has characterized as a definitive German practice of "negative memory."[6]

However, the year 2005 was not restricted to the commemoration of the Holocaust. The anniversary of the liberation of Auschwitz, on 27 January, was soon followed, on 13 February, by the anniversary of the destruction of Dresden – a context in which a politician of the right-wing National-Democratic Party (NPD) used the slogan "bombing holocaust."[7] In October of the same year, the inauguration of the Frauenkirche, destroyed in the firestorm of Dresden and rebuilt as a promise that the wounds of the past would be healed, created no less of a stir than the inauguration of the Holocaust Memorial. Thus, the 'super memorial year' raised questions about the coordinates of collective memory in Germany. It became apparent that contradictory templates of memory were being superimposed on each other, creating complex and contradictory discourses of memory.

---

5 See Matthias Weiß, "Vom 'Zivilisationsbruch' zu einer Kultur des 'negativen Gedächtnisses'," in *Shylock nach dem Holocaust: Zur Geschichte einer deutschen Erinnerungsfigur*, ed. Zeno Ackermann and Sabine Schülting (Berlin: De Gruyter, 2011), 36. See also Aleida Assmann, *Der lange Schatten der Vergangenheit: Erinnerungskultur und Geschichtspolitik* (München: Beck 2006); Torben Fischer and Matthias N. Lorenz, eds., *Lexikon der 'Vergangenheitsbewältigung' in Deutschland: Debatten- und Diskursgeschichte des Nationalsozialismus nach 1945*, 2nd ed. (Bielefeld: transcript, 2009); Peter Reichel, Harald Schmid, and Peter Steinbach, eds., *Der Nationalsozialismus – die zweite Geschichte: Überwindung – Deutung – Erinnerung* (Munich: Beck 2009).
6 Reinhart Kosselleck, "Formen und Traditionen des negativen Gedächtnisses," in *Verbrechen erinnern: Die Auseinandersetzung mit Holocaust und Völkermord*, ed. Volkhard Knigge and Norbert Frei (Munich: Beck 2002), 21–32.
7 Anon., "Skandal im Sächsischen Landtag: NPD-Mann spricht von Dresdner 'Bomben-Holocaust'," *Spiegel Online*, 21 January 2005, accessed 8 September 2018, http://www.spiegel.de/politik/deutschland/skandal-im-saechsischen-landtag-npd-mann-spricht-von-dresdner-bomben-holocaust-a-337894.html. See also Zeno Ackermann, "*Der Untergang* und die erinnerungskulturelle Rahmung des Zivilisationsbruchs," *Geschichte in Wissenschaft und Unterricht* 58.3 (2007): 148–162.

In 2005, the chronological distance of the historical events had reached the crucial mark that Walter Scott highlighted in the subtitle to *Waverley* (1814): "'Tis Sixty Years Since." In an essay on the significance of the 'super memorial year,' Micha Brumlik played on this formula in order to raise a series of questions:

> The number 'sixty' apparently marks a threshold between epochs. On the far side, the past eventually begins to turn into history. What lies in wait on this side of the threshold? Is it a new era for Germany and the Germans in which they will be at peace with themselves and with their past?[8]

From the perspective of memory studies, the historical distance of sixty years defines the breaking point of communicative memory.[9] Soon after, the last witnesses who experienced the events as adults cease to participate in the discourse. As a consequence, remembrance turns into a completely mediated process. This is the beginning of 'memory culture' in the narrow sense of the term, i.e. as a dynamic, multimedia process in which the significance of the past is constantly being emphasized and negotiated at the same time.

In this process, national frameworks of memory and accountability have been both transcended and affirmed.[10] The present chapter investigates the roles of *Merchant* and especially of the Shylock figure in relation to such transformations and evocations of the past. Performance numbers indicate that the popularity of the play abated neither in the wake of reunification nor with the emergence of a firmly established 'memory culture.' At the same time, the actual implications of Shakespeare's fraught comedy, its significance in relation to the past or to the present, may have become less clear than ever.

4.1 Against Identification: Peter Zadek's 1988 Burgtheater Production

In our introductory remarks on Erich Auerbach's engagement with Shylock, we have suggested that his struggle with 'Shakespeare's Jew' can be linked to his examination of *figura* and *figuratio*, of figure and figuration. According to our

---

8 Micha Brumlik, "Jenseits der Schwelle: Auschwitz im 21. Jahrhundert," *Newsletter zur Geschichte und Wirkung des Holocaust – Informationen des Fritz Bauer Instituts* 27 (2005): 12.
9 For a useful introduction to memory studies, see Astrid Erll, *Memory in Culture*, trans. Sara B. Young (Houndmills: Palgrave, 2011).
10 For an engaged analysis of current German memory discourses, see Aleida Assmann, *Das neue Unbehagen an der Erinnerungskultur: Eine Intervention* (Munich: Beck, 2013).

interpretation, both the potentials and the problems of *Merchant* are due to the play's complicated aesthetics, its pronounced tendency of inviting figurative and representational readings simultaneously. In viewing or in producing the play, it remains vexingly unclear whether the logic of abstraction and allegory or the logic of concretization and identification applies. In contemporary productions and reviews, the problem of Shylock's two-fold dimensions as figure and as character seems particularly acute. Should a performance foreground Shylock's identification as a 'Jew'? Or should this identification be dealt with as a mere label, a heterostereotypical imposition that needs to be interrogated and is open for topical re-articulations?

Moreover, the confusion about the dramatic status of Shylock goes along with a confusion about the historical status of the Holocaust. The imperative of stressing the uniqueness and specificity of the Holocaust is challenged by an urge to stress its tremendous transhistorical significance, its implications as a *figura*.[11] Paradoxically, it is exactly the recognition of the Holocaust as a 'rupture in civilization' ('Zivilisationsbruch'[12]), which makes it accessible for processes of allegorization. This is one of the reasons why 'memory culture' runs the danger of what Lawrence Langer terms "preempting the Holocaust," of "shifting the focus of Holocaust discussion from the central issue of mass murder to any number of auxiliary matters that skirt the question of how it was done, and why."[13]

If these are the pitfalls encountered by contemporary takes on *Merchant*, we are opening this chapter with a production that stands out by virtue of having actively engaged the aesthetic, epistemological, and ideological problems that have been at the heart of the play's reception. Peter Zadek's Burgtheater production – his fourth and last take on Shakespeare's comedy – proves illuminating exactly because it is so different from the majority of other productions. In the context of our present concerns, this *Merchant* has indeed a special standing also in terms of its chronological and geographical position. Premiering on 10 December 1988, the production was brought onto the stage not even a year before the momentous events that would culminate in the reunification of

---

[11] One of the most important deliberations on this question is Imre Kertész's essay "The Holocaust as Culture," originally published in Hungarian in 1993. For an English translation with much additional material, see Kertész, *The Holocaust as Culture*, trans. and ed. Thomas Cooper (New York: Seagull, 2011).

[12] The term was introduced by Dan Diner. See esp. Diner, ed., *Zivilisationsbruch: Denken nach Auschwitz* (Frankfurt/M.: Fischer, 1988).

[13] Lawrence L. Langer, *Preempting the Holocaust* (New Haven: Yale University Press, 1998), xi. See also Peter Novick, *The Holocaust in American Life* (Boston: Houghton Mifflin, 1999).

Germany. Premiering in the capital of Austria, moreover, it was realized at a remove from the theatrical practices and socio-political discourses of the FRG.

However, as one West German reviewer pointed out, the 1988 *Merchant* resembled "a guest performance, put on the stage of the Burgtheater by a who-is-who of the FRG's theatre scene."[14] Zadek, at the time, was managing director of the Deutsches Schauspielhaus in Hamburg. Claus Peymann, the director of the Burgtheater who had invited Zadek to produce the play, was also German. And the star of the evening, Gert Voss, who played the role of Shylock, had come from Bochum to the Austrian capital in Peymann's train. During the following years, the hugely successful production was also taken to Germany. After guest performances at the Berliner Ensemble (in March 1993), the host theatre decided to recreate, or take over, the production (premiere: 8 January 1994).

Zadek's re-imagination of the play's Venice alluded to a newly prominent international world of business. This was indicated in the titles of many reviews, such as "Zadek takes Shylock to the world of Wall Street,"[15] "Shylock among the Stock Brokers,"[16] "The Profiteers of Trump Tower,"[17] and "Yuppies on the Rialto."[18] The director had been inspired by the setting and atmosphere of Oliver Stone's *Wall Street* (1987), a film drama about the unscrupulous ethics of the contemporary American world of finance which had captured large audiences during the previous year. The Burgtheater stage designed by Wilfried Mink resembled the foyer of a business tower. Everybody was constantly handling the gadgets of financial professionalism – not only the *Financial Times*, business diaries, and cigars, but also the large mobile phones of the time. However, the production counteracted effects of direct referentiality. Shakespeare's drama about "moneys," "bonds," and the machinery of justice was not really transferred to the present business world. Rather, the performance was set in a space that resembled contemporary imaginaries of such a world. The Venetian Lions embossed on the iron doors of the elevator were reminders that this was not quite an American scene.

The provocation of the production was in how naturally Shylock moved in this setting. Gert Voss as Shylock (see figure 9) was a broker among brokers.

---

[14] Dietmar Grieser, "Shylock im Nadelstreif," *Rhein-Neckar-Zeitung*, 12 December 1988.
[15] Klaus Gruber, "Zadek bringt 'Shylock' ins Wallstreet-Milieu," *Westfälische Rundschau*, 13 December 1988.
[16] Otto F. Beer, "Shylock bei den Börsianern," *Hannoversche Allgemeine Zeitung*, 14 December 1988.
[17] Karin Katherein, "Geschäftemacher vom Trump Tower," *Die Welt*, 12 December 1988.
[18] Wolfgang Höbel, "Yuppies am Rialto, Geldhaie unter sich," *Badische Zeitung*, 13 December 1988.

Figure 9: Gert Voss (Shylock) in Peter Zadek's 1988 production at Vienna's Burgtheater. © Gisela Scheidler, Archiv Burgtheater.

He wore the same suit, read the same newspaper, and boasted the same briefcase as his competitors. If he differed at all, it was by being just a trifle more at home in the environs, just a trifle more sure of himself, and more confidently in possession of the world around him. Indeed, when Portia asked, "Which is the merchant here, and which the Jew?" (4.1.169), she first addressed Antonio, who was so shocked that he let the cigar drop from his mouth. Judging from reviews, the theatre audience was as startled as Antonio. "A Jew like you and me" was the provocative heading of a review in the *Frankfurter Allgemeine Zeitung*: "No caftan, no gaberdine, no synagogue scarf – not even a beard, even though it is known that the Christians need one to spit at: in Vienna, Peter Zadek has liberated the Jew Shylock from all the attributes that theatre tradition has made so familiar to us."[19] In a similar vein, an Austrian critic pointed out:

> [Shylock] explains that he has been spat at and slandered as a Jew. But who might be able to imagine such things happening to this self-assured, arrogant man – a man whose confidence is evidently bolstered by a huge fortune? [...] Peter Zadek has managed to de-Jew *The Merchant of Venice*; he has cleansed the play from its taboo topic and thus from its provocative power.[20]

While the critical reception of the production resulted in a number of worrying formulations (the expression "de-Jew" was of course part of the National Socialist vocabulary), many reviewers also came up with stimulating reflections. Indeed, rather than "de-Jewing" and defusing Shakespeare's play, Zadek had taken away the frames of reference according to which Shylock's Jewishness had traditionally been identified and codified. Thus, the reviewer of the *Stuttgarter Zeitung* claimed that Zadek's achievement lay in refusing to adjust Shylock to the needs of the audience, that this was "not a Shylock for us but a Shylock for Shylock."[21]

In an interview with the influential Austrian journalist and critic Sigrid Löffler, Zadek claimed that he had wanted to "cast away all the paraphernalia of the Ghetto that over the centuries had accumulated around the Shylock figure." Instead, he had been motivated to "tell the story of an assimilated Jew," of "a banker who jokes about anti-Semitic remarks – and yet, at the back of his mind, there is the consciousness of 3,000 years of suffering and

---

19 Georg Hensel, "Ein Jude wie du und ich," *Frankfurter Allgemeine Zeitung*, 12 December 1988.
20 Heinz Hans Hahnl, "Der unerschütterliche Businessman," *Arbeiterzeitung Wien*, 12 December 1988.
21 Gerhard Stadelmaier, "Der Jude Jedermann," *Stuttgarter Zeitung*, 12 December 1988.

persecution."[22] What may sound like a rather uncomplicated idea resulted in a production that exploded the limitations of a discourse defined by the interdependent routines of 'anti-Semitism' and 'philo-Semitism.' It seems that Zadek stepped back from the force fields of contemporary discourses on the Holocaust and on identity. However, he certainly did not do so in order to withdraw the play into a utopian safe haven beyond the pressures of history. Rather, he meant to activate the play's potential of looking awry at the processes of representation, figuration, and identification. Indeed, the Shylock created by Zadek and Voss provoked exactly because he was a Jew and yet defied identification. The mask of his fascinating personality proved impermeable, so that neither the markings nor the meanings of his Jewishness could be made out and nailed down. As Bernd Sucher observed in his review for the *Süddeutsche Zeitung*, Zadek allowed Shylock "to keep his secret."[23]

Accordingly, Shylock's defeat was the failure of a businessman who accepted his bankruptcy almost without batting an eyelid. When, at the end of the trial scene, he dropped to his knees, this did not resemble an act of submission. Rather than asking for mercy, Shylock simply bowed down to sign the cheque for Antonio. Commenting on Shylock's exit from the stage, one critic remarked:

> Shylock goes – but this time he does not bear his people's tragedy on his shoulders. He does not go (like other Shylocks) to gloomily meet his destruction, he also does not go towards Auschwitz. The Christians know (and this is why they are so embarrassed) that they will not easily get rid of this Jew. [...] Shylock goes – but he will always return again.[24]

It is debatable whether the Burgtheater Shylock was or was not meant to carry the burdens of anti-Jewish persecution on his shoulders (note Zadek's previously quoted remark about "3,000 years of suffering and persecution"). If he did carry the burden, however, he certainly refrained from offering the act as a spectacle in which the majority society might participate. In any case, the reviewer was right in pointing out that Zadek's production undercut a resilient discourse in Germany and Austria: the representation of minorities and immigrants as accidental and disposable addenda to the essence of the nation. With the Burgtheater *Merchant*, there was no denying that Shylock was a full member of the 'Venetian' society. The outsider refused to be identified, and thus simply could not be warded off. The Vienna Shylock had lost the deal, but he was not

---

22 Peter Zadek in an interview with Sigrid Löffler, "Den Shylock kriegste nicht ekelhaft," *profil*, 19 December 1988, 102.
23 Bernd C. Sucher, "Shylock Jude fehlen die Worte," *Süddeutsche Zeitung*, 12 December 1988.
24 Benjamin Henrichs, "Das Messer im Koffer," *Die Zeit*, 16 December 1988.

destroyed. He was not a victim to be pitied and excluded, but remained a member of society.

4.2 The "Shylock Syndrome": Dietrich Schwanitz's Close Reading of Anti-Semitism

The 1988 Burgtheater production of *Merchant* can be fruitfully related to another important negotiation of the Shylock figure which appeared on the threshold of the 1990s. In 1989, Dietrich Schwanitz, a professor of English Literature at the University of Hamburg, published a book entitled *Shylock: Von Shakespeare bis zum Nürnberger Prozeß* ("Shylock: From Shakespeare to the Nuremberg Trials").[25] His proposition was to locate the Shylock figure at the very heart of the long history of European and German anti-Semitism. As Schwanitz suggested, *Merchant* had to be read as a condensed articulation of ideological configurations that had produced barbarous results. However, the real point of the study was that Shakespeare had transposed these ideologies into the realm of "art" – a realm where their deep structure becomes accessible. As it seemed to Schwanitz, the play was thus a privileged site for working through anti-Semitism and the Holocaust in a combined effort of ideology critique, psychological self-analysis, and memory work.

The following passage from the beginning of his book does not only elucidate Schwanitz's design of cathartic analysis, but also stands as an example of German mnemonic dispositions at the end of the 1980s. Commenting on a seminar he had taught at the University of Hamburg, Schwanitz explained:

> The crucial moment in our joint experience with the topic was when the discussion suddenly revealed that our perception had undergone a major shift, such as in contemplating a picture puzzle ("wie bei einem Vexierbild"): *The Merchant of Venice* had stopped being the 'object' of our analysis. Rather, we were now looking at reality *through* the play. For many seminar participants the experience was similar to looking at the moon through a telescope for the first time. For the first time they were glancing at the German-Jewish trauma without immediately freezing in horror and looking away again. [...] One cannot contemplate the horrible face of Medusa without being paralyzed. However, great art helps us to keep looking against all odds. Of course, we will then see the face of Medusa only indirectly, but we will be able to look without flinching.[26]

---

25 Dietrich Schwanitz, *Shylock: Von Shakespeare bis zum Nürnberger Prozeß* (Hamburg: Krämer 1989).
26 Schwanitz, *Shylock: Von Shakespeare bis zum Nürnberger Prozeß*, 14. Cf. the revised version of Schwanitz's study, *Das Shylock-Syndrom oder die Dramaturgie der Barbarei* (Frankfurt/M.: Eich-

A revised version of the Shylock study that Schwanitz published in 1997 under the title *Das Shylock-Syndrom oder die Dramaturgie der Barbarei* ("The Shylock Syndrome or the Dramaturgy of Barbarism") received considerable attention in the German press. Schwanitz had left the main body of the book unchanged. However, the study now terminated in a polemical essay on contemporary German practices of remembrance – an essay that the reviewer of the *Frankfurter Allgemeine Zeitung* found both "brilliant" and "absurd."[27] And it began with a more systematic explication of the concepts applied in Schwanitz's reading. Here he introduced the keyword "dramatic scenario" ("dramatisches Szenario").

Pointing out that his book was intended for "all those who are looking for ways of relaxing the cramp" and who wish to "face the collapse of their civilization without demoralising themselves and others," Schwanitz explained:

> The way that this book suggests is via reaching back to the language of forms that has been devised by great literature. In this language the abyss of experience is combined with a wealth of perspectives that is bound to loosen our paralysis. Therefore, the book is centred on the concept of the dramatic scenario. This is taken to be the form in which the anti-Semitic phantasm appears and takes on a *gestalt*. A scenario cannot be explained by reference to external causes. Rather, it stabilizes itself by force of a dramaturgy that organizes social and semantic energies into a dynamic figure. Here is the reason for the enigmatic character of the dramatic scenario, which cannot be reduced to external causes. Its form is autonomous. In consequence, one has to understand its structure. This is the objective of the present book. In the following, many stories will be told. Within the dramatic scenario, these stories are tied into a single story – the story of a European obsession. Having read this story we will perhaps feel the effect of that aesthetic purgation that we call catharsis.[28]

Schwanitz's study is driven by a twofold vision. The emphatic tone of the book (including the repeated image of looking at the unbearable) underline the resolution of confronting not only anti-Semitism and the Holocaust but also the rootedness of both within German and "European" cultural history. At the same time, Schwanitz is inspired by a redemptive fantasy built on the twin concept of figuration and scenario. This is why he insists on looking indirectly, on using "great literature" or "great art" as a mirror that will deflect some of the destructive energy. Indeed, Schwanitz claims that the indirect approach

---

born, 1997), 20, where the reference to the seminar is deleted but the ideas about looking at the face of Medusa are repeated verbatim.

27 Karl Markus Michel, "Von den Fremden magst du Zins nehmen – Gegen die Priester vor der Bundeslade: Dietrich Schwanitz erforscht das 'Shylock-Syndrom'," *Frankfurter Allgemeine Zeitung*, 2 December 1997.

28 Schwanitz, *Das Shylock-Syndrom*, 7–8.

4.2 The "Shylock Syndrome": Dietrich Schwanitz's Close Reading — 173

can lead into the heart of the matter, to a place where "work on the myth"[29] will coincide with the labour of working through, where historical analysis and psychoanalysis will be achieved within a single effort of close reading. In consequence, Schwanitz views social or political history as after-effects of a dramatic psychological game whose mysterious rules can be unravelled through the powers of a rigorously formalist structuralism. This relegation is the precondition for the therapeutic effect envisaged: only if the history of figures and affects can be isolated from the material rest of history will it prove possible to cure the illness of anti-Semitism.

The costs of this reductionism become apparent in the concluding chapters of *Das Shylock-Syndrom*, where anti-Semitism, anti-capitalism, and "anti-Americanism" are all too easily identified with each other. Here is how Schwanitz, writing simultaneously about the students' movement and the opposition against the Gulf War, summarily accuses "the German left" of inheriting key ideologemes from the German right: "[R]ight-wing anti-Semitism turned into left-wing anti-Zionism, and the anti-materialist cultural critique of the right transformed into the anti-capitalist anti-Americanism of the left."[30] Schwanitz's approach to contemporary memory practices is equally pithy and equally broad, bringing him close to sentiments that Martin Walser would express in his (in)famous speech in acceptance of the Peace Price of the German Book Trade in 1998 (see below):

> The curse that used to lie on the Jews is now lying on them [i. e. on the Germans]. And it will continue to do so until the high priests of the art of memory will be clearly exposed as what they really are: not agents of enlightenment or intellectuals, but priests. Self-empowered legislators for dealing with horror. Special agents of an abysmal power. Wardens of intimidating secrets and ambassadors of demonic forces. In sum, figures who run Holocaust memory in the manner of running a power plant from which they draw energy to increase their own influence.[31]

In spite of such diatribes, Schwanitz's analysis is certainly insightful. His achievement lies in breaking loose from a long German tradition of functionalizing *Merchant* in the name of a majoritarian social ethos. One might perhaps claim that Schwanitz was the first non-Jewish German who systematically used the play as a touchstone for defining a social vision that would be resilient to the "syndrome" of anti-Semitism. In doing so, Schwanitz presumed to commu-

---

[29] Schwanitz, *Das Shylock-Syndrom*, 7. Cf. Hans Blumenberg, *Arbeit am Mythos* (Frankfurt/M.: Suhrkamp, 1979).
[30] Schwanitz, *Das Shylock-Syndrom*, 266.
[31] Schwanitz, *Das Shylock-Syndrom*, 278–279.

nicate at eye-level with earlier German-Jewish approaches, especially with Hermann Sinsheimer's *Shylock: The History of a Character* / *Shylock: Die Geschichte einer Figur* (1947/1960) and with the Shylock chapter in Hans Mayer's *Außenseiter* (1975; *Outsiders: A Study in Life and Letters*, 1982).

Schwanitz reads *Merchant* as "a play on the contrast between (archaic) community and (modern) society."[32] Within this polarity, he argues, the drama develops an ambivalent solution. On the one hand, it follows the drift of modernization in "opting for differentiating a wider society of strangers from a closely defined realm of intimacy." On the other hand, Shakespeare's comedy – like European social ideology more generally – is not consistent in performing the transition that Schwanitz (slipping into English even in the German original of his study) defines as the transition "from tribal brotherhood to universal otherhood." Rather, it is suggested, Shakespeare's conservative stance on the question of interest caused him to hold on to the doctrine that love might continue to serve as an all-embracing social ideal.[33]

One may say that Zadek's 1988 Burgtheater production mended what Schwanitz felt to be the half-hearted character of the play – that it pushed Shakespeare across the limits of his conservative social ideology. Although the Shylock played by Gert Voss was personally vanquished by the trial, he was still successful in redefining Venetian society as a society of strangers, a society where the template of otherness and tolerance rather than the template of brotherhood and hate must grudgingly be applied. In contrast to Schwanitz, however, Zadek and Voss did not limit Shylock to his dimension as a figure. In the Burgtheater production, the history of anti-Semitism was evidently more than a riddle solved by means of structuralist psychoanalysis. Rather, anti-Semitism was present as a continued given with which certain people did have to live. Indeed, while the ideas of dramaturgy and theatre are central in Schwanitz's two books, there is almost no mention of the stage history of *Merchant*. This lack of interest is revealing, for the catharsis Schwanitz looks for is to be had only in terms of an *imaginary* dramaturgy revealed by close reading, and not in terms of real theatrical performance. Schwanitz does not explicitly say so, but his book suggests that the real performance of *Merchant* should be avoided if redemptive figurations are looked for.

---

[32] Schwanitz, *Das Shylock-Syndrom*, 66–67, and (verbatim) *Shylock: Von Shakespeare bis zum Nürnberger Prozeß*, 56.

[33] Schwanitz, *Das Shylock-Syndrom*, 123, and (verbatim) *Shylock: Von Shakespeare bis zum Nürnberger Prozeß*, 106.

4.3 The Theatre of Remembrance: Imperatives, Denials, and Transferences

Transcending the Holocaust?

"Those were glorious times when *The Merchant of Venice* could still be staged by a Jewish director as a colourful fairytale!"[34] With these words, Shakespeare scholar Wilhelm Hortmann introduced a 2003 review essay on German productions of the play. The reference, of course, was to Max Reinhardt's lavish interpretations during the first decades of the twentieth century (see Chapter 1). Hortmann interpreted these as manifestations of an innocence that had been lost. He argued that attempts at introducing Holocaust consciousness into the performance of Shakespeare's comedy distorted the dramatic balance of the play. However, the reviewer felt that one recent interpretation could be seen as a new departure.

The respective production had opened at the Munich Residenztheater on 11 October 2001. It was directed by Dieter Dorn, the well-known proponent of a dramatic style which was praised for its forcefulness but also criticized for its aesthetic conservatism.[35] It may be indicative of the significance of *Merchant* on the German stage that Dorn chose this play to open the first season in his new theatre, after having been ousted from the directorship of the Munich Kammerspiele, and then – by the grace of other political agents – reinstalled in yet grander style as manager of the Munich Residenztheater. According to Hortmann, it had been on the basis of an "absolute respect for the text" that Dorn's well-received production had found a way out of the theatrical "dilemma" caused by the Holocaust.[36] In this context, the reviewer came up with a suggestive pair of terms: "This production," he claimed, "was not a post-Holocaust but rather a trans-Holocaust interpretation."[37]

The compound "Trans-Holocaust-Darstellung" sounds as unusual in German as it does in English. It wavers between two meanings. On the one hand, a "trans-Holocaust-production" abstracts from the specificity of the genocide, universalizing the Holocaust by rendering it a *figura* of general significance.

---

[34] Wilhelm Hortmann, "Wo, bitte, geht's nach Belmont? Über ein Dilemma von Inszenierungen des *Kaufmann von Venedig* nach dem Holocaust," *Shakespeare Jahrbuch* 139 (2003): 217.
[35] For a discussion of the tendency to see Dorn's aesthetics as past-oriented, see Yvonne Poppek, *Was ist ein Dorn? Die Shakespeare-Inszenierungen des Theaterregisseurs Dieter Dorn* (Munich: Utz, 2007), 9–10.
[36] Hortmann, "Wo, bitte, geht's nach Belmont?," 220.
[37] Hortmann, "Wo, bitte, geht's nach Belmont?," 223.

On the other hand, transcending the Holocaust might also mean to break free from the imperative of remembrance. This ambivalent movement of universalizing and, at the same time, diluting significance is characteristic of 'memory culture' in the narrow sense of the term. Indeed, although published two years earlier, Hortmann's pronouncements read like an affirmative response to the questions posed by Micha Brumlik in 2005: "What lies in wait on this side of the threshold? Is it a new time for Germany and the Germans in which they will be at peace with themselves and with their past?"[38] In Hortmann's essay, the hope for "peace" surfaces as the desire to recover the Belmont scenes, using them as the site for a salvation from the burden of the past. Hortmann's title – "Wo, bitte, geht's nach Belmont?" – translates as "Could you show us the way to Belmont, please?" Interestingly, this functionalization of Belmont re-enacts tendencies inherent in the early post-war reception of *Merchant* (see Chapter 1).

Both Hortmann (born in 1929) and Dorn (born in 1935) had not yet come of age by 1945. They are neither members of the 'first generation,' which often resisted Holocaust remembrance, nor of the 'second generation,' which enforced such remembrance in a revolt against the parents. Accordingly, Hortmann's review essay can partly be understood as stating the dispositions of an in-between age-group – a group whose members, exactly because their consciousness of the painful implications of the Holocaust is relatively immediate, may be unable to submit to the constant mediation of the genocide.

Martin Walser (born in 1927), the writer who shocked the public with his 1998 speech in acceptance of the Peace Price of the German Book Trade, also is a member of this generation. In his reaction to 'memory culture,' Walser had declared:

> No one who can be taken seriously would deny Auschwitz. No one in his right wits would relativize the horror of Auschwitz. But when the media confront me, day in and day out, with this past, I realize how something within me is stirring to revolt against such a constant presentation of our shame. [...] It is not adequate to make Auschwitz into a habitually delivered threat, a handy means of intimidation, a moral cudgel or compulsive routine exercise. What is achieved by ritualization can only have the quality of lip service.[39]

---

38 Brumlik, "Jenseits der Schwelle," 12.
39 Martin Walser, "Erfahrungen beim Verfassen einer Sonntagsrede," *Friedenspreis des Deutschen Buchhandels – 1998: Martin Walser*, 11–12, accessed 8 September 2018, https://www.friedenspreis-des-deutschen-buchhandels.de/sixcms/media.php/1290/1998_walser_mit_nachtrag_2017.pdf.

4.3 The Theatre of Remembrance: Imperatives, Denials, and Transferences — 177

Was Dorn's 2001 production of *Merchant* motivated by similar qualms? Did the performance offered on the stage of Munich's Residenztheater help to keep the "moral cudgel" at bay? At first, the discourse generated around the production seems to suggest exactly this. Before the premiere, Dorn had made it clear that *Merchant* needed to be dissociated from Holocaust memory: "I cannot use Shylock to explain the Holocaust. In my view [the play] is a parable of capitalism."[40] Along these lines, the theatre had avoided the word "Jew" in a conspicuous and belaboured manner. The synopsis of the play on the theatre's website read:

> The story of the fight between the two Saturnine brothers Antonio and Shylock, which begins to escalate in the thicket of the city of Venice and in which the two contenders are both completely in the right and just as completely in the wrong, is among the most passionate and most accurately calculated stage texts by Shakespeare.[41]

In her review of Dorn's *Merchant*, Barbara Reitter highlighted both the status of the director's style and the implications of its application to Shakespeare's play. While stage and auditorium were considerably larger in the Residenztheater, she suggested, "all the rest" remained "true to what we are used to from the Kammerspiele":

> [Dorn] not only continues to work with his congenial stage designer Jürgen Rose but also sticks to his old style in all other respects. And this still means: the best actors in the republic; the highest culture of elocution; a meticulous attention to the classical texts; images and stories that possess a dream-like beauty and that unfold their full and timeless epic potential. Accordingly, Dorn allowed Shakespeare's *The Merchant of Venice* to remain in that remote century when anti-Semitism was not yet known. When it comes to a play that has been abused by all kinds of interest groups for various purposes this is a bold decision. Certainly, it is politically correct. However, being conscious of hundreds of years of history that finally led to Auschwitz, one would have wished that the director had come up with a more decided statement.[42]

The phrase about a "remote century when anti-Semitism was not yet known" reiterates the distinction between anti-Judaism as the context of Shakespeare's

---

40 Dieter Dorn, qtd. in Andres Müry, "Die Straßenschlacht. Shakespeare zum Auftakt: Dieter Dorn eröffnet das Münchner Residenztheater mit *Der Kaufmann von Venedig*," *Focus* 41 (8 December 2001), accessed 8 September 2018, https://www.focus.de/kultur/medien/theater-die-strassenschlacht_aid_192952.html.
41 Bayerisches Staatsschauspiel, "Der Kaufmann von Venedig, Regie: Dieter Dorn," accessed 13 March 2009, http://www.bayerischesstaatsschauspiel.de.
42 Barbara Reitter, "Jede Geste fast zu schön," *Neue Osnabrücker Zeitung*, 15 October 2001.

play and anti-Semitism as the context of the Holocaust. Indeed, Dorn's production may have proceeded from an intention to re-insert *Merchant* into the pre-Holocaust universe from which the play had originally evolved. Evoking "images and stories that possess a dream-like beauty" and that are allowed to "unfold their full and timeless epic potential," the director's style certainly had a tendency toward insulating drama against history.

Moreover, the production veered towards presenting the "Saturnine brothers" Shylock and Antonio as counterparts. Both were shown as gruff old men, social outsiders in spite of the economic or social power they wield. This resulted in an emphasis on Antonio's dramatic weight. Thomas Holtzmann provided the role with a towering presence: his Antonio appeared dominant, irritable, and arrogant. During the curtain call, Antonio and Shylock – the latter played by the equally imposing Rolf Boysen – stood on either side of the stage, jointly embodying dark reminiscences, framing and haunting the new society that had emerged during the play. Indeed, the ploy of the production was to insist that both Shylock *and* Antonio needed to be exiled into the realm of the past. Hortmann reads this as demonstrating "how a deeply entrenched hostility has wrought havoc since times immemorial and will continue through eternity – if the younger generation does not put an end to it."[43] In sum, Dorn's *Merchant* could be considered a "trans-Holocaust production" in that it revealed a pressing consciousness of the genocide while simultaneously containing this consciousness within a timeless plot of conflict, punishment and social transformation.

Nevertheless, the production also admitted different perspectives. It is true that memory was staged as a destructive inability to forget. Antonio and Shylock, who embodied memory, were clad in pitch black, while the young people wore brighter colours. However, the trial scene blurred such optimistic distinctions. When Portia (Sibylle Canonica) put on the black garb of the young doctor, she was drawn into the conflict. There was no longer any way in which she might remain impartial or innocent. When Shylock cried "[Y]ou take my life / When you do take the means whereby I live" (4.1.371–372), the clever heiress of Belmont suddenly seemed to realize what she had done. As if she were struck by Shylock's plight, she asked Antonio what mercy he might render his opponent. Having asked Shylock whether he was "contented" (4.1.383), Portia embarrassedly stared at the floor. When Shylock looked at her, that look could be felt as the startled and startling look of the Other – a look that, according to Derrida, suddenly lays bare the full reality of power relationships and fundamentally calls into question established chronology:

---

43 Hortmann, "Wo, bitte, geht's nach Belmont?," 223.

> This spectral *someone other looks at us*, we feel ourselves being looked at by it, outside of any synchrony, even before and beyond any look on our part, according to an absolute anteriority (which may be on the order of generation, of more than one generation) and asymmetry, according to an absolutely unmasterable disproportion.[44]

This rendering of the trial scene muffled the standard resolution of comedy. The fifth act indicated how the younger people had been infected with the aggressions of the old men. Jessica's and Lorenzo's dialogue in 5.1 oscillated between a battle of wits between lovers and the altercations of a couple torn apart by fundamental dislike. Gratiano's double-entendres on Nerissa's "ring" evidently embarrassed all parties involved. Rather than providing room for carefree celebration, Portia's estate proved to be inseparably entwined with Venice life – a fact that the stage design had made evident from the beginning. Indeed, Belmont was constantly present on the stage as a large black shrine, which was opened for the scenes set in Portia's realm. On these occasions, the shrine showed the faded image of a Renaissance palace. Even during the fifth act, this contraption was kept hanging over the scene, revealing that Belmont was primarily an image – the utopian dream of a better world, which would never come. Right at the beginning of the new millennium, Shylock and the play in which he served as the antagonist still frustrated the beginning of "a new era for Germany and the Germans in which they will be at peace with themselves and with their past."[45]

There are significant similarities between the two outstanding productions offered by Zadek in 1988 and Dorn in 2001. Both can be seen as attempts at probing the potentials of the play from a new angle. But the differences between them are just as evident. While Zadek wanted to bracket in routine identifications, he still professed that he was interested in the play as a Jew – specifically as a Jew who had been born in Germany in 1926, had then been forced to emigrate, and had since returned to the country of his birth. Dorn, on the other hand, clearly staged the play from the perspective of the German majority society. However, the force of his production is due to the fact that the director was alert to the resistance that the play, and the history that had accumulated around it, offered against restorative intentions. As a drama that is energized by a yearning for comedic resolutions as well as by an awareness of their shortcomings, *Merchant* offered a platform for acting

---

44 Jacques Derrida, *Specters of Marx: The State of the Debt, the Work of Mourning and the New International*, trans. Peggy Kamuf (1993; Abingdon: Routledge, 1994), 7.
45 Brumlik, "Jenseits der Schwelle," 12.

out the contradictions inherent within as well as in between "post-Holocaust" and "trans-Holocaust" approaches.

The Imperative of Remembrance and the Crisis of Figuration

In Chapter 2 of our study, Hanan Snir's production of *Merchant* at the Weimar Nationaltheater (premiere: 8 April 1995) has been briefly discussed in relation to George Tabori's and Peter Zadek's path-breaking work during the 1970s. Although Snir's *Merchant* was put on the stage after Zadek's Burgtheater production of 1988, the mimetic representation of the context of a concentration camp may appear as a return to older (i.e. 'post-Holocaust') practices of engagement. These were the very paradigms of representation from which Zadek had tried to break free. Although critics were disposed to appreciate Snir's 1995 production as an attempt to do much-needed memory work, the praise was often muffled. Thus, a critic writing for both Berlin's *Morgenpost* and Bonn's *General-Anzeiger* felt that the Nationaltheater's various efforts to commemorate the fiftieth anniversary of the liberation of Buchenwald were characterized not only by "seriousness, dignity, and sensitivity," but also by an "unorthodox boldness." The last predicate was directed at Snir's *Merchant*, which, according to the review, was based on an "almost alarmingly daring approach" (the German word "tollkühn," which was used in this context, might also be translated as "foolhardy").[46]

Quite in keeping with the rhetoric of Shakespeare's play, many reviewers used the German term "Wagnis" ("risk" or "venture"), frequently combined with an expression of relief that the "venture" seemed to have "gone well."[47] However, others posed the question of whether *Merchant* was an appropriate platform for confronting the Holocaust:

> Even after having watched the Weimar performance doubts remain. Of course, remarkable achievements can be listed on the plus side of the production. The framing action retrieves the play from its aesthetic and historical distance, making its painfulness concretely understandable. [...] On the other hand, it is evident that the Weimar version of *Merchant* frequently twists the play and lacks sufficient motivation. This adds weight to the question

---

46 Lorenz Tomerius, "Der 'Kaufmann von Venedig' spielt im Vernichtungslager," *Berliner Morgenpost*, 12 April 1995. Cf. (with slight editorial changes) Tomerius, "Shylock in Weimar: Die Mörder lassen spielen," *General-Anzeiger* (Bonn), 12 April 1995.
47 Michael Plote, "'Tanz auf dem Vulkan' menschlicher Gefühle," *Freies Wort*, 10 April 1995. For similar turns of phrase, see e.g. Thomas Bickelhaupt, "Der Shakespeare der SS," *Frankfurter Allgemeine Zeitung*, 11 April 1995.

why exactly we should try to discuss our problems with this Shakespearean play – a play that is quite problematic in and of itself.[48]

Among the negative reviews, the one by Maik Hamburger for *Shakespeare Jahrbuch* was the most detailed and pertinent. Starting out from an overview of the play's reception in post-war Germany, Hamburger observed: "In Weimar, the Israeli director Hanan Snir has taken the bull by the horns. He has superimposed the real genocide committed by the National Socialists onto the discrimination against the Jew that is implicit in the poetry of the play."[49] Hamburger conceded that, "in spite of its clichéd manner," Snir's use of Buchenwald for framing the play certainly had emotive power. However, he also felt that it resulted in an aporia:

> Naturally, Shakespeare does not have a chance. [...] Snir stages a concentration camp play which has neither been written nor invested with a dramaturgical logic but which has been improvised around Shakespeare's play. The director presumes to map a simulated reality onto the work of art. [...] However, for both actors and audience this reality is already history and cannot be matched with the material of unmediated experience. The "reality of history" [to which Snir had referred in the theatre programme] turns out to be merely a naïve and frequently mistaken mimesis of the Nazi period [...]. However, it is still real enough to smother the imagination of the poetry.[50]

This suggests that the attempt to represent and work through the Holocaust by means of performing *Merchant* failed not only because the vaunted "reality of history" had not really been taken seriously enough, but also because the tension of play and world had been "smothered" by an inadequate presumption of realist mimesis.

Writing for the *Thüringer Allgemeine*, an East German daily, Henryk Goldberg conceptualized this problem as a crisis of figuration. According to Goldberg, by representing Shakespeare's moneylender as a camp inmate who eventually is killed by the SS, Snir had moved the audience towards fully accepting Shylock: "Now we are able to completely understand the Jew Shylock because we identify him as the Jewish prisoner." However, such identification also seemed to Goldberg to destroy Shylock's dynamic and potential. In this context, Goldberg came up with an interesting metaphor:

---

48 Lothar Schmidt-Mühlisch, "Wie der Jude bei der Taufe ertränkt wird," *Die Welt*, 10 April 1995.
49 Maik Hamburger, "Regisseure aus Israel und England in Thüringen," *Shakespeare Jahrbuch* 132 (1996): 174.
50 Hamburger, "Regisseure aus Israel und England," 176.

> Taking away the unexplained mystery of the play's characters, Snir is also taking away their vitality. This vitality is inherent in a tightrope act, not in a firm stride forward. It is as if what has been announced as a tightrope act were now to take place on the flat ground, with the hemp rope painted on stone. [...] Primarily, the production fails because of its inability to offer the actors adequate room in which a dramatic character can be developed.[51]

Of course, director Hanan Snir and dramaturge Gad Kaynar had started out from a different definition of theatrical space than that implied by Goldberg's insistence on "adequate room" in which to "develop" a "character" (the German term used in the review is "Figur").

Looking back in 2010, Kaynar explained that the Weimar *Merchant* "should be viewed as a psycho-social and not merely as a textual-performative undertaking."[52] In other words, the theatrical space was supposed to comprise Weimar in its entirety. The actors involved were not only the ensemble of the Nationaltheater, but all of Weimar's citizens. And the drama to be performed was limited neither to *Merchant* nor to the added frame, but in fact extended much further: it was the open-ended drama of German – particularly East German – attempts and refusals to work through the past. As Kaynar concludes in an essay published in 2017, "the contaminated memory patterns of the Holocaust featured, mostly unintentionally, as the real protagonist of the double-edged stage allegory and theatrical event directed by Snir."[53]

This remark by Kaynar indicates an awareness that he and Snir had underrated the complexity of memory discourses and overestimated the powers of theatrical performance. Shortly before the premiere, Snir confessed: "The past three months of working in this place have been the most difficult months in my entire life." He felt that the people of Weimar had "difficulties in dealing with strangers," and that they easily considered themselves "disturbed or cornered." Moreover, the director regretted that he had been unable to enter into a dialogue with the ensemble. According to Snir, the distance of the actors

---

[51] Henryk Goldberg, "Das Seil, auf Stein gemalt," *Thüringer Allgemeine*, 10 April 1995.

[52] Hans-Peter Bayerdörfer and Gad Kaynar, "'Jedem das Seine' oder Buchenwald in Weimar," in *Shylockgestalten*, ed. Patric Blaser and Brigitte Dalinger, special issue of *Maske und Kothurn* 56.3 (2010): 39. Cf. also Kaynar's recent essay on the Weimar production, in which the dramaturge explains that he and Snir "opted for a metatheatrical framework which involved several planes of reality," including "a play-within-a-play within present-day German reality." Gad Kaynar-Kissinger, "*The Merchant of Venice* on the German Stage and the 1995 'Buchenwald' Production in Weimar," in *Wrestling with Shylock: Jewish Responses to* The Merchant of Venice, ed. Michael Shapiro and Edna Nahshon (Cambridge: Cambridge University Press, 2017), 262.

[53] Kaynar-Kissinger, "*The Merchant of Venice* on the German Stage and the 1995 'Buchenwald' Production in Weimar," 271.

4.3 The Theatre of Remembrance: Imperatives, Denials, and Transferences — 183

had been due to both aesthetic and psychological reasons. On the one hand, the Brechtian aesthetics prevalent in the GDR had "weaned the actors from an emotional approach to theatre playing." On the other hand, they had strongly disliked having to play SS men.[54] As Snir indicated, general professional dissatisfaction, xenophobia, and memory blockades among the Germans were among the reasons for his negative experiences. At the same time, rather than really offering a space in which the German audience might have pondered its relationship to a guilty past, Snir's and Kaynar's rigorously mimetic and identitarian approach hampered productive processes of figuration, both within and without the world of Shakespeare's play.

In the last two decades, there have been a few widely noted guest productions of *Merchant* by Jewish directors from abroad: in addition to Snir's Weimar *Merchant* (1995), they comprise, for example, Avishai Milstein's Freiburg (2011) and Barrie Kosky's Frankfurt (Main) (2012) productions. Because of the thematic focus of our book, we have not systematically studied the reverse scenario, i.e. the impact of German productions on the stage history of *Merchant* in the Anglophone world. And yet, the story of one German actor playing Shylock on a London stage deserves closer attention because it offers a brief insight into differences between national stage traditions in relation to Shylock.

In 1998, Norbert Kentrup, a German actor and director, played Shylock on the stage of the Globe Theatre, which had been opened in the previous year. Fifteen years earlier, Kentrup had been among the founding members of the bremer shakespeare company. Inspired by the concept of the early modern "popular theatre," as described by Robert Weimann in *Shakespeare and the Popular Tradition in the Theatre* (1976; German original 1967), the bremer shakespeare company started out to break with the tradition of the proscenium stage and naturalistic acting, developing a theatre that includes the audience.

At the opening of the Globe Theatre Neuss (in North Rhine-Westphalia) in 1991, Kentrup had met Sam Wanamaker, the American actor and director who was the driving force behind the reconstruction of the Globe in London.[55] They became friends, sharing the same fascination with the theatrical potential of Shakespeare's Globe. In 1993, Kentrup was involved in the foundation of the International Shakespeare-Globe-Zentrum Deutschland, and he also became a member of The Globe Council. Wanamaker developed the wish that Kentrup

---

54 Hanan Snir in an interview with Lothar Schmidt-Mühlisch, *Die Welt*, 10 April 1995.
55 Shakespeare's Globe, "Germany," accessed 8 September 2018, http://www.shakespearesglobe.com/about-us/todays-globe/international/germany. The following passages are based on a talk with Norbert Kentrup, in June 2016, as well as unpublished notes generously provided by Kentrup.

would play Shylock at the reconstructed Globe, but Wanamaker died before this idea could be realized. For the celebrations of Shakespeare's birthday in April 1993, the bremer shakespeare company was invited to perform, in German, *The Merry Wives of Windsor* on the construction site of the Globe. Kentrup was present at the opening ceremony of the Globe Theatre in 1997 and returned to the Globe in the following year to play the role of Shylock in a production directed by Richard Olivier.

One major difficulty Kentrup had to master was English. He had learnt the language only for this role, but his command of it was far from perfect. The actor was aware of his strong German accent, and the effect it might have on the role of Shylock, marking him also linguistically as an outsider. Moreover, Kentrup knew that a lack of concentration might be disastrous because there was no prompter and his English was not good enough to improvise. For this reason, he decided to always carry his own prompt-book with him, which he would build into the role. It became Shylock's book, in which he took notes about the behaviour of the Christians, to make them litigable, as it were. Shylock thus transformed into a character who was scrupulously precise and constantly alert, incessantly turning his head here and there like a bird, so that no danger would escape his watchful eye.

Another difficulty faced by Kentrup were his disagreements with Olivier. The director apparently wanted an 'authentic' Shylock, supported by a large red hat (which Kentrup resented) and 'Jewish' gestures. For Kentrup, who felt obliged to the memory of Sam Wanamaker, himself a Jew, the idea of such an 'authentic' Shylock ran the danger of reiterating anti-Semitic ideology. After decades in which directors and actors in Germany had deconstructed the figure of the stage Jew, Kentrup feared that this stereotype was exactly what Olivier had in mind. Two years previously, Kentrup had been involved in a production of *Merchant* by the bremer shakespeare company (directed by Andres Perez from Chile; premiere: 7 February 1996). In this context, he had learnt to see Shylock not as a coherent character but as a figure who changes from scene to scene, and sometimes even from one line to the next. In Bremen, each act featured a Shylock played by a different actor.

Compared to this study of figuration, Olivier's approach seemed too psychological. For the Globe production, Kentrup eventually decided to develop his own take on the role, which would challenge both the stereotypes piled up around Shylock and the idea of a coherent character. He had a Jewish teacher with whom he read the text and who confirmed him in his understanding of Shylock as a figure "without flesh." This teacher also introduced him into Jewish culture and organized meetings with British Jews, among them survivors who had come to the United Kingdom as children, rescued by the Refugee Children's

Movement on the so-called *Kindertransport* ('children's transport') in the last months before the Second World War. Kentrup's approach to the role was inspired by his new knowledge about Judaism, but also by his awareness of his own identity as a German.

What seems to have been paramount, however, was Kentrup's wish to play Shylock as an obvious outsider. The architecture of the Globe, open to the skies, invited him to think of Shylock as a Jew, who would raise his eyes to heaven, as if in mute dialogue with his God. Kentrup also resisted Olivier's suggestion of a broken and truly converted Shylock at the end of the trial scene. Against Olivier's explicit instructions, Kentrup decided to play Shylock's exit not unlike Kortner had done in the 1968/69 TV version; he spoke Shylock's lines, "I am content," then drew his tallit over his head, and slowly left the stage. Lois Potter, in his review article published in *Shakespeare Quarterly*, attests Kentrup a "finely nuanced interpretation," which "gave the character not only dignity but an element of mystery." "Unlike most Shylocks," Potter adds, "this one did not seem terminally ill when he left the courtroom, and it was possible to feel that the story was not yet over."[56]

Many of the productions discussed in this chapter show an increasing insistence on the non-identitarian dynamic of theatrical figuration. They do so despite the fact that *Merchant* has continued to be produced as a vehicle of Holocaust memory. Indeed, the example of Kentrup may suggest particularly clearly that the one does not necessarily exclude the other. This is also true of many directors who represent a 'third generation' in relation to National Socialism and the Holocaust. They still respond to the imperative of remembrance by striving to relate the play – directly, as it were – to the past and to the processes of remembering the past. This is evident, for example, from a fairly recent production that Malte Kreutzfeldt realized for the Landestheater Coburg (premiere: 3 October 2008). In stark contrast to Hortmann's restorative concept of a "trans-Holocaust interpretation," Kreutzfeldt's work clearly lacked an "absolute respect for the text," rigorously updating *Merchant* to present ways of feeling and speaking, including a plethora of contemporary racist insults. Belmont was almost totally absent. Of the fifth act, only Jessica's and Lorenzo's dialogue on the lovers of myth and story (5.1.1–24) remained, designated as an "Epilogue" by a projection on the proscenium arch. Accordingly, Portia did not serve as a salvational figure, but was rather played by Dagmar Poppy as a problematic minor character who was drawn into the plot and its guilty implications.

---

[56] Lois Potter, "A Stage Where Every Man Must Play a Part," *Shakespeare Quarterly* 50.1 (1999): 76.

Snir had wanted to activate and direct the mnemonic potentials of *Merchant* by adding the framing play and by implicitly extending the stage into the audience. He thus imbued the theatrical performance with a complex temporality, evoking at least three layers of historical significance: the distant early modern past from which the play originally emerged, the past of the Holocaust, and the present of the production. These layers were intertwined by a theatrical performance that suggested and revealed various links between them – for example, posing questions about the relations between the traditional anti-Jewish discourse of the play, the anti-Semitism of the National Socialists, and the xenophobia evident in contemporary Germany.

The mnemonic design of Kreutzfeldt's production likewise resulted in complex temporalities. On the one hand, the on-stage occurrences seemed to be set in the present, as when Antonio declared at the very beginning: "The financial crisis does not concern me." On this level, the production displayed a contemporary society that, even and especially after the Holocaust, was morbidly xenophobic and anti-Semitic. Lancelot, for example, concluded his monologue in 2.2 with the words: "Scheiß Itzig!" – an old-fashioned expression that might be translated as "fucking Jew."[57] On the other hand, Kreutzfeldt also implied a second historical time frame. When, after the trial scene, Jessica and Lorenzo were speaking their "Epilogue" at the back of the stage, Shylock remained up front, folding his invalidated contract into a paper boat and sending it adrift on a pool of water. The scene was accompanied by a recording of the 1948 Israeli Declaration of Independence. While the historical words were played over the audio system, a German translation was projected onto the proscenium arch. It froze on the words "in hope," which were still visible during the curtain call. This activated an extra-theatrical history in which the State of Israel was finally realized in reaction to the Holocaust. In consequence, the society portrayed in the course of the play seemed to acquire a manifold temporality. 'Venice' seemed to be situated simultaneously before, during, and after the Holocaust. This circuitous temporality underscored the permanent latency of the genocide as a 'rupture in civilization.' However, it also de-historicized and de-realized the Holocaust. Arguably, in Coburg, the imperative of remembrance resulted in a dramatic configuration in which history and memory, representational and figurative evocations of the Holocaust clashed.

---

[57] 'Itzig' is a shortened version of the family name *Jitzchak* (Isaac), which in some German dialects was used as a synonym for 'Jew.' See Hans Peter Althaus, *Mauscheln: Ein Wort als Waffe* (Berlin: De Gruyter, 2002), 257–258.

Another production that opened in the same year, Elmar Goerden's *Merchant* at the Schauspielhaus Bochum (premiere: 10 October 2008), deserves particular attention because few directors can be expected to be as acutely aware of the play's implications as Goerden. He has published on the British and German stage histories of Shylock, commenting on both the precariousness and the potentials of the role.[58] Moreover, he has researched, written, and directed an acclaimed dramatic investigation into the problems of Lessing's *Nathan*. In the resultant play, *Lessings Traum von Nathan dem Weisen* ("Lessing's Dream of Nathan the Wise"), which premiered at the Staatstheater Stuttgart in 1999, Goerden wished to interrogate "the potentials and suitability of *Nathan* in light of our historical experience."[59] Interestingly, *Lessings Traum* introduced Shylock into Lessing's play, where he confronted the playwright's universalist "dream" of tolerance with the reality of the Holocaust.

A press release by the theatre described Goerden's production as a project that "had been close to his heart for a long time."[60] However, it received mixed reviews. The reviewer for the *Westfälische Rundschau* was impressed by Shylock, who had been played by the actress Renate Becker – not, indeed, as a woman but as an elderly man: "In particular, there is one veritable, deeply conceived character, and that, alas, is Shylock. Renate Becker plays him as an unsteady figure, gnarled but also vulnerable, wooden but also fragile, dry as dust but also driven by demons." However, the same review stated that Goerden had invoked too many "particles of ideas and more or less clever pronouncements on the subject that loosely accumulate[d] here and there."[61] Along similar lines, Sarah Heppekausen reviewing the production for the online magazine *nachtkritik.de* felt that the many topics addressed in the performance, and the wealth of additional material, resulted in a loss of dramatic direction: "The

---

58 See Elmar Goerden, "Der Andere: Fragmente einer Bühnengeschichte Shylocks im deutschen und englischen Theater des 18. und 19. Jahrhunderts," in *Theatralia Judaica: Emanzipation und Antisemitismus als Momente der Theatergeschichte. Von der Lessing-Zeit bis zur Shoah*, ed. Hans-Peter Bayerdörfer (Tübingen: Niemeyer, 1992) 129–163.
59 Elmar Goerden, "Nathan findet nicht statt," in Staatstheater Stuttgart, *Lessings Traum von Nathan dem Weisen: Collage mit Passagen aus Nathan der Weise und Der Kaufmann von Venedig, sowie modernen Texten von Elmar Goerden*, theatre programme (Staatstheater Stuttgart, 1999), 5.
60 Schauspielhaus Bochum, "Der Kaufmann von Venedig," press release, accessed 18 September 2008, http://www.schauspielhausbochum.de/presse/.
61 Bernd Berke, "Ein Mitbewerber wird eiskalt erledigt," *Westfälische Rundschau*, 13 October 2008.

numerous approaches mutually impede their respective effectiveness or peter out into insignificance."[62]

Goerden's 2008 *Merchant* also met with criticism by members of Bochum's Jewish community who felt hurt by the portrayal of Shylock.[63] In light of Becker's empathetic performance, this may seem surprising. Indeed, her Shylock was the most fragile person on the stage. He was also the one with the most delicate voice. It seemed plausible that such a Shylock could only stand up to the contempt that he was constantly encountering by insisting on the letter of the law – and also by wielding a knife. The only provocation that Shylock offered before the trial scene was his refusal to conform to the all-pervading logic of a power-hungry and entertainment-addicted society.

Indeed, Goerden clearly had set his *Merchant* in the present. The stage represented an open-air bar, reminiscent of a typical street café in emulation of Italian lifestyles, as it can be found almost everywhere in contemporary Germany. The customers were mostly well dressed, and there was plenty of music and celebration. Occasional references to the financial crisis could not really disturb the general mirth. In this atmosphere, Shylock was the odd one out. Dressed in a conspicuously inconspicuous, old-fashioned manner, he was a constant reminder of a half-forgotten history. In conversation with Tubal, who was represented as a fully assimilated Jew, Shylock spelt out his insistence on remembrance. When Tubal – emulating a line from the Nathan of Goerden's Stuttgart production – insisted that Jewishness was merely a "religion," Renate Becker's Shylock answered: "So you think it was on religious grounds that we were forbidden to go to symphonic concerts and to listen to the radio?"

It seems that the production's potential to offend was grounded in its dual functionalization of the Shylock figure, positing Becker's version of Shakespeare's moneylender as both an "acid test" of modern society's potentials for "humanity and tolerance"[64] *and* as a figuration of the presence of the Holocaust. Indeed, the question of why the Bochum production was deemed hurtful elucidates general problems of performing the play in contemporary Germany. To begin with, there is the problem of Shylock's Jewishness. Learning to 'understand' his desire for revenge may be a productive exercise in empathy. However,

---

62 Sarah Heppekausen, "Jenseits der Finanzkriese," *nachtkritik.de*, 10 October 2008, accessed 8 September 2018, http://nachtkritik.de/index.php?option=com_content&view=article&id=1864&Itemid=0.
63 The performance on 24 January 2009 was followed by a public discussion in response to complaints addressed to Goerden. Several participants renewed their statement that, as Jews living in Germany after the Holocaust, they felt "hurt" by the production's portrayal of Shylock.
64 Elmar Goerden in his introduction to the performance of the production on 24 January 2009.

4.3 The Theatre of Remembrance: Imperatives, Denials, and Transferences — 189

Figure 10: Renate Becker (Shylock) and Benno Ifland (Antonio) in Elmar Goerden's 2008 production at the Schauspielhaus Bochum. Photograph by Matthias Horn. Courtesy of Matthias Horn.

the process is also bound to trigger precarious associations in that it makes 'Jewishness' connote a desire for revenge. The realization of the trial scene in Goerden's production, which had Renate Becker literally climb onto the outstretched Antonio, dangerously wielding a pair of poultry shears (see figure 10), is a case in point. Obviously, the presentation was meant to highlight the outrageous sensationalism with which Shakespeare tapped into the collective (un)consciousness as well as the asymmetrical power relationship between Shylock and the Christians.

However, the self-reflection at work in Goerden's realization of the scene may not have been immediately clear to everybody. Certainly, the playful investigation of the history of the Shylock figure was complicated and confounded by the contemporaneity of the theatrical setting. This resulted in a clash of temporalities as well as in a clash of representational and figurative approaches. Suggesting that Shylock is a contemporary Jew who lives with the consciousness of the Holocaust in a society that skirts such consciousness, Goerden obviously intended to acknowledge the challenges that the Holocaust poses for the entire German society of today. However, the production necessarily ran the risk of representing Holocaust remembrance as the need of a social minority, as an idiosyncrasy that should be 'understood' and 'tolerated.'

4.4 The Politics of Identity

Jessica's Tragedy

Goerden devoted particular attention to Jessica, testing the potentials of her role, adapting it to present concerns, and extending its dramatic weight.[65] Her function in the play as a subject in whom "the contrary discourses of race, nation, and religion meet"[66] was graphically played out. Staggering over the stage in very high heels, Elisabeth Hart constantly communicated a sense of exposure, fragility, and insecurity. In the fifth act, Jessica's difficulties in expressing her

---

[65] Contemporary scholarship has also devoted increasing attention to Jessica. See Mary Janell Metzger, "'Now by My Hood, a Gentle and No Jew': Jessica, *The Merchant of Venice*, and the Discourse of Early Modern English Identity," *PMLA* 113 (1998): 52–63; John Drakakis, "Jessica," In *The Merchant of Venice: New Critical Essays*, ed. John W. Mahon and Ellen Macleod Mahon (London: Routledge, 2002), 145–164; Janet Adelman, "Her Father's Blood: Race, Conversion, and Nation in *The Merchant of Venice*," *Representations* 81 (2003): 4–30; Lara Bovilsky, "'A Gentle and No Jew': Jessica, Portia, and Jewish Identity," *Renaissance Drama* 38 (2010): 47–76.
[66] Adelman, *Blood Relations*, 70.

position and needs gave rise to desperate demonstrations. She poured milk over herself and called herself "a latte macchiato without macchiato." Building on the image of milk mixing with coffee – 'latte macchiato' literally means 'spotted' or 'blotched milk' – this was evidently intended as a bitter joke about Jessica's assumed seamless religious or 'racial' convertibility. Making the performance yet more absurd, Jessica then squeezed out lemons over her hair, commenting: "I am a brimstone butterfly" (the German name of the insect is 'Zitronenfalter', which literally means 'lemon butterfly'). This heightened attention to Jessica can be observed in many contemporary productions,[67] which shift the implications of the play and the focus of its reception from the old man to the young woman, from the first generation to the second and third generations, and from the problem of remembering the Holocaust to the problem of contemporary identity politics.

Such an emphasis on Shylock's daughter usually goes along with considerable textual and structural changes. Malte Kreutzfeldt's Coburg production, discussed above, foregrounded the sexist subtexts of the play's discourse about religion and race by showing how Gratiano tried to make Lancelot rape Jessica. In her production of the play for the bremer shakespeare company (premiere: 27 September 2007), Nora Somaini cut Lancelot and gave most of his text, including the monologue about running away from his master (2.2.1–24), to Jessica – a ploy that worked surprisingly well. Insinuating that Jessica was being sexually abused by her father, this production made it clear why she thought that her family home was "hell" (2.3.2). At the Landestheater Tübingen (premiere: 18 April 2008) Clemens Bechtel boldly transformed the young Jewish woman into a Muslim, locked by her father in the straight-jacket of tradition. As this Jessica ran away with Lorenzo, her declaration "I am much ashamed of my exchange" (2.6.35) took on a novel meaning: in contrast to the Shakespearean text, she did not don the "lovely garnish of a boy," but rather exchanged her headscarf for a purple feather boa, and her oriental slippers for a pair of fashionable boots. Jessica's new life in the majority society was spent at Portia's side, where she took the place usually reserved for Nerissa. This also meant that it was Jessica rather than Nerissa who assisted in Shylock's defeat during the trial scene – a modification that one enraged reviewer called "a

---

[67] See Franziska Reinfeldt, "'Nimm dich dieser Fremden an': Die Figur der Jessica in aktuellen Inszenierungen des *Kaufmann von Venedig*," in *Shylock nach dem Holocaust: Zur Geschichte einer deutschen Erinnerungsfigur*, ed. Zeno Ackermann and Sabine Schülting (Berlin: De Gruyter, 2011), 143–158; Sabine Schülting, "'Schön, dass ihr da seid. Und jetzt habt viel Spaß!' – Jessica und die Spaßgesellschaft," in *Wer lacht, zeigt Zähne: Spielarten des Komischen*, ed. Johann N. Schmidt, Felix C. H. Sprang, and Roland Weidle (Trier: wvt, 2014), 41–48.

monstrous quid pro quo."⁶⁸ In fact, all the productions mentioned here, including Goerden's, admitted Shylock's daughter to the courtroom. In Bremen, she was given Gratiano's lines so that she hurled insults at her defeated father.

Karin Beier's 1994 production of *Merchant* at Düsseldorf's Schauspielhaus (premiere: 24 September) was an early instance of this systematic revaluation of Jessica. In contrast to her other projects, Beier's *Merchant* was not celebrated by the reviewers, many of whom seemed to feel that the play's dramatic urgency had somehow been eliminated. One critic thought that the production "evade[d] the Christian-Jewish antithesis of the drama."⁶⁹ Writing for the important weekly *Die Zeit*, Benjamin Henrichs facetiously described the muffled effect of Horst Mendroch's Shylock:

> [He] plays Shylock as an everyman and as an upright citizen. [...] Neither the Jewish God of vengeance whom Fritz Kortner had given of yore nor the grandiosely impertinent player and stock market wizard played by Gert Voss in Zadek's production. Even when Mendroch confesses his "hate" against the Christians and against his Christian competitor, he resembles the administrative head of the Venice health maintenance organization who is worried about his balances.⁷⁰

There seemed to be a reason why Beier downsized Shylock's hate and pain so relentlessly, and that reason was the moneylender's daughter: "Karin Beier tells Jessica's story with such ambition and passion that the rest of the performance necessarily has turned out mildly stimulating or even harmless rather than dramatic."⁷¹ Indeed, everybody who had seen the production seemed to agree that this was "Jessica's Tragedy," as the *Frankfurter Allgemeine Zeitung* titled its review.⁷²

A theatregoer who feared that Shakespeare's comedy was permeated with old anti-Semitic stereotypes wrote a detailed reflection on the production and posted it to Volker Canaris, the managing director of the Schauspielhaus. The text, which resembled an engaged theatre review, foregrounded its writer's posi-

---

68 Reinhard Schulte, "Die Haare zu Berge: Meta-Kritiker Reinhard Schulte über den LTT-*Kaufmann von Venedig* und Wilhelm Triebolds Besprechung vom Montag," *Schwäbisches Tagblatt*, 24 April 2008.
69 Andreas Wilink, "Welt am Draht," *Solinger Tagesblatt*, 26 September 1994.
70 Benjamin Henrichs, "Kein Messer im Fleisch – Shakespeare in Stuttgart und in Düsseldorf: Jürgen Kruse inszeniert *Richard den Zweiten*, Karin Beier den *Kaufmann von Venedig*," *Die Zeit*, 7 October 1994.
71 Henrichs, "Kein Messer im Fleisch."
72 Andreas Rossmann, "Die Tragödie der Jessica," *Frankfurter Allgemeine Zeitung*, 29 September 1994.

Figure 11: Caroline Ebner (Jessica) in Karin Beier's 1994 production at the Düsseldorfer Schauspielhaus. Photograph by Sonja Rothweiler. Courtesy of Sonja Rothweiler.

tion as a member of Düsseldorf's Jewish community and expressed concern that Beier's *Merchant* promulgated anti-Semitic stereotypes because it failed to oppose the problematic potential of Shakespeare's play. Canaris responded with a long and careful explanation of why he would not stop the production. Emphasizing the fact that he had been closely involved in the realization of Beier's *Merchant*, he explained its interrogation of stigmatization and exclusion. Significantly, the character of Jessica was at the centre of Canaris's defence:

> Dwelling on her, the young girl, the performance tells the strongly accentuated story of a destruction: the love for her father *and* the yearning for freedom, the search for her own identity between her roots and the society in which she lives, the love for the father *and* for Lorenzo. And how does all this develop and end? In (near) rape, in a nightmare, in the bitter disillusionment about her future as wife and Christian, in loneliness and fear. A Jewish girl is mistreated by Christian society – and desperately fights to survive.[73]

---

[73] We are basing our discussion on photocopies of the exchange between Canaris and his correspondent. Cf. Jörg Monschau, *Der Jude nach der Shoah: Zur Rezeption des* Kaufmann von Venedig

Indeed, Beier's production postulated a new approach to the play. With a very strong performance by Caroline Ebner as Jessica (see figure 11), this approach resulted in some compelling theatrical moments. However, virtually all reviews indicated that the novelty of the production came at the price of emptying out the role of Shylock. The "Explanatory Remarks" that dramaturge Joachim Lux placed at the beginning of the detailed programme suggest that this downsizing of Shylock may actually have been systematic. This is how Lux introduced an extensive collage of passages from Northrop Frye's 1965 study *A Natural Perspective:*[74]

> *The Merchant of Venice* primarily has to be seen as a Shakespearean comedy, not as a tragedy about the Jewish question. [...] There is no other Shakespeare play where the habit of looking through the lens of historical experience has so inadequately narrowed our perception as in case of *The Merchant of Venice*. The special Shylock question, which for us has always been the question of anti-Semitism and the Holocaust, must be subordinated to the comic-melancholy stories of the Venetian and Belmontian society. [...] By elucidating the structural foundations of Shakespearean comedy, Frye does not only contribute to a deeper understanding of Shakespeare, but he also helps us to yet again view *The Merchant of Venice* in a less fraught manner than that which seems to be admitted by our historical (and also our present) situation.[75]

Lux's use of the term "Jewish question" seems presumptuously naïve. Signalling and performing historical obliviousness, it makes it apparent that attempts to insulate *Merchant* against the inferences of the Holocaust can never be quite innocent. The urge, evident in the passage from the Düsseldorf programme, to dissociate the play from the imperative of remembrance seems yet more significant if one considers historical constellations in the German reception history of *Merchant*. After all, Beier's production was put on the stage in the year before the fiftieth anniversary of the war's end, and its premiere took place barely seven months before that of Snir's weighty production at Weimar. One might be led

---

auf dem Theater der Bundesrepublik Deutschland und der Deutschen Demokratischen Republik 1945–1989, doctoral dissertation, Ruprecht-Karls-Universität Heidelberg, 2002, accessed 7 September 2018, https://archiv.ub.uni-heidelberg.de/volltextserver/3530/, 495. Monschau also quotes the German original of the translated passage.

74 Northrop Frye, *A Natural Perspective: The Development of Shakespearean Comedy and Romance* (New York: Columbia University Press, 1965). The programme quotes from the German translation, *Shakespeares Vollendung: Eine Einführung in die Welt seiner Komödien*, trans. Helmut Haug (Munich: Nymphenburger Verlagshandlung, 1966).

75 Joachim Lux, "Vorbemerkung," in Düsseldorfer Schauspielhaus, *Der Kaufmann von Venedig*, theatre programme (Düsseldorf, 1994), n. p.

to interpret such a conjunction of radically different productions as evidence of a bifurcation of German reception or memory discourses.

It should be stressed that Beier's *Merchant* did not tell "the comic-melancholy stories of the Venetian and Belmontian society," but really unfolded what Canaris termed "the strongly accentuated story of a destruction." However, as the passage quoted from Canaris's letter also shows, Beier's *Merchant* certainly re-accentuated and transformed the basic logic and direction of the plot. Shylock's tragedy had been that of a flawed revolt against the hegemony and the hypocrisy of the Christians: "I will not eat with you, drink with you, nor pray with you" (1.3.31–32). Jessica's tragedy was that of the betrayed promise of emancipation and assimilation. Beier's production transformed an ambiguity in the play's dramatic economy into a fundamental movement between two interpretations: from Shylock's stubborn resistance against his integration into the majority society to Jessica's desperate attempt at breaking through into the multicultural or even transnational society promised as the flip-side of the Venetian money-economy.

Shylock's Ethnicity

What exactly happens to Shylock if the role of Jessica is so significantly upgraded and updated? With respect to this question, the 2007 production by the bremer shakespeare company is particularly suggestive. Nora Somaini, a guest director from Switzerland, expanded not only Jessica's role but also that of the eponymous "royal merchant" (3.2.238), explicitly presenting the play "from the radically subjective perspective of Antonio."[76] At first, Antonio was seen in a wheelchair. It did not take long, however, before the hypochondriac jumped up and raced across the stage. In the course of Antonio's living out his manic depression, Shylock was almost turned into his victim. Somaini even had the merchant instead of the moneylender come up with the hair-raising idea about the pound of flesh.

Judging by his outward appearance, Peter Lüchinger's Shylock could be taken for a descendant of the Shylock played by Gert Voss in Peter Zadek's 1988 Vienna production. However, whereas that production had drawn attention to the arbitrariness of stigmatization, Somaini's approach resulted in actually downsizing or even hiding Shylock's Jewishness. This became startlingly evident

---

[76] bremer shakespeare company, "Der Kaufmann von Venedig," accessed 8 September 2018, https://www.shakespeare-company.com/repertoire/der-kaufmann-von-venedig.

in Shylock's monologue (3.1.45–61), from which the word 'Jew' had been cut entirely. Having enumerated the wrongs sustained at the hands of Antonio, which led up to the question "and what's his reason?," Shylock did not come up with the well-known answer "I am a Jew," but could be heard uttering the words: "Ich bin ich" ("I am I" or "I am myself").

It is probably no mere coincidence that a production realized by Clemens Bechtel for Tübingen's Landestheater (LTT) in the following year likewise 'cleansed' Shylock's monologue from explicit references to Jewishness. A newspaper article in which dramaturge Inge Zeppenfeld explained the basic design of the production similarly took care to avoid or abstract from the word 'Jew': "Shylock is a member of a cultural and religious minority, a minority that has become the target of hostility mainly for the reason that it signifies economic competition."[77] Such downsizing of Jewish specificity may be described as a process of universalization, but it was through the highly stereotyped portrayal of Jessica as a young Muslim woman that the play's thematics of alterity came to be re-articulated in a new, very specific, context. In the trial scene, Jessica spoke not only Nerissa's text but also passages from Portia's so that the two women presided over Shylock's destruction as almost equal partners. And it was Jessica's revelation of her true identity that triggered Shylock's famous last words: "I pray you give me leave to go from hence. I am not well (4.1.391–92).

The LTT production played out Shylock's forced conversion in a harrowing manner. However, it also raised the question of whether the social murder of the outsider father may not be a prerequisite for the daughter's emancipation. More explicitly, the production adopted the popular argument that young Muslimas who wear the hijab in Germany are invariably the victims of patriarchal family structures. In this intertwining of Islamophobia with Western feminism, a young woman's religious faith (if it is not a Christian faith) is constructed as the medium of patriarchal tyranny, authoritarian rule or irrational (if not terrorist) violence.[78]

In the context of contemporary German politics and media, the analogy between traditional anti-Semitic stereotypes and current debates on the 'integration' of Muslim immigrants is not entirely off the mark. Moreover, the manner in which the debate on 'integration' versus 'multiculturalism' has come to be organ-

---

77 Inge Zeppenfeld, "Ein Pfund Fleisch aus Antonios Brust," *Reutlinger Generalanzeiger*, 17 April 2008.
78 Wendy Brown, "Subjects of Tolerance: Why We Are Civilized and They Are the Barbarians," in *Political Theologies: Public Religions in a Post-Secular World*, ed. Hent de Vries and Lawrence E. Sullivan (New York: Fordham University Press, 2006), 298–299, 301.

ized around stock images of the 'Muslim daughter' may in fact be comparable to the way in which the stereotype of the young 'Jewess' is articulated in Shakespeare's text. The problem about Bechtel's strategy of topicality, however, was that it displaced the traumatic memories connoted by the play, transferring the emotional energies of Holocaust remembrance to the contentious issues surrounding the immigration society. For, in spite of the numerous changes to the plot and text of *Merchant*, the thematics of Jewish alterity, anti-Semitism, and the Holocaust certainly remained present as a suppressed text.

The production thus ran the danger of playing Muslims off against Jews, Islamophobia against anti-Semitism, and the issue of cultural integration against Holocaust remembrance. Interestingly, Bechtel's *Merchant* featured a Brechtian sequence that foregrounded this problem. After Jessica's elopement, two actors stepped up to microphones at either side of the stage. One of them declaimed charged opinions concerning Muslim immigrants.[79] As a counterpoint, the other actor sonorously enounced slogans from German memory discourses, such as "year of remembrance," "memorial stone" or "virtual memory." This battle of discourses seemed to denounce the failure of Holocaust remembrance to provide, in Aleida Assmann's programmatic terms, "a generally agreed-upon frame of reference that is needed to communicate and negotiate conflicting memories [...] in order to diminish the destructive differences of national memories by making them compatible with each other."[80]

The fringe ensemble, a theatre project based in Bonn, followed a completely different tactic in order to articulate *Merchant* with and within current discourses about Germany as an immigration society. The production premiered at Bonn's independent Theater im Ballsaal on 14 January 2010 and was later taken to the studiobühneköln, a theatrical space at the University of Cologne. Director Severin von Hoensbroech worked with a mixed cast consisting not only of a small group of professional actors but also of five young members of the local hip-hop scene. Of the latter group of performers, dancer and acrobat Jilou Rasul played Jessica. The others, Nebil Erdogan, Faruk Haziri, Miguel Inserra, and the Cologne Gangsta rapper S-Dog all played Shylock. The realization of Shylock shifted between the performance of a series of individual Shylocks

---

[79] The quotations came from a debate between German-Jewish author Ralph Giordano and the Minister of the Interior, Wolfgang Schäuble, on the planned building of a mosque in Cologne. See Landestheater Tübingen, *Der Kaufmann von Venedig*, theatre programme (2008), n. p.
[80] Aleida Assmann, "Response to Peter Novick," *GHI Bulletin* 40 (2007): 38.

and the performance of a 'corporate' Shylock who consisted of a group of people.[81]

This Shylock – or rather, these Shylocks – were played as German Muslims. This group was frequently referred to, both by the Christian characters and by themselves, as "Kanaken" – an offensive German term for people of Southern origin that urban youths with a Turkish background have increasingly appropriated for their self-identification. The four Shylocks spoke 'Kanak Spraak,' or 'Kiez German,' a subcultural sociolect that emerged among, but is no longer restricted to, young people with a Turkish background. According to this manner of articulation, the high-German "Ich bin Shylock" ("I am Shylock," "My name is Shylock") was rendered as *"Isch* bin Shylock." The Shakespearean play's concern with Christian-Jewish encounters and Christian anti-Semitism was translated into the logic of contemporary confrontations between the German majority society and German Muslims. Indeed, the short announcement published on the website of the fringe ensemble explicitly identified Shakespeare's problematic comedy as an ideal vehicle for addressing current issues:

> *The Merchant of Venice* applies to the here and now. It probably suits the open discussion about integration and assimilation better than any contemporary play. This is why in this production Gangsta rappers, breakdancers, and hip-hoppers find themselves on the stage beside the actors of the fringe ensemble.[82]

The idea that the amateurs should "find themselves on the stage" ("finden sich [...] auf der Bühne wieder") was carefully put. On the one hand, it was designed to carve out a specific space for the performance of the non-professional actors. On, the other, it almost seemed to imply that these exponents of a minority subculture happened to be on stage against their will, having been put there either by virtue of the director's artistic design or by the sheer force of cultural necessity. Therefore, the participation of the "Gangsta rappers, breakdancers, and hip-hoppers" had a special figurative quality: they were and were not part of the play, were and were not themselves, did and did not act.

In this production, Shylock was undoubtedly at the centre. Sometimes directly with the audience, he was a narrator of sorts, an observer and commentator of the setting, the plot and the other characters. All the Venetians were

---

[81] On the fringe ensemble *Merchant*, see also Sabine Schülting, "'Imagined Communities': Reconsidering European Shakespeares," *Cahiers Élisabéthains: A Journal of English Renaissance Studies* 96.1 (2018): 166–168.
[82] fringe ensemble, "Der Kaufmann von Venedig," accessed 8 September 2018, http://www.fringe-ensemble.de/der-kaufmann-von-venedig-in-vorbereitung/.

played by the same three actors – Leopold Altenburg, David Fischer, and Tina Seydel – who did not have fixed roles, and whose roles were not always congruent with their gender. Indeed, from the beginning, the production denaturalized identities. In contrast to Jessica and the four Shylocks, the 'Christians' closely adhered to the diction of the Shakespearean text, creating a contrast between two mutually alienating cultural codes: on the one hand, the language of Shakespeare and the social rites of the Renaissance upper crust; and on the other, the articulation of 'Kiez German' and the artistic figures of rap, breakdance, and hip-hop. In addition, the multiplication of Shylock had strong effects. He was no longer a solitary outsider in Venice but outnumbered the three Venetians. The confrontation sometimes gained a physically aggressive character, which was reinforced by the spatial opposition between the Venetians and the Shylock performers on stage.

Hip-hop emerged in the US street subculture of the 1970s and 1980s. Originally, it was an artistic form developed by young African Americans and Hispanic Americans in order to give expression to their experience of violence, dispossession, and disenfranchisement. Sociologists have argued that "part of what was at stake during the early period of recorded rap was not merely a retelling of ghetto stories, but recuperation and recasting of the meaning of black life in 'the hood.'"[83] In the terminology of Michel de Certeau, which we cited in Chapter 2, hip-hop can be described as a tactic for reclaiming urban space. Hip-hop, including rap and breakdance, emerged from the 'ghetto,' and despite their world-wide dissemination, these forms have kept their original associations. As Michael P. Jeffries explains, contemporary hip-hop urbanism should be seen as "a recasting and preservation of its prior incarnation as a floating signifier bound by race, gender and class. It is invoked to confer a certain type of authenticity, respect and status upon the performer, and is materially anchored in late-twentieth-century American urban history."[84]

By adapting Shylock's lines to the musical performance of rap and to the bodily performance of breakdance, the Bonn *Merchant* gave expression to the frustration of youths with a Turkish or Arab background in contemporary Germany. This was particularly effective in the rap adaptation of the monologue in 3.1 that the four Shylocks, sometimes singing together and sometimes taking turns, hurled at the 'Christians,' narrating the story of their exclusion and disempower-

---

[83] Michael P. Jeffries, "Hip-Hop Urbanism Old and New," *International Journal of Urban and Regional Research* 38.2 (2014): 707.
[84] Jeffries, "Hip-Hop Urbanism," 708.

ment and, at the same time, expressing their self-identification: "Isch [i.e.: ich] bin Shylock, isch bin, isch bin Shylock."

Signalling his awareness that the majority wanted him to go, this collective Muslim Shylock from the fringes of German city life declared that he would never do so because he had his "heart and soul in Venice." Only the song's refrain, delivered to an Oriental melismatic musical line, was a straight translation of the Shakespearean text: "If you prick us, do we not bleed? If you tickle us, do we not laugh? If you poison us, do we not die? And if you wrong us, shall we not revenge?" (3.1.54–56). However, the refrain was introduced by a rising sequence of more pithy images:

> Wir essen das Gleiche, trinken das Gleiche,
> Pissen das Gleiche, kacken das Gleiche.
> Ihr wollt, dass ich Schweine fresse, ihr falschen Christen?
> Aber ich bin ein Moslem und pass nicht in eure Kisten.[85]

Hip hop culture thus turned out to provide a dynamic language for a translation of *Merchant* into the here and now, and yet it remained a foreign element, jarring with the Shakespearean text.

The conclusion of the performance reinforced the fact that the two aesthetic traditions and sociocultural routines at play in the production did not admit of any easy integration. The fringe ensemble played a fairly conventional trial scene, at the end of which Shylock exited. But then he did not disappear from the stage. Act 5 was projected on a screen, watched by all four Shylocks as if it were a TV soap opera. The performance was concluded with the repetition of Shylock's rap monologue. However, it now included the final words "warum nicht Rache?" ("why not revenge?"), thus thwarting naïve hopes of simple integration yet more emphatically. At the same time, the ending stressed the determination of the supposed cultural others to claim their space in society and in the discourse that they entered by participating in the Shakespearean play.

In a yet more pronounced manner than the other productions discussed in this subchapter, the fringe ensemble's 2010 *Merchant* brought the play to bear on current discourses of identity. However, in terms of political and theatrical tactics, significant differences are evident. This is particularly true if we compare

---

[85] "We eat the same, drink the same, / Piss the same, and shit the same. / You want me to gorge myself on pork, false Christians? / But I am a Muslim and don't fit your narrow ideas [literally: your boxes]." A recording of the 'Shylock-Rap' is available at http://www.fringe-ensemble.de/der-shylock-rap/, accessed 8 September 2018.

the production that Severin von Hoensbroech put on the stage in Bonn and Cologne to that presented by Clemens Bechtel in Tübingen. Bechtel seemed to project a rigid as well as highly stereotyped conception of contemporary topics and identities onto the Shakespearean text, fundamentally changing the plot of the drama and emptying out its potentials for refiguration. His production represented an instance of rigorous identification and confrontational topicality, quite explicitly playing present concerns and remembrance off against each other.

In contrast, von Hoensbroech and the fringe ensemble refrained from forcing *Merchant* into a stunted representation of present scenarios. Rather, they invited contemporary performances onto the stage set by the text. In the process, the signatures of the Shakespearean text offered provocations to which the contemporary performance responded through its own kind of stylization. This enabled a dialectical process of figuration that turned out to be illuminating, both with regard to the discursive sediments of the text and with regard to contemporary strategies of identification, othering, and self-expression. Although the construction of Jewishness in the Shakespearean text was suspended and transposed into contemporary constructions of Muslim identity, both heterostereotypical and autostereotypical, the fringe ensemble's *Merchant* threw some fresh light onto the complex relationships between anti-Semitism and Islamophobia. This was possible exactly because such relationships were neither posited nor suggested.

5 "Forced Companionability": Conclusion

The setting is a cemetery in the north of England, "a stage unsuited to tragedy." Enter two men: Simon Strulovitch, a Jewish art dealer with "a passion for Shakespeare" and "a daughter going off the rails," and Shylock, "an infuriated and tempestuous Jew."[1] This is the introductory scene of Howard Jacobson's *Shylock Is My Name* (2016), a novelistic re-telling of Shakespeare's *The Merchant of Venice*, commissioned for Hogarth's Shakespeare series, which was launched in late 2015, in time for the quatercentenary of Shakespeare's death. Jacobson's version of Shakespeare's comedy takes the confrontation between the Jewish outsider and the Christian majority society to the contemporary world, and in doing so, it resembles many of the productions of *Merchant* we have discussed in the preceding chapters.

What is new about this retelling of the story is not only Jacobson's focus on humour and comedy. More importantly perhaps, his novel splits the figure of Shakespeare's Shylock up into Strulovitch, a lapsed Jew living in contemporary England, and Shylock, a revenant from early modern Venice. Surprisingly, however, Jacobson's Shylock is not a ghost, even though his presence in contemporary England, as well as his eventual disappearance, remain unaccounted for. "'I'm here because I'm here,' Shylock answers to Strulovitch's question. "What other explanation could satisfy an unbeliever such as you?"[2] It is in the discussions between the two that the retelling of Shakespeare's story or, rather, the assessment of its relevance for the present day slowly unfolds. Shylock provides a blueprint for Strulovitch's struggles, and their lives show considerable parallels: both their daughters have fallen in love with gentiles; both men communicate with wives that cannot respond (Shylock's is dead, Strulovitch's is paralysed after a stroke); and both try, or have tried, to avenge themselves on the Christians. For a while, their fates become entangled – and yet, as Strulovitch realizes at the end of "Act Four": "He will never be my friend. [...] But then I will never be his."[3] They are 'fellow travellers' for a while, and when they first meet at the cemetery, the narrator notices the "forced companionability"[4] with which they walk to Strulovitch's home.

Jacobson's novel develops a (con)figuration of Shylock that lends itself as a foil for our concluding reflections on the various realizations of the figure in

---

1 Howard Jacobson, *Shylock Is My Name* (London: Hogarth, 2016), 1–3.
2 Jacobson, *Shylock Is My Name*, 65.
3 Jacobson, *Shylock Is My Name*, 250.
4 Jacobson, *Shylock Is My Name*, 49.

twentieth- and early twenty-first-century Germany. The precarious bond between Strulovitch and Shylock draws attention to the ways in which modern productions enter into a dialogue with the figure of Shakespeare's Jewish moneylender, a dialogue that in Jacobson's novel is taken literally when the two men discuss "Shylock's own original intentions": "How merry was your bond?" "Was I acting out my desires or theirs?" "He could have killed his enemy and joined his wife? So why hadn't he?"[5] But their conversations are also concerned with what it means to live as a Jew in a Western (Christian) society. In other words, they explore the possible implications of Shakespeare's play for the present, as well as gauging the historical changes since the early modern age. To Strulovitch's question, "[W]hat's the biggest change," Shylock responds drily: "They used to spit on me, now they tell me Jewish jokes."[6]

The attention to the impact of the respective historical moment is certainly not exclusive to *Merchant*, and the concept of 'figuration' does not only lend itself to an analysis of Shakespeare's Shylock, but can also be applied to the contradictory afterlives of other canonical dramatic characters, such as Othello and Caliban, both of whom have been thoroughly transformed under the influence of Postcolonial Theory and, perhaps even more importantly, adaptations and rewritings in the former colonies. As in the case of *Merchant*, the political and cultural dislocations of the twentieth century have thoroughly affected the meaning of these texts and posed the question as to the plays' present-day signification with unusual urgency.

Throughout the book we have discussed examples in which critics, actors, and directors have interpreted Shakespeare's *Merchant* as a figuration of the Holocaust, or, more generally, of the fate of outsiders in contemporary society. Indeed, many of the earlier post-war productions seem to have been driven by the hope that *Merchant* would offer a solution to, or even a redemption from, racist exclusion and genocidal violence. But our discussions of *Merchant* productions during the National Socialist era as well as during the Cold War should have proven this trust in the classics at best a naïve belief, disregarding the fact that the complexities of the play have prevented its full appropriation for any single interpretation or ideology.

Jacobson complicates these simplistic approaches to *Merchant*, refusing to suggest Shakespeare's play as a solution for present-day conflicts. At first glance, the novel's Shylock seems to be a *figura* of Strulovitch in Auerbach's sense of the

---

5 Jacobson, *Shylock Is My Name*, 149, 147, 151, 183.
6 Jacobson, *Shylock Is My Name*, 63.

term – a real figure, separate in time, and yet connected.[7] However, the novel simultaneously deviates from a figurative logic since it offers no redemption whatsoever. "There's no Act Six," Shylock tells Strulovitch. "For me there wasn't even an Act Five. But at least no resolution means no final rejection. Anything could be. There is no knowing."[8] There is no concluding answer either to the question of Shylock's identity, past and present, or to what it means to be Jewish or be called a Jew in a society of Gentiles. Strulovitch does not 'learn' from Shylock's example but chooses the same path as Shylock did – and also fails. Jacobson's enigmatic Shylock is and is not Shakespeare's, and the same holds true for Strulovitch. Indeed, there are some surprising changes: towards the end of *Shylock Is My Name*, it is Shylock who speaks Portia's words about the "quality of mercy." There is a farcical revelation (rather than a trial) that prevents Strulovitch's victory over his adversary D'Anton, and yet he enjoys some kind of reconciliation with his daughter. Jacobson thus highlights the differences between the two characters, and between them and the Shakespearean Shylock figure, just as much as the parallels.

It is exactly this gap opened up by figuration – the tensions between the various interpretations of the figure and its different historical layers, the "figure's/character's space of possibility in the continuum of different spatiotemporal perspectives"[9] – that we have tried to explore in this book. Understood in this way, figuration is less a redeeming fulfilment than a tentative variation or even a counterpoint to Shylock, exploring a variety of alternatives rather than presenting one single resolution. Many interpretations of Shylock that we have discussed – by Auerbach, Deutsch, Kortner, Tabori, Zadek, and others – can be read as the outcome of such a thorough investigation of a figure that has haunted the Western imagination since the early modern age and that has achieved a new topicality after the Holocaust.

Perhaps the most innovative and thought-provoking strand of twentieth-century figurations of Shylock is the struggle of Jewish writers, scholars, actors, and directors with the figure. "These Jews," Jacobson's Shylock says in one of his dialogues with his dead wife, "these Jews! They don't know whether to cry for

---

[7] Cf. Erich Auerbach "Figura," in *Time, History and Literature: Selected Essays of Erich Auerbach*, ed. James I. Porter, trans. Jane O. Newman (Princeton: Princeton University Press, 2014), 96.
[8] Jacobson, *Shylock Is My Name*, 56.
[9] Gabriele Brandstetter, "SchnittFiguren: Intersektionen von Bild und Tanz," in *Figur und Figuration: Studien zu Wahrnehmung und Wissen*, ed. Gottfried Boehm, Gabriele Brandstetter and Achatz von Müller (Munich: Fink, 2007), 13–14.

me, disown me or explain me."[10] On stage as well as in criticism, this struggle has often involved a seemingly paradoxical turn: a radical rejection of the stereotype, combined with an emphatic acknowledgement of Shylock as a "tragic brother,"[11] and the tension between figurative and identitarian approaches to Shylock. Like Auerbach, with whom we started this book, Jewish actors and directors have looked awry at Shylock, resisting simplistic identification with the figure while simultaneously accepting and embracing it – further instances of their "forced companionability." This ambiguous perspective on Shylock is of course not the effect of an ethnic or religious disposition, but the result of speaking, writing, performing, or directing as Jews, of positioning themselves with respect to a powerful anti-Semitic stereotype, "the ancient stain."[12] The 2010 fringe ensemble production of *Merchant*, with which we ended the last chapter, is a recent example suggesting a new development in the reception of the play in which strategic companionship with Shylock also proves productive for other minorities (in Germany).

To end this book with Jacobson's retelling seems apposite because the novel opens up the predominantly German focus of the preceding chapters. It shifts attention away from the narcissistic self-reflection of the majority society that has characterized so many even of the well-intended productions at minor and major theatres in Germany, and offers a broader view of the international or even global configurations at stake. In *Shylock Is My Name*, the Holocaust is not at the centre of the narrative, but it establishes its uncanny undercurrent, which impacts even the most mundane aspects of the characters' lives: from anti-Semitic jokes to a discussion of *The Guardian's* stance against Israel, from Strulovitch's decision to buy a German car to the fact that Beatrice, Strulovitch's daughter, has fallen in love with a popular football player who likes to show the Nazi salute on the pitch. Jacobson's novel is set in England, and deals with the implications of *Merchant* for Jewish life in the contemporary UK, but it does so by situating the plot in a larger historical and geographical context – from early modern Venice to contemporary Israel – than most German productions of *Merchant* have done.

"Anything could be. There is no knowing." As some of the more recent productions of *Merchant* suggest, it may be such an entanglement of histories

---

10 Jacobson, *Shylock Is My Name*, 194. For Jewish responses to the Shylock figure see also the collection of essays *Wrestling with Shylock: Jewish Responses to* The Merchant of Venice, ed. Michael Shapiro and Edna Nahshon (Cambridge: Cambridge University Press, 2017).
11 Ernst Simon, "Lessing und die jüdische Geschichte," *Jüdische Rundschau*, 22 January 1929; repr. in Simon, *Brücken: Gesammelte Aufsätze* (Heidelberg: Lambert Schneider, 1965), 218.
12 Jacobson, *Shylock Is My Name*, 15.

and cultures in a globalised world that will offer new frames for refigurations of Shylock and *The Merchant of Venice* in the twenty-first century. Parallel to this, it seems as if the figure of Jessica is currently gaining new pertinence. As has been shown in the preceding chapters, in many productions since the Second World War, Jessica has been used to challenge the 'happy ending' of the play, which reconfirms both patriarchy and the exclusion of Others from the majority society. Jessica has often turned into a witness of Shylock's defeat, mourning his social death, silently accusing the 'Venetians,' and simultaneously realizing that she will forever be barred from full integration into the community of the Christians. In 1979, in his production at Cologne, the Israeli director Arie Zinger revised the ending of Shakespeare's play and imagined a reconciliation of Jessica and Shylock. A similar conclusion is offered in Jacobson's novel, where Beatrice, Strulovich's daughter, also returns home – but neither as a mourner nor as a victim. Instead, adopting Malvolio's last lines from Shakespeare's *Twelfth Night*, she has transformed into a new, female figuration of Shylock, as precarious and uncompromising as the Shakespearean model:

> In her stony unforgiveness she resembles Shylock, Strulovitch thought. Were he to ask her what she was thinking he had little doubt how she would answer.
>
> I will be revenged on the whole pack of you.[13]

---

13 Jacobson, *Shylock Is My Name*, 277.

Works Cited

1 Primary Texts and Critical Studies

Abusch, Alexander. *Shakespeare: Realist und Humanist, Genius der Weltliteratur.* Berlin: Aufbauverlag, 1964.
Ackermann, Zeno. "Anglistik und Amerikanistik." In *Kulturwissenschaften und Nationalsozialismus*, edited by Jürgen Elvert and Jürgen Nielsen-Sikora, 647–668. Stuttgart: Steiner, 2008.
Ackermann, Zeno. "'Ease and Deliciousness': *The Merchant of Venice* and the Performance of Ethical Continuity in National Socialist Germany." In *Renaissance Shakespeare / Shakespeare Renaissances: Proceedings of the Ninth World Shakespeare Congress*, edited by Martin Procházka, Michael Dobson, Andreas Höfele, and Hanna Scolnicov, 238–248. Newark: University of Delaware Press, 2014.
Ackermann, Zeno. "Performing Oblivion / Enacting Remembrance: *The Merchant of Venice* in West Germany, 1945 to 1961." *Shakespeare Quarterly* 62.3 (2011): 364–395.
Ackermann, Zeno. "Shakespearean Negotiations in the Perpetrator Society: German Productions of *The Merchant of Venice* during the Second World War." In *Shakespeare and the Second World War: Memory, Culture, Identity*, edited by Irena R. Makaryk and Marissa McHugh, 35–62. Toronto: University of Toronto Press, 2012.
Ackermann, Zeno. "*Der Untergang* und die erinnerungskulturelle Rahmung des Zivilisationsbruchs." *Geschichte in Wissenschaft und Unterricht* 58.3 (2007): 148–162.
Adelman, Janet. *Blood Relations: Christian and Jew in* The Merchant of Venice. Chicago: University of Chicago Press, 2008.
Adelman, Janet. "Her Father's Blood: Race, Conversion, and Nation in *The Merchant of Venice*." *Representations* 81 (2003): 4–30.
Adorno, Theodor W. "Was bedeutet: Aufarbeitung der Vergangenheit" (1959/60). Translated as "The Meaning of Working Through the Past." In *Critical Models: Interventions and Catchwords*, translated by Henry W. Pickford, 89–103. New York: Columbia University Press, 1998.
Akademie der Künste Berlin, ed. *Fritz Wisten: Drei Leben für das Theater: Stuttgart 1919–1933. Jüdischer Kulturbund 1933–1941. Berlin 1945–1962.* Berlin: Hentrich, 1990.
Alter, Robert. "Who Is Shylock?" *Commentary* 96.1 (1993): 29–34.
Althaus, Hans Peter. *Mauscheln: Ein Wort als Waffe.* Berlin: De Gruyter, 2002.
Anikst, Alexander. "Shakespeare – A Writer of the People" (1959). In *Shakespeare in the Soviet Union: A Collection of Articles*, edited by Roman Samarin and Alexander Nikolyukin, translated by Avril Pyman, 113–139. Moscow: Progress Publishers, 1966.
Anon. "Affäre Filbinger: Was Rechtens war…" *Der Spiegel* 20 (15 May 1978): 23–27.
Anon. "Skandal im Sächsischen Landtag: NPD-Mann spricht von Dresdner 'Bomben-Holocaust.'" *Spiegel Online*, 21 January 2005, http://www.spiegel.de/politik/deutschland/skandal-im-saechsischen-landtag-npd-mann-spricht-von-dresdner-bomben-holocaust-a-337894.html (accessed 8 September 2018).
Arendt, Hannah. *Eichmann in Jerusalem: A Report on the Banality of Evil.* New York: Viking Press, 1963.
Armstrong, Gareth. *A Case for Shylock: Around the World with Shakespeare's Jew.* London: Nick Hern, 2004.

Assmann, Aleida. *Der lange Schatten der Vergangenheit: Erinnerungskultur und Geschichtspolitik.* Munich: C. H. Beck 2006.
Assmann, Aleida. *Das neue Unbehagen an der Erinnerungskultur: Eine Intervention.* Munich: C. H. Beck, 2013.
Assmann, Aleida. "Response to Peter Novick." *GHI Bulletin* 40 (2007): 33–38.
Auerbach, Erich. "Figura." *Archivum Romanicum* 22 (1938): 436–489.
Auerbach, Erich. "Figura." Translated by Ralph Mannheim. In *Scenes from the Drama of European Literature: Six Essays*, 11–76. New York: Meridian Books, 1959.
Auerbach, Erich. "Figura." In *Time, History and Literature: Selected Essays of Erich Auerbach*, edited by James I. Porter, translated by Jane O. Newman, 65–113. Princeton: Princeton University Press, 2014.
Auerbach, Erich. "The Idea of the National Spirit as the Source of the Modern Humanities." In *Time, History, and Literature: Selected Essays of Erich Auerbach*, edited by James I. Porter, translated by Jane O. Newman, 56–61. Princeton: Princeton University Press, 2014.
Auerbach, Erich. *Mimesis: Dargestellte Wirklichkeit in der abendländischen Literatur* (1946). Tübingen: A. Francke, 2001.
Auerbach, Erich. *Mimesis: The Representation of Reality in Western Culture.* Fiftieth Anniversary Edition. Translated by Willard R. Trask, introduced by Edward Said. Princeton: Princeton University Press, 2003.
Bachmann, Michael. "Fritz Kortner on the Post-War Stage: The Jewish Actor as a Site of Memory." In *Jews and Theater in an Intercultural Context*, edited by Edna Nahshon, 197–217. Leiden: Brill, 2012.
Badische Landesbühne Bruchsal. "Einige Vorüberlegungen zur Inszenierung: Vor Probenbeginn." In *Ib Texte: William Shakespeare: Der Kaufmann von Venedig. Eine Komödie*, theatre programme, 19–22. Bruchsal, 1981/82.
Baumgart, Reinhard. "Shakespeares krauser Reichtum." *Süddeutsche Zeitung*, 3 January 1973.
Bayerdörfer, Hans-Peter. "'Ewiger Jude' und 'Israeli': Stationen der 'Nathan'-Rezeption in der Bundesrepublik." In *Theatralia Judaica II: Nach der Shoah. Israelisch-deutsche Theaterbeziehungen seit 1949*, edited by Hans-Peter Bayerdörfer, 71–99. Tübingen: Niemeyer, 1996.
Bayerdörfer, Hans-Peter. "Shylock auf der deutschen Bühne nach der Shoah." In *Shylock? Zinsverbot und Geldverleih in jüdischer und christlicher Tradition*, edited by Johannes Heil and Bernd Wacker, 261–280. Frankfurt/M.: Fink, 1997.
Bayerdörfer, Hans-Peter. "Shylock on the German Stage in the Post-Shoah Era." In *German Shakespeare Studies at the Turn of the Twenty-First Century*, edited by Christa Jansohn, 205–223. Newark: University of Delaware Press, 2006.
Bayerdörfer, Hans-Peter, and Gad Kaynar. "'Jedem das Seine' oder Buchenwald in Weimar." *Maske und Kothurn* 56.3 (2010), special issue: *Shylockgestalten*, edited by Patric Blaser and Brigitte Dalinger, 33–54.
Becker, Peter von. "Fast verspielt: Das Theater als unmoralische Anstalt? Beobachtungen und Fragen zum Frankfurter Fassbinder-Streit." *Theater heute* 26.12 (1985): 3–9.
Bennewitz, Fritz, and Dieter Görne. "Konzeptionelle Überlegungen." Unpublished typescript. In the theatre documentation for Fritz Bennewitz's production of *Merchant* at Deutsches

Nationaltheater Weimar (premiere: 11 April 1976). Archiv der Akademie der Künste Berlin, Inszenierungsdokumentationen 173.
Bennewitz, Fritz, and Dieter Görne. "Shakespeares *Kaufmann von Venedig* im Deutschen Nationaltheater Weimar." *Shakespeare Jahrbuch* 113 (1977): 56–63.
Bennewitz, Fritz. "Ein Theater stellt sich den Forderungen unserer Zeit." Interview. *Wochenpost* 41 (1976).
Berg, Nicolas. "Lesarten des Judenmords." In *Wandlungsprozesse in Westdeutschland: Belastung, Integration, Liberalisierung 1945–1980*, edited by Ulrich Herbert, 91–139. Göttingen: Wallstein, 2002.
Biedrzynski, Richard. *Schauspieler, Regisseure, Intendanten*. Heidelberg: Hüthig & Co., 1944.
Bliersbach, Gerhard. *So grün war die Heide: Der deutsche Nachkriegsfilm in neuer Sicht*. Weinheim: Beltz, 1985.
Blumenberg, Hans. *Arbeit am Mythos*. Frankfurt/M.: Suhrkamp, 1979.
Boehm, Gottfried, Gabriele Brandstetter, and Achatz von Müller, eds. *Figur und Figuration: Studien zu Wahrnehmung und Wissen*. Munich: Fink, 2007.
Bonnell, Andrew G. *Shylock in Germany: Antisemitism and the German Theatre from the Enlightenment to the Nazis*. London: Tauris Academic Studies, 2008.
Bösch, Frank. "Film, NS-Vergangenheit und Geschichtswissenschaft." *Vierteljahrshefte für Zeitgeschichte* 54 (2007): 1–32.
Bovilsky, Lara. "'A Gentle and No Jew': Jessica, Portia, and Jewish Identity." *Renaissance Drama* 38 (2010): 47–76.
Brandl-Risi, Bettina, Wolf-Dieter Ernst, and Meike Wagner, eds. *Figuration: Beiträge zum Wandel der Betrachtung ästhetischer Gefüge*. Munich: Epodium, 2000.
Brandstetter, Gabriele, and Sibylle Peters, eds. *De figura: Rhetorik – Bewegung – Gestalt*. Munich: Fink, 2002.
Brandstetter, Gabriele. "SchnittFiguren: Intersektionen von Bild und Tanz." In *Figur und Figuration: Studien zu Wahrnehmung und Wissen*, edited by Gottfried Boehm, G. Brandstetter and Achatz von Müller, 13–32. Munich: Fink, 2007.
Braulich, Heinrich. "Das romantische Traumtheater der bürgerlichen Vorkriegsgesellschaft." In *Max Reinhardt*, 63–157. Berlin: Henschelverlag, 1969.
Brinkmann, Karl. "Bühnenbericht 1964." *Shakespeare Jahrbuch* (West) (1964): 326–348.
Brockmann, Stephen. *German Literary Culture at the Zero Hour*. Rochester: Camden House, 2009.
Brown, Wendy. "Subjects of Tolerance: Why We Are Civilized and They Are the Barbarians." In *Political Theologies: Public Religions in a Post-Secular World*, edited by Hent de Vries and Lawrence E. Sullivan, 298–317. New York: Fordham University Press, 2006.
Browning, Christopher. *The Origins of the Final Solution: The Evolution of Nazi Jewish Policy, September 1939 – March 1942*. Jerusalem: Yad Vashem / Lincoln: University of Nebraska Press, 2004.
Brumlik, Micha. "Jenseits der Schwelle: Auschwitz im 21. Jahrhundert." *Newsletter zur Geschichte und Wirkung des Holocaust – Informationen des Fritz Bauer Instituts* 27 (2005): 12–14.
Busse, Sylta. "Vorschläge für Erwin Piscator zur Kostümgestaltung der 'Clique' ... im *Kaufmann von Venedig*." In *Theaterarbeit: Eine Dokumentation*, by Hans-Ulrich Schmückle and Sylta Busse, edited by Eckehart Nölle, 90–95. Munich: Theatermuseum, c. 1975.

Canaris, Volker. *Peter Zadek: Der Theatermann und Filmemacher*. Munich: Hanser, 1979.
Carlson, Marvin. *The Haunted Stage: The Theatre as Memory Machine* (2001). Ann Arbor: The University of Michigan Press, 2011.
Carlson, Marvin. *Theatre Is More Beautiful than War: German Stage Directing in the Late Twentieth Century*. Iowa City: University of Iowa Press, 2009.
Certeau, Michel de. *The Practice of Everyday Life*. Translated by Steven Rendall. Berkeley: The University of California Press, 1984.
Chow, Rey. "'I Insist on the Christian Dimension': On Forgiveness ... and the Outside of the Human." *Differences: A Journal of Feminist Cultural Studies* 20.2/3 (2009): 224–249.
Claussen, Detlev. "Nach Auschwitz: Ein Essay über die Aktualität Adornos." In *Zivilisationsbruch: Denken nach Auschwitz*, edited by Dan Diner, 54–68. Frankfurt/M.: Fischer, 1988.
Cohen, Robert. "The Political Aesthetics of Holocaust Literature: Peter Weiss's *The Investigation* and Its Critics." *History and Memory* 10.2 (1998): 43–67.
Critchfield, Richard D. "Fritz Kortner's *Aller Tage Abend*: Self-Discovery as the Discovery of the Other or a Life and Career as Shylock." In *When Lucifer Cometh: The Autobiographical Discourse of Writers and Intellectuals Exiled during the Third Reich*, 75–82. New York: Peter Lang, 1994.
Critchfield, Richard D. *From Shakespeare to Frisch: The Provocative Fritz Kortner*. Heidelberg: Synchron, 2008.
Daiber, Hans. *Schaufenster der Diktatur: Theater im Machtbereich Hitlers*. Stuttgart: Neske, 1995.
Damrosch, David. "Auerbach in Exile." *Comparative Literature* 47.2 (1995): 97–117.
Darf der Jude wieder böse sein? TV-round table on the occasion of the screening of Otto Schenk's *Der Kaufmann von Venedig* on German TV. Westdeutscher Rundfunk, 2 March, 1969.
Derrida, Jacques. *Specters of Marx: The State of the Debt, the Work of Mourning and the New International* (1993). Translated by Peggy Kamuf. Abingdon: Routledge, 1994.
Deutsch-Schreiner, Evelyn. "Die Opfer schützen die Täter." In *Theatralia Judaica II: Nach der Shoah. Israelisch-deutsche Theaterbeziehungen seit 1949*, edited by Hans-Peter Bayerdörfer, 100–114. Tübingen: Niemeyer, 1996.
Diner, Dan, ed. *Zivilisationsbruch: Denken nach Auschwitz*. Frankfurt/M.: Fischer, 1988.
Dische, Irene. "Die reichen Juden in Deutschland." *TransAtlantik* 6 (1981): 14–25. Reprinted in Schauspielhaus Düsseldorf. *Der Kaufmann von Venedig*, theatre programme, n. p. Düsseldorf, 1981.
Drakakis, John. "Introduction." In William Shakespeare, *The Merchant of Venice*, edited by John Drakakis. The Arden Shakespeare, Third Series, 1–159. London: Methuen, 2010.
Drakakis, John. "Jessica." In *The Merchant of Venice: New Critical Essays*, edited by John W. Mahon and Ellen Macleod Mahon, 145–164. London: Routledge, 2002.
Drössler, Stefan. "Der Fall *Nathan der Weise*." Booklet accompanying the DVD of *Nathan der Weise*. Munich: Filmmuseum München, 2006.
Dubiel, Helmut. *Niemand ist frei von der Geschichte: Die nationalsozialistische Herrschaft in den Debatten des Deutschen Bundestages*. Munich: Hanser, 1999.
Dudley Edwards, Ruth. *Victor Gollancz: A Biography*. London: Gollancz, 1987.

Düren, Fred. "Angst gibt es nicht: Fred Düren in Gesprächen, Berlin, November 2004." In Fred Düren. *Ich muß ja den Weg gehen, den ich gehen kann: Schauspieler in Berlin – Jahre in Jerusalem*, edited by Karl-Heinz Müller, 55–131. Berlin: Das Neue Berlin, 2007.

Ebert, Gerhard. "Die humanistische Aussage eines klassischen Werkes neu entdeckt." *Neues Deutschland*, 23/24 March 1985.

Edelman, Charles. "Introduction." In *Shakespeare in Production: The Merchant of Venice*, edited by Charles Edelman, 1–93. Cambridge: Cambridge University Press, 2002.

Egervari, Tibor. "Shakespeare's *Merchant of Venice* in Auschwitz." In *Shakespeare and the Second World War: Memory, Culture, Identity*, edited by Irena R. Makaryk and Marissa McHugh, 274–285. Toronto: University of Toronto Press, 2012.

Eicher, Thomas. "Spielplanstrukturen 1929–1944." In *Theater im "Dritten Reich": Theaterpolitik, Spielplanstruktur, NS-Dramatik*, edited by Henning Rischbieter, 285–486. Seelze-Velber: Kallmeyer, 2000.

Elias, Norbert. *What is Sociology?* Translated by Stephen Mennell and Grace Morrissey. London: Hutchinson / New York: Columbia Press, 1978.

Endriss, Beate-Ursula. *Shakespeare-Inszenierungen in Berlin 1933–1944*. Doctoral dissertation, Freie Universität, Berlin, 1994.

Engler, Balz. "The Noise That Banish'd Martius: *Coriolanus* in Post-War Germany." In *Renaissance Refractions: Essays in Honour of Alexander Shurbanov*, edited by Boika Sokolova and Evgenia Pancheva, 179–186. Sofia: St Kliment Ohridski University Press, 2001.

Enzensberger, Christian. "Das Schöne im Warentausch: William Shakespeares *Kaufmann von Venedig*." In *Literatur und Interesse*, vol. 2, 15–89. Munich: Hanser, 1977.

Erll, Astrid. *Memory in Culture*. Translated by Sara B. Young. Houndmills: Palgrave, 2011.

Fassbinder, Rainer Werner. *Der Müll, die Stadt und der Tod. Nur eine Scheibe Brot.* Frankfurt/M.: Verlag der Autoren, 1998.

Feinberg, Anat. "Against 'False Piety': George Tabori and *The Merchant of Venice*." *Shakespeare Jahrbuch* 149 (2013): 104–116.

Feinberg, Anat. *Embodied Memory: The Theatre of George Tabori*. City: The University of Iowa Press, 1999.

Feinberg, Anat. "Vom bösen Nathan und edlen Shylock: Überlegungen zur Konstruktion jüdischer Bühnenfiguren in Deutschland nach 1945." In *Shylock nach dem Holocaust: Zur Geschichte einer deutschen Erinnerungsfigur*, edited by Zeno Ackermann and Sabine Schülting, 41–61. Berlin: De Grutyer, 2011.

Feinberg, Anat. *Wiedergutmachung im Programm: Jüdisches Schicksal im deutschen Nachkriegsdrama*. Cologne: Prometh, 1988.

Fest, Joachim. "Reicher Jude von links." *Frankfurter Allgemeine Zeitung*, 19 March 1976.

Fischer, Torben, and Matthias N. Lorenz, eds. *Lexikon der 'Vergangenheitsbewältigung' in Deutschland: Debatten- und Diskursgeschichte des Nationalsozialismus nach 1945*. 2007, 2nd edition, Bielefeld: transcript, 2009.

Frei, Norbert. *Adenauer's Germany and the Nazi Past: The Politics of Amnesty and Integration*. Translated by Joel Golb. New York: Columbia University Press, 2002.

Frei, Norbert. *1945 und wir: Das Dritte Reich im Bewußtsein der Deutschen*. 2005, extended edition, Munich: Beck, 2009.

Frei, Norbert, and Sybille Steinbacher, eds. *Beschweigen und Bekennen: Die deutsche Nachkriegsgesellschaft und der Holocaust*. Göttingen: Wallstein, 2001.

Freydank, Ruth. "Die Klassiker als Herausforderung an eine Vorstadtbühne." In *Das Rose-Theater: Ein Volkstheater im Berliner Osten 1906–1944*, edited by Michael Baumgarten and Ruth Freydank, 126–154. Berlin: Hentrich, 1991.

fringe ensemble. "Shylock-Rap." http://www.fringe-ensemble.de/der-shylock-rap/ (accessed 8 September 2018).

Frye, Northrop. *A Natural Perspective: The Development of Shakespearean Comedy and Romance*. New York: Columbia University Press, 1965.

Frye, Northrop. *Shakespeares Vollendung: Eine Einführung in die Welt seiner Komödien*. Translated by Helmut Haug. Munich: Nymphenburger Verlagshandlung, 1966.

Gillman, Abigail. "Shylock in German-Jewish Historiography." In *Wrestling with Shylock: Jewish Responses to The* Merchant of Venice, edited by Edna Nahshon and Michael Shapiro, 51–73. Cambridge: Cambridge University Press, 2017.

Goerden, Elmar. "Der Andere: Fragmente einer Bühnengeschichte Shylocks im deutschen und englischen Theater des 18. und 19. Jahrhunderts." In *Theatralia Judaica: Emanzipation und Antisemitismus als Momente der Theatergeschichte. Von der Lessing-Zeit bis zur Shoah*, edited by Hans-Peter Bayerdörfer, 129–163. Tübingen: Niemeyer, 1992.

Goerden, Elmar. "Nathan findet nicht statt." In Staatstheater Stuttgart. *Lessings Traum von Nathan dem Weisen: Collage mit Passagen aus* Nathan der Weise *und* Der Kaufmann von Venedig, *sowie modernen Texten von Elmar Goerden*, theatre programme, 5. Stuttgart, 1999.

Gollancz, Victor. *Let My People Go: Some Practical Proposals for Dealing with Hitler's Massacre of the Jews and an Appeal to the British Public*. London: Gollancz, 1943.

Görtz, Hans-Helmut. *Hermann und Christobel Sinsheimer: Briefe aus England und der Pfalz*. Edited by Gabriele Giersberg and Erik Giersberg. Neustadt/Weinstraße: Selbstverlag, 2012.

Goschler, Constantin. *Schuld und Schulden: Die Politik der Wiedergutmachung für NS-Verfolgte seit 1945*. Göttingen: Wallstein, 2005.

Granach, Alexander. "Shylock." In *Da geht ein Mensch: Autobiographischer Roman*, 421–428. Stockholm: Neuer Verlag, 1945.

Greiner, Bernhard. "Is that the Law? Die Metaphorisierung des Rechts als Problem der Interpretation des *Kaufmann von Venedig*." In *Shylock nach dem Holocaust: Zur Geschichte einer deutschen Erinnerungsfigur*, edited by Zeno Ackermann and Sabine Schülting, 189–200. Berlin: De Gruyter, 2011.

Gross, John. *Shylock: A Legend and Its Legacy*. New York: Simon & Schuster, 1992.

Gross, John. *Shylock: Four Hundred Years in the Life of a Legend*. London: Chatto & Windus, 1992.

Gundolf, Friedrich. "*Der Kaufmann von Venedig*." In *Shakespeare: Sein Wesen und sein Werk*, vol. 1: 561–588. Berlin: Bondi, 1928.

Günther, Hans F. K. "Shakespeares Mädchen und Frauen: Ein Vortrag vor der Deutschen Shakespeare-Gesellschaft." *Shakespeare Jahrbuch* 73 (1937): 85–108.

Guntner, Lawrence. "In Search of a Socialist Shakespeare: *Hamlet* on East German Stages." In *Shakespeare in the Worlds of Communism and Socialism*, edited by Irena R. Makaryk and Joseph G. Price, 177–204. Toronto: University of Toronto Press, 2006.

Guntner, Lawrence. "Introduction. Shakespeare in East Germany: Between Appropriation and Deconstruction." In *Redefining Shakespeare: Literary Theory and Theater Practice in the German Democratic Republic*, edited by Lawrence Guntner and Andrew M. McLean,

29–57. Newark: University of Delaware Press / London: Associated University Presses, 1998.
Guntner, Lawrence. "Preface." In *Redefining Shakespeare: Literary Theory and Theater Practice in the German Democratic Republic*, edited by Lawrence Guntner and Andrew M. McLean, 11–14. Newark: University of Delaware Press / London: Associated University Presses, 1998.
Hacohen, Malachi Haim. "Typology and the Holocaust: Erich Auerbach and Judeo-Christian Europe." *Religions* 3 (2012): 600–645.
Hamburger, Maik. "Regisseure aus Israel und England in Thüringen." *Shakespeare Jahrbuch* 132 (1996): 174–179.
Hamburger, Maik. "Shakespeare on the Stages of the German Democratic Republic." In Wilhelm Hortmann. *Shakespeare on the German Stage: The Twentieth Century*, 369–434. Cambridge: Cambridge University Press, 1998.
Hamburger, Maik. "Unser Shakespeare – Ein Judenfeind? *Der Kaufmann von Venedig* auf den Bühnen der DDR." In *Shylock nach dem Holocaust: Zur Geschichte einer deutschen Erinnerungsfigur*, edited by Zeno Ackermann and Sabine Schülting, 85–99. Berlin: De Gruyter, 2011.
Harlan, Veit. *Im Schatten meiner Filme*. Gütersloh: Mohn, 1966.
Hartlage-Laufenberg, Barbara. *Hermann Sinsheimer*. Berlin: Hentrich & Hentrich, 2012.
Hausmann, Frank-Rutger. *Anglistik und Amerikanistik im "Dritten Reich."* Frankfurt/M.: Klostermann, 2003.
Hausmann, Frank-Rutger. *Die Geisteswissenschaften im 'Dritten Reich.'* Frankfurt/M.: Vittorio Klostermann, 2011.
Heimpel, Hermann. "'Zur Lage': Eine Vorlesung des Professors für Englische Philologie, Herbert Schöffler, gehalten im Oktober 1945." In *Geschichtswissenschaft in Göttingen*, edited by Hartmut Boockmann and Hermann Wellenreuther, 364–399. Göttingen: Vandenhoek & Ruprecht, 1987.
Heine, Heinrich. *Shakespeare's Maidens and Women*. Vol. 1 of *The Works of Heinrich Heine*. Translated by Charles Godfrey Leland. London: Heinemann, 1906.
Heiseler, Bernt von. "Zu Shakespeares Komödie 'Der Kaufmann von Venedig'." In Stadttheater Gießen. *Der Kaufmann von Venedig*, theatre programme, 71. Gießen, 1968.
Heiseler, Bernt von. "Unser Dienst am Frieden: Ansprache auf der Herbsttagung 1951 der 'Deutschen Akademie für Sprache und Dichtung'." In *Zwischen Kritik und Zuversicht: 50 Jahre Deutsche Akademie für Sprache und Dichtung*, edited by Michael Hackmann and Herbert Heckmann, 292–294. Göttingen: Wallstein, 1999.
Hensel, Georg. "Laudatio auf Peter Zadek." In Peter Zadek, *My Way: Eine Autobiographie 1926–1969*, 544–555. Cologne: Kiepenheuer & Witsch, 1998.
Herbert, Ulrich. *Geschichte der Ausländerpolitik in Deutschland: Saisonarbeiter, Zwangsarbeiter, Gastarbeiter, Flüchtlinge*. Munich: Beck, 2001.
Herbold, Astrid. *Vom Elefanten zum Intendanten: Peter Zadeks Shakespeare-Inszenierungen am Schauspielhaus Bochum*. Herne: Verlag für Wissenschaft und Kunst, 1997.
Herf, Jeffrey. *Divided Memory: The Nazi Past in the Two Germanys*. Cambridge, MA: Harvard University Press, 1997.
Heschel, Susannah. "From Jesus to Shylock: Christian Supersessionism and 'The Merchant of Venice'." *Harvard Theological Review* 99.4 (2006): 407–431.

Höfele, Andreas. *No Hamlets: German Shakespeare from Nietzsche to Schmidt*. Cambridge: Cambridge University Press, 2016.

Hockerts, Hans Günther. "Wiedergutmachung in Deutschland: Eine historische Bilanz 1945–2000." *Vierteljahrshefte für Zeitgeschichte* 49 (2001): 167–214.

Hollstein, Dorothea. *Jud Süß und die Deutschen: Antisemitische Vorurteile im nationalsozialistischen Spielfilm*. Frankfurt/M.: Ullstein, 1983.

Holmes, Jonathan, and Adrian Streete, eds. *Refiguring Mimesis: Representation in Early Modern Literature*. Hatfield: University of Hertfordshire Press, 2005.

Honecker, Erich. "Für das Wohl des arbeitenden Menschen all unsere Kraft: Bericht des Zentralkomitees an den VIII. Parteitag der Sozialistischen Einheitspartei Deutschlands, 15. bis 19. Juni 1971." In *Reden und Aufsätze*, vol. 1, 134–225. Berlin: Dietz Verlag, 1975.

Hortmann, Wilhelm. *Shakespeare on the German Stage: The Twentieth Century*. Cambridge: Cambridge University Press, 1998.

Hortmann, Wilhelm. "Wo, bitte, geht's nach Belmont? Über ein Dilemma von Inszenierungen des *Kaufmann von Venedig* nach dem Holocaust." *Shakespeare Jahrbuch* 139 (2003): 217–225.

Huesmann, Heinrich. *Welttheater Reinhardt: Bauten, Spielstätten, Inszenierungen*. Munich: Prestel, 1983.

Ihering, Herbert. *Werner Krauß: Ein Schauspieler und das neunzehnte Jahrhundert*. Berlin: Vorwerk 8, 1997.

International Military Tribunal. *Der Prozeß gegen die Hauptkriegsverbrecher vor dem Internationalen Militärgerichtshof: Amtlicher Wortlaut in deutscher Sprache*. Nuremberg: Internationaler Militärgerichtshof, 1947.

Jacobi, Johannes. "Wohin steuert das Theater?" *Die ZEIT*, 16 October 1952.

Jacobson, Howard. *Shylock Is My Name*. London: Hogarth, 2016.

Jauslin, Christian. "Bühnenbericht 1973 und Verzeichnis der Shakespeare-Aufführungen 1973." *Shakespeare Jahrbuch* (West) (1974): 223–237.

Jauslin, Christian. "Zu Gustav Rudolf Sellners Shakespeare-Inszenierungen: Gespräch mit dem Regisseur." *Shakespeare Jahrbuch* (West) (1984): 32–43.

Jeffries, Michael P. "Hip-Hop Urbanism Old and New." *International Journal of Urban and Regional Research* 38.2 (2014): 706–715.

Jellonnek, Burkhard. *Homosexuelle unter dem Hakenkreuz: Die Verfolgung von Homosexuellen im Dritten Reich*. Paderborn: Schöningh, 1990.

Kahane, Arthur. "Max Reinhardt's Shakespeare-Zyklus im Deutschen Theater zu Berlin." *Shakespeare Jahrbuch* 50 (1914): 107–120.

Kaiser, Joachim. *Kleines Theatertagebuch*. Reinbek: Rowohlt, 1965.

Karasek, Hellmuth. "Revue der Arbeitslosen." *Die ZEIT*, 29 September, 1972.

Karasholi, Adel. "Die Figur des Shylock in heutiger Sicht." *Shakespeare Jahrbuch* 113 (1977): 64–73.

Der Kaufmann von Venedig. TV adaptation, directed by Otto Schenk. Austria/Germany: ORF/ARD, 1968.

Kaynar, Gad. "Pragmatic Dramaturgy: Text as Context as Text." *Theatre Research International* 31.3 (2006): 245–259.

Kaynar-Kissinger, Gad. "*The Merchant of Venice* on the German Stage and the 1995 'Buchenwald' Production in Weimar." In *Wrestling with Shylock: Jewish Responses to* The

Merchant of Venice, edited by Edna Nahshon and Michael Shapiro, 243–272. Cambridge: Cambridge University Press, 2017.
Kennedy, Dennis. *Looking at Shakespeare: A Visual History of Twentieth-Century Performance.* Cambridge: Cambridge University Press, 1994.
Kertész, Imre. *The Holocaust as Culture.* Translated and edited by Thomas Cooper. New York: Seagull, 2011.
Koberg, Roland, Bernd Stegemann, and Henrike Thomsen, eds. *Max Reinhardt und das Deutsche Theater.* Berlin: Deutsches Theater/Henschel, 2005.
Korte, Karl-Rudolf. "Die deutsche Wiedervereinigung." In *Die Bundesrepublik Deutschland: Eine Bilanz nach 60 Jahren*, edited by Hans-Peter Schwarz, 181–203. Cologne: Böhlau, 2008.
Kortner, Fritz. *Aller Tage Abend.* 1959, 4th edition, Munich: dtv, 1972.
Kosselleck, Reinhart. "Formen und Traditionen des negativen Gedächtnisses." In *Verbrechen erinnern: Die Auseinandersetzung mit Holocaust und Völkermord*, edited by Volkhard Knigge and Norbert Frei, 21–32. Munich: Beck 2002.
Kuckhoff, Armin-Gerd. *Das Drama William Shakespeares.* Berlin: Henschel, 1964.
Kuckhoff, Armin-Gerd. "Erbe – Gegenwart – Prognose." *Shakespeare Jahrbuch* 106 (1970): 29–62.
Kuckhoff, Armin-Gerd. "Shakespeare auf den Bühnen der DDR im Jahre 1975." *Shakespeare Jahrbuch* 133 (1977): 186–199.
Kujawińska-Courtney, Krystyna. "'In this Hour of History: Amidst these Tragic Events' – Polish Shakespeare during the Second World War." In *Shakespeare and the Second World War: Memory, Culture, Identity*, edited by Irena R. Makaryk and Marissa McHugh, 122–142. Toronto: University of Toronto Press, 2012.
Landauer, Gustav. "Der Kaufmann von Venedig." In *Shakespeare: Dargestellt in Vorträgen*, vol. 1, 42–90. Frankfurt/M.: Rütten und Loening, 1920.
Landauer, Gustav. "Der Fall Shylock." In Württembergisches Staatstheater, *Der Kaufmann von Venedig*, theatre programme, 3–4. Stuttgart, 1956/57.
Landestheater Darmstadt. "Die Musik im *Kaufmann von Venedig.*" *Das Neue Forum* 5 (1955/56): 1–2.
Lange, Wigand. *Theater in Deutschland nach 1945: Zur Theaterpolitik der amerikanischen Besatzungsbehörden.* Frankfurt/M.: Lang, 1980.
Langer, Lawrence L. *Preempting the Holocaust.* New Haven: Yale University Press, 1998.
Langhoff, Thomas, and Eva Walch. Theatre documentation for Thomas Langhoff's production of *Merchant* at Deutsches Theater Berlin (premiere: 17 March 1985), 2 vols. Unpublished typescript. Archiv der Akademie der Künste Berlin, Inszenierungsdokumentationen 584.
Latham, Alison. "Figuration." In *The Oxford Companion to Music.* Oxford: Oxford University Press, 2011. http://www.oxfordreference.com/view/10.1093/acref/9780199579037.001.0001/acref-9780199579037-e-2510.
Ledebur, Ruth von. *Der Mythos vom deutschen Shakespeare: Die Deutsche Shakespeare-Gesellschaft zwischen Politik und Wissenschaft 1918–1945.* Cologne: Böhlau, 2002.
Ledebur, Ruth von. *Deutsche Shakespeare-Rezeption seit 1945.* Frankfurt/M.: Akademische Verlagsgesellschaft, 1974.
Lemcke, Heinrich. "Zur Einführung." In William Shakespeare, *Der Kaufmann von Venedig*, iii–vii. Bielefeld: Velhagen und Klasing, 1940.

Leo, Annette. "Als antifaschistischer Staat nicht betroffen? Die DDR und der Holocaust." In *Deutschland, Israel und der Holocaust: Zur Gegenwartsbedeutung der Vergangenheit*, edited by Bernd Faulenbach and Helmuth Schütte, 98–104. Essen: Klartext, 1998.

Lerer, Seth. "Auerbach's Shakespeare." *Philological Quarterly* 90.1 (2011): 21–44.

Ludewig, Alexandra. *Screening Nostalgia: 100 Years of German Heimat Film*. Bielefeld: transcript, 2011.

Lühe, Irmela von der. "'Sogar das Sterben ist hier wunderschön': Grenzgänge des Schauspielers und Schriftstellers Alexander Granach." In *Anthropologien der Endlichkeit: Stationen einer literarischen Denkfigur seit der Aufklärung*, edited by Friederike Felicitas Günther and Torsten Hoffmann, 208–218. Göttingen: Wallstein 2011.

Lux, Joachim. "Vorbemerkung." In Düsseldorfer Schauspielhaus. *Der Kaufmann von Venedig*, theatre programme, n. p. Düsseldorf, 1994.

Malkin, Jeanette R. "Fritz Kortner and Other German-Jewish Shylocks before and after the Holocaust." In *Wrestling with Shylock: Jewish Responses to* The Merchant of Venice, edited by Edna Nahshon and Michael Shapiro, 198–223. Cambridge: Cambridge University Press, 2017.

Mandelkow, Karl Robert. "Die literarische und kulturpolitische Bedeutung des Erbes." In *Die Literatur der DDR*, edited by Hans-Jürgen Schmitt, 78–119. Munich: dtv, 1983.

Markovits, Andrei S., Seyla Benhabib, and Moishe Postone. "Rainer Werner Fassbinder's *Garbage, the City and Death:* Renewed Antagonisms in the Complex Relationship between Jews and Germans in the Federal Republic of Germany." *New German Critique* 38 (1986): 3–27.

Marx, Peter W. "Die drei Gesichter Shylocks: Zu Max Reinhardts Projekt eines metropolitanen, liberalen Theaters vor dem Hintergrund seiner jüdischen Herkunft." In *Max Reinhardt und das Deutsche Theater*, edited by Roland Koberg, Bernd Stegemann, and Henrike Thomsen, 51–59. Berlin: Deutsches Theater/Henschel, 2005.

Marx, Peter W. *Max Reinhardt: Vom bürgerlichen Theater zur metropolitanen Kultur*. Tübingen: Francke, 2006.

Matzke, Annemarie. *Arbeit am Theater: Eine Diskursgeschichte der Probe*. Bielefeld: transcript, 2012.

Mayer, Hans. *Außenseiter*. 1975, Frankfurt/M.: Suhrkamp, 1981.

Mayer, Hans. *Outsiders: A Study in Life and Letters*. Translated by Denis M. Sweet. Cambridge, MA: MIT Press, 1982, paperback reprint 1984.

Melchinger, Siegfried. "Shakespeare heute." *Shakespeare Jahrbuch* (West) (1965): 59–79.

The Merchant of Venice. Film adaptation, directed by John Sichel (based on the National Theatre production directed by Jonathan Miller). UK/USA: National Theatre/ATV, 1973.

Mertz, Peter. *Das gerettete Theater: Die deutsche Bühne im Wiederaufbau*. Weinheim: Quadriga, 1990.

Metzger, Mary Janell. "'Now by My Hood, a Gentle and No Jew': Jessica, *The Merchant of Venice*, and the Discourse of Early Modern English Identity." *PMLA* 113 (1998): 52–63.

Michel, Karl Markus. "Von den Fremden magst du Zins nehmen – Gegen die Priester vor der Bundeslade: Dietrich Schwanitz erforscht das 'Shylock-Syndrom'," *Frankfurter Allgemeine Zeitung*, 2 December 1997.

Moeller, Robert G. *War Stories: The Search for a Usable Past in the Federal Republic of Germany*. Berkeley: University of California Press, 2001.

Moninger, Markus. "Auschwitz erinnern: *Merchant*-Inszenierungen im Nachkriegsdeutschland." In *Das Theater der Anderen: Alterität und Theater zwischen Antike und Gegenwart*, edited by Christopher Balme, 229–248. Tübingen: Francke, 2001.

Moninger, Markus. "Die Dramaturgie von *Merchant*-Inszenierungen in der Weimarer Republik." 2005, last modified 20 August 2018. In *Zukunft braucht Erinnerung*. http://www.zukunft-braucht-erinnerung.de/die-dramaturgie-von-merchant-inszenierungen-in-der-weimarer-republik/ (accessed 8 September 2018).

Moninger, Markus. *Shakespeare inszeniert: Das westdeutsche Regietheater und die Theatertradition des 'dritten deutschen Klassikers.'* Tübingen: Max Niemeyer Verlag, 1996.

Monschau, Jörg. *Der Jude nach der Shoah: Zur Rezeption des Kaufmann von Venedig auf dem Theater der Bundesrepublik Deutschland und der Deutschen Demokratischen Republik 1945–1989*. Doctoral dissertation, Ruprecht-Karls-Universität Heidelberg, 2002. https://archiv.ub.uni-heidelberg.de/volltextserver/3530/ (accessed 8 September 2018).

Mühlbach, Egon. "Statistischer Überblick über die Aufführungen Shakespearescher Werke auf den deutschen und einigen außerdeutschen Bühnen in den Jahren 1941 und 1942." *Shakespeare Jahrbuch* 80/81 (1946): 113–121.

Müller, Karl-Heinz. "Stationen des Schauspielers Fred Düren." In Fred Düren, *Ich muß ja den Weg gehen, den ich gehen kann: Schauspieler in Berlin – Jahre in Jerusalem*, edited by Karl-Heinz Müller, 7–19. Berlin: Das Neue Berlin, 2007.

Müthel, Lothar. "Zur Dramaturgie des *Kaufmann von Venedig*." *Neues Wiener Tagblatt*, 13 May 1943.

Nachmann, Werner. "Warum? Offener Brief an den Intendanten des Düsseldorfer Schauspielhauses, Günther Beelitz." *Berliner Allgemeine jüdische Wochenzeitung*, 9 October 1981.

Nahshon, Edna. "Preface." In *Wrestling with Shylock: Jewish Responses to* The Merchant of Venice, edited by Edna Nahshon and Michael Shapiro, xxi–xxiv. Cambridge: Cambridge University Press, 2017.

Nahshon, Edna, and Michael Shapiro, eds. *Wrestling with Shylock: Jewish Responses to* The Merchant of Venice. Cambridge: Cambridge University Press, 2017.

Novick, Peter. *The Holocaust in American Life*. Boston: Houghton Mifflin, 1999.

Onuki, Atsuko, and Thomas Pekar, eds. *Figuration – Defiguration: Beiträge zur transkulturellen Forschung*. Munich: Iudicium, 2006.

Papsdorf, Werner, Ernst Leopold Stahl, and Carl Niessen. "Shakespeare auf der deutschen Bühne 1940/42." *Shakespeare Jahrbuch* 78/79 (1943): 128–137.

Pfeiffer, Ludwig. "Anglistik." In *Die Rolle der Geisteswissenschaften im Dritten Reich 1933–1945*, edited by Frank-Rutger Hausmann, 57–62. Munich: Oldenbourg, 2002.

Picker, Henry. *Hitlers Tischgespräche im Führerhauptquartier*. Stuttgart: Seewald, 1983.

Piscator, Erwin. "Die Bühne als moralische Anstalt in der Prägung dieses Jahrhunderts." In *Theater der Auseinandersetzung: Ausgewählte Schriften und Reden*, 138–141. Frankfurt/M.: Suhrkamp, 1977.

Piscator, Erwin. "Regiebuch" (*Der Kaufmann von Venedig*, Freie Volksbühne Berlin, premiere: 1 December 1963). Unpublished typescripts. Archiv der Akademie der Künste Berlin, Piscator 556–560.

Piscator, Erwin. "Vorwort zum 'Stellvertreter'." In *Aufsätze – Reden – Gespräche*, vol. 2 of *Schriften*, edited by Ludwig Hoffmann, 301–305. Berlin: Henschelverlag, 1968.

Poppek, Yvonne. *Was ist ein Dorn? Die Shakespeare-Inszenierungen des Theaterregisseurs Dieter Dorn.* Munich: Utz, 2007.

Porter, James I. "Introduction." In *Time, History, and Literature: Selected Essays of Erich Auerbach*, edited by James I. Porter, ix–xlix. Princeton: Princeton University Press, 2014.

Potter, Lois. "A Stage Where Every Man Must Play a Part." *Shakespeare Quarterly* 50.1 (1999): 74–86.

Rathkolb, Oliver. *Führertreu und gottbegnadet: Künstlereliten im Dritten Reich.* Wien: Österreichischer Bundesverlag, 1991.

Reichel, Peter. *Erfundene Erinnerung: Weltkrieg und Judenmord in Film und Theater.* Munich: Hanser, 2004.

Reichel, Peter, Harald Schmid, and Peter Steinbach, eds. *Der Nationalsozialismus – die zweite Geschichte: Überwindung – Deutung – Erinnerung.* Munich: Beck 2009.

Reichert, Klaus. "William Shakespeare. Der Kaufmann von Venedig." In Schauspielhaus Düsseldorf. *Der Kaufmann von Venedig*, theatre programme. Düsseldorf, 1981.

Reinfeldt, Franziska. "'Nimm dich dieser Fremden an': Die Figur der Jessica in aktuellen Inszenierungen des *Kaufmann von Venedig*." In *Shylock nach dem Holocaust: Zur Geschichte einer deutschen Erinnerungsfigur*, edited by Zeno Ackermann and Sabine Schülting, 143–158. Berlin: De Gruyter, 2011.

Richardson, Michael D. *Revolutionary Theater and the Classical Heritage: Inheritance and Appropriation from Weimar to the GDR.* Bern: Peter Lang, 2007.

Riewoldt, Otto F. "Theaterarbeit: Über den Wirkungszusammenhang von Bühne, Dramatik, Kulturpolitik und Publikum." In *Die Literatur der DDR*, edited by Hans-Jürgen Schmitt, 133–186. Munich: dtv, 1983.

Rischbieter, Henning. "NS-Theaterpolitik." In *Theater im "Dritten Reich": Theaterpolitik, Spielplanstruktur, NS-Dramatik*, edited by Henning Rischbieter, 9–278. Seelze-Velber: Kallmeyer, 2000.

Rühle, Günther. "Rückkehr in ein verwüstetes Land." *Theater heute* 45.12 (2004): 26–35.

Said, Edward W. "Introduction to the Fiftieth-Anniversary Edition." In Erich Auerbach, *Mimesis: The Representation of Reality in Western Culture*, Fiftieth Anniversary Edition. Translated by Willard R. Trask, ix–xxxii. Princeton: Princeton University Press, 2003.

Schaller, Rudolf. Letter to Gert Hillesheim, Deutsche Akademie der Künste, Sektion Dichtkunst und Sprachpflege (Academy of Arts, Section Literature and Language), 7 December, 1959. Unpublished typescript. In "Vorgänge um Shakespeare-Übersetzung von Rudolf Schaller." Archiv der Akademie der Künste Berlin, AdK-O 0858.

Schlegel, August Wilhelm. *Lectures on Dramatic Art and Literature.* Translated by John Black. 1809–1811, 2nd ed. London: George Bell & Sons, 1892.

Schlösser, Anselm. "Zur Dialektik in *Der Kaufmann von Venedig*." *Zeitschrift für Anglistik und Amerikanistik* 23.1 (1975): 5–11. Reprinted in *Shakespeare Jahrbuch* 113 (1977): 135–144.

Schlösser, Anselm. *Shakespeare: Analysen und Interpretationen.* Berlin: Aufbau-Verlag, 1977.

Schlösser, Anselm, ed. *Shakespeare Jubiläum: Festschrift zu Ehren des 400. Geburtstages William Shakespeares und des 100jährigen Bestehens der Deutschen Shakespeare-Gesellschaft.* Weimar: Hermann Böhlaus Nachfolger, 1964.

Schlösser, Rainer. "Der deutsche Shakespeare." *Shakespeare Jahrbuch* 74 (1938): 20–30.

Schmückle, Hans-Ulrich, and Hermann Kleinselbeck. "Notizen für die Szene zu 'Der Kaufmann von Venedig' von William Shakespeare." In *Theaterarbeit: Eine Dokumentation*, by

Hans-Ulrich Schmückle and Sylta Busse, edited by Eckehart Nölle, 75–89. Munich: Theatermuseum, c. 1975.

Schnauder, Ludwig. "'The poor man is wronged!' Die Figur des Shylock in Inszenierungen am Burgtheater." In *Die Rezeption anglophoner Dramen auf Wiener Bühnen im 20. Jahrhundert.* Vol. 2 of *Weltbühne Wien / World Stage Vienna*, edited by Ewald Mengel, Ludwig Schnauder, and Rudolf Weiss, 119–147. Trier: WVT, 2010.

Schöffler, Herbert. "*Der Kaufmann von Venedig:* Zu den kommenden Aufführungen in Göttingen." *Göttinger Tageblatt*, 26/27 September 1942.

Schülting, Sabine. "Evoking the Holocaust in George Tabori's Productions of *The Merchant of Venice*." In *Wrestling with Shylock: Jewish Responses to* The Merchant of Venice, edited by Michael Shapiro and Edna Nahshon, 224–242. Cambridge: Cambridge University Press, 2017.

Schülting, Sabine. "'I am not bound to please thee with my answers': *The Merchant of Venice* on the Post-War German Stage." In *World Wide Shakespeares: Local Appropriations in Film and Performance*, edited by Sonia Massai, 65–71. London: Routledge, 2005.

Schülting, Sabine. "'Imagined Communities': Reconsidering European Shakespeares," *Cahiers Élisabéthains: A Journal of English Renaissance Studies* 96.1 (2018): 160–171.

Schülting, Sabine. "'Remember Me': Shylock on the Postwar German Stage." *Shakespeare Survey* 63 (2010): 290–300.

Schülting, Sabine. "'Schön, dass ihr da seid. Und jetzt habt viel Spaß!' – Jessica und die Spaßgesellschaft." In *Wer lacht, zeigt Zähne: Spielarten des Komischen*, edited by Johann N. Schmidt, Felix C. H. Sprang, and Roland Weidle, 41–48. Trier: wvt, 2014.

Schülting, Sabine. "Shylock als Erinnerungsfigur." In *Shylock nach dem Holocaust: Zur Geschichte einer deutschen Erinnerungsfigur*, edited by Zeno Ackermann and Sabine Schülting, 103–116. Berlin: De Gruyter, 2011.

Schütze, Peter. *Fritz Kortner.* Reinbek bei Hamburg: Rowohlt, 1994.

Schwanitz, Dietrich. *Shylock: Von Shakespeare bis zum Nürnberger Prozeß.* Hamburg: Krämer, 1989.

Schwanitz, Dietrich. *Das Shylock-Syndrom oder die Dramaturgie der Barbarei.* Frankfurt/M: Eichborn, 1997.

Sehrt, Ernst Theodor. "Der Shylock Fritz Kortners." *Shakespeare Jahrbuch* (West) (1973): 78–96.

Sellner, Gustav Rudolf. "Zu Gustav Rudolf Sellners Shakespeare-Inszenierungen: Gespräch mit dem Regisseur." Interview by Christian Jauslin. *Shakespeare Jahrbuch* (West) (1984): 32–43.

Sellner, Gustav Rudolf, and Werner Wien. *Theatralische Landschaft.* Bremen: Carl Schünemann, 1962.

Shakespeare, William. *The Norton Shakespeare.* Edited by Stephen Greenblatt, Walter Cohen, Jean E. Howard, and Katharine Eisaman Maus. New York: W. W. Norton & Company, 1997.

Shapiro, Marianne. "Figuration." In *The Princeton Encyclopedia of Poetry and Poetics*, 4th ed., edited by Roland Greene et al., 486–487. Princeton: Princeton University Press, 2012. https://www.degruyter.com/view/books/9781400841424/9781400841424.476/9781400841424.476.xml.

Simon, Ernst. "Lessing und die jüdische Geschichte." *Jüdische Rundschau*, 22 January 1929. Reprinted in Ernst Simon, *Brücken: Gesammelte Aufsätze*, 215–219. Heidelberg: Lambert Schneider, 1965.
Sinsheimer, Hermann. *Shylock: The History of a Character.* London: Gollancz, 1947.
Sinsheimer, Hermann. *Shylock: Die Geschichte einer Figur.* Munich: Ner-Tamid-Verlag, 1960.
Sinsheimer, Hermann. *Shylock: The History of a Character.* New York: Benjamin Blom, 1963.
Sinsheimer, Hermann. "Shylock." In Landestheater Ballhof, Hannover, *Der Kaufmann von Venedig*, theatre programme, n. p. Hannover, 1963.
sle. "Der Schauspieler Fred Düren ist tot: Eine deutsche Theaterlegende." *nachkritik de*, 8 March 2015. https://www.nachtkritik.de/index.php?option=com_content&view=article&id=10655:2015-03-08-15-51-34&catid=126:meldungen-k&Itemid=100089 (accessed 6 August 2018).
Slights, Camille. "In Defense of Jessica: The Runaway Daughter in *The Merchant of Venice.*" *Shakespeare Quarterly* 31 (1980): 357–368.
Snir, Hanan. Interview by Lothar Schmidt-Mühlisch. *Die Welt*, 10 April 1995.
Sokolyansky, Mark. "The Half-Forbidden Play in Soviet Shakespeare Criticism of the 1920s–50s." *Multicultural Shakespeare: Translation, Appropriation and Performance* 6/7 (2010): 71–79. http://dspace.uni.lodz.pl:8080/xmlui/handle/11089/1508 (accessed 8 September 2018).
Sokolova, Boika. "'Mingled Yarn': Perspectives on *The Merchant of Venice* in East European Contexts." Unpublished paper given at the World Shakespeare Congress 2016 at Stratford-upon Avon.
Sorge, Thomas. "'Jew' und 'usury' in der Shakespeare-Zeit und in *Der Kaufmann von Venedig*." *Shakespeare Jahrbuch* 113 (1977): 45–55.
Stahl, Ernst Leopold. "Shakespeare im Aufführungsjahr 1943/44." *Shakespeare Jahrbuch* 80/81 (1946): 108–112.
Stahl, Ernst Leopold. *Shakespeare und das deutsche Theater: Wanderung und Wandelung seines Werkes in dreiundeinhalb Jahrhunderten.* Stuttgart: Kohlhammer, 1947.
Stern, Frank. *Im Anfang war Auschwitz: Antisemitismus und Philosemitismus im deutschen Nachkrieg.* Gerlingen: Bleicher, 1991.
Stolten, Inge. *Das alltägliche Exil: Leben zwischen Hakenkreuz und Währungsreform.* Berlin: Dietz, 1982.
Strobl, Gerwin. "The Bard of Eugenics: Shakespeare and Racial Activism in the Third Reich." *Journal of Contemporary History* 34.3 (1999): 323–336.
Stroedel, Wolfgang. "Bühnenbericht 1954." *Shakespeare Jahrbuch* 91 (1955): 217–224.
Syberberg, Jürgen. *Fritz Kortner spricht Monologe für eine Schallplatte.* Syberberg Filmproduktion / Preiserrecords, 1966. Accessible on YouTube at https://www.youtube.com/watch?v=9GB6Jaas3o0 (accessed 8 September 2018).
Symington, Rodney. *The Nazi Appropriation of Shakespeare: Cultural Politics in the Third Reich.* Lewiston, NY: Edwin Mellen, 2005.
Tabori, George. "Regiearbeiten: *The Merchant of Venice* (As performed in Theresienstadt)" (Stockbridge, Berkshire Theatre Festival, premiere: 19 July 1966). Unpublished typescripts. Archiv der Akademie der Künste Berlin, Tabori 3065–3079.
Tabori, George. "Das Einmalige wiederholen: Gespräch mit George Tabori über sein Münchner Shylock-Projekt." *Süddeutsche Zeitung*, 17 November 1978.

Tabori, George. *Ich wollte meine Tochter läge tot zu meinen Füßen und hätte die Juwelen in den Ohren: Improvisationen über Shakespeares Shylock. Dokumentation einer Theaterarbeit*, edited by Andrea Welker and Tina Berger. Munich: Hanser, 1979.
Tabori, George. *Unterammergau oder Die guten Deutschen*. Frankfurt/M.: Suhrkamp, 1981.
Taylor, Brandon. "Socialist Realism: 'To depict reality in its revolutionary development'." In *Adventures in Realism*, edited by Matthew Beaumont, 142–157. Hoboken: Wiley, 2008.
Tollini, Frederick. *The Shakespeare Productions of Max Reinhardt*. Lewiston, NY: Edwin Mellen, 2004.
Ubermann, Iwona. *Auschwitz im Theater der "Peinlichkeit": George Taboris Holocaust-Stücke im Rahmen der Theatergeschichte seit dem Ende der 60er Jahre*. Munich: Dissertationsverlag NG Kopierladen, 1995.
Vietta, Egon, ed. *Darmstädter Gespräch: Theater*. Darmstadt: Neue Darmstädter Verlags-Anstalt, 1955.
Volbach, Walther. "Berliner Shakespeare-Vorstellungen: Spielzeit 1920/21." *Shakespeare Jahrbuch* 57 (1921): 145–148.
Völker, Klaus. "Berthold Viertels dramatische Opposition und sein Bemühen um ein Theater der Ensemblekunst im Berlin der Zwanziger Jahre." In *Der Traum von der Realität: Berthold Viertel*, edited by Siglinde Bolbecher, Konstantin Kaiser, and Peter Roessler, 99–120. Vienna: Döcker, 1998.
Völker, Klaus. *Peter Zadek: Mit dem "Fertigen" gab er sich nicht zufrieden*. Berlin: Hentrich & Hentrich, 2011.
Walch, Eva. "Dramaturgische Blicke auf zwei Inszenierungen von Thomas Langhoff am Deutschen Theater." *Shakespeare Jahrbuch* 140 (2004): 151–164.
Walser, Martin. "Erfahrungen beim Verfassen einer Sonntagsrede." *Friedenspreis des Deutschen Buchhandels – 1998: Martin Walser*. https://www.friedenspreis-des-deutschen-buchhandels.de/sixcms/media.php/1290/1998_walser_mit_nachtrag_2017.pdf (accessed 8 September 2018).
Wannemacher, Klaus. "Der Amnesie des Publikums begegnen: Nachkriegstheater als Inkubator des 'Aufarbeitungs'-Diskurses." In *Erfolgsgeschichte Bundesrepublik? Die Nachkriegsgesellschaft im langen Schatten des Nationalsozialismus*, edited by Stephan A. Glienke, Volker Paulmann, and Joachim Perels, 263–291. Göttingen: Wallstein, 2008.
Wannemacher, Klaus. *Erwin Piscators Theater gegen das Schweigen: Politisches Theater zwischen den Fronten des Kalten Kriegs (1951–1966)*. Tübingen: Niemeyer, 2004.
Warnke, Nina, and Jeffrey Shandler. "Yiddish Shylocks in Theater and Literature." In *Wrestling with Shylock: Jewish Responses to* The Merchant of Venice, edited by Edna Nahshon and Michael Shapiro, 74–104. Cambridge: Cambridge University Press, 2017.
Weigel, Sigrid. "Shylocks Wiederkehr: Die Verwandlung von Schuld in Schulden oder: Zum symbolischen Tausch der Wiedergutmachung." *Zeitschrift für Deutsche Philologie* 114 (1995): 3–22.
Weimann, Robert. "A Divided Heritage: Conflicting Appropriations of Shakespeare in (East) Germany." In *Shakespeare and National Culture*, edited by John J. Joughin, 173–205. Manchester: Manchester University Press, 1997.
Weimann, Robert. "Ideology and Performance in East German Versions of Shakespeare." In *Shakespeare in the Worlds of Communism and Socialism*, edited by Irena R. Makaryk and Joseph G. Price, 328–348. Toronto: University of Toronto Press, 2006.

Weisker, Jürgen. "Theaterschau: Shakespeare auf der deutschen Bühne 1932/33." *Shakespeare Jahrbuch* 69 (1933): 200–225.

Weiß, Matthias. "Sinnliche Erinnerung: Die Filme *Holocaust* und *Schindlers Liste* in der bundesdeutschen Vergegenwärtigung der NS-Zeit." In *Beschweigen und Bekennen: Die deutsche Nachkriegsgesellschaft und der Holocaust*, edited by Norbert Frei and Sybille Steinbacher, 71–102. Göttingen: Wallstein, 2001.

Weiß, Matthias. "Vom 'Zivilisationsbruch' zu einer Kultur des 'negativen Gedächtnisses.'" In *Shylock nach dem Holocaust: Zur Geschichte einer deutschen Erinnerungsfigur*, edited by Zeno Ackermann and Sabine Schülting, 13–39. Berlin: De Gruyter, 2011.

Wenzel, Mirjam. *Gericht und Gedächtnis: Der deutschsprachige Holocaust-Diskurs der sechziger Jahre*. Göttingen: Wallstein, 2009.

Whisnant, Clayton J. *Male Homosexuality in West Germany: Between Persecution and Freedom, 1945–69*. Basingstoke: Palgrave Macmillan, 2012.

White, Hayden. "Auerbach's Literary History: Figural Causation and Modernist Historicism." In *Figural Realism: Studies in the Mimesis Effect*, 87–100. Baltimore: Johns Hopkins University Press, 1999.

Wiesel, Elie. "Trivializing the Holocaust: Semi-Fact and Semi-Fiction." *New York Times*, 16 April 1978.

Wilharm, Irmgard. "Filmwirtschaft, Filmpolitik und der 'Publikumsgeschmack' im Westdeutschland der Nachkriegszeit." *Geschichte und Gesellschaft* 28.2 (2002): 267–290.

Wulf, Joseph. *Theater und Film im Dritten Reich: Eine Dokumentation*. 1964, Frankfurt/M.: Ullstein, 1989.

Zadek, Peter. "Den Shylock kriegste nicht ekelhaft." Interview by Sigrid Löffler. *profil*, 19 December 1988.

Zadek, Peter. "Ein Interview für das *profil* mit Sigrid Löffler anläßlich der Inszenierung von *Der Kaufmann von Venedig* in Wien (1988)." Reprinted in *Das wilde Ufer: Ein Theaterbuch*, edited by Laszlo Kornitzer, 253–260. Cologne: Kiepenheuer & Witsch, 1994.

Zadek, Peter. "Fritz Kortner: The Last of the Lions." *AJR Information* 14.9 (1959): 8–9.

Zadek, Peter, and Karsten Schälike. "Gespräch mit Peter Zadek und Karsten Schälike." Interview by Hartmut Gehrke. In Schauspielhaus Bochum, *Der Kaufmann von Venedig*, theatre programme, 28. Bochum, 1972/73.

Zadek, Peter. "Holocaust (1979)." Reprinted in *Das wilde Ufer: Ein Theaterbuch*, edited by Laszlo Kornitzer, 244. Cologne: Kiepenheuer & Witsch, 1994.

Zadek, Peter. *My Way: Eine Autobiographie 1926–1969*. Cologne: Kiepenheuer & Witsch, 1998.

Zakai, Avihu, and David Weinstein, "Erich Auerbach and His 'Figura': An Apology for the Old Testament in an Age of Aryan Philology." *Religions* 3 (2012): 320–338.

Zivier, Georg. *Ernst Deutsch und das deutsche Theater: Fünf Jahrzehnte deutscher Theatergeschichte. Der Lebensweg eines großen Schauspielers*. Berlin: Haude & Spenersche Verlagsbuchhandlung, 1964.

Zweig, Arnold. *Juden auf der deutschen Bühne*. Berlin: Welt-Verlag, 1928.

2 Reviews of Stage Productions of *The Merchant of Venice*

A. S. V. [= Albert Schulze Vellinghausen]. "Nach jenen Jahren – Hut ab vor Shylock! Shakespeares *Kaufmann von Venedig* in Bochum." *Der Mittag*, 26 September 1952.
A. W. "Shylock im Souterrain." *Die Welt*, 23 November 1978.
Anon. "Des Lebens ganze Fülle: Shakespeares *Kaufmann von Venedig* im Göttinger Stadttheater." *Südhannoversche Zeitung*, 28 September 1942.
Anon. "Der Versöhnung mitten ins Herz." *Allgemeine Wochenzeitung der Juden in Deutschland*, 26 January 1973.
Anon. "Ein Shylock wie aus Hitlers Zeiten." *Der Spiegel* 2 (8 January 1973): 96–97.
Anon. "Tragische Elemente bestimmten Sinn der Komödie: Shakespeares 'Kaufmann von Venedig in der Aula'." *Neustädter Zeitung*, 22 January 1986.
Anon. "Rüdigers Shylock kann nicht mehr mißbraucht werden." *Hannoversche Allgemeine Zeitung*, 22 January 1986.
Anon. "'Der Kaufmann von Venedig' – ein Schauspiel in Vers und Prosa." *Helmstedter Blitz*, 12 February 1986.
Anon. "Shylock." *Schwäbisches Tagblatt Tübingen*, 3 October 1986.
Anon. "Utopisches Illyrien und Pandämonium der Liebe: George Tabori über seine Entdeckungsreise durch Shakespeares Leidenschaften, Kulturpolitik und experimentelles Theater." *Der Standard*, 13 March 1989.
Anon. "Mitten ins System: *Gomorra* und *Der Kaufmann von Venedig*." *Berliner Zeitung*, Sonderseiten der Berliner Bühnen, 25 September 2009.
Antosch, Georg. "Anregung zu erneuter Erprobung: Gedanken zu Shakespeares 'Kaufmann von Venedig'." *Neue Zeit*, 26 May 1976.
Beer, Otto F. "Shylock bei den Börsianern." *Hannoversche Allgemeine Zeitung*, 14 December 1988.
Belzner, Emil. "Karenzzeit abgelaufen." *Rhein-Neckar-Zeitung*, 2 May 1953.
Berke, Bernd. "Ein Mitbewerber wird eiskalt erledigt." *Westfälische Rundschau*, 13 October 2008.
Bickelhaupt, Thomas. "Der Shakespeare der SS." *Frankfurter Allgemeine Zeitung*, 11 April 1995.
Braun, Hanns. "Der Kaufmann von Venedig." *Süddeutsche Zeitung*, 25 July 1964.
Brockmann, Hagmuth W. "Wahrheit zwischen vielen Gags." *Spandauer Volksblatt*, 20 May 1973.
Butzlaff, Wolfgang. "Kiel: Ein nachdenklicher 'Kaufmann von Venedig'." *Lübecker Nachrichten*, 17 April 1985.
Cwojdrak, Günther. "Shakespeares Kaufmann, Barlachs Boll." *Weltbühne* 14 (2 April 1985): 426–428.
ERES. "'Ich steh' hier auf meinen Schein!' Coburger Neuinszenierung des *Kaufmanns von Venedig*." *Neue Presse*, Coburg, 23 January 1954.
Eschmann, Wolfgang. "Sieg der Liebe und der Gnade: Der Jude Shylock als tragische Figur." *Rhein-Zeitung*, 17 January 1967.
G. "'Der Kaufmann von Venedig': Richard Flatters Neuübersetzung im Großen Haus des Badischen Staatstheaters." *Badische Neueste Nachrichten*, 8 March 1966.
Gersch, Wolfgang. "Die Welt des Geldes und die Welt des Schönen: 'Der Kaufmann von Venedig' am Deutschen Theater Berlin." *Tribüne* 58 (22 March 1985): 4.
Giese, Karen. "Shylock als Projektion." *Rheinische Post*, 11 November 1986.

Gleiß, Jochen. "Ein Kaufmann für Belmont." *Theater der Zeit* 7 (1976): 10–12.
Gleiß, Jochen. "Masken des Realen: Thomas Langhoff inszenierte Shakespeares 'Der Kaufmann von Venedig'." *Theater der Zeit* 6 (1985): 14–15.
Goldberg, Henryk. "Das Seil, auf Stein gemalt." *Thüringer Allgemeine*, 10 April 1995.
Grack, Günter. "Spektakel um Shylock." *Tagesspiegel*, 20 May 1973.
Grieser, Dietmar. "Shylock im Nadelstreif." *Rhein-Neckar-Zeitung*, 12 December 1988.
Gruber, Klaus. "Zadek bringt 'Shylock' ins Wallstreet-Milieu." *Westfälische Rundschau*, 13 December 1988.
Hahnl, Heinz Hans. "Der unerschütterliche Businessman." *Arbeiterzeitung Wien*, 12 December 1988.
Hartmann, Rainer. "Der Schmerz des Außenseiters." *Frankfurter Neue Presse*, 29 September 1981.
Henrichs, Benjamin. "Das Messer im Koffer." *Die ZEIT*, 16 December 1988.
Henrichs, Benjamin. "Kein Messer im Fleisch – Shakespeare in Stuttgart und in Düsseldorf: Jürgen Kruse inszeniert *Richard den Zweiten*, Karin Beier den *Kaufmann von Venedig*," *Die Zeit*, 7 October 1994.
Hensel, Georg. "Ein Jude wie du und ich." *Frankfurter Allgemeine Zeitung*, 12 December 1988.
Hensel, Georg. "Shakespeare, Jazz und Judenhaß: George Taboris Shylock-Improvisationen." *Frankfurter Allgemeine Zeitung*, 23 November 1978.
Heppekausen, Sarah. "Jenseits der Finanzkrise." nachtkritik.de, 10 October 2008, http://nachtkritik.de/index.php?option=com_content&view=article&id=1864&Itemid=0 (accessed 8 September 2018).
Herchenröder, Jan. "Shakespeares 'Kaufmann von Venedig'." *Lübecker Nachrichten*, 1 September 1964.
Höbel, Wolfgang. "Yuppies am Rialto, Geldhaie unter sich." *Badische Zeitung*, 13 December 1988.
Hübner, Paul. "Herrliches Welttheater um ein Pfund Fleisch." *Rheinische Post*, 9 September 1957.
Hübner, Paul. "Porzias Heiratslotterie." *Rheinische Post*, 28 September 1964.
Hübner, Paul. "Wie steht es mit Shylock nach 'Holocaust'?" *Badisches Tagblatt* (Baden-Baden), 19 February 1979.
Jacobi, Johannes. "Der aktuelle Shakespeare." *Die ZEIT*, 5 February 1960.
k. u. "Das Problem läßt sich nicht überspielen." *Die Rheinpfalz*, 22 October 1962.
Karasek, Hellmuth. "Shylock im Ghetto." *Stuttgarter Zeitung*, 13 February 1961.
Katherein, Karin. "Geschäftemacher vom Trump Tower." *Die Welt*, 12 December 1988.
Keisch, Henryk. "Nochmals zum 'Kaufmann von Venedig'." *Weltbühne* 23 (4 June 1985): 716–718.
Keisch, Henryk. "Nochmals zum 'Kaufmann von Venedig' (II)." *Weltbühne* 24 (11 June 1985): 745–747.
Kerndl, Rainer. "Shakespeares 'Kaufmann' wieder auf der Bühne." *Neues Deutschland*, 4 May 1976.
Kersch, Walther. "Shakespeare ohne jede Poesie." *Der Tagesspiegel*, 2 December 1983.
Kill, Reinhard. "Ein Macht-Spiel?" *Rheinische Post*, 28 September 1981.
Koch, Heinz. "Das Spiel vom geprellten Juden: Shakespeares *Kaufmann von Venedig* im Stadttheater." *Göttinger Tageblatt*, 28 September 1942.
Krieger, Hans. "Melancholisches Märchen." *Nürnberger Nachrichten*, 16 January 1984.

Krug, Hartmut. "Konflikte im Weichzeichner: Shakespeares 'Kaufmann von Venedig' in Ost-Berlin." *Zitty*, 7 June 1985.
Krüger, Michael. "Menschen-Spiele: Anmerkungen zum Münchner Shylock." *Theater heute* 20.2 (1979): 4.
kth. "Buckwitz kommt doppelt." *Abendzeitung*, 8 April 1964.
Laaths, Erwin. "Der elisabethanische Shylock – ehedem und heute." *Der Mittag*, 9 September 1957.
Lahm, Karl. "Shylock der Ostjude." *Deutsche Allgemeine Zeitung*, 19 May 1943.
Langner, Rainer Kurt. Radio review of *Der Kaufmann von Venedig* at the Schauspielhaus Leipzig (dir. Fritz Bennewitz, premiere: 2 September 1988), *Stimme der DDR*, 11 September 1988. Deutsches Rundfunkarchiv.
Lentz, Georg. "Der Clown von Venedig." *Berliner Zeitung*, 21 May 1973.
Loskill, Hans-Jörg. "Nur Wigger überzeugt als Shylock." *Westdeutsche Allgemeine Zeitung* (Essen), 14 October 1981.
Luckow, Heinz. "Siebzehn Jahre danach wird uns der Shylock wiedergegeben." *Heidelberger Tageblatt*, 18 October 1962.
Luft, Friedrich. "Wie man Shakespeare schändet." *Die Welt*, 3 December 1963.
Melchinger, Siegfried. "*Der Kaufmann von Venedig:* Müthels Neuinszenierung im Burgtheater." *Neues Wiener Tagblatt*, 17 May 1943.
Menchén, Georg. "Von der Notwendigkeit menschlicher Bewährung." *Thüringische Landeszeitung*, 17 April 1976.
Missenharter, Hermann. "Shylock der Weise." *Stuttgarter Nachrichten*, 17 September 1956.
Müller, Christoph. "Tübingen: Vom Rialto direkt nach Auschwitz." *Theater heute* 27.11 (1986): 53–54.
Müry, Andres. "Die Straßenschlacht. Shakespeare zum Auftakt: Dieter Dorn eröffnet das Münchner Residenztheater mit *Der Kaufmann von Venedig*." *Focus* 41 (8 December 2001). https://www.focus.de/kultur/medien/theater-die-strassenschlacht_aid_192952.html (accessed 8 September 2018).
Nyssen, Leo. "Lustspiel – dicht an der Tragödie." *Bochumer Anzeiger*, 24 September 1952.
Pesel, Jens. "Shylock ist in erster Linie Kaufmann." Interview. *Darmstädter Echo*, 28 May 1986.
Platzeck, Wolfgang. "Blick durchs Teleobjektiv." *Westdeutsche Allgemeine Zeitung*, 25 November 1986.
Plote, Michael. "'Tanz auf dem Vulkan' menschlicher Gefühle." *Freies Wort*, 10 April 1995.
Plunien, Eo. "Außenseiter gegen Playboys." *Die Welt*, 28 September 1981.
R. K. "Oldenburgisches Staatstheater: 'Der Kaufmann von Venedig' von Shakespeare." *Münsterländische Tageszeitung*, 16 January 1963.
Reblitz, Irma. "Piscators 'Kaufmann von Venedig'." *Rhein-Neckar Zeitung*, 13 December 1963.
Reitter, Barbara. "Jede Geste fast zu schön." *Neue Osnabrücker Zeitung*, 15 October 2001.
Ringelband, Wilhelm. "Abschied vom Old Vic." *Bergsträßer Anzeiger*, 19 May 1981.
Ritter, Heinz. "Ein Märchen-Unhold." *Der Abend*, 19 May 1973.
Ritter, Heinz. "Nur Ernst Deutsch." *Der Abend*, 2 December 1963.
Rossmann, Andreas. "Die Tragödie der Jessica." *Frankfurter Allgemeine Zeitung*, 29 September 1994.
Rühle, Günther. "Wie zeigt man auf Wunden: Arie Zinger inszeniert in Köln Shakespeare's 'Kaufmann von Venedig'." *Theater heute* 20.12 (1979): 6–9.

Sachse, Peter. "'Der Kaufmann von Venedig' als bunte Commedia dell'arte." *Heilbronner Stimme*, 11 January 1982.
Scheller, Bernhard. "Düstere Komödie – Römerdrama – Trauerspiel: Welttheater? Shakespeare-Inszenierungen in Erfurt, Leipzig und Weimar." *Theater der Zeit* 12 (1988): 19–21.
Schmidt-Mühlisch, Lothar. "Wie der Jude bei der Taufe ertränkt wird." *Die Welt*, 10 April 1995.
Schön, Gerhard. "Deutschs Shylock: Ein Mono-Drama." *Frankfurter Nachtausgabe*, 15 September 1957.
Schulte, Gerd. "Shakespeares Shylock und die Taugenichtse." *Hannoversche Allgemeine Zeitung*, 22 June 1963.
Schulte, Reinhard. "Die Haare zu Berge: Meta-Kritiker Reinhard Schulte über den LTT-*Kaufmann von Venedig* und Wilhelm Triebolds Besprechung vom Montag." *Schwäbisches Tagblatt*, 24 April 2008.
Schumacher, Ernst. "Gewagt, doch nicht gewonnen: Shakespeares 'Kaufmann von Venedig' im DT." *Berliner Zeitung*, 22 March 1985.
Schwirten, Ethel. "Piscators politischer Shylock." *Frankfurter Rundschau*, 5 December 1963.
Sellenthin, H. G. "Die Angst vor Shylock." *Neue Presse Coburg*, 14 April 1960.
Stadelmaier, Gerhard. "Shylock hat keine Chance." *Stuttgarter Zeitung*, 27 October, 1979.
Stadelmaier, Gerhard. "Kein Visum für Shylock: Thomas Langhoff inszeniert Shakespeare in Ost-Berlin." *Stuttgarter Zeitung*, 23 March 1985.
Stadelmaier, Gerhard. "Der Jude Jedermann." *Stuttgarter Zeitung*, 12 December 1988.
Stone, Michael. "Nicht zu rechtfertigen – Premiere in Ost-Berlin: 'Der Kaufmann von Venedig'." *Der Tagesspiegel*, 24 March 1985.
Sucher, Bernd C. "Shylock Jude fehlen die Worte." *Süddeutsche Zeitung*, 12 December 1988.
Tomerius, Lorenz. "Der 'Kaufmann von Venedig' spielt im Vernichtungslager." *Berliner Morgenpost*, 12 April 1995.
Tomerius, Lorenz. "Shylock in Weimar: Die Mörder lassen spielen." *General-Anzeiger* (Bonn), 12 April 1995.
Trauth, Doris M. "Das Spiel von Liebe und Haß." *Die Rheinpfalz*, 15 May 1981.
Tschechne, Wolfgang. "So viele Venezianer: Zu Shakespeares 'Kaufmann von Venedig' in Hannover." *Hannoversche Rundschau*, 22 June 1963.
U. R. "Shylock heute." *Stuttgarter Zeitung*, 16 January 1964.
Ullrich, Helmut. "Da ist ein Mensch in seinem Widerspruch: Zu Shakespeares 'Kaufmann von Venedig'." *Neue Zeit*, 20 March 1985.
Unger, Wilhelm. "Die Tragödie des venezianischen Juden ist keine Tändelei." *Kölner Stadt-Anzeiger*, 30 July 1964.
Werth, Wolfgang. "Shylock gegen Shakespeare." *Deutsche Zeitung*, 9 December 1963.
Westecker, Dieter. "Die Pause ist der einsame Höhepunkt." *Westdeutsche Zeitung*, 28 September 1981.
Wilink, Andreas. "Welt am Draht." *Solinger Tageblatt*, 26 September 1994.
Winderboth, Horst. "Shakespeare – heiß umstritten." *Berliner Morgenpost*, 20 May 1973.
Winters, Hans-Christian. "Frühshakespearesche Unschuld gibt es nicht mehr." *Göttinger Tageblatt*, 14 January 1986.
Zeppenfeld, Inge. "Ein Pfund Fleisch aus Antonios Brust." *Reutlinger Generalanzeiger*, 17 April 2008.

3 Theatre Programmes and Theatre Websites

Berlin, Deutsches Theater. *Der Kaufmann von Venedig* (premiere 17 March 1985), theatre documentation. Unpublished typescript. 2 vols. Archiv der Akademie der Künste Berlin, Inszenierungsdokumentationen 584.
Berlin, Freie Volksbühne. *Der Kaufmann von Venedig*, theatre programme. Berlin, 1963/64.
Bochum, Schauspielhaus. *Der Kaufmann von Venedig*, theatre programme. Bochum, 1972/73.
Bochum, Schauspielhaus. "Der Kaufmann von Venedig." http://www.schauspielhausbochum.de/presse/ (accessed 18 September 2008).
bremer shakespeare company. "Der Kaufmann von Venedig." https://www.shakespeare-company.com/repertoire/der-kaufmann-von-venedig (accessed 8 September 2018).
Bruchsal, Badische Landesbühne. *Ib Texte: William Shakespeare: Der Kaufmann von Venedig. Eine Komödie*, theatre programme. Bruchsal, 1981/82.
Darmstadt, Staatstheater. *Shakespeare, William. Der Kaufmann von Venedig*, theatre programme. Darsmstadt, 1986.
Düsseldorf, Städtische Theater. "Zur Inszenierung des *Kaufmann von Venedig*." *Die Theaterwelt* 16 September 1925.
Düsseldorfer Schauspielhaus. *Der Kaufmann von Venedig*, theatre programme. Düsseldorf, 1981.
Düsseldorfer Schauspielhaus, *Der Kaufmann von Venedig*, theatre programme. Düsseldorf, 1994.
fringe ensemble. "Der Kaufmann von Venedig." http://www.fringe-ensemble.de/der-kaufmann-von-venedig-in-vorbereitung/ (accessed 8 September 2018).
Gießen, Stadttheater. *Der Kaufmann von Venedig*, theatre programme. Gießen, 1968.
Hannover, Landesbühne. *Der Kaufmann von Venedig*, theatre programme. Hannover, 1985/86.
Hannover, Landestheater Ballhof. *Der Kaufmann von Venedig: Komödie von William Shakespeare*, theatre programme. Hannover, 1963.
Hannover, Niedersächsisches Staatsschauspiel. *Der Kaufmann von Venedig*, theatre programme. Hannover, 1972.
Leipzig, Schauspielhaus. *Der Kaufmann von Venedig*, theatre programme. Leipzig, 1988.
München, Bayerisches Staatsschauspiel. "Der Kaufmann von Venedig, Regie: Dieter Dorn." www.bayerischesstaatsschauspiel.de (accessed 13 March 2009).
Shakespeare's Globe. "Germany." http://www.shakespearesglobe.com/about-us/todays-globe/international/germany (accessed 8 September 2018).
Stuttgart, Staatstheater. *Lessings Traum von Nathan dem Weisen: Collage mit Passagen aus Nathan der Weise und Der Kaufmann von Venedig, sowie modernen Texten von Elmar Goerden*, theatre programme. Stuttgart, 1999.
Stuttgart, Württembergischen Staatstheater. *Der Kaufmann von Venedig*, theatre programme. Stuttgart, 1956/57.
Tübingen, Landestheater. "Der Kaufmann von Venedig." http://alt2.landestheater-tuebingen.de/spielplan/der-kaufmann-von-venedig-1953 (accessed 8 September 2018).
Tübingen, Landestheater. *Der Kaufmann von Venedig*, theatre programme. Tübingen, 2008.
Weimar, Deutsches Nationaltheater. *Der Kaufmann von Venedig* (premiere 11 April 1976). theatre documentation. Unpublished typescript. Archiv der Akademie der Künste Berlin, Inszenierungsdokumentationen 173.

Stage Productions of *The Merchant of Venice* in Germany and Austria (1933 – 2010)

This list of German and Austrian productions of *The Merchant of Venice* comprises the period between 1933 and 2010, which has been at the centre of our research. Our major source for compiling this list was the theatre section in *Shakespeare Jahrbuch*, complemented by theatre programmes, reviews, and references in other scholarly studies. We have tried to bring together as much information as possible, but information on pre-war productions is sparse. The respective issues of *Jahrbuch* offer statistics of Shakespeare productions and performances but they do not name directors or actors. Wherever possible, we have added dates for the opening night of the respective production (in brackets).

For the years between 1938 and 1945, German productions in the occupied/annexed parts of Poland and the Czechoslovak Republic are also listed. For these towns, their current names as well as the country to which they belong today are added in brackets. For the period of the German separation (1949 – 1990), the towns in the GDR are identified.

1933

Bonn, Schauspielhaus.
Darmstadt: Hessisches Landestheater.
Detmold, Lippisches Landestheater.
Düsseldorf: Deutsches Theater am Rhein.
Elbing (Elbląg, Poland), Stadttheater.
Gotha, Landestheater.
Hagen, Stadttheater.
Hamburg, Kleines Schauspielhaus
Hannover, Schauspielhaus.
Heidelberg, Stadttheater.
Hildesheim, Stadttheater.
Ingolstadt, Stadttheater.
Karlsbad (Karlovy Vary, Czech Republic), Stadttheater.
Konstanz, Stadttheater.
Leipzig, Altes Theater.
Plauen, Stadttheater.
Regensburg, Stadttheater.
Schwäbisch-Hall, Kurtheater.
Vienna (Austria), Volksoper.

1934

Breslau (Wrocław, Poland), Lobe-Theater.
Brünn (Brno, Czech Republic), Schauspielhaus.
Chemnitz, Schauspielhaus.

Coburg, Landestheater.
Darmstadt, Hessisches Landestheater.
Dessau, Friedrich-Theater.
Gotha-Sondershausen, Vereinigte Landestheater.
Hannover, Schauspielhaus.
Konstanz, Stadttheater.
Leipzig, Altes Theater.
Meiningen, Landestheater.
Stolp (Słupsk, Poland), Stadttheater.

1935
Bremen, Staatstheater.
Coburg, Landestheater.
Freiberg, Stadttheater.
Hanau, Stadttheater.
Hannover, Schauspielhaus.
Koblenz, Stadttheater.
Königsberg i. Pr. (Kaliningrad, Russia), Schauspielhaus.
Linz (Austria), Landestheater.

1936
Bremen, Staatstheater.
Freiberg, Stadttheater.
Kaiserslautern, Landestheater Saarpfalz.
Schaffhausen, Stadttheater.

1937
Bremerhaven, Stadttheater.
Hannover, Schauspielhaus.
Offenburg, Badische Bühne.

1938
Elbing (Elbląg, Poland), Stadttheater.
Hannover, Schauspielhaus.
Hildesheim, Städtische Bühne.
Lübeck, Stadttheater. Dir.: Wulf Leisner.

1939
Erfurt, Deutsches Volkstheater (18 April).
Breslau (Wrocław, Poland), Schlesische Landesbühne.
Lübeck, Stadttheater.

1940
Reichenberg (Liberec, Czech Republic), Stadttheater. Dir.: Friedrich Neubauer.
Aachen, Stadttheater. Dir.: Otto Kirchner; Shylock: Otto Hermann Kempert.
Brüx (Most, Czech Republic), Stadttheater.
Halberstadt, Stadttheater.
Meiningen, Meininger Theater.
Teplitz-Schönau (Teplice-Šanov, Czech Republic), Kleine Bühne.
Troppau (Opava, Czech Republic), Stadttheater.
Regensburg, Stadttheater.

1941
Regensburg, Stadttheater.

1942
Berlin, Rose-Theater. Dir.: Paul Rose; Shylock: Georg August Koch (31 August).
Göttingen, Stadttheater. Dir.: Gustav Rudolf Sellner; Shylock: Wilhelm Meyer-Ottens (23 or 26 September).
Görlitz, Stadttheater.

1943
Vienna (Austria), Burgtheater. Dir.: Lothar Müthel; Shylock: Werner Krauß (15 May).
Minsk (Belarus), German front theatre (September).

1948
Graz (Austria), Opernhaus. Dir.: Richard Eggarte (3 February).
Siegburg, Westdeutsches Landestheater.

1949
Hamm, Theater der Stadt. Dir.: Hans Harnier.

1951–1959

Bregenz (Austria), Theater für Vorarlberg. Dir.: Fritz Klingenbeck; Shylock: Otto Bolesch (1950).
Klagenfurt (Austria). Dir.: Willy Dunkl; Shylock: Anton Gaugl (2 March 1951).
Kaiserslautern, Pfalztheater. Dir.: Rolf Weidenbrück; Shylock: Felix Lademann (9 November 1951).
Schleswig, Nordmark-Landestheater. Dir.: Dr. Horst Gnekow; Shylock: Karl Striebeck (26 December [?] 1951).
Detmold, Landestheater. Dir.: Franz Wirtz; Shylock: Walter Hartung (8 February 1952).
Bochum, Städtische Bühne / Duisburg, Bühne der Stadt. Dir.: Hans Schalla; Shylock: Hanns-Ernst Jäger (22 September 1952).
Linz (Austria), Linzer Landestheater. Dir.: Eduard Volters; Shylock: Arthur Fischer-Colbrie (June 1953).
Heidelberg, Städtische Bühne. Dir.: Rudolf Meyer; Shylock: Franz Rücker (24 September 1953).
Freiburg, Städtische Bühnen. Dir.: Günther Sauer; Shylock: Heinz Suhr (28 December [?] 1953).
Coburg, Landestheater. Dir.: Stefan Dahlen; Shylock: Stefan Dahlen (21 January 1954).
Osnabrück, Osnabrücker Theater am Domhof. Dir.: Erich Pabst; Shylock: Hans Eick (1 April 1954).
Ulm, Städtische Bühne. Dir.: Peter Wackernagel; Shylock: Willy Court (10 September 1954).
Konstanz. Dir.: Klaus Bremer; Shylock: Hans Madin (13 October 1954).
Bruchsal, Unterländer Volksbühne. Dir.: Franz Mosthav; Shylock: Franz Mosthav (30 October 1954).
Darmstadt, Landestheater. Dir.: Gustav Rudolf Sellner; Shylock: Max Noack (7 May 1955).
Obermoschel, open air (1956).
Trier, Theater der Stadt. Dir.: Hanns König; Shylock: Wilhelm Meyer-Ottens (3 March 1956).
Hannover, Landesbühne. Dir.: Jöns Andersson; Shylock: Werner Leonhard (22 March 1956).
Bonn, Theater der Stadt. Dir.: Dr. Karl Pempelfort; Shylock: Paul Gogel (2 May 1956).
Lüneburg, Lüneburger Bühne. Dir.: Willie Schmidt; Shylock: Hermann Schober (5 September 1956).
Stuttgart, Württembergisches Staatstheater / Stuttgarter Staatsschauspiel. Dir.: Werner Kraut; Shylock: Erich Ponto (15 September 1956).
Innsbruck (Austria), Tiroler Landestheater (before 1 December 1956).
Düsseldorf, Schauspielhaus. Dir.: Karl Heinz Stroux; Shylock: Ernst Deutsch (7 September 1957).
Landshut, Stadttheater. Dir.: Hans-Heinz Franckh; Shylock: Jürgen von Alten (4 October 1958).

1960–1969

Ulm, Städtische Bühne. Dir.: Peter Zadek; Shylock: Norbert Kappen (10 February 1961).
Rendsburg, Landesbühne Schleswig-Holstein. Dir.: Joachim von Groeling; Shylock: Will Court (11 February 1961).

Salzburg (Austria), Landestheater. Dir.: Klaus Heydenreich; Shylock: Eduard Cossovel
    (7 September 1961).
Bregenz (Austria), Theater für Vorarlberg. Dir.: Rolf Kautek; Shylock: Richard Rieß
    (23 September 1961).
Pforzheim, Stadttheater. Dir.: Hanno Lunin; Shylock: Bruno Karl (spring 1962).
Kaiserslautern, Pfalztheater. Dir.: Willie Schmitt; Shylock: Felix Lademann (April 1962).
Heidelberg, Stadttheater. Dir.: Martin Ankermann; Shylock: Günter Boehnert
    (16 October 1962).
Ingolstadt, Stadttheater. Dir.: Friedrich Brandenburg; Shylock: Kurt Eggers-Kestner (1963).
Oldenburg, Oldenburgisches Staatstheater. Dir.: Ernst Dietz; Shylock: Raimund Bucher
    (11 January 1963).
Hannover, Landestheater, Ballhof. Dir.: Peter Palitzsch; Shylock: Kurt Ehrhardt (20 June 1963).
St. Gallen, Stadttheater/Kurtheater Baden. Dir.: Siegfried Meisner; Shylock: Karl Ferber
    (17 November 1963).
Berlin, Freie Volksbühne. Dir.: Erwin Piscator; Shylock: Ernst Deutsch (1 December 1963).
Esslingen, Württembergische Landesbühne. Dir.: Joachim von Groeling; Shylock: Will Court
    (11 January 1964).
München, Deutsches Theater. Dir.: Harry Buckwitz; Shylock: Ernst Deutsch (23 July 1964).
Lübeck, Bühnen der Hansestadt. Dir.: Jöns Andersson; Shylock: Joachim Wichmann
    (9 September 1964).
Krefeld, Vereinigte Städtische Bühnen Krefeld Mönchengladbach. Dir.: Herbert Decker;
    Shylock: Alfred Melchior (22 September 1964).
Cuxhaven, Stadttheater. Dir.: Bernd Rademaker; Shylock: Toni Graschberger
    (29 November 1964).
Braunschweig, Staatstheater. Dir.: Jörg Buttler; Shylock: Dirk Dautzenberg (12 March 1965).
Augsburg, Städtische Bühnen. Dir.: Helmut Gaick; Shylock: Otto Preuß (28 September 1965).
Karlsruhe, Badisches Staatstheater. Dir.: Hans-Georg Rudolph; Shylock: Karl A. Jakoby
    (6 March 1966).
Celle, Schlosstheater. Dir.: Hannes Razum; Shylock: Orf Leo Betz (2 April 1966).
Kassel, Staatstheater. Dir.: Pierre Léon; Shylock: Karl Meixner (29 June 1966).
Hildesheim, Stadttheater. Dir.: Victor Warsitz; Shylock: Günter Witte (3 September 1966).
Koblenz, Theater der Stadt. Dir.: Heinz Joachim Klein; Shylock: Manfred Schindler
    (13 January 1967).
Erlangen, Markgrafentheater. Dir.: Keith Hack; Shylock: Karl-Heinz Burger (22 February 1967).
Vienna (Austria), Burgtheater. Dir.: Adolf Rott; Shylock: Ernst Deutsch (4 November 1967).
Bremerhaven, Stadttheater. Dir.: Rudolf Debiel; Shylock: Ferdinand Dux (31 May 1968).
Feuchtwangen, Kreuzgangspiele. Dir.: Ludwig Bender; Shylock: Erik Jelde / Willy Lindberg
    (22 June 1968).
Landshut, Südostbayerisches Städtetheater. Dir.: Ludwig Bender; Shylock: Willy Lindberg
    (30 September 1968).
Würzburg, Stadttheater. Dir.: Herbert Decker; Shylock: Kurt Lasin (31 October 1968).
Gießen, Stadttheater. Dir.: Dietrich Taube; Shylock: Arthur Bauer (3 November 1968).
Schleswig, Nordmark-Landestheater. Dir.: Walter Vorberg; Shylock: Toni Graschberger
    (10 November [?] 1968).
TV-version (Austria/Germany). Dir.: Otto Schenk; Shylock: Fritz Kortner (ORF:
    26 October 1968, WDR: 2 March 1969).

Münster, Studiobühne. Dir.: Wolfgang Kühnhold; Shylock: Peter Otten (January 1969).
Mannheim, Nationaltheater. Dir.: Ernst Dietz; Shylock: Raimund Bucher (16 April 1969).
Bamberg, Theater am Schillerplatz. Dir.: Otto Schmidt; Shylock: Gerd Gutbier
    (11 September 1969).
Freiburg, Städtische Bühnen. Dir.: Friedhelm Schauwienhold; Shylock: Günter Erich Martsch
    (3 October 1969).

1970–1979

Hohenlimburg, Schlossspiele. Dir.: Panejotu Haritoglu (27 June 1970).
Hof, Städtebundtheater. Dir.: Hannes Keppler; Shylock: Willi Meyer-Fürst (14 September 1971).
Marburg, Schauspiel. Dir.: Heinrich Buchmann (19 September 1971).
Linz (Austria) Landestheater Linz. Dir.: Bernd Rademaker; Shylock: Manfred Schinder
    (6 April 1972).
Heilbronn, Stadttheater. Dir.: Walter Bison; Shylock: Walter Bison (7 September 1972).
Graz (Austria), Vereinigte Bühnen. Dir.: Rudolf Kautek; Shylock: Anton Lehmann
    (30 September 1972).
Hannover, Niedersächsische Staatstheater. Dir.: Herbert Kreppel; Shylock: Will Quadflieg
    (1 October 1972).
Bochum, Schauspielhaus. Dir.: Peter Zadek; Shylock: Hans Mahnke (30 December 1972).
Bonn, Theater der Stadt. Dir.: Hans-Joachim Heyse; Shylock: Oswald Fuchs (12 April 1973).
Göttingen, Deutsches Theater. Dir.: Walter Davy; Shylock: Eberhard Müller-Elmau (16 February
    1974).
Tübingen, Landestheater Tübingen. Dir.: Conny Hannes Meyer; Shylock: Heinz Schubert
    (12 September 1974).
Weimar (GDR), Deutsches Nationaltheater. Dir.: Fritz Bennewitz; Shylock: Viktor Dräger
    (11 April 1976).
Greifswald (GDR), Theater Greifswald. Dir.: Eugen Dovides und Fred Grasnick; Shylock: Rudolf
    Reinhardt (17 June 1978).
Weimar (GDR), Deutsches Nationaltheater. Guest performance, South Bohemian Theatre of
    Ceské Budejovice. Dir.: Jaromir Pleskot (July [?] 1978).
Lübeck, Bühnen der Hansestadt. Dir.: Reinhold K. Olszewski; Shylock: Roderich Wehnert
    (14 October 1978).
Munich, Kammerspiele. *Ich wollte meine Tochter läge tot zu meinen Füßen und hätte die
    Juwelen in den Ohren: Improvisationen über Shakespeares Shylock.* Dir.: George Tabori.
    Shylock: Richard Beek; Klaus Fischer; Michael Greza; Michael Habeck; Rüdiger Hacker;
    Ursula Höpfner; Fred Klaus; Felix von Manteuffel; Edwin Noël; Helmut Pick; Siemen
    Rühaak; Arnulf Schumacher; Stanley Walden (19 November 1978).
Baden-Baden, Theater der Stadt. Dir.: Friedhelm Schauwienhold; Shylock: Wolfgang
    Breitenstein (16 February 1979).
Bielefeld, Theater. Dir.: Kai Braak; Shylock: Horst A. Fechner (15 September 1979).
Würzburg, Stadttheater. Dir.: Joachim von Groeling; Shylock: Karl Worzel (4 October 1979).
Cologne, Schauspiel. Dir.: Arie Zinger; Shylock: Hermann Lause (24 October 1979).

1980–1989

Innsbruck (Austria), Tiroler Landestheater. Dir.: Heinz Possberg; Shylock: Heinz Joachim Klein
(28 September 1980).
Lüneburg, Stadttheater. Dir.: Alexander de Montléart; Shylock: Dieter G. Knichel
(7 March 1981).
Düsseldorf, Schauspielhaus. Dir.: Peter Palitzsch; Shylock: Stefan Wigger
(26 September 1981).
Bruchsal, Badische Landesbühne. Dir.: Eberhard Peiker; Shylock: Jürgen Wolfram
(6 October 1981).
Heilbronn, Stadttheater. Dir.: Jaroslav Gillar; Shylock: Karl Straub (9 January 1982).
Koblenz, Theater der Stadt. Dir.: Hannes Maeder; Shylock: Hermann Motschach
(23 April 1982).
Meiningen (GDR), Theater Meiningen. Dir.: Albert R. Pasch. Shylock: Wolfgang Dietrich
(3 December 1982).
Neuss, Rheinisches Landestheater. Dir.: Karl Wesseler; Shylock: Waldemar Stutzmann
(17 April 1983).
Munich, Bayerisches Staatsschauspiel, Residenztheater. Dir.: Alfred Kirchner; Shylock: Walter
Schmidinger (13 January 1984).
Schwäbisch Hall, Haller Treppen-Spiele (open air). Dir.: Kurt Hübner; Shylock: Wolf Kaiser
(24 June 1984).
Münster, Städtische Bühnen. Dir.: Karl Wesseler; Shylock: Waldemar Stutzmann
(7 September 1984).
Dresden (GDR), Staatsschauspiel. Dir.: Klaus Dieter Kirst; Shylock: Hans Teuscher
(11 January 1985).
Hamburg, Altonaer Theater. Dir.: Jöns Andersson; Shylock: Franz-Josef Steffens
(11 March 1985).
Berlin (GDR), Deutsches Theater. Dir.: Thomas Langhoff; Shylock: Fred Düren (17 March 1985).
Kiel, Theater der Stadt. Dir.: Reinhard Hinzpeter; Shylock: Hermann-Josef Geiger
(13 April 1985).
Nordhausen (GDR), Bühnen der Stadt. Dir.: Claus Martin Winter; Shylock: Henning Orphal
(24 January 1986).
Hannover, Landesbühne, Theater am Aegi. Dir.: Reinhold Rüdiger; Shylock: Gerd Peiser
(8 January 1986).
Darmstadt, Staatstheater. Dir.: Jens Pesel; Shylock: Wolf Flüs (13 June 1986).
Tübingen, Landestheater Tübingen (LTT). Dir.: Johannes Klaus; Shylock: Michael Wittenborn
(12 September 1986).
Moers, Schlosstheater. Dir.: Holk Freytag; Shylock: Hans-Christian Seeger
(21 November 1986).
St. Pölten (Austria), Stadttheater. Dir.: Leopold Neustifter (20 December 1986).
Ettlingen, Schlossfestspiele. Dir.: Jörg Cossardt; Shylock: Pinkas Braun (20 June 1987).
Bad Hersfeld, Festspiele. Dir.: Tom Toelle; Shylock: Karl-Heinz Martell (21 June 1988).
Leipzig (GDR), Schauspielhaus Leipzig. Dir.: Fritz Bennewitz; Shylock: Günter Grabbert
(2 September 1988).
Hanau, Hohe Landesschule. Dir.: Erland Schneck; Shylock: Witold Riedel
(26 September 1988).
Vienna (Austria), Burgtheater. Dir.: Peter Zadek; Shylock: Gert Voss (10 December 1988).

Bremen, Schauspielhaus. Dir.: Kurt Hübner; Shylock: Benno Iffland (20 January 1989).
Dortmund, Städtische Bühnen. Dir.: Annegret Ritzel; Shylock: Hartmut Stanke
    (11 February 1989).
Vienna (Austria), Theater Der Kreis. *William Shakespeare: Verliebte und Verrückte – Eine Collage.* Dir.: George Tabori and Martin Fried. Shylock: George Tabori (14 March 1989).
Freiburg, Städtische Bühnen. Dir.: Jan Maagaard; Shylock: Heiner Stadelmann
    (29 April 1989).

1990–1999

Marburg, Schauspiel (open air). Dir.: Volkmar Kamm (20 June 1990).
Ulm, Theater. Dir.: Markwart Müller-Elmau; Shylock: Hartmut Schories (30 September 1990).
Celle, Schlosstheater. Dir.: Werner Pohl; Shylock: Helmut Dicke (9 February 1991).
Lahr, Tournee Euro-Studio Landgraf. Dir.: Edwin Zbonek; Shylock: Karl Heinz Martell
    (11 September 1991).
Frankfurt/Main, Schauspielhaus. Dir.: Wolfgang Engel; Shylock: Jürgen Holtz
    (26 February 1992).
Bad Godesberg, Kleines Theater. Dir.: Kurt Hübner; Shylock: Walter Ullrich (29 March 1992).
Greifswald, Theater. Dir.: Dieter Wagner; Shylock: Johannes Rhein (2 October 1992).
Ingolstadt, Stadttheater. Dir.: Ernst Seiltgen; Shylock: Werner Schnitzer (30 January 1993).
Bregenz (Austria), Theater für Vorarlberg. Dir.: Bernd Bartoszewski (13 November 1993).
Bayreuth, Studiobühne. Dir.: Thomas Krauß; Shylock: Ralf Berghofer (27 November 1993).
Bonn, Endenicher Theater im Ballsaal. Dir.: Rhys Martin (19 September 1993).
Berlin, Berliner Ensemble. Dir.: Peter Zadek; Shylock: Gert Voss (8 January 1994).
Hildesheim, Stadttheater Hildesheim. Dir.: Ralf Knapp (24 September 1994).
Düsseldorf, Düsseldorfer Schauspielhaus. Dir.: Karin Beier; Shylock: Horst Mendroch
    (24 September 1994).
Wiesbaden, Hessisches Staatstheater Wiesbaden. Dir.: Annegret Ritzel (6 October 1994).
Freiburg, Großes Haus des Freiburger Theaters. Dir.: Urs Troller (15 October 1994).
Saarbrücken, Saarländisches Staatstheater. Dir.: Gerhard Weber (21 January 1995).
Weimar, Nationaltheater Weimar. Dir.: Hanan Snir; Shylock: Karl Merkatz (8 April 1995).
Neustrelitz, Landestheater Mecklenburg. Dir.: Peter Lüdi; Shylock: Klaus-Dieter Ulrich
    (9 September 1995).
Bremen, bremer shakespeare company. Dir.: Andrés Pérez Araya; Shylock: Christian Aumer
    und Erik Roßbander (7 February 1996).
Plauen, Vogtland Theater. Dir.: Klaus Krampe; Shylock: Dieter Maas (18 February 1996).
Koblenz, Theater der Stadt. Dir.: Eberhard Johow; Shylock: Hannes Houska (21 March 1996).
Schleswig, Schleswig Holsteinisches Landestheater. Dir.: Klaus Hoser; Shylock: Uwe Michael
    Wiebking (14 April 1996).
Aachen, DAS DA Theater / Burg Frankenberg. Dir.: Tom Hirtz; Shylock: Bernd Büttgens
    (11 July 1996)
Schwerin, Mecklenburgisches Staatstheater. Dir.: David Levin; Shylock: Horst Westphal
    (29 August 1997).
Krefeld / Mönchengladbach, Theater Krefeld Mönchengladbach. Dir.: Urs Schaub; Shylock:
    Matthias Oelrich (13 September / 19 December 1997).

Detmold, Landestheater. Dir.: Barbara Abend (27 September 1997).
Mayen, Burgfestspiele. Dir.: Hans-Joachim Heyse; Shylock: Hans-Joachim Heyse
    (26 June 1998).
Stuttgart, Staatstheater Stuttgart / Kleines Haus. *Lessings Traum von Nathan dem Weisen.*
    Dir.: Elmar Goerden; Shylock: Thomas Loibl (19 February 1999).
Hamburg, Thalia Theater. Dir.: Jens-Daniel Herzog; Shylock: Hans Christian Rudolph
    (17 April 1999).
Würzburg, Stadttheater. Dir.: Johannes Klaus; Shylock: Dirk Bender (19 May 1999).
Ludwigsburg, Theatersommer im Cluss-Garten. *Die Kaufmänner von Venedig.* Dir.: Christiane
    Wolff / Peter Kratz (11 June 1999).

2000–2010

Feuchtwangen, Kreuzgangspiele. Dir.: Lis Verhoeven (23 June 2000).
Mülheim, Theater an der Ruhr. Dir.: Roberto Ciulli (29 November 2000).
Stuttgart, Theater der Altstadt. Dir.: Uwe Hoppe; Shylock: Susanne Heydenreich
    (27 March 2001).
Linz (Asutria), Landestheater. Dir.: Dominik von Gunten (20 April 2001).
Lübeck, Theater Lübeck. Dir.: Gabriele Gysi; Shylock: Norbert Stöß (27 April 2001).
Recklinghausen, Ruhrfestspiele. Co-production with Teatro de La Abadía (Madrid), in Spanish
    with German subtitles. Dir.: Hansgünther Heyme (13 May 2001).
Munich, Residenztheater. Dir.: Dieter Dorn; Shylock: Rolf Boysen (11 October 2001).
Darmstadt, Staatstheater. Dir.: Heinz Kreidl; Shylock: Till Sterzenbach (23 February 2002).
Baden-Baden, Theater Baden-Baden. Dir.: Axel Richter; Shylock: Bernd-Michael Baier
    (11 April 2002).
Nordhausen, Theater. Dir.: Oliver Vorwerk; Shylock: Peter Hausmann (27 September 2002).
Bochum, Schauspielhaus. Dir.: Georg Schmiedleitner; Shylock: Friedrich-Karl Praetorius
    (16 October 2002).
Karlsruhe, Badisches Staatstheater. Dir.: Hasko Weber; Shylock: Sebastian Kreutz
    (18 October 2002).
Frankfurt/Main, Theater am Turm. Collage with fragments of *The Merchant of Venice.* Dir.: Ute
    Rauwald; Shylock: Ilja Richter. (5 December 2002).
Hannover, Schauspielhaus. Dir.: Thomas Bischoff; Shylock: Wolfgang Michalek, Roland
    Renner (5 April 2003).
Kiel, Schauspielhaus. Dir.: Daniel Karasek; Shylock: Sascha Nathan (27 September 2003).
Aachen, Grenzlandtheater. Dir.: Manfred Langner; Shylock: Ernst Wilhelm Lenik
    (7 March 2004).
Hof, Theater Hof. Dir.: Michael Blumenthal; Shylock: Wolfgang Kaiser (30 April 2004).
Koblenz-Ehrenbreitstein, Konradhaus. Dir.: Michael John Hamlett; Shylock: Karl-Heinz
    Hofmann (9 May 2004).
Klingenberg, Clingenburg Festspiele. Dir.: Udo Schürmer; Shylock: Burkhard Heim
    (23 June 2004).
Dresden, Staatsschauspiel. Dir.: Holk Freytag and Constanze Kreusch; Shylock: Holger Bülow
    (25 June 2004).
Braunschweig, Staatstheater. Dir.: Holger Berg; Shylock: Günter Hutsch (2 October 2004).

Koblenz, Stadttheater. Dir.: Annegret Ritzel; Shylock: Olaf Schaeffer (12 February 2005).
Berlin, Deutsches Theater. Dir.: Tina Lanik; Shylock: Ulrich Matthes (16 September 2005).
Cologne, Bühnen der Stadt. Dir.: Michael Talke; Shylock: Markus Scheumann
  (24 September 2005).
Kaiserslautern, Pfalztheater. Dir.: Thomas Krauß; Shylock: Thorsten Danner (8 October 2005).
Cottbus, Staatstheater. Dir.: Bettina Jahnke; Shylock: Gunnar Golgowski (1 April 2006).
Konstanz, Stadttheater. Dir.: Reinhard Gröber; Shylock: Hans Helmut Straub (13 May 2006).
Bremen, Bremer Theater. Dir.: David Mouchtar-Samorai; Shylock: Dirk Audehm (2 June 2006).
Bamberg, E.T.A.-Hoffmann Theater. Co-production with the New Traid Theatre Company
  (London). Dir.: John Strehlow; Shylock: Eckhart Neuberg (10 March 2007).
Leipzig, Schauspielhaus. Dir.: Wolfgang Engel; Shylock: Matthias Hummitzsch
  (22 September 2007).
Bremen, bremer shakespeare company. Dir.: Nora Somaini; Shylock: Peter Lüchinger
  (27 September 2007).
Göttingen, Deutsches Theater. Dir.: Mark Zurmühle; Shylock: Paul Wenning
  (29 September 2007).
Oberhausen, Theater Oberhausen. Dir.: Valentin Jeker (2 November 2007).
Wilhelmshaven, Landesbühne Niedersachsen Nord. Dir.: Philipp Kochheim; Shylock: Stefan
  Ostertag (3 November 2007).
Tübingen, Landestheater Tübingen. Dir.: Clemens Bechtel; Shylock: Udo Rau (18 April 2008).
Rosenburg, Shakespeare-Festspiele. Dir.: Birgit Doll; Shylock: Alexander Waechter (4 July –
  10 August 2008).
Coburg, Landestheater Coburg. Dir.: Malte Kreuzfeld; Shylock: Stephan Mertl
  (3 October 2008).
Bochum, Schauspielhaus. Dir.: Elmar Goerden; Shylock: Renate Becker (10 October 2008).
Cologne, Severins-Burg-Theater. Dir.: Burkhard Schmiester; Shylock: Gerd Buurmann
  (9 January 2009).
Munich, Theater Viel Lärm Um Nichts / Pasinger Fabrik. *Shylock-Variationen: Schauspiel
  in 14 Bildern*. Dir.: Heike Anna Koch; Shylock: Alexander Adler, Betim Bojaxhiu, Elisabeth
  Englmüller, Maryan Said (1 February 2009).
Erfurt, Neues Schauspiel / Erfurt summer theatre. Dir.: C.W. Olafson; Shylock: Karl-Heinz
  Krause (10 July 2009).
Berlin, Maxim Gorki Theater. Dir.: Armin Petras; Shylock: Regine Zimmermann
  (25 October 2009).
Salzburg (Austria), TriBühne Lehen. Dir.: Alexander Linse (5 November 2009).
Bonn / Cologne, fringe ensemble. Dir.: Severin von Hoensbroech; Shylock: S-Dog, Nebil
  Erdogan, Faruk Haziri, Miguel Inserra, Jilou Rasul (14 January 2010 / 2 March 2010).
Osnabrück, Theater Osnabrück. Dir.: Holger Schultze; Shylock: Thomas Schneider
  (4 September 2010).

Index

Abusch, Alexander 143
Adelman, Janet 7, 190
Adenauer, Konrad 65, 68
Adorno, Theodor W. 67, 95, 127
Akademie der Künste, Berlin (Academy of the Arts) 97, 147
Allio, René 109
Altenburg, Leopold 199
Alter, Robert 8
Althaus, Hans Peter 186
Anikst, Alexander 140
Antonio (character in *The Merchant of Venice*) 11, 27, 55, 57, 69, 80, 91, 103, 112, 120, 124, 126–129, 138, 150–152, 158–160, 162, 169–170, 177–178, 186, 189–190, 195–196
Antosch, Georg 154–155
Aragon (character in *The Merchant of Venice*) 22
Arendt, Hannah 91, 108, 121
Armstrong, Gareth 46
Arts Council of Great Britain 121
Assmann, Aleida 164–165, 197
Association of Jewish Refugees 100
Auerbach, Erich 1–11, 56, 111, 165, 203–205
Aufricht, Ernst Josef 34

Baader-Meinhof-Gruppe, see RAF
Bachmann, Michael 104–105
Baden-Baden, Theater der Stadt 122, 129
Balthazar (character in *The Merchant of Venice*) 32
Barton, John 157
Bassanio (character in *The Merchant of Venice*) 24, 27, 55, 57, 59, 103, 113
Bassermann, Albert 20, 30, 107, 126, 154
Bassnett, Susan 144
Bayerdörfer, Hans-Peter 63, 78–79, 90, 182
Bechtel, Clemens 191, 196–197, 201
Becker, Peter von 133, 135–136
Becker, Renate 187–190

Beelitz, Günther 126
Beier, Karin 13, 192–195
Benhabib, Seyla 132, 135
Bennewitz, Fritz 13, 137–138, 148, 150–157, 160
Benrath, Martin 129
Berg, Nicolas 81
Berger, Tina 115
Berlin
– Berliner Ensemble 147, 167
– Deutsches Theater 19–26, 78, 137–138, 145, 147, 154, 157–161
– (Freie) Volksbühne 31, 80, 84–85, 90–94, 107, 154
– Großes Schauspielhaus 20, 39–41
– Lustspielhaus 34
– Maxim Gorki Theater 162–163
– Rose-Theater 48–50, 53, 61
– Schillertheater 91, 105
– Staatstheater 36, 58, 100, 105, 107, 157
– Theatertreffen 119
Biedrzynski, Richard 51–52, 61
Bielefeld, Theater 122
Biermann, Wolf 144
Bliersbach, Gerhard 102
Bochum, Schauspielhaus (Städtische Bühne) 65, 69–72, 86–88, 98, 107–110, 118–119, 133, 143, 154, 157, 187–191
Boehm, Gottfried 10
Bonn
– fringe ensemble 197–201, 205
– Theater der Stadt 66
– Theater im Ballsaal 197
Bonnell, Andrew G. 19, 43, 47–50, 61–62
Borchert, Wolfgang
– *Draußen vor der Tür (The Man Outside)* 65
Bösch, Frank 122–123
Bovilsky, Lara 190
Boyd-Brent, Jack 98
Boysen, Rolf 178
Brandl-Risi, Bettina 10
Brandt, Willy 130

Brandstetter, Gabriele   10, 204
Braulich, Heinrich   20–21, 29
Brecht, Bertolt   83–85, 94, 183, 197
Bremen
– bremer shakespeare company   183–184, 191–192, 195–196
– Schauspielhaus   129
Brockmann, Stephen   65
Broder, Henryk M.   134
Brook, Peter   85
Brown, John Russell   157
Brown, Wendy   196
Browning, Christopher   49
Bruchsal, Badische Landesbühne   128
Brumlik, Micha   165, 176, 179
Bubis, Ignatz   125, 132
Buchmann, Heinrich   55
Buchmann, Josef   125
Bunge, Hans-Joachim   84
Busse, Sylta   92

Canaris, Volker   108, 120–121, 192–193, 195
Canonica, Sibylle   178
Carlson, Marvin   11, 79, 83–84, 86
Carpaccio, Vittore
– *Miracle of the Cross at the Ponte di Rialto*   91–92
Certeau, Michel de   99–100, 199
Cervantes, Miguel de
– *Don Quixote*   4
Chomsky, Marin J.
– *Holocaust*   122–123, 129, 156
Coburg, Landestheater   67, 185–186, 191
Chow, Rey   6
Claussen, Detlev   95
Cohen, Robert   85–86
Cohen, Walter   144
Cologne
– Schauspiel   119–122, 206
– studiobühneköln   197
Critchfield, Richard D.   34–36, 39, 41
Cuxhaven, Stadttheater   97

Dahlen, Stefan   67
Daiber, Hans   52, 57–59
Damrosch, David   2–5

Dante Alighieri
– *Divina Comedia*   4, 86
Darmstadt, Staatstheater (formerly Hessisches Landestheater)   66, 73, 129, 134
Derrida, Jacques   178–179
Deutsch, Ernst   63, 66, 71, 76–82, 83, 89–91, 93–96, 98, 107, 115, 126, 128–129, 154, 204
Deutsche Akademie für Sprache und Dichtung (German Academy for Language and Literature)   97
Deutsch-Schreiner, Evelyn   76–78
Deutsche Shakespeare Gesellschaft   22, 39, 43–47, 50, 96, 139, 141, 143–144, 155
Deutsches Theater am Rhein   42–43
Devrient, Ludwig   107
Dietel, Günter   153
Diner, Dan   12, 166
Dische, Irene   125–126, 132
Dorn, Dieter   13, 159, 175–180
Dorst, Tankred   118
Dortmund, Städtische Bühnen   129
Dräger, Victor   154
Drakakis, John   144, 190
Dresden, Staatsschauspiel   137
Drese, Claus Helmut   105
Dresen, Alfred   145
Drössler, Stefan   40
Dubiel, Helmut   68
Duke of Venice (character in *Merchant of Venice*)   36, 78, 93, 103
Düren, Fred   158–159
Düsseldorf
– Schauspielhaus   76–80, 83, 123–126, 129, 132, 157, 192–195
– Stadttheater   42

Ebner, Caroline   193–194
Edelman, Charles   58
Edwards, Ruth Dudley   14
Egervari, Tibor   112
Ehrhardt, Kurt   89
Eicher, Thomas   46–48
Eichmann, Otto Adolf   83, 91, 95, 135, 150
Elias, Norbert   10–11
Endriss, Beate-Ursula   49
Engler, Balz   64

Enzensberger, Christian 127–128
Enzensberger, Hans Magnus 125, 127
Epstein, Alan 112
Erdogan, Nebil 197
Erfurt, Gerhard 147
Erll, Astrid 165
Ernst, Wolf-Dieter 10
Esslingen, Württembergische Landesbühne 97
Everding, August 100

Fallada, Hans
– *Kleiner Mann, was nun* ("Little Man, What Now?") 118–119
Fassbinder, Rainer Werner
– *Der Müll, die Stadt und der Tod* ("Garbage, the City, and Death") 131–136, 158
Fehling, Jürgen 36, 38–39, 73, 100, 107
Feinberg, Anat 78, 98–99, 111, 113, 116–117
Fest, Joachim 132, 135
Filbinger, Hans 122–123
Fischer, David 199
Fischer, Torben 164
Frank, Anne
– *The Diary of Anne Frank* 66, 77–79
Frank, Otto 77–79
Frankfurt/Main
– Alte Oper 132
– Schauspielhaus 58, 64, 132, 183
– Theater am Turm 131
Frei, Norbert 65, 67, 71
Freiburg, Theater 183
Freydank, Ruth 48
Freytag, Holk 135
fringe ensemble, see Bonn
Frye, Northrop 194

Gehrke, Hartmut 108
Geldern, Rainer 69
George, Stefan 29
Gersch, Wolfgang 160
Giehse, Therese 83
Gielgud, John 50–51
Gießen, Stadttheater 97
Gillar, Jaroslav 128
Gillman, Abigail 14

Giordano, Ralph 197
Gleiß, Jochen 153, 155
Globe Council 183
Goebbels, Joseph 48, 61–62, 102
Goerden, Elmar 13, 187–192
– *Lessings Traum von Nathan dem Weisen* ("Lessing's Dream of Nathan the Wise") 187–188
Goethe, Johann Wolfgang von 73, 140
Gollancz, Victor 14
Goodrich, Frances
– *The Diary of Anne Frank* (dramatization) 78
Gorky, Maxim 142
Görlitz, Stadttheater 50
Görne, Dieter 151–155
Görtz, Hans-Helmut 15
Goschler, Constantin 72
Göttingen, Deutsches Theater (formerly: Stadttheater) 50–57, 61, 66, 84
Graetz, Heinrich 14
Granach, Alexander 31–33, 35, 42, 45, 82
Grass, Günter 105–106, 130
– "Was gesagt werden muss" 106
Gratiano (character in *The Merchant of Venice*) 27, 91, 93, 103, 179, 191–192
Greenblatt, Stephen 144
Greifswald, Theater 137, 145
Greiner, Bernhard 56
Gross, John 8, 22, 46, 51
Gründgens, Gustaf 73, 84
Gundolf, Friedrich 29–30
Günther, Hans F. K. 44, 61
Guntner, Lawrence 139, 143–145

Habermas, Jürgen 130
Hackett, Albert
– *The Diary of Anne Frank* (dramatization) 78
Hacohen, Malachi Haim 2, 4, 12
Haider, Jörg 110
Hamburg, Deutsches Schauspielhaus 167
Hamburger, Maik 139, 147, 181
Hamm, Theater der Stadt 64–65
Hannover
– Ballhof 89–90, 96
– Landesbühne 133–134

Harlan, Veit   62
– *Jud Süß*   40, 49, 62
– *Kolberg*   62
Hart, Elisabeth   190–191
Hausmann, Frank-Rutger   44, 54
Haziri, Faruk   197
Heidelberg, Stadttheater   95–96
Heilbronn, Stadttheater128
Heimpel, Hermann   54
Hein, Pieter   158
Heine, Heinrich   17–18, 25, 44, 70, 89, 124, 149
– *Shakespeare's Mädchen und Frauen (Shakespeare's Maidens and Women)*   17, 44, 124
Heinz, Wolfgang   83
Heiseler, Bernt von   97
Hensel, Georg   108
Hentig, Hartwig von   105
Herbert, Ulrich   163
Herbold, Astrid   107, 118–119
Herder, Johann Gottfried   140
Herf, Jeffrey   149
Heschel, Susanne   6, 10
Hillesheim, Gert   147
Hilpert, Heinz   68, 73
Himmler, Heinrich   57
Hippler, Fritz
– *Der ewige Jude*   53, 62
Hitler, Adolf   5, 39, 43–44, 91, 119, 123, 130
Hochhuth, Rolf   123
– *Der Stellvertreter (The Deputy)*   85, 90, 94
Hockerts, Hans Günther   72
Hoensbroech, Severin von   197–201
Höfele, Andreas   43
Holl, Fritz   31, 42
Hollstein, Dorothea   62
Holst, Maria   52
Holtzmann, Thomas   178
Höring, Klaus   104
Horn, Matthias   189
Holderness, Graham   144
Holmes, Jonathan   10
Homer
– *Odyssey*   4–5
Honecker, Erich   143–144, 156

Hortmann, Wilhelm   63, 71, 107, 175–176, 178, 185
Hübner, Kurt   129
Huesmann, Heinrich   20, 32, 36, 40,
Humperdinck, Engelbert   21

Iffland, August Wilhelm   107
Ifland, Benno   189
Ihering, Herbert   40–41
Inserra, Miguel   197
Irving, Henry   22

Jacobi, Johannes   78–79, 84, 88
Jacobson, Howard
– *Shylock Is My Name*   202–206
Jacobsohn, Siegfried   31
Jäger, Hanns-Ernst   88
Jauslin, Christian   74, 119
Jeffries, Michael P.   199
Jellonnek, Burkhard   130
Jesserer, Gertraud   104
Jessica (character in *The Merchant of Venice*)   11, 26–29, 34, 47–48, 59, 92–93, 104, 114, 160, 185–186, 190–197, 199, 206
Jüdischer Kulturbund (Cultural Federation of Jews)   139

Kahane, Arthur   20–25
Kaiser, Joachim   74–75
Kaliningrad (Königsberg), Schauspielhaus   66
Kappen, Norbert   107
Karasek, Hellmuth   107, 119
Karasholi, Adel   148–150, 155
Karlsruhe, Badisches Staatstheater   98
Kaynar(-Kissinger), Gad   58, 118, 182–183
Kean, Edmund   22
Keller, Wolfgang   44–45
Kennedy, Dennis   7
Kentrup, Norbert   183–185
Kertész, Imre   166
Kiel, Theater der Stadt   128
Kipphardt, Heinar
– *Shakespeare dringend gesucht* ("Desperately Seeking Shakespeare")   145
Kirchner, Alfred   129

Klaus, Johannes 134
Knorr, Heinz 88
Koblenz, Theater der Stadt 98
Koch, Georg August 49
Kohl, Helmut 130, 162
Königsberg, see Kaliningrad
Korczak, Janus 88
Körner, Hermine 31
Korte, Karl-Rudolf 162
Kortner, Fritz 20, 33–39, 41, 45, 59, 63, 83–84, 86, 98–108, 113–114, 122, 126, 128, 134, 149, 157–158, 185, 192, 204
Kosky, Barrie 183
Kosselleck, Reinhart 164
Kott, Jan 86
Krahl, Hilde 80
Krämer-Badoni, Rudolf 105
Krauß, Werner 20, 39–41, 51–52, 61–62, 126, 155
Kraut, Werner 75
Krefeld, Städtische Bühnen Krefeld-Mönchengladbach 97
Kreutzfeldt, Malte 185–186, 191
Krieger, Murray 144
Kroepelin, Hermann 47
Kuckhoff, Armin-Gerd 139–142, 146, 148, 150–151, 154–155
Kujawińska-Courtney, Krystyna 61

Lancelot Gobbo (character in *The Merchant of Venice*) 40, 107, 120, 134, 160, 186, 191
Landauer, Gustav 27–29, 45–46, 54, 69–70, 73, 75, 155
Lang, Jochen von 135
Lange, Wigand 64
Langer, Lawrence 166
Langhoff, Thomas 13, 137–138, 145, 157–161
Langhoff, Wolfgang 83, 147
Langner, Rainer Kurt 157
Lause, Hermann 120
Ledebur, Ruth von 44, 141
Leipzig, Schauspielhaus 137, 150, 155–157, 160
Lemcke, Heinrich 45–47
Leo, Annette 149–150, 156

Lerer, Seth 4
Lessing, Gotthold Ephraim 140
– *Die Juden (The Jews)* 158
– *Nathan der Weise (Nathan the Wise)* 14, 35, 40, 52, 66, 71, 75–79, 90, 94, 99, 106, 139, 187
Löffler, Sigrid 99, 169–170
London
– Royal National Theatre 104
– Shakespeare's Globe (Globe Theatre) 183–185
– Queen's Theatre 50–51
Lorenz, Matthias N. 164
Lorenzo (character in *The Merchant of Venice*) 27, 47, 93, 104, 179, 185–186, 191, 193
Lübeck, Bühnen der Hansestadt 97, 122
Lüchinger, Peter 195–196
Ludewig, Alexandra 102
Luft, Friedrich 94
Lühe, Irmela von der 32
Lux, Joachim 194

Macklin, Charles 22
Mahnke, Hans 108–109, 133, 154
Malkin, Jeanette R. 19–20, 33
Mandelkow, Karl Robert 141–143
Mannheim, Nationaltheater 88
Mannheim, Ralph 9
Marburg, Schauspielhaus 90
Markovits, Andrei S. 132, 135
Marlowe, Christopher
– *The Jew of Malta* 4, 158
Martegna, Andrea
– *Saint Sebastian* 108
Marx, Karl 127–128, 140
Marx, Peter W. 20, 26, 28–29, 31, 40,
Matzke, Annemarie 151
Mayer, Hans 17–18, 127–128, 174
Meiningen, Theater 137
Melchinger, Siegfried 59–61, 86
Menchén, Georg 154
Mendroch, Horst 192
Mertz, Peter 52, 66, 73
Metzger, Mary Janell 190
Meyer-Ottens, Wilhelm 51, 55
Michal, Robert 73

Miller, Jonathan 104, 159
Milstein, Avishai 183
Mink, Wilfried 167
Mitterand, François 130
Mitterwurzer, Friedrich 107
Moeller, Robert G. 71
Moers, Schlosstheater 134–135
Moissi, Alexander 20
Mönchengladbach, Städtische Bühnen Krefeld-Mönchengladbach 97
Moninger, Markus 1, 2, 20, 22, 24–25, 34–36, 62–63, 81, 85
Monschau, Jörg 46–48, 58, 60, 64, 67–69, 73, 76–77, 79–80, 88, 119–120, 122, 125–126, 193
Morocco (character in *The Merchant of Venice*) 22
Mühe, Ulrich 160
Mühlheim/Ruhr, Theater an der Ruhr 133
Müller, Achatz von 10
Müller, Heiner
– *Hamletmaschine* 145
– *Hamlet/Maschine* 145
Müller, Karl-Heinz 158
Münch, Josef 42
Munich
– Deutsches Theater 95–97
– Kammerspiele 98–100, 111, 113–116, 118, 122, 175
– Residenztheater 129, 175, 177
– Schauspielhaus 31–32
Murnau, Friedrich Wilhelm
– *Nosferatu* 32
Müthel, Lothar 13, 52, 57–61, 73

Nachmann, Werner 126
Nahshon, Edna 8, 205
Nerissa (character in *The Merchant of Venice*) 61, 103, 179, 191, 196
Neuss, Globe Neuss 183
Newman, Jane O. 9
Noa, Manfred
– *Nathan der Weise* ("Nathan the Wise", film adaptation) 40
Noack, Max 74
Nordhausen, Bühnen der Stadt 137
Novelli, Ermete 59

Novick, Peter 166
Nyssen, Leo 69–71

Old Vic 121
Oldenburg, Staatstheater 95
Olivier, Laurence 104, 113, 159
Olivier, Richard 184–185
Onuki, Atsuko 10
Orgler, Joseph 125
Orth, Elisabeth 107

Palitzsch, Peter 85, 89, 123–126, 132, 157
Peiser, Gerd 133
Pekar, Thomas 10
Pempelfort, Karl 66
Pepys, Samuel 115
Perel, Simon 125
Perez, Andres 184
Pesel, Jens 129
Peters, Sibylle 10
Peymann, Claus 167
Pfeiffer, Ludwig 54
Picker, Henry 44
Piscator, Erwin 80, 83–86, 89–94, 107, 154
Pius XII, Pope 85
Polgar, Alfred 107
Ponto, Erich 66, 71, 75–77, 81
Poppek, Yvonne 175
Poppy, Dagmar 185
Porter, James I. 6
Portia (character in *The Merchant of Venice*) 11, 22–24, 27, 32, 45, 52–54, 56, 70, 72–73, 75, 80, 93, 103, 107–108, 110, 113, 116–117, 121, 129, 169, 178–179, 185, 191, 196, 204
Postone, Moishe 132, 135
Potter, Lois 185
Purnell, Louise 104

Quadflieg, Will 84

Rabelais, François 4
RAF (Rote Armee Fraktion, a.k.a. Baader-Meinhof-Gruppe) 122
Reagan, Ronald 130
Rasul, Jilou 197

Rathkolb, Oliver 60
Reed, Carol
– *The Third Man* 77
Refugee Children's Movement (RCM) 184–185
Reichel, Peter 63, 84–86, 123, 164
Reichert, Klaus 126–127
Reiffenstein, Bruno 37
Reinfeldt, Franziska 191
Reinhardt, Max 12–13, 19–37, 39, 40, 42, 45, 126, 138, 154–155, 175
Reinhold, Rüdiger 133
Richardson, Michael D. 141
Richter, Walther 42–43
Riewoldt, Otto F. 144–145
Ritzel, Annegret 129
Rose, Jürgen 177
Rose, Paul 48
Rosenberg, Alfred 45, 61
Roth, Cecil 107
Rothweiler, Sonja 193
Rowe, Nicholas 157
Royal Shakespeare Company 85
Rüdiger, Reinhold 133–134
Rühle, Günther 104, 121, 132, 134–135
Ryan, Kiernan 144

Said, Edward 6
Salerio (character in *The Merchant of Venice*) 92, 120
Schälike, Karsten 87, 108
Schalla, Hans 69, 85, 88, 118
Schaller, Rudolf 147
Schallück, Paul 105
Schäuble, Wolfgang 197
Scheidler, Gisela 168
Schenk, Otto 98, 100–106, 126, 134
Schereschewsky, Emanuel 105–106, 126
Schildkraut, Joseph 19, 25
Schildkraut, Rudolf 19, 26–31, 33–34, 107
Schiller, Friedrich 140
– *Don Carlos* 91, 105
Schirach, Baldur von 58
Schlegel, August Wilhelm 59–60, 92, 108, 113
Schlösser, Anselm 141, 143, 150–153, 155
Schlösser, Rainer 44, 47–49

Schmahl, Hildegard 116–117
Schmid, Daniel
– *Schatten der Engel (Shadow of Angels)* 131
Schmid, Harald 164
Schmidinger, Walter 129
Schmitt, Saladin 118
Schmückle, Hans Ulrich 91–92
Schnauder, Ludwig 58, 60
Schöffler, Herbert 54, 56
Schröder, Gerhard 162
Schüler, Hans 88–89
Schumacher, Ernst 160
Schümmer, Karl 45
Schütze, Peter 101
Schwanitz, Dietrich 171–174
Scott, Walter
– *Waverley* 165
S-Dog 197
Seeger, Hans-Christian 135
Sehrt, Ernst Theodor 33
Sellner, Gustav Rudolf 50–58, 66, 73–74, 84–85
Seydel, Tina 199
Shakespeare, William
– *Antony and Cleopatra* 116
– *As You Like It* 65
– *The Comedy of Errors* 65
– *Hamlet* 1–2, 65, 96, 139–140, 145
– *Henry IV* 2
– *Julius Caesar* 29
– *King Lear* 1–2, 96, 143
– *Macbeth* 1–3, 96
– *Measure for Measure* 65
– *The Merry Wives of Windsor* 46, 184
– *A Midsummer Night's Dream* 14, 65, 96
– *Much Ado about Nothing* 65
– *Othello* 65, 203
– *Romeo and Juliet* 117
– *The Taming of the Shrew* 65
– *The Tempest* 2, 29, 203
– *Twelfth Night* 65, 206
Shakespeare Globe Zentrum Deutschland 183
Shandler, Jeffrey 33
Shapiro, Michael 8, 205
Sichel, John 104

Siegburg, Westdeutsches Landestheater   64
Simon, Ernst   106, 205
Sinsheimer, Eugenie   15
Sinsheimer, Hermann   14–18, 32, 41, 89, 107, 174
Sinsheimer, Ludwig   15
Snir, Hanan   13, 118, 180–183, 186, 194
Sokolova, Boika   146
Sokolyansky, Mark   146, 149
Solanio (character in *The Merchant of Venice*)   92, 120
Somaini, Nora   191–192, 195–196
Sorge, Thomas   155
Spier, Wolfgang   80
SS   57, 111, 123, 130, 183
Stadelmaier, Gerhard   120–121, 137, 159, 169
Stahl, Ernst Leopold   49, 53, 64, 67–68
Stalin, Joseph   146, 149
Stein, Peter   105
Steinbach, Peter   164
Steinbacher, Sybille   71
Stern, Ernst   23
Stern, Frank   66
Stewart, Patrick   157
Stockbridge, MA, Berkshire Theater Festival   98, 111–113, 115
Stolten, Inge   61
Stone, Oliver
– *Wall Street*   167
Stratford-upon-Avon, The Other Place   157
Streete, Adrian   10
Strobl, Gerwin   44
Stroux, Karl Heinz   76–78, 85, 90, 129
studiobühneköln, see Cologne
Stuttgart, Württembergisches Staatstheater   75–76, 187
Syberberg, Hans Jürgen   100, 103
Sylvanus, Erwin
– *Korczak und die Kinder (Korczak and the Children)*   88
Symington, Rodney   43, 47

Tabori, George   13, 63, 83, 86, 98–100, 110–118, 122–123, 136, 141, 180, 204
– *The Cannibals (Die Kannibalen)*   111

– *Ich wollte, meine Tochter läge tot zu meinen Füßen und hätte die Juwelen in den Ohren: Improvisationen über Shakespeares Shylock* ("I would my daughter were dead at my foot and the jewels in her ear: Improvisations on Shakespeare's Shylock")   99, 110–116, 118, 122
– *Jubiläum* ("Jubilee")   111
– *Mein Kampf* ("My Struggle")   111
– *Verliebte und Verrückte* ("Lovers and Lunatics")   99, 116–117
– *Mutters Courage* ("My Mother's Courage")   111
– *Unterammergau oder Die guten Deutschen* ("Unterammergau or The Good Germans")   111
Taylor, Brandon   142
Tollini, Frederick   24–25
Die Truppe (theatre company)   34–36
Tubal (character in *The Merchant of Venice*)   11, 188
Tübingen, Landestheater (LTT)   134–135, 162, 191–192, 196–197, 201

Ubermann, Iwona   114
Ulbricht, Walter   143
Ulm, Städtische Bühne   92, 98, 106–108
UNESCO   64

Venice
– Biennale   27
– Campo San Trovaso   29
Verband der Theaterschaffenden der DDR (Federation of Theatre Professionals of the GDR)   139, 151
Vienna
– Burgtheater   13, 39–41, 51–52, 57–61, 83, 98–99, 110, 159, 165–171, 174, 180, 195
– Theater Der Kreis   99, 116–117
– Theater in der Josefstadt   20, 35–37
Viertel, Berthold   34–36, 59, 83
Völker, Klaus   34, 118
Voss, Gert   110, 167–168, 170, 174, 192, 195

Wagner, Meike   10
Walch, Eva   145, 157–160

Waldheim, Kurt 110
Walser, Martin 173, 176
Wanamaker, Sam 183–184
Wangenheim, Gustav von 138–140
Wannemacher, Klaus 83–85, 90–91, 94
Warnke, Nina 33
Waschneck, Erich
– *Die Rothschilds* 66
Wehrmacht 110
Weigel, Sigrid 72
Weimann, Robert 138, 140, 142–145, 183
Weimar, Deutsches Nationaltheater 58, 118, 137, 148, 150–156, 180–183, 194
Weinstein, David 5
Weiß, Matthias 122, 164
Weiss, Peter
– *Die Ermittlung (The Investigation)* 85, 94
Welker, Andrea 115
Wenzel, Mirjam 95
Wesker, Arnold
– *The Merchant* 158
West, Timothy 121
Whisnant, Clayton J. 130
White, Hayden 9, 111
Wien, Werner 73
Wiesbaden, Hessisches Staatstheater 58
Wiesel, Elie 123
Wigger, Stefan 123, 125
Wildgruber, Ulrich 107
Wilharm, Irmgard 102

Winterstein, Eduard von 24
Wisten, Fritz 139
Wittenborn, Michael 134
Wolf, Andreas 55
Wulf, Joseph 48, 66
Würzburg, Stadttheater 122

Zadek, Peter 13, 50–51, 63, 81–82, 83, 86–87, 92, 98–100, 106–111, 114, 118–120, 122–124, 133, 135–136, 141, 154, 157, 159, 165–171, 174, 179–180, 192, 195, 204
Zakai, Avihu 5
Zech, Rosel 108
Zentralrat der Juden in Deutschland (Central Council of Jews in Germany) 126, 132
Zeppenfeld, Inge 196
Zinger, Arie 119–121, 206
Zivier, Georg 79
Znamenacek, Wolfgang 50
Zuckmayer, Carl
– *Des Teufels General (The Devil's General)* 65
Zweig, Arnold 30–31, 34
Zwerenz, Gerhard
– *Die Erde ist unbewohnbar wie der Mond* ("The Earth Is Uninhabitable as the Moon") 131
Zwickau, Theater 147

www.ingramcontent.com/pod-product-compliance
Lightning Source LLC
Chambersburg PA
CBHW031806220426
43662CB00007B/550